DIGITAL BUSINESS

Navigating the Digital Landscape and Thriving in the Digital Economy

Patrice Seuwou

Routledge
Taylor & Francis Group
LONDON AND NEW YORK

Designed cover image: Eoneren / Getty Images

First published 2026
by Routledge
4 Park Square, Milton Park, Abingdon, Oxon OX14 4RN

and by Routledge
605 Third Avenue, New York, NY 10158

Routledge is an imprint of the Taylor & Francis Group, an informa business

British Library Cataloguing-in-Publication Data
A catalogue record for this book is available from the British Library

ISBN: 978-1-032-67243-4 (hbk)
ISBN: 978-1-032-67244-1 (pbk)
ISBN: 978-1-032-67245-8 (ebk)

DOI: 10.4324/9781032672458

Typeset in Times New Roman
by codeMantra

Access the Support Material: www.routledge.com/9781032672441

Digital Business: Navigating the Digital Landscape and Thriving in the Digital Economy

Contents

About the Author

Dr Patrice Seuwou is an accomplished academic and thought leader at the intersection of computing, business, and education, making him uniquely positioned to author a book on digital business. Holding a distinguished PhD in Computer Science & Informatics from London South Bank University, Dr Seuwou has dedicated his career to understanding and advancing the role of technology in transforming business landscapes. Complementing his technological expertise, he pursued a second PhD in Sociology of Education at The University of Northampton, deepening his understanding of the human and societal dimensions of innovation and education.

Dr Seuwou is an Associate Professor in Learning and Teaching at the University of Northampton, where he also serves as Director of the Centre for the Advancement of Racial Equality. Over the years, he has designed and led transformative MBA programmes across private and public institutions in the UK and taught modules on digital business and digital transformation. His experience in higher education includes pivotal leadership roles such as Academic Registrar, Quality Manager, Head of Department, and Programme Leader for both undergraduate and postgraduate portfolios.

As a Senior Fellow of the Higher Education Academy and a nominee for the prestigious National Teaching Fellow award, Dr Seuwou's commitment to academic excellence is recognised widely. He is an active member of the academic community, serving as a reviewer for several educational journals and an external examiner for multiple UK universities. Additionally, as a Quality Assurance Agency reviewer, he contributes to maintaining academic and institutional standards across the UK.

Beyond his work in the UK, Dr Seuwou's influence extends internationally. He has taught Executive MBA students in China, delivered guest lectures at Kathmandu University in Nepal, and engaged with academic and business communities globally. His writing has appeared in *Times Higher Education*, where he shares insights on education, leadership, and digital transformation.

Dr Patrice Seuwou's rare combination of technological expertise, business acumen, and educational leadership positions him as an authoritative voice on the digital business revolution. His deep understanding of both the technological and human dimensions of digital transformation ensures that his insights are both visionary and practical, offering readers a unique perspective on navigating the future of business in a rapidly evolving digital world.

Preface

The purpose of this book, *Digital Business: Navigating the Digital Landscape and Thriving in the Digital Economy*, is to provide a comprehensive exploration of the transformative power of digital technologies, their profound impact on businesses, and the emerging trends reshaping industries. It is designed to meet the needs of both undergraduate and postgraduate students while offering valuable insights for educators and professionals navigating the complexities of the digital economy. Covering key topics such as Digital Revolution, Digital Business Models, Digital Transformation and Innovation, Digital Business Strategy, Digital Marketing, Artificial Intelligence, Blockchain, the Internet of Things (IoT), 5G Connectivity, Cybersecurity, and Extended Reality, this book bridges the gap between theoretical foundations and practical applications. It ensures that readers not only understand these technologies but also grasp their implications for businesses striving to thrive in today's digital-first world.

This book has been crafted for a diverse audience, including students aiming to master the principles of digital business, educators seeking a robust teaching resource, and professionals keen to remain competitive in an ever-evolving landscape. Whether you are a student exploring strategies for digital transformation or a business leader seeking to incorporate emerging technologies into your operations, this book offers a structured, insightful, and practical guide to understanding and capitalising on the opportunities afforded by the digital economy.

The motivation to write this book stems from my academic journey and professional experience, which have afforded me an intimate view of the sweeping changes brought about by digitalisation. As businesses increasingly depend on technology to innovate, adapt, and grow, it became evident that there was a need for a resource that combines rigorous academic analysis with actionable insights. The proliferation of digital platforms, interconnected systems, and intelligent automation underscores the urgency for individuals and organisations to adapt to the challenges and opportunities of this rapidly evolving environment. This book was created to help readers develop the knowledge, skills, and strategies required to navigate and succeed in the digital business landscape.

Organised into chapters, this book explores distinct yet interconnected themes within digital business. It begins by establishing a foundational understanding of emerging technologies, then delves into transformative innovations such as AI and blockchain, before moving on to critical topics such as data privacy, cybersecurity, and ethical considerations in technology. Practical case studies, reflective questions, and insights into forward-looking trends ensure that readers can contextualise theoretical concepts within real-world applications.

Each chapter is designed with clear learning objectives to enable readers to grasp essential concepts, analyse their implications for businesses, and develop actionable strategies for harnessing their potential. This book includes pedagogical features such as concise chapter summaries, definitions of key terms, and discussion prompts, all of which enhance the learning process and encourage critical thinking.

Students are encouraged to engage deeply with the reflective questions and apply their insights to real-world scenarios, while educators can use the structured content and examples to frame lectures and discussions. By combining theoretical perspectives with practical applications, this book serves as both a foundational guide and an invaluable forward-looking resource for those seeking to navigate and thrive in the dynamic world of digital business.

Acknowledgements

I would like to express my deepest gratitude to Routledge and the University of Northampton for fostering an incredibly supportive and enriching environment in which this book was conceived and written. Their encouragement, resources, and belief in this project have provided the perfect foundation for bringing this vision to life. The commitment to academic excellence and innovation that both institutions uphold has been a continual source of inspiration throughout this journey.

To my delightful MBA, Executive MBA, and MSc students, I owe a special debt of gratitude. Your curiosity, insights, and boundless energy have not only shaped the content of this book but also deepened my own understanding of the ever-evolving field of digital business. The vibrant class discussions, the thought-provoking questions, and the countless hours spent in office meetings have been an invaluable source of inspiration. Your feedback and suggestions, often shared with enthusiasm and passion, have been instrumental in making this book practical, engaging, and relevant to today's fast-changing digital landscape. This book, in many ways, is as much yours as it is mine.

A profound and heartfelt thank you goes to my wife, Cece, whose unwavering love and support have been my anchor through the highs and lows of this writing journey. You have been my partner, cheerleader, and constant source of strength, always believing in me when the challenges seemed insurmountable. To my wonderful children, Willyam, Alanys, Robin, and Riley, you have been my greatest joy and inspiration. Your patience, understanding, and endless encouragement have lifted my spirits and reminded me of the importance of perseverance and passion. Each word of this book carries a piece of the love and strength you all have given me.

This book is not just a culmination of research, teaching, and professional experiences; it is a testament to the incredible people who have walked this path with me. To every mentor, colleague, student, friend, and family member who has been a part of this journey, thank you for your unwavering support, guidance, and belief in this project. It is because of all of you that this book exists, and I will forever be grateful.

CHAPTER 1

The Rise of Digital Business

An Introduction

Learning Objectives

By the end of this chapter, you will be able to:

1. Gain a comprehensive understanding of the digital revolution, its past, present, and the transformation of business models in the digital economy.
2. Analyse how digital disruption has reshaped industries, consumer behaviour, and the competitive landscape.
3. Understand the legal and regulatory considerations surrounding digital business, including how businesses adapt to the evolving landscape in a post-pandemic world.

1.1 INTRODUCTION

The fast integration of digital technologies into various elements of business and society is causing a revolutionary shift in the world. This chapter digs into the diverse digital business world, thoroughly examining its definition, evolution, and critical position in today's fast-changing market. This chapter aims to provide readers with essential insights for navigating the digital landscape and thriving in the digital economy by reviewing the digital revolution's past and present, comprehending the digital economy's dynamics, and analysing the impact of digital disruption.

BOX 1.1

Defining a Digital Business

A digital business is an organisation that leverages digital technologies to generate, deliver, and capture value in ways that significantly differ from traditional businesses. This concept highlights several key elements that distinguish digital businesses.

DOI: 10.4324/9781032672458-1

One of the most crucial elements is the extensive use of digital technology. Digital businesses rely heavily on various technologies such as the internet, mobile devices, social media, and cloud computing. These tools enable companies to interact with consumers, suppliers, and partners in innovative ways, often resulting in more efficient and effective communication channels.

Value creation is another defining characteristic of digital businesses. These organisations create value by offering new products, services, and experiences that are made possible through the use of digital technologies. For example, digital businesses can use these technologies to personalise customer experiences, provide real-time support, and optimise supply chains. By doing so, they can offer unique value propositions that are difficult for traditional businesses to replicate.

In addition to creating value, digital businesses also excel at value capture. They achieve this by monetising data and insights collected from customers and users. This information can be used to improve products and services, design targeted marketing campaigns, and personalise customer interactions. Such capabilities enable digital businesses to not only understand their customers better but also to continuously adapt and refine their offerings based on real-time feedback.

The definition of a digital business also highlights the fundamental differences between digital and traditional organisations. While traditional businesses may use digital technologies to enhance their existing operations, digital businesses integrate these technologies into the core of their business strategy. This fundamental distinction shapes how digital businesses operate and compete in the market, often giving them a strategic advantage over more conventional counterparts.

1.1.1 The Evolution of Business in the Digital Age

The early days of the internet (the 1990s): Businesses largely used the internet to reach new clients and market their products and services in the early days of the internet. This was the era of the "dot-com bubble," when many new firms were formed to profit quickly from the internet.

The rise of e-commerce in the 2000s: E-commerce began to take off in the 2000s, and firms began to use the internet to offer products and services directly to consumers. This resulted in the rise of online merchants such as Amazon and eBay and the demise of traditional brick-and-mortar storefronts.

The era of mobile internet (the 2010s): The mobile internet became increasingly popular in the 2010s, and businesses began to employ mobile devices to reach clients. This resulted in the developing of mobile apps, social networking, and mobile payments.

The present digital epoch (the 2020s): The current digital era is distinguished by the growing convergence of digital technology. This means organisations can now create, deliver, and collect value using diverse digital technologies. As a result, new business models, such as the sharing economy, have emerged along with the change of old firms.

Various factors have influenced the evolution of business in the digital age, including the rise of the internet, the proliferation of mobile devices, and the increasing convergence of digital technologies. These variables have given businesses new opportunities, but they have also given them new obstacles. Businesses that can adapt to the digital world will be well-positioned for success in the coming years.

1.1.2 Important Trends Affecting Company Evolution in the Digital Age

Artificial intelligence (AI) is rapidly becoming a mainstream technology, with organisations increasingly adopting it to automate tasks, enhance decision-making processes, and develop innovative products and services. Its integration is transforming traditional business models and operations, enabling companies to operate more efficiently and create more personalised customer experiences.

The surge in big data is another significant trend, as the volume of data being generated is growing exponentially. Businesses are leveraging this vast amount of information to gain deeper insights into customer behaviour, refine product development, and optimise marketing strategies. The ability to analyse and utilise data effectively is becoming a crucial competitive advantage in the digital landscape.

Security is a pressing concern as companies become more reliant on digital technologies. As cyber threats grow in both number and sophistication, businesses must implement robust measures to safeguard their data and ensure the integrity of their systems. Protecting sensitive information and maintaining trust with customers are essential aspects of operating in the digital age.

The evolution of business in the digital era is still in its nascent stages, and predicting the future remains challenging. However, it is clear that digital technologies are fundamentally altering how businesses operate. Companies that embrace and adapt to these changes will be better positioned to thrive and succeed in this dynamic environment.

1.1.3 Importance of Understanding Digital Business

Understanding digital businesses is critical for firms seeking to thrive and remain competitive in today's fast-changing environment. Organisations that fail to embrace digital technology and strategies risk slipping behind their competition. Embracing digital transformation is critical for corporate survival and competitiveness because it allows organisations to experiment with new business models, find growth possibilities, and adapt to meet changing customer expectations.

Improved customer involvement is one of the primary benefits of understanding digital businesses. Digital channels enable organisations to create personalised and engaging experiences with their customers, fostering better relationships and increased customer loyalty. Furthermore, digital technologies enable data-driven decision-making. Organisations that understand digital enterprises may use analytics to make educated decisions, optimise operations, and drive business growth with massive amounts of data from multiple sources.

The digital age has also torn geographic borders, allowing firms to reach worldwide audiences. Understanding digital enterprises enables organisations to broaden their market reach

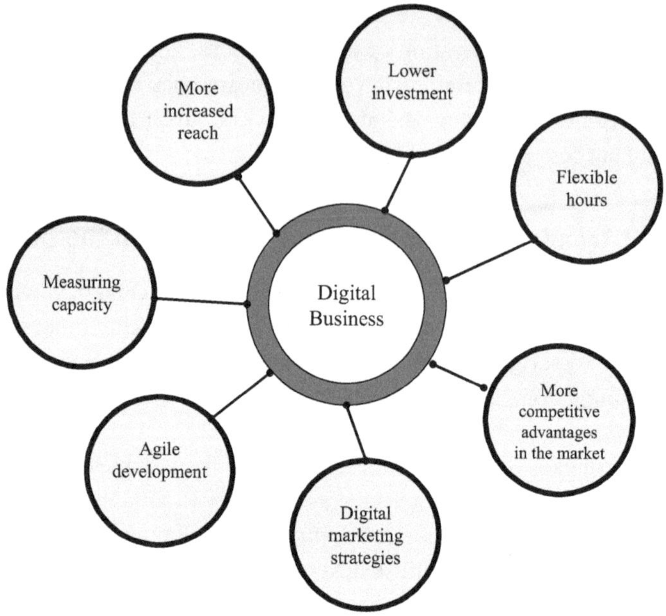

FIGURE 1.1 Benefits of a Digital Business

and reach new client segments worldwide. Furthermore, it fosters agility and adaptability, critical characteristics in today's rapidly changing digital landscape. Staying competitive and relevant requires responding swiftly to market trends, consumer preferences, and emerging technology.

The adoption of digital technologies improves the cost-effectiveness and efficiency of corporate operations. Process automation and streamlining can help to decrease operational costs and maximise resources. Furthermore, digital disruption is altering industries and opening up new opportunities. Organisations that understand digital enterprises can better negotiate disruption, embrace change, and position themselves for success in an ever-changing world (Figure 1.1).

Understanding digital businesses attracts tech-savvy individuals and helps organisations prepare for the future. By embracing digital transformation, firms can remain relevant and adaptable as technology evolves. Because of the fast-changing nature of the digital world, knowing digital business is a requirement rather than a choice. Failure to adopt digital practices may result in missed opportunities, loss of market share, and decreased long-term sustainability.

1.2 DIGITAL REVOLUTION: PAST AND PRESENT

The Digital Revolution, a transformative age of technical developments, has significantly altered how people live, work, and communicate. This revolution has transformed industries, revolutionised communication, and upset old business models since the advent of computers in the mid-20th century through the widespread adoption of the internet in recent decades. The Digital Revolution's trajectory represents a never-ending drive of innovation, with important milestones such as the birth of the World Wide Web and the proliferation of smartphones. We see the immense impact of digital technologies on society as we delve into the past and present of this transformative era, setting the way for a future marked by limitless possibilities and ever-accelerating change.

1.2.1 The Emergence of Computers and the Internet

Computers and the internet have a lengthy and complicated history, although they can be traced back to the early 20th century. The original computers were big, expensive equipment utilised for study by scientists and engineers. However, in the 1950s and 1960s, computers began to shrink and become more affordable, making them more accessible to a larger range of individuals. In the 1960s, the internet arose for scientists and researchers to share knowledge. The original internet networks were government-funded, but the internet began to open up to the public in the 1980s. The World Wide Web, the graphical interface through which we now access the internet, was invented in 1990. The introduction of computers and the internet had a significant impact on society. Computers have altered how we work, communicate, and learn. The internet has enabled individuals worldwide to connect with one another, and it has given rise to new enterprises and industries (Table 1.1).

TABLE 1.1 Significant Milestones in the History of Computers and the Internet

Year	Event	Description
1946	Construction of ENIAC	The Electronic Numerical Integrator and Computer (ENIAC) was completed. It was the first digital electronic computer, marking a significant milestone in computing.
1957	Launch of Sputnik	The Soviet Union launched Sputnik, the first artificial satellite. This event prompted the United States to develop the ARPANET, a precursor to the modern internet.
1969	First ARPANET Message	The first message was transmitted over the ARPANET, establishing a foundation for the future development of the internet.
1983	Division of ARPANET	The ARPANET split into two separate networks: MILNET, reserved for military communication, and ARPANET, dedicated to academic and civilian use.
1990	Creation of the World Wide Web	Tim Berners-Lee developed the World Wide Web, a system of interlinked hypertext documents accessible via the internet, revolutionising information sharing.
1993	Introduction of Mosaic	Mosaic, the first graphical web browser, was launched. It provided a user-friendly interface that significantly boosted public interest in the World Wide Web.
1995	Establishment of First Commercial ISPs	The first commercial internet service providers (ISPs) were established, making the internet accessible to the general public and fostering its rapid growth.

The introduction of computers and the internet had a significant impact on society. Computers have altered how we work, communicate, and learn. The internet has enabled individuals worldwide to connect, giving rise to new enterprises and industries. Computers and the internet's future are uncertain, but these technologies will continue to play a significant role in our lives.

1.2.2 Major Technological Milestones in the Digital Revolution

Several important technological achievements fuelled the digital revolution, including the birth of the transistor, the microprocessor's development, the internet's advent, and the growth of mobile devices. In 1947, the transistor was invented, revolutionising how computers were built. Transistors are smaller and more efficient than vacuum tubes, the prior computer technology. This enabled the development of smaller, more powerful computers. In 1971, the microprocessor was invented, hastening the pace of the digital revolution. Microprocessors are small computers that can be installed on other devices like cell phones and automobiles. This has resulted in an increase in the number of digital devices in our lives. The internet was created in the 1960s and has significantly impacted how we communicate and share information. The internet has enabled individuals worldwide to connect with one another, and it has given rise to new enterprises and industries. Smartphones and tablets have become increasingly common in recent years. Thanks to mobile smartphones, people may now access the internet and digital content on the go. This has altered how we work, learn, and play. These are just a few important technological breakthroughs that have propelled the digital revolution. These technologies have significantly impacted our lives and will continue to shape our world in the coming years (Table 1.2).

The digital revolution is still unfolding, and the future is impossible to foresee. These technologies, however, will undoubtedly continue to play an important role in our lives.

1.2.3 Impact of Digital Revolution on Traditional Business Models

The rise of e-commerce has profoundly transformed traditional brick-and-mortar businesses. By enabling companies to sell products and services online, e-commerce has allowed customers to shop from virtually anywhere in the world. This shift has disrupted conventional retail models and changed consumer expectations about the availability and convenience of shopping.

The growth of mobile commerce has further reshaped traditional business practices. With the increasing use of smartphones and tablets, customers can now make purchases on the go, making it easier than ever for them to shop wherever they are. This trend has forced businesses to adapt their strategies to provide seamless and responsive mobile shopping experiences.

New business models, such as the sharing economy, have emerged as a direct result of the digital revolution. Platforms like Airbnb and Uber have redefined how services are delivered by connecting customers directly with one another, bypassing traditional service providers. This has led to the creation of entirely new industries and has presented both opportunities and challenges for established businesses.

TABLE 1.2 Major Technological Milestones in the Digital Revolution

Year	Milestone	Description
1971	Microprocessor Invented	Intel introduces the first microprocessor, the Intel 4004, paving the way for personal computers (PCs) and digital devices.
1973	Invention of Ethernet	Robert Metcalfe invents Ethernet, revolutionising data communication and networking capabilities in computer systems.
1981	Introduction of IBM PC	IBM launches the first PC, which standardises the PC market and popularises computer use in homes and businesses.
1984	Launch of the Macintosh	Apple introduces the Macintosh, the first mass-market PC with a graphical user interface (GUI).
1989	World Wide Web Conceptualised	Tim Berners-Lee proposes the concept of the World Wide Web, which would enable users to navigate and share information globally.
1991	Launch of the World Wide Web	The World Wide Web has become publicly accessible, revolutionising how information is shared and consumed online.
1998	Google Founded	Google is founded, becoming one of the most influential search engines and a cornerstone of the digital age.
2001	Introduction of the iPod	Apple releases the iPod, revolutionising digital music consumption and paving the way for mobile digital devices.
2004	Launch of Facebook	Facebook is launched, signalling the rise of social media and fundamentally changing how people connect and communicate.
2007	Introduction of the iPhone	Apple introduces the iPhone, redefining the smartphone industry and revolutionising mobile computing and communication.
2010	Introduction of the iPad	Apple launches the iPad, popularising tablet computing and expanding the digital device ecosystem.
2014	Rise of Artificial Intelligence	AI technologies, such as deep learning and neural networks, gain traction, leading to advancements in machine learning and automation.
2017	Mainstream Adoption of Cloud Computing	Cloud computing has become mainstream, enabling businesses to store, process, and manage data more efficiently and flexibly.
2020	Acceleration of Digital Transformation	COVID-19 pandemic accelerates digital transformation across industries, boosting remote work, e-commerce, and digital collaboration tools.

Customer expectations have also evolved in response to the digital revolution. Consumers now demand round-the-clock availability and personalised services from companies. Businesses must be agile and responsive to meet these heightened expectations or risk losing customers to more adaptive competitors.

Another significant impact of the digital revolution is the diminishing role of intermediaries. As it becomes easier for businesses to communicate directly with customers through digital channels, the traditional role of middlemen is being challenged. This shift has disrupted industries that rely heavily on intermediaries and has forced many businesses to rethink their value propositions.

Data has become increasingly valuable in the digital age. Companies that can collect, analyse, and leverage data effectively gain critical insights into consumer behaviour, enabling them to refine their products and services and make more informed business decisions. The ability to harness data is becoming a key differentiator in the competitive landscape.

Innovation is more crucial than ever as the digital revolution continuously evolves. Businesses must innovate to keep pace with technological advancements and changing consumer preferences. Those that fail to innovate risk being overtaken by more agile competitors who can effectively leverage new technologies.

The digital revolution is a powerful force reshaping traditional business practices. It is driving the evolution of business models and challenging companies to adapt and innovate. Organisations that can navigate this rapidly changing landscape and embrace digital transformation will be well-positioned for success in the future.

1.3 THE DIGITAL ECONOMY: A GLOBAL PERSPECTIVE

The digital economy is a revolutionary force in the fast-changing world of the 21st century, transcending borders and reshaping established corporate models. The digital economy has grown as a dynamic and interconnected global ecosystem as digital technology and the internet continue penetrating every area of our lives. In this section, we will look at the digital economy globally, delving into its essential components, the players driving its expansion, and the dynamic market dynamics at work. From the rise of e-commerce to the revolutionary power of digital marketing, we explore how the digital economy has transformed how businesses function and how consumers interact in an increasingly interconnected world. As we negotiate the complexities of this digital ecosystem, we acquire insights into the digital economy's far-reaching impact and its role in determining the future of global trade and innovation.

1.3.1 Understanding the Digital Economy

The digital economy refers to economic activities that are enabled by digital technologies, encompassing areas such as e-commerce, online banking, social media, and cloud computing. This sector is rapidly growing and has become a significant driver of economic growth. Several factors are contributing to the expansion of the digital economy. These include increased access to broadband internet, the widespread use of mobile devices, and the growing adoption of cloud computing. Furthermore, the development of emerging technologies such as AI and blockchain is also accelerating the growth of the digital economy.

The impact of the digital economy on business operations is profound. Companies that adapt to the demands of the digital economy are more likely to succeed, while those that fail to do so risk being overtaken by newer enterprises that are better equipped to leverage these technologies. To fully grasp the digital economy, it is essential to understand several key concepts.

Firstly, digital technologies form the foundation of the digital economy. This includes the internet, mobile devices, cloud computing, and AI. These technologies enable new ways of conducting business and interacting with customers.

Secondly, digital platforms play a crucial role in connecting businesses with their customers. Platforms such as Amazon, eBay, and Facebook act as intermediaries, facilitating transactions and communication between different parties.

Data is another essential component of the digital economy, often referred to as its fuel. Businesses that can effectively collect and analyse data gain valuable insights into customer behaviour, which can be used to refine products and services, enhancing their overall value proposition.

Innovation is also a cornerstone of success in the digital economy. Companies that are able to innovate can stay ahead of their competitors and carve out new market opportunities. Being at the forefront of technological advancements and creative business solutions is key to thriving in this dynamic environment.

1.3.2 Key Players in the Digital Economy

The digital economy is a complex and dynamic environment, characterised by a diverse array of influential players who are shaping its development. Among the most prominent are the tech giants such as Google, Amazon, and Meta (formerly Facebook). These companies wield significant influence across multiple sectors and are continually pushing the boundaries of innovation. Their expansive reach extends from search engines and e-commerce to social media and cloud computing, making them central pillars of the digital landscape.

FinTech companies have also become key players by leveraging technology to revolutionise the financial services sector. These firms provide innovative financial products and services, such as peer-to-peer lending, digital wallets, and mobile payment solutions, challenging traditional banking models and enhancing accessibility and convenience for consumers.

E-commerce companies are rapidly transforming the retail industry by enabling the sale of goods and services online. Their growth has fundamentally altered consumer behaviour, offering unprecedented convenience and choice and driving significant shifts in how products are marketed and sold.

Social media companies play a pivotal role in connecting people online. Platforms such as Instagram, Twitter, and LinkedIn serve not only as social networks but also as powerful tools for businesses to engage with customers and build brand loyalty. These platforms have become essential for marketing, customer service, and community building.

Data companies, which specialise in collecting and selling information, are another crucial component of the digital economy. They provide valuable insights that businesses use to refine products and services, while governments utilise this data for monitoring and policymaking. The ability to analyse large datasets has become a critical competitive advantage across various industries.

Telecommunications companies are indispensable in providing the infrastructure that underpins the digital economy. They build and maintain the networks that enable connectivity for both individuals and businesses, supporting everything from basic internet access to advanced digital services.

Cloud computing firms offer scalable computing resources and storage solutions, allowing organisations to expand their operations without significant upfront investment in their own infrastructure. This has been transformative for businesses of all sizes, enabling greater flexibility, cost-efficiency, and innovation.

Cybersecurity companies are increasingly vital as the threat of cyberattacks grows. These firms work to protect businesses and individuals from a range of digital threats, safeguarding sensitive data and ensuring the continuity of operations in an increasingly connected world.

Regulatory bodies also play a crucial role in the digital economy by overseeing compliance with laws and regulations. They work to ensure fair competition, protect consumer rights, and address issues such as data privacy and cybersecurity. Their influence is critical in shaping the ethical and legal framework within which digital businesses operate.

These entities represent just a portion of the major forces driving the digital economy. As the landscape continues to evolve, new players will emerge, and existing ones will adapt, but the impact of these key participants will continue to shape the future of digital innovation and economic growth.

1.3.3 Digital Business and Global Market Dynamics

Digital business and global market dynamics are inextricably linked in today's interconnected world. With the introduction of digital technologies and the internet, geographical barriers have been broken down, allowing firms to expand their reach beyond local markets to a worldwide scale. Digital platforms have evolved into entry points for businesses to reach out to a wide range of customers, facilitating cross-border transactions and interactions. Furthermore, the digital landscape has heralded a new era of competitiveness in which both startups and established firms can disrupt old markets and grasp opportunities on a global scale. Factors such as quickly changing consumer behaviour, developing technologies, regulatory regimes, and cultural nuances impact global market dynamics in the digital arena. Understanding these dynamics is critical for organisations seeking to manage the intricacies of foreign marketplaces, adapt to various client tastes, and employ digital tools to establish a worldwide competitive advantage.

1.4 DIGITAL DISRUPTION AND ITS EFFECTS

Digital disruption has become a potent force affecting sectors, business structures, and consumer behaviour in an age of rapid technological breakthroughs. The disruptive impact of breakthrough technology, digital platforms, and data-driven initiatives that challenge old conventions and create new paradigms is called digital disruption. No business is immune to the far-reaching consequences of digital disruption, from traditional retail to financial services, healthcare to transportation. This section delves into digital disruption and its far-reaching consequences for businesses and society. We look at real-world examples of industries disrupted by digital pioneers, why traditional organisations need to adapt, and what opportunities and problems this revolutionary wave brings. Businesses can embrace change, capture emerging opportunities, and position themselves for success in an ever-changing digital landscape by comprehending digital technology's disruptive impact.

1.4.1 Examples of Disrupted Industries

Table 1.3 illustrates the profound impact of digital technology on a wide range of industries, transforming traditional business models and creating new opportunities and challenges. The music industry, for example, has seen a seismic shift from physical media to digital streaming platforms, altering revenue streams and consumer behaviour. Similarly, the rise of e-commerce has revolutionised the retail landscape, enabling customers to shop online and diminishing the relevance of brick-and-mortar stores. Traditional service sectors such as taxis and hotels have also been disrupted by the advent of ride-hailing apps and home-sharing platforms, which offer consumers more flexible and cost-effective alternatives. The finance, healthcare, and education sectors are not immune either, as FinTech, telemedicine, and online learning platforms reshape the way services are delivered. These disruptions illustrate the ongoing evolution of the digital economy, where adaptability and innovation are crucial for businesses to thrive in an increasingly competitive environment (Table 1.3).

TABLE 1.3 Examples of Disrupted Industries

Industry	Disruption Cause	Impact
Music	Digital technology, such as MP3 players and streaming services	Digital platforms like Spotify and Apple Music have transformed how people access music, leading to a significant decline in physical media sales and reshaping revenue models for artists and record labels.
Print Media	Internet and social media	Traditional newspapers and magazines have experienced a drop in readership due to the ease of accessing news and information online, resulting in reduced advertising revenues and closures of print outlets.
Retail	E-commerce platforms like Amazon and eBay	E-commerce has revolutionised shopping habits, leading to a decline in physical store sales, store closures, and the rise of logistics and warehousing to support online retail operations.
Taxi Services	Ride-hailing apps such as Uber and Lyft	These platforms have made personal transport more accessible, reducing the market share and profitability of traditional taxi services while introducing new regulatory and labour issues.
Hospitality	Home-sharing platforms like Airbnb	Short-term rental services have disrupted the hotel industry by providing more flexible and often cheaper accommodation options, impacting hotel occupancy rates and pricing strategies.
Travel	Online booking sites like Expedia and Priceline	The traditional travel agency model has been largely replaced by online platforms, which offer consumers the ability to compare and book flights, hotels, and car rentals independently, reshaping the travel industry

(Continued)

TABLE 1.3 (Continued)

Industry	Disruption Cause	Impact
Telecommunications	Smartphones and mobile internet	The decline of landlines and traditional cable TV has accelerated due to the widespread adoption of mobile phones and streaming services, forcing telecom companies to adapt to new service demands.
Financial Services	FinTech companies such as Square and PayPal	FinTech innovations have made transactions, lending, and financial management more accessible, challenging traditional banking models and encouraging traditional banks to innovate or partner with tech firms.
Healthcare	Telemedicine technologies	Virtual consultations and remote monitoring are becoming more common, not only making healthcare more accessible but also challenging traditional patient care models and healthcare facility utilisation.
Education	Online learning platforms	The rise of Massive Open Online Courses (MOOCs) and online degree programmes allows students to learn from anywhere, challenging traditional classroom-based education and institutional funding models.

The digital economy is upending sectors around the world. Enterprises that cannot adapt to these developments risk being disrupted by new enterprises that can leverage new technologies.

1.4.2 Why Traditional Businesses Need to Adapt

For various reasons, traditional businesses must adapt to the digital age, including the advent of e-commerce, which poses a serious threat to brick-and-mortar firms. Expanding e-commerce allows firms to offer items and services online, making it easier for customers to shop abroad. Similarly, the increasing growth of mobile commerce adds to the convenience of online buying by allowing users to purchase from their smartphones and tablets. Customer expectations have shifted in the digital age, with 24/7 access and personalised care becoming the standard.

Data have become the digital economy's lifeblood, and firms that can collect and analyse data receive important insights into client behaviour, allowing them to improve their offers. Staying ahead of the competition in the fast-paced digital world needs ongoing innovation. Businesses that fail to innovate are subject to disruption from new initiatives that use developing technologies.

Furthermore, because the internet has broken geographical barriers, conventional firms must adapt to reach a larger audience through a strong online presence. Embracing the digital world also allows for cost savings through internet marketing, which eliminates the need for traditional advertising expenses. Businesses can boost productivity by accessing processing power and storage without investing heavily in infrastructure.

Traditional firms have both challenges and opportunities in the digital age. On the other hand, those that adapt and embrace the digital transition will be better positioned to succeed in the changing terrain of the future.

1.4.3 Opportunities and Challenges of Digital Disruption

The influence of digital technologies on traditional business structures and industries, revolutionising how businesses operate and compete, is referred to as digital disruption. This phenomenon creates many opportunities and challenges for organisations in the digital age.

With the introduction of digital technologies, new markets and options for enterprises open up. E-commerce, for example, allows you to offer products and services online to a larger customer base. Digital technologies also increase efficiency by enabling organisations to use cloud computing for computing power and storage without making significant infrastructure investments. Furthermore, increased customer service is achievable with chatbots, which provide round-the-clock help. Furthermore, digital technologies stimulate innovation, allowing firms to create new products and services suited to individual customers' demands.

However, digital disruption brings with it new obstacles that organisations must overcome. The increased ease of entrance for new enterprises due to digital technologies increases market competitiveness. The regulatory involvement of governments in digital spheres provides compliance issues for enterprises. Cybersecurity dangers are becoming more prevalent as digital technologies advance, necessitating strengthening firms' security procedures. Furthermore, data privacy issues need rigorous data management in order to comply with rules.

Businesses face new hurdles as the digital era progresses. A skills gap occurs, necessitating hiring workers with digital capabilities, prompting organisations to invest in training or hiring individuals with the necessary skills. The digital age necessitates a cultural transformation in firms to keep up with the rate of change and become more agile and adaptable. Understanding the potential and difficulties of digital disruption is required to embrace the digital age fully. Businesses should position themselves for success in the dynamic digital landscape of the future by capitalising on opportunities and proactively tackling problems.

CASE STUDY 1

McDonald's Digital Transformation—A Recipe for Success in the Digital Age

McDonald's, the world's largest fast-food chain, has long been recognised for its consistency, efficiency, and global reach. However, in the face of increasing competition from digital-first food service companies and shifting consumer expectations, the company realised that it needed to evolve. Customers were demanding faster service, greater personalisation, and seamless digital ordering options, while digital-native competitors such as Uber Eats, Deliveroo, and Domino's Pizza were redefining customer engagement. Additionally, McDonald's was facing operational inefficiencies, long wait times, order inaccuracies, and rising labour costs. These challenges made it clear that digital transformation was not just an option but a necessity for the company's continued success.

To address these challenges, McDonald's implemented a multi-faceted digital strategy, integrating technology into various aspects of its operations. A major shift came with the introduction of self-service kiosks, which allowed customers to place their orders independently, reducing queues and improving order accuracy. Alongside this, the company launched its mobile ordering and loyalty app, which enabled customers to pre-order food, customise their meals, and earn rewards through a digital points system. McDonald's also embraced AI by acquiring *Dynamic Yield*, an AI-driven personalisation company, which allowed them to introduce smart menu recommendations based on factors such as weather conditions, time of day, and purchasing behaviour. This use of AI further streamlined the customer journey and increased average spending per order.

In addition to enhancing its in-store and mobile experiences, McDonald's capitalised on the booming food delivery market by forming strategic partnerships with platforms such as Uber Eats and DoorDash. This expanded the company's reach beyond physical stores, allowing them to serve customers who preferred home delivery. At the same time, the company optimised its kitchen operations with AI-powered systems that improved food preparation times, reduced waste, and enhanced overall efficiency.

The results of this digital transformation were significant. By 2023, digital sales accounted for nearly 40% of McDonald's total revenue in key markets, demonstrating the success of its digital-first approach. Customers benefitted from faster service, increased personalisation, and greater convenience, while McDonald's saw higher engagement through its app, improved operational efficiency, and an expanded market reach. The integration of AI and data analytics also provided valuable insights into consumer preferences, enabling the company to refine its offerings and further enhance customer satisfaction.

McDonald's transformation provides several key takeaways for businesses navigating digital change. Firstly, it underscores the importance of adaptation and innovation, even for well-established brands.

No business, regardless of its legacy, can afford to ignore digital disruption. Secondly, the case highlights the significance of a customer-centric approach, where personalisation and convenience drive engagement. Furthermore, it demonstrates how technology and data analytics can create a competitive advantage by optimising operations and enhancing decision-making. Finally, it reinforces the importance of an omnichannel presence, where businesses leverage multiple digital platforms to reach and serve customers effectively.

McDonald's success in digital transformation serves as a powerful case study for companies looking to modernise their operations and improve customer experiences in an increasingly digital world.

Discussion Questions for Students (with Indicative Answers)

1. **What were the key factors driving McDonald's digital transformation?**
   Indicative Answer: McDonald's needed to meet changing customer expectations, improve efficiency, reduce labour costs, and compete with digital-first brands like Uber Eats and Domino's.
2. **How did self-service kiosks and AI-driven menu recommendations improve customer experience?**
   Indicative Answer: Self-service kiosks reduced wait times and order errors, while AI-driven recommendations offered personalised promotions and enhanced sales.
3. **What role did partnerships with third-party delivery platforms play in McDonald's strategy?**
   Indicative Answer: These partnerships helped McDonald's expand its reach beyond physical stores, capturing the growing market for food delivery services.
4. **What potential risks or challenges could arise from McDonald's reliance on digital technology?**
   Indicative Answer: Challenges include cybersecurity risks, potential loss of human interaction, and the risk of alienating customers who prefer traditional ordering methods.
5. **What lessons can other traditional businesses learn from McDonald's digital transformation?**
   Indicative Answer: Businesses should embrace digital innovation to improve customer experience, leverage data analytics for better decision-making, and integrate technology seamlessly into operations.

1.5 ADVANTAGES OF DIGITAL BUSINESS

The benefits of digital business have transformed how businesses function and connect with their clients in the digital age. In this section, we will look at the revolutionary benefits that digital technology provides to firms in a variety of industries. Digital business models have evolved as significant instruments for gaining a competitive edge in today's fast-paced and interconnected world, from cost-effectiveness and scalability to better accessibility and reach. Furthermore, the part discusses how digital platforms improve consumer engagement by providing personalised experiences, creating strong customer relationships, and increasing brand loyalty. Embracing the benefits of digital business enables organisations to improve productivity, broaden their market reach, and provide unmatched value to their clients, setting them up for success in the ever-changing digital marketplace.

1.5.1 Cost-Effectiveness and Scalability

Compared to traditional brick-and-mortar installations, digital business models provide considerable cost advantages. By embracing digital technologies, businesses can minimise operational costs connected with physical infrastructure, rent, utilities, and staff. Online transactions and automated processes reduce the need for manual involvement, streamlining operations and saving money. Furthermore, digital platforms allow organisations to develop quickly without making large upfront investments. Digital enterprises can extend their operations effectively, whether catering to a local audience or reaching a worldwide market, making scalability a vital advantage in today's fast-paced economy.

1.5.2 Accessibility and Reach

Digital business eliminates time and geography constraints, allowing customers and clients to access products and services 24 hours a day, 7 days a week from nearly anywhere in the world. Geographical barriers are becoming outdated as online platforms connect firms with a worldwide audience, allowing them to enter previously untouched areas. The simplicity of shopping online or accessing services remotely improves the customer experience, leading to higher customer satisfaction and loyalty. Furthermore, digital marketing methods allow businesses to efficiently target specific consumers, optimising reach and engagement with personalised content.

1.5.3 Improved Customer Engagement and Personalisation

Digital technologies enable organisations to develop more meaningful interactions with their customers. Businesses can engage in real-time dialogues, handle customer queries, and gain vital feedback through social media, email marketing, and interactive websites. Customer engagement increases brand loyalty and trust. Furthermore, data analytics and AI allow firms to analyse client behaviour and preferences, enabling personalised product suggestions and targeted marketing campaigns. Personalisation improves the total consumer experience, giving digital firms a competitive advantage.

1.6 IMPACT ON CONSUMER BEHAVIOUR

Digitalisation has transformed consumer behaviour, transforming how people engage with brands and make purchasing decisions. The development of the connected consumer, armed with digital gadgets and immediate access to information, has changed how individuals research products, compare alternatives, and interact with businesses. Peer recommendations increasingly carry enormous weight in social media and online reviews, which play key roles in influencing consumer choices. Furthermore, the customer journey has evolved into a complicated and non-linear process that includes several encounters across digital platforms. Understanding these changes in consumer behaviour is critical for organisations hoping to flourish in the fast-paced digital economy.

1.6.1 The Connected Consumer: How Has Digitalisation Changed Consumer Behaviour?

Digitalisation has ushered in the connected consumer era, profoundly altering how people interact with brands and make purchasing decisions. Thanks to internet access and a plethora of digital devices, consumers are more aware, empowered, and connected than ever. The internet is a wonderful research tool, allowing people to acquire information, compare items, read reviews, and make informed decisions. Consumers may instantly access product specifications, pricing, and customer comments at home, on the go, or in-store, impacting their purchasing decisions.

Furthermore, technology has altered the purchasing process. Consumers now have multi-channel and omnichannel shopping experiences, fluidly switching between online and offline touchpoints. They might come across a product through a social media ad, investigate it on a brand's website, read online reviews, and then buy it in-store or through a mobile app. Customers' pleasure and loyalty can be increased by brands understanding the connected consumer journey and providing consistent experiences across channels.

1.6.2 The Contribution of Social Media and Online Reviews

In the digital age, social media and online reviews significantly impact customer behaviour. Social media platforms such as Facebook (Meta), Instagram, Twitter, and YouTube have evolved into effective marketing channels, allowing firms to reach a large audience and interact directly with customers. Influencer marketing, social media advertising, and user-generated content all play important roles in moulding brand views and generating purchase intent. Consumers frequently use social media for product recommendations, brand updates, and real-time interactions with businesses; therefore, businesses must maintain an active and engaging social media presence.

Online reviews have also become an important factor in consumer decision-making. Consumers trust their peers' opinions more than traditional advertising, and internet reviews provide accurate information about product quality, customer service, and general business reputation. Positive reviews can help a brand's credibility, but negative ones might hurt it. Businesses must actively manage and respond to online reviews to effectively create trust and handle customer problems.

1.6.3 Recognising the Customer Journey in the Digital Age

The digital era has changed the typical customer journey, making it more complex and non-linear. Customers now interact with brands through several touchpoints on various devices and platforms. The customer journey can begin with a Google search and progress to social media interactions, website visits, and in-store sales or online transactions. Understanding this disjointed journey is crucial for organisations to create consistent experiences and exceed customer expectations at each point.

Data-driven insights and analytics are critical for understanding the consumer journey. Companies use data to map client touchpoints, identify pain points, and optimise interactions in order to increase customer happiness. Businesses that use customer journey mapping methodologies obtain a full understanding of the consumer's path to buy, allowing them to deliver personalised messaging and bespoke experiences. Such insights enable organisations to engage customers in a proactive manner, anticipate their requirements, and make relevant recommendations, boosting the likelihood of conversion and client retention.

1.7 LEGAL AND REGULATORY CONSIDERATIONS

Businesses must traverse a complicated web of legal and regulatory considerations as the digital economy evolves to assure compliance and protect their operations. This section goes into three essential areas of digital-age legal and regulatory frameworks: data privacy and protection laws, cybersecurity rules, and intellectual property (IP) rights.

1.7.1 Data Privacy and Protection Legislation

Data have evolved as a significant asset in the digital era, propelling business growth and providing personalised client experiences. On the other hand, personal data collection, storage, and processing are major responsibilities to protect persons' privacy and prevent misuse. Data privacy and protection legislation, such as the General Data Protection Regulation of the European Union and the California Consumer Privacy Act, impose rigorous requirements on firms that handle personal data. These laws require express consent for data collection, comprehensive privacy practices, and the right of individuals to access, correct, and remove their data.

Compliance with data privacy rules is not only a legal requirement but also builds consumer trust. Data breaches and privacy violations can result in significant reputational harm and costly fines. Businesses must adopt robust data protection measures, encrypt sensitive information, conduct frequent security audits, and guarantee that data are only used for authorised purposes to comply with data privacy requirements.

1.7.2 Cybersecurity Policies and Procedures

Businesses are vulnerable to a wide range of cyber threats in the digital realm, including data breaches, ransomware attacks, and phishing schemes. Governments and regulatory agencies worldwide have enacted cybersecurity legislation and standards in response to the rising cybersecurity risks. These restrictions require organisations to protect their systems and networks proactively.

Implementing cybersecurity best practices to reinforce the digital business infrastructure is critical. This includes employing multi-factor authentication, routinely upgrading software, performing employee cybersecurity awareness training, and establishing intrusion detection systems. Furthermore, businesses should develop incident response plans to quickly address and mitigate cyber problems while maintaining the trust of consumers and partners.

1.7.3 Rights to Intellectual Property in the Digital Age

IP rights have become increasingly important in the digital era as digital assets, content, and inventions are shared and accessible throughout the internet. Patents, trademarks, copyrights, and trade secrets are all forms of IP that provide legal protection for creative works, inventions, and brand identities. Businesses must protect their IP in order to avoid unauthorised usage or infringement by competitors or harmful actors.

Because content may be easily reproduced and shared in the digital age, protecting IP offers new issues. Content creators and brand owners face major dangers from digital piracy and counterfeiting. Businesses must register patents, trademarks, and copyrights to protect their IP and rigorously pursue their rights against infringement. They should also consider utilising digital rights management technologies to govern digital material access and distribution.

1.8 DIGITAL BUSINESS IN THE POST-PANDEMIC WORLD

The COVID-19 epidemic caused a seismic upheaval in the corporate landscape, forcing organisations to quickly embrace digital strategies to survive and grow. As the world transitions into the post-pandemic era, digital business models have proven critical in navigating problems and capitalising on emerging opportunities. This part delves into the faster adoption of digital technology during the crisis, as well as the ongoing influence of COVID-19 on digital business strategies, to examine the tremendous impact of digitalisation in the post-pandemic environment. Businesses leverage digital transformation to change their operations and meet the shifting needs of a dynamic and resilient future, from hybrid business models to e-commerce innovation and remote work arrangements.

1.8.1 The Acceleration of Digital Adoption During the Pandemic

The COVID-19 epidemic has presented businesses worldwide with unprecedented obstacles, needing rapid adaption to survive in the face of lockdowns, social distancing measures, and disruptions to typical operations. In this scenario, digital business models have emerged as saviours, allowing organisations to stay connected with customers, run operations remotely, and manage to alter consumer behaviour.

The pandemic has pushed digital adoption across industries, forcing businesses to embrace technology in ways they have never done before. E-commerce saw a boom in demand as consumers sought safety and convenience in online shopping. Companies that formerly relied on physical stores quickly shifted their focus to digital platforms in order to contact clients electronically. The adoption of contactless payment technologies has accelerated the shift away from cash transactions, assuring a sanitary shopping experience.

Telecommuting has become the new normal, with remote work technologies such as video conferencing and collaboration software allowing for smooth communication and cooperation among remote teams. Traditional gatherings were supplanted by virtual events, webinars, and online conferences, which kept firms linked with customers and stakeholders.

Furthermore, the pandemic has increased the use of digital health technologies, including telemedicine and health monitoring applications, to meet healthcare demands remotely. The education and entertainment industries embraced online learning platforms and streaming services to appeal to a captive audience confined to their homes.

1.8.2 The Ongoing Impact of COVID-19 on Digital Business Strategies

As the world moves beyond the immediate repercussions of the pandemic, the long-term effects of COVID-19 continue to reshape digital business strategies in profound ways. The post-pandemic landscape demands strategic agility, resilience, and an unwavering commitment to meet evolving customer expectations.

Many organisations have adopted hybrid business models that blend digital and physical elements to cater to a diverse array of customer needs. This approach facilitates the development of omnichannel experiences, allowing customers to engage with brands either online or in person, depending on their preferences. By integrating the efficiency and reach of digital platforms with the essential face-to-face interactions that nurture customer relationships, businesses can optimise their service offerings and foster deeper connections with their clientele.

E-commerce has become a cornerstone of the post-pandemic economy, compelling businesses to innovate continually to stand out in an increasingly competitive digital marketplace. Companies are focusing on enhancing user experiences through intuitive website designs, personalised product recommendations, and streamlined checkout processes. Innovations such as augmented reality (AR) and virtual try-on features are being employed to replicate the tactile elements of in-store shopping, bridging the gap between online and physical retail environments and providing customers with a more immersive shopping experience.

Remote work, which surged during the pandemic, is likely to remain a significant aspect of business operations as organisations recognise the benefits of a more flexible workforce. Digital collaboration tools and cloud-based platforms are crucial for enabling seamless communication and effective project management, facilitating smooth collaboration among geographically dispersed teams. Many companies are also reimagining their office spaces to support hybrid working arrangements, prioritising employee well-being and creating environments that accommodate both remote and in-office work.

In this new business environment, data and analytics have become indispensable tools for informed decision-making. Businesses are increasingly relying on data analytics to gain insights into shifting consumer behaviour, emerging industry trends, and potential disruptions to the supply chain. Advanced analytics and AI are being used to predict customer preferences, optimise inventory management, and forecast demand fluctuations, thereby allowing companies to make proactive adjustments to their strategies and operations.

The pandemic has underscored the importance of resilience and crisis preparedness, prompting many businesses to revisit their risk management frameworks and invest in comprehensive business continuity plans. These plans now account for a range of potential future disruptions, ensuring that organisations are better equipped to navigate unforeseen challenges. Cloud-based infrastructure and remote access capabilities have become vital components in these strategies, enabling companies to maintain operations and adapt rapidly to changing circumstances. As a result, digital technologies have become essential for ensuring business continuity and safeguarding against future crises.

Overall, the pandemic has acted as a catalyst for significant transformations in digital business strategies. Organisations that can effectively adapt to these changes while maintaining a focus on innovation and resilience will be well positioned to thrive in the evolving digital landscape.

BOX 1.2

The Benefits and Challenges of Working from Home

The shift to remote work, accelerated by the COVID-19 pandemic, has fundamentally transformed how businesses and employees view productivity and workplace flexibility. One of the most significant benefits observed is an increase in productivity. Many employees have reported that working from home allows them to focus better, with fewer interruptions compared to the traditional office environment. The absence of long commutes and rigid schedules has also contributed to improved work-life balance, enabling employees to manage their time more effectively and engage in healthier routines.

However, the shift to remote work is not without its challenges. One of the primary concerns is the blurring of boundaries between personal and professional life. This can lead to longer working hours, increased stress, and a potential for burnout if not managed carefully. Moreover, the lack of face-to-face interactions can hinder team cohesion and the spontaneous collaboration often sparked in a physical office. Communication tools and digital platforms have bridged some of this gap, but they cannot fully replicate the dynamic and social aspects of in-person interactions.

Looking ahead, the future of work is likely to be hybrid, combining the flexibility of remote work with the benefits of occasional in-office presence. This model allows organisations to cater to diverse employee preferences, enhance productivity, and reduce overhead costs associated with maintaining large office spaces. Companies are also likely to continue investing in digital tools and technologies to support this hybrid workforce, ensuring seamless communication and collaboration.

As businesses adapt to this new normal, it is crucial to establish clear policies and support systems to manage the unique challenges of remote work, fostering an environment that promotes both productivity and well-being. This approach will be key to harnessing the benefits of remote work while mitigating its potential drawbacks.

1.9 CHAPTER SUMMARY

This chapter explores digital business in-depth, covering everything from its definition and evolution to its impact on customer behaviour, regulatory considerations, and post-pandemic solutions. The introduction of computers, the internet, and other major technological milestones has tremendously impacted traditional business strategies. The global perspective of the digital economy, important actors, and market dynamics are critical considerations for organisations functioning in this context. Examples of digital disruption highlight the need for adaptability and present both opportunities and problems. Cost-effectiveness, scalability, accessibility, and improved client involvement are all advantages of digital business. Case studies and various digital business models provide insights into successful deployments. Cloud computing and big data analytics, two key technologies driving digital business, play critical roles. Businesses must understand the drivers and actions involved in digital transformation to survive. Data privacy, cybersecurity, and IP rights are all legal and regulatory considerations. The chapter finishes by emphasising the relevance of the pandemic's rapid digital adoption and the continued impact of COVID-19 on digital business strategies. This chapter offers critical insights on navigating the digital landscape for long-term success.

Key Questions for Discussion

1. How has the digital revolution evolved over the past few decades, and what key moments have significantly shaped the current digital landscape? Can you identify any parallels between historical industrial revolutions and today's digital transformation?
2. In what ways has the digital economy impacted global business operations and trade? How can businesses in developing countries leverage digital technologies to compete in the global marketplace?
3. What are some real-world examples of industries that have been significantly disrupted by digital advancements? How can businesses adapt to or anticipate digital disruption in order to remain competitive?
4. With the rapid growth of digital businesses, what challenges do governments face in creating effective legal and regulatory frameworks? How can digital businesses ensure compliance while fostering innovation?
5. The COVID-19 pandemic accelerated the adoption of digital business practices. What long-term changes do you foresee in consumer behaviour and business operations as a result? How can companies prepare for a post-pandemic digital economy?

BIBLIOGRAPHY

Barker, M., Barker, D.I., Bormann, N.F. and Neher, K.E. (2023). *Social Media Marketing: A Strategic Approach*. 3rd ed. Cengage Learning.

Chaffey, D. and Ellis-Chadwick, F. (2022). *Digital Marketing: Strategy, Implementation & Practice*. 8th ed. Pearson.

Chaffey, D., Hemphill, T. and Edmundson-Bird, D. (2023). *Digital Business and E-Commerce Management*. 7th ed. Pearson.
Charlesworth, A. (2023). *Digital Marketing: A Practical Approach*. 3rd ed. Routledge.
Dodson, I. (2023). *The Art of Digital Marketing: The Definitive Guide to Creating Strategic, Targeted, and Measurable Online Campaigns*. Wiley.
Godin, S. (2023). *Permission Marketing: Turning Strangers into Friends and Friends into Customers*. Simon & Schuster.
Kannan, P.K. (2023). *Digital Marketing: A Practical Approach*. Routledge.
Kingsnorth, S. (2023). *Digital Marketing Strategy: An Integrated Approach to Online Marketing*. 3rd ed. Kogan Page.
Kotler, P., Kartajaya, H. and Setiawan, I. (2023). *Marketing 5.0: Technology for Humanity*. Wiley.
Pulizzi, J. (2023). *Epic Content Marketing: How to Tell a Different Story, Break Through the Clutter, and Win More Customers by Marketing Less*. McGraw-Hill Education.
Ryan, D. (2023). *Understanding Digital Marketing: Marketing Strategies for Engaging the Digital Generation*. 5th ed. Kogan Page.
Tuten, T.L. and Solomon, M.R. (2023). *Social Media Marketing*. 4th ed. Sage Publications.
Vaynerchuk, G. (2023). *Jab, Jab, Jab, Right Hook: How to Tell Your Story in a Noisy Social World*. Harper Business.
Wirtz, B.W. (2023). *Digital Business and Electronic Commerce: Strategy, Business Models and Technology*. Springer.
Wymbs, C. (2023). *Digital Marketing: Integrating Strategy and Tactics with Values*. Routledge.

CHAPTER 2

Understanding Digital Business Models

Learning Objectives

By the end of this chapter, you will be able to:

1. Understand the role of various digital business models in driving success in the digital economy and how they influence business strategy.
2. Learn about various models, such as e-commerce, sharing economy, subscription, freemium, and platform-based approaches, and how to select the most suitable model for different business contexts.
3. Explore emerging trends in digital business models, including hybrid models and data monetisation, and understand how to adapt traditional models to stay competitive in the digital landscape.

2.1 INTRODUCTION

Businesses today are navigating a complex terrain where creative models fuel success and establish their competitive edge. This chapter is a detailed reference that explains the varied landscape of digital business models. As technology continues transforming sectors, the chapter aims to familiarise readers with these models' complexities, characteristics, and profound impact on the digital economy. The chapter digs into the possibilities organisations can embrace to prosper in the dynamic digital arena, from e-commerce and sharing economy models to subscription-based, freemium, ad-based, and on-demand service models. Moreover, the chapter offers readers the tools to handle the complexity of the digital economy by taking them on a tour of digital business models. It also provides insights to help businesses make informed decisions in selecting, adapting, and optimising their business models, whether exploring the nuances of e-commerce, sharing economy, subscription-based, freemium, ad-based, on-demand service, platform, data monetisation, or hybrid models. The investigation concludes by imagining a future in which rising trends, artificial intelligence (AI), and automation are set to redefine and reconfigure the very fabric of digital business models.

DOI: 10.4324/9781032672458-2

Understanding these models will surely be a cornerstone of success in the ever-changing digital landscape as technology pulls us forward.

2.2 NAVIGATING THE DIGITAL ECONOMY: THE STRATEGIC ROLE OF BUSINESS MODELS

Digital business models are strategic frameworks that define how organisations create value, generate revenue, and operate within the increasingly complex digital ecosystem. These models are vital in leveraging technology to foster growth, enhance customer engagement, and achieve sustainable success in the digital age. For companies striving to navigate this rapidly evolving landscape, understanding and implementing digital business models is essential. By aligning their strategies with the dynamics of the digital ecosystem, businesses can optimise operations, seize emerging opportunities, and secure long-term growth.

The fundamental difference between digital and traditional business models lies in their approach to value creation and customer interaction. While traditional models typically rely on physical infrastructure and localised operations, digital business models leverage virtual platforms, data analytics, and online interactions to deliver value. They are designed for scalability and global outreach, enabling rapid expansion and heightened customer engagement. Unlike traditional linear value chains, digital models operate within interconnected ecosystems, prioritising personalised experiences, real-time interactions, and data-driven insights. This transformation fosters innovation and allows businesses to adapt swiftly to shifting market demands.

In the context of the digital economy, business models serve as critical tools for directing organisations towards sustainable growth, innovation, and competitive advantage. They are not merely static blueprints but dynamic strategies that respond to rapid technological advancements and evolving consumer behaviours. Effective business models enable organisations to identify and capitalise on new opportunities, ensuring agility and adaptability in a constantly changing environment. By defining how value is created, delivered, and monetised, these models empower organisations to optimise their operations, enhance customer experiences, and forge meaningful relationships within a globally connected marketplace.

The seamless integration of technology and data-driven insights is a cornerstone of successful business models in the digital economy. As digital disruption becomes the norm and traditional boundaries blur, these models facilitate the development of ecosystems that promote collaboration, co-creation, and partnerships, ultimately amplifying impact and value delivery. They provide a solid foundation for sustained revenue growth and profitability, even amid uncertainty. By aligning revenue streams with evolving customer preferences and market dynamics, organisations can cultivate resilience and longevity.

In essence, business models in the digital age act as strategic compasses, guiding organisations through the complexities of the digital economy with foresight and precision. They are instrumental in driving efficiency, fostering innovation, and nurturing a forward-thinking mindset, all of which are crucial for harnessing opportunities and building a prosperous future in an ever-changing digital world.

2.3 E-COMMERCE BUSINESS MODELS: UNVEILING DIGITAL COMMERCE LANDSCAPES

The digital revolution has heralded a new era of commerce, altering how organisations interact with their customers and partners. E-commerce business models have arisen as dynamic tactics enabling transactions, promoting connectivity, and redefining market dynamics in this transformational environment. This section digs into the intricate fabric of these models, unravelling their intricacies and demonstrating how they have revolutionised how goods and services are purchased, sold, and traded in the digital era (Table 2.1).

TABLE 2.1 Key Models of E-Commerce: B2C and B2B Approaches

Category	Model	Description
Business-to-Consumer (B2C)	Direct Sales Model	This model enables businesses to directly engage with customers through digital channels, eliminating intermediaries. It facilitates real-time communication, personalised offerings, and transparency, enhancing customer experiences and expanding global reach.
	Subscription Model	This model focuses on providing ongoing value through recurring subscriptions, such as subscription boxes or streaming services. It offers consumers personalised experiences and ensures steady revenue streams for businesses, fostering long-term customer relationships.
	Marketplace Model	A digital platform where multiple sellers offer a variety of products and services, exemplified by giants like Amazon and eBay. It allows businesses to access a global customer base, leveraging established infrastructure and brand recognition.
Business-to-Business (B2B)	Platform as a Service (PaaS)	PaaS enables businesses to develop, deploy, and manage digital solutions without complex infrastructure concerns. It supports innovation by allowing developers to build on existing platforms, facilitating digital transformation and customised solutions.
	Software as a Service (SaaS)	SaaS offers businesses access to software applications through the cloud, eliminating extensive installation and maintenance requirements. It enhances productivity and collaboration while reducing operational complexities.
	Infrastructure as a Service (IaaS)	IaaS provides a digital infrastructure by outsourcing hardware components like servers and storage. This model allows organisations to optimise resource allocation and scalability, focusing on core competencies while relying on a robust digital foundation.

These models showcase the versatility and innovation within the e-commerce landscape, transforming traditional commerce into a dynamic, interconnected ecosystem.

2.4 SHARING ECONOMY BUSINESS MODELS: REDEFINING COLLABORATIVE COMMERCE

The sharing economy has emerged as a significant disruptor in the digital transformation landscape, fostering new channels of cooperation, consumption, and wealth generation. This part follows the features of these creative sharing economy models, revealing how they have reshaped traditional company paradigms and enabled individuals to leverage the power of technology for mutual gain (Table 2.2).

The P2P and B2P sharing economy models have prompted a paradigm shift, showcasing the power of collaborative consumption and decentralised corporate operations. These models are not only disrupting existing sectors, but they are also sparking a new era of entrepreneurship, empowerment, and community-driven commerce. The sharing economy

TABLE 2.2 Peer-to-Peer and Business-to-Peer Models: Transforming Access and Opportunity

Category	Model	Description
Peer-to-Peer (P2P) Model	Ride-Hailing Services	Ride-hailing platforms, such as Uber and Lyft, connect individuals seeking transport with drivers using their personal vehicles. By leveraging smartphone apps and GPS technology, these services offer a seamless and affordable alternative to traditional taxi services, transforming the transportation industry.
	Accommodation Services	Platforms like Airbnb enable homeowners to rent out their properties or spare rooms to travellers. This model provides unique lodging options and allows property owners to monetise underutilised spaces, offering a more personalised and cost-effective alternative to traditional hotels.
Business-to-Peer (B2P) Model	Crowdfunding Platforms	Platforms such as Kickstarter and Indiegogo facilitate innovation by connecting entrepreneurs with a global audience of potential supporters. Individuals present their projects, products, or ideas to secure funding, democratising access to capital and allowing backers to become active participants in realising creative ventures.
	Freelance Marketplaces	Sites like Upwork and Fiverr have revolutionised the job market by providing platforms where skilled individuals can offer their services to businesses worldwide. These marketplaces support the exchange of global talent, enabling businesses to access diverse expertise and offering freelancers flexible earning opportunities.

has expanded economic involvement and value exchange by employing technology to bridge barriers and unleash underutilised resources.

2.5 CULTIVATING CONTINUOUS ENGAGEMENT: THE EVOLUTION OF SUBSCRIPTION-BASED BUSINESS MODELS

Subscription-based business models have become emblematic of the evolving consumer preferences and the innovative approaches that organisations adopt to meet these expectations in the digital marketplace. These models signify a shift in how products and services are delivered, consumed, and monetised, offering an ongoing value proposition that resonates deeply with modern customers.

At the heart of this transformation are membership-based models, which transcend traditional one-off transactions. These frameworks are designed to foster long-term relationships by offering exclusive benefits and experiences that are often structured in tiers. Each level of membership unlocks unique privileges, creating a sense of exclusivity and belonging. This strategy not only enhances customer loyalty but also secures a stable foundation for sustainable engagement and predictable revenue streams. By cultivating a sense of community and aligning offerings with customer values, businesses can nurture a deep-seated loyalty that extends beyond the initial purchase.

In the realm of digital information and entertainment, content subscription models have gained immense popularity. These models provide subscribers with access to an extensive, curated library of digital content, ranging from articles and e-books to movies and music. Platforms like Netflix and Spotify epitomise this approach, offering on-demand access to vast collections that cater to diverse tastes and interests. By prioritising convenience and choice, these models enable customers to tailor their consumption experiences to personal preferences. For businesses, the result is a robust and consistent revenue stream supported by a highly engaged user base.

Meanwhile, product subscription models redefine ownership by transforming the act of purchasing into an ongoing service. Rather than a one-time transaction, customers receive products or digital offerings on a regular basis, such as curated subscription boxes or software-as-a-service (SaaS) platforms. This approach marries consumption with convenience, eliminating the need for significant upfront investment and aligning company revenues with the sustained delivery of value. These models have proven particularly effective in creating a seamless and hassle-free consumer experience, allowing businesses to remain an integral part of their customers' lives.

The evolution of subscription-based business models across membership, content, and product categories highlights their capacity to deliver ongoing engagement and value. By focusing on continuous interaction, personalisation, and effortless access, these models cater to the desires of modern consumers who seek seamless and enriching experiences. As digital technologies continue to shape and reshape consumer behaviour, the flexibility and innovation inherent in subscription-based models position them as powerful tools for businesses navigating the complexities of the ever-evolving marketplace.

CASE STUDY 2

Netflix's Subscription-Based Model—Transforming the Entertainment Industry

Netflix has become a dominant force in the global entertainment industry, but its journey began as a DVD rental service in 1997. Initially, the company operated on a pay-per-rental model, mailing DVDs to customers, which provided convenience over traditional brick-and-mortar rental stores like Blockbuster. However, as digital technologies advanced, consumer preferences shifted towards on-demand entertainment. By the early 2000s, broadband internet and digital media consumption were growing rapidly, and Netflix recognised an opportunity to transition from physical rentals to a subscription-based digital streaming service. The challenge was to move away from a traditional revenue model and create a sustainable digital-first business model while competing with established media companies and emerging streaming services.

To address this challenge, Netflix pioneered a subscription-based model, offering unlimited access to digital content for a fixed monthly fee. This approach eliminated late fees associated with DVD rentals and provided users with an uninterrupted entertainment experience. The company invested heavily in licensing content from major studios and gradually shifted toward original content production, giving it greater control over its library and reducing reliance on third-party providers. By leveraging data analytics and AI-driven recommendations, Netflix personalised content suggestions for users, improving customer retention and engagement. Furthermore, the company expanded globally, ensuring that its content library was tailored to different regions through multilingual options and culturally relevant programming.

The results of this transformation were remarkable. By 2023, Netflix had over 230 million global subscribers, with revenue exceeding $30 billion annually. The company's ability to scale internationally allowed it to capture new markets, while its focus on original content—including hits like *Stranger Things* and *Squid Game*—helped differentiate it from competitors. The subscription model provided a predictable and recurring revenue stream, enabling continued investment in content creation and platform enhancements. Additionally, the use of AI-driven personalisation increased user engagement, with many subscribers watching suggested content rather than actively searching for titles.

Netflix's success offers several key takeaways for businesses navigating the digital economy. Firstly, it highlights the importance of business model innovation—Netflix did not simply digitise its DVD rental service; it reimagined the entire entertainment experience. Secondly, the case study demonstrates the power of subscription models in fostering customer loyalty and predictable revenue streams. Thirdly, Netflix's emphasis on data-driven decision-making underscores the significance of leveraging analytics to enhance user experiences. Lastly, the company's global expansion strategy showcases the need for localisation and adaptability in an increasingly interconnected world.

Netflix's evolution from a DVD rental service to a subscription-based streaming giant exemplifies the transformative potential of digital business models, offering valuable insights for organisations seeking to adapt and thrive in the digital economy.

Discussion Questions for Students (with Indicative Answers)

1. **How did Netflix's transition from a DVD rental service to a subscription-based streaming platform exemplify digital business model innovation?**
   Indicative Answer: Netflix did not merely digitise its existing DVD rental business; instead, it completely reimagined the entertainment experience by shifting to an on-demand, subscription-based model. This move allowed users to access unlimited content for a fixed monthly fee, eliminating late fees and the inconvenience of physical rentals. By leveraging digital distribution, Netflix disrupted traditional media consumption and reshaped industry norms.
2. **What role did data analytics and AI-driven recommendations play in Netflix's success?**
   Indicative Answer: Netflix used data analytics and AI to personalise content recommendations, increasing user engagement and satisfaction. By analysing viewing habits, search behaviour, and ratings, Netflix's algorithm curated tailored content for each user, reducing churn and improving retention. This data-driven approach enhanced customer experience, drove higher watch times, and maximised subscription renewals.
3. **What are the key advantages of the subscription-based model that Netflix adopted, and how do they benefit the company and consumers?**
   Indicative Answer: The subscription-based model provides Netflix with predictable and recurring revenue, allowing it to reinvest in content production and platform development. For consumers, it offers unlimited access to a vast content library at a fixed price, making entertainment more accessible and affordable. The model also

encourages customer loyalty, as users tend to stay subscribed due to the continuous addition of new content.

4. **How did Netflix's strategy of creating original content contribute to its competitive advantage?**
Indicative Answer: By producing original content, such as Stranger Things *and* Squid Game, *Netflix differentiated itself from competitors and reduced its reliance on third-party studios. This strategy ensured exclusive content ownership, allowing Netflix to attract and retain subscribers who could not access these shows elsewhere. Additionally, original productions gave Netflix global appeal, as it invested in localised content for diverse audiences worldwide.*
5. **What challenges does Netflix face in maintaining its dominance in the streaming industry, and how might it continue to evolve?**
Indicative Answer: Netflix faces challenges such as intensifying competition from Disney+, Amazon Prime, and HBO Max, increasing content production costs, and subscription fatigue among consumers. To maintain its dominance, Netflix must continue innovating through interactive content, gaming, and AI-driven engagement strategies. Expanding ad-supported subscription tiers and investing in new technologies like virtual reality (VR) streaming could also help sustain growth.

2.6 THE FREEMIUM PARADIGM: HARMONISING FREE AND PREMIUM OFFERINGS

The freemium business model has emerged as a compelling strategy that skilfully integrates the allure of free access with the appeal of premium services, thriving amid the digital transformation sweeping through various industries. At its core, this model leverages consumer psychology and value perception to navigate the complexities of monetisation in the digital age. It presents a unique approach to engaging users by offering a fundamental version of a product or service at no cost, while simultaneously enticing them with a premium tier that promises enhanced features and experiences.

Central to the freemium concept is the art of choice. By providing a basic version free of charge, businesses invite potential customers to explore and familiarise themselves with the essential functionalities, thereby reducing entry barriers. Alongside this, a premium version is made available, often featuring advanced capabilities, additional content, or an ad-free experience, which is accessible through a subscription or one-time purchase. This strategic dichotomy taps into the "try-before-you-buy" mentality, allowing users to appreciate the product's value before making a financial commitment. The challenge lies in crafting this premium offering to be sufficiently compelling, ensuring it meets user needs while enhancing their overall experience.

Monetisation within the freemium framework involves a delicate balance between accessibility and value. Businesses must carefully delineate between free and premium features, ensuring the latter are attractive enough to justify an upgrade. Tiered pricing models often play a pivotal role, offering various levels of access, such as unlocking additional functionality, increased storage, or priority customer support. Additionally, time-limited trials of premium features are commonly employed to provide users with a taste of the elevated experience they would receive as paying subscribers. These tactics are interwoven with the user journey, fostering a harmonious relationship between free users and subscribers, where each group benefits from the other's engagement and revenue contribution.

However, navigating the freemium model is not without its challenges. Monetisation can be complex, requiring a careful evaluation of what features remain free and which are premium. Conversion rates from free users to paid subscribers are often modest, necessitating clear communication of value and targeted incentives. Resource allocation poses another dilemma, as companies must invest in both free and premium versions to maintain and enhance their appeal. Moreover, businesses must ensure that the perceived value of the premium tier is strong enough to warrant the cost, without alienating users who remain on the free tier. Achieving a seamless transition between these tiers is critical to avoiding a disjointed user experience that could undermine overall satisfaction.

The freemium model, therefore, represents a sophisticated interplay of psychology, value proposition, and revenue strategy. It capitalises on the initial draw of free access to build a broad user base while cultivating a community of loyal paying subscribers. As digital landscapes continue to evolve, the freemium approach exemplifies how businesses can effectively balance user engagement, value creation, and sustainable revenue in an ever-shifting ecosystem.

2.7 AD-BASED REVENUE MODELS: NAVIGATING THE COMPLEX LANDSCAPE OF DIGITAL ADVERTISING

Ad-based business models have become a fundamental strategy for generating revenue within the intricate digital economy, offering users free access to content, services, and platforms while capitalising on advertising opportunities. This approach involves deploying various advertising techniques designed to engage users and promote brands effectively while simultaneously overcoming the inherent challenges of the digital landscape.

Central to this model is display advertising, a long-standing pillar of digital marketing characterised by the strategic positioning of visual ads across digital platforms. These ads, which can range from static banners to interactive rich media, are crafted to capture users' attention and deliver brand messages through compelling visual narratives. The success of display advertising lies in the ability to create visually engaging content that resonates with target audiences, thereby boosting brand visibility and driving engagement.

In contrast, native advertising represents a more subtle approach, integrating sponsored content seamlessly into the user experience of digital platforms. Unlike traditional adverts, native ads are designed to blend in with the surrounding content, offering value through informative or entertaining material that aligns with the platform's format and user behaviour.

This technique minimises disruption, fostering organic user engagement while preserving trust and credibility. By appearing as a natural part of the user journey, native ads facilitate a smoother interaction between brands and audiences.

Video advertising has gained significant traction in the digital era, harnessing the power of motion and storytelling to captivate viewers. This format, which includes short clips, pre- and mid-roll ads, and video content embedded within social media, provides brands with an immersive medium to communicate narratives, showcase products, and establish emotional connections. The dynamic nature of video advertising makes it an effective tool for creating memorable brand experiences and engaging diverse audiences across various platforms.

However, the rise of ad-blockers presents a formidable challenge to ad-based business models, as users increasingly seek to limit their exposure to disruptive or irrelevant advertising. To navigate this obstacle, businesses are adopting innovative strategies aimed at enhancing ad relevance and user engagement. Crafting targeted and personalised ads that align with user preferences can reduce the likelihood of ad-blocker usage. Embracing native ad formats that integrate seamlessly with content allows advertisers to bypass ad-blocker filters. Furthermore, providing users with the ability to customise their ad preferences or offering premium, ad-free experiences can empower users and incentivise engagement. Businesses are also exploring interactive and gamified ad formats to encourage genuine user interest and participation.

The evolving landscape of digital advertising requires businesses to strike a delicate balance between promoting brands and ensuring a positive user experience. By curating engaging content, leveraging innovation, and prioritising user-centric strategies, ad-based business models are continually adapting to the dynamic demands of the digital market. As the advertising environment continues to evolve, these models will play a crucial role in fostering meaningful connections, delivering resonant messages, and securing sustainable revenue streams.

2.8 ON-DEMAND SERVICE MODELS: REVOLUTIONISING ACCESS AND EFFICIENCY

In an age characterised by the pursuit of immediacy and personalised experiences, on-demand service models have emerged as transformative forces, reshaping the way services are accessed, delivered, and experienced. These models have permeated various industries, from food delivery and household tasks to professional consultancy, offering a seamless blend of convenience and customisation that meets the evolving needs of modern consumers and businesses alike.

On-demand delivery services have redefined the food and retail sectors, transforming the way people order and receive their favourite meals and products. Platforms such as DoorDash and Postmates have bridged the gap between restaurants, retailers, and consumers, offering quick and convenient deliveries that cater to the growing demand for hassle-free experiences. This model thrives on the promise of speed and accessibility, providing users with an array of options that can be tailored to their preferences, thus making culinary and shopping experiences more dynamic and flexible.

Expanding beyond the realm of food and retail, on-demand task services have become an essential part of navigating daily challenges. Platforms like TaskRabbit and Thumbtack have revolutionised how individuals and households manage their workload by creating a virtual marketplace for outsourcing a range of services. From handyman work to specialised professional tasks, these platforms empower users to delegate responsibilities to skilled personnel, enhancing efficiency and allowing individuals to focus on their core priorities. This shift towards a more flexible and task-specific workforce reflects the changing nature of employment, where gig-based models are increasingly embraced for their adaptability and resourcefulness.

The disruption extends further into professional realms with on-demand services reimagining traditional consultation frameworks. Platforms such as UpCounsel and Uber for Business have made it possible for individuals and organisations to access expert advice and specialised services with unprecedented agility. Whether it's legal guidance, marketing strategies, or project management, these platforms provide targeted expertise without the need for long-term commitments or cumbersome contracts. This model offers a new level of flexibility and cost-effectiveness, enabling clients to engage with professionals as and when required, thereby optimising their resource allocation and strategic planning.

These on-demand service models signify a profound transformation in consumer expectations and workplace dynamics, driven by the ubiquity of digital connectivity and the relentless pursuit of efficiency. By breaking down traditional barriers and enabling services to be delivered precisely when and where they are needed, these models embody a new era of service delivery. However, the success of these models depends not only on their ability to meet consumer demand but also on their capacity to manage a flexible workforce effectively. The challenge lies in recruiting, training, and retaining a dynamic pool of service providers who can uphold the quality and reliability that on-demand services promise.

From the swift delivery of gourmet meals to the seamless assembly of furniture or the strategic input of seasoned consultants, on-demand service models showcase the growing role of technology in shaping contemporary lifestyles. They offer consumers unprecedented levels of customisation and control, transforming traditional service industries and empowering individuals in ways previously unimagined. As we continue to explore the implications of these models, it becomes clear that the on-demand revolution is not merely a trend but a fundamental shift in how services are conceived, executed, and valued in a world where time and personalisation are paramount.

2.9 PLATFORM BUSINESS MODELS: SHAPING ECOSYSTEMS AND REDEFINING CONNECTIVITY

Platform business models have emerged as transformative forces within the digital economy, fundamentally reshaping how value is created, exchanged, and amplified. These models transcend traditional business frameworks by acting as digital intermediaries, facilitating interactions and transactions between diverse parties across various industries. They are not merely facilitators but orchestrators of intricate ecosystems where users, businesses, and service providers converge to create a dynamic, interconnected web of relationships and exchanges.

At the core of platform dynamics lies the two-sided marketplace, a model that exemplifies the seamless integration of distinct user groups to foster interactions. Platforms such as Airbnb and Uber serve as quintessential examples, linking hosts with guests and drivers with riders, respectively. These marketplaces thrive on the delicate balance of supply and demand, leveraging sophisticated digital interfaces to synchronise the interests and needs of their users. The success of these platforms hinges on their ability to create a mutually beneficial environment, where both sides of the market find value in their participation, thus driving sustained engagement and growth.

Moving beyond the binary nature of two-sided marketplaces, multi-sided platforms add layers of complexity by enabling interactions among a broader spectrum of participants. Payment gateways like PayPal exemplify this model, connecting consumers, businesses, and merchants in a secure financial ecosystem. These platforms do more than just facilitate transactions; they create a unified space where diverse stakeholders can interact seamlessly. By employing advanced technology to streamline processes and bridge various needs, multi-sided platforms enhance the value proposition for all involved, fostering a network of interconnected users whose collective engagement fuels the platform's expansion and resilience.

The concept of platform ecosystems further elevates the potential of these business models by cultivating an intricate web of interconnected entities that collectively enhance the platform's value. In such ecosystems, the value of the platform grows exponentially with the addition of each new participant, a phenomenon known as network effects. The Apple App Store and Google Play Store are prime examples of this dynamic, where developers, users, and app providers coalesce to enrich digital experiences. As more developers create and contribute applications, the platform becomes increasingly attractive to users, which in turn draws even more developers—creating a self-sustaining cycle of growth and innovation. This virtuous circle not only amplifies the platform's impact but also cements its position as a central hub within the digital ecosystem.

Platform business models represent a sophisticated interplay of technology, user engagement, and ecosystem development. They transcend traditional linear business structures by fostering connectivity, organising interactions, and harnessing the power of network effects to create expansive digital economies. Through careful orchestration, platforms facilitate value creation and exchange in ways that were previously unimaginable. They redefine how businesses interact with stakeholders, shaping the digital landscape and unlocking new realms of possibility.

In exploring the intricate strategies that underpin the success of two-sided marketplaces, multi-sided platforms, and platform ecosystems, we gain insights into the unique capabilities of these models to transform industries. By cultivating vibrant ecosystems and leveraging network effects, platforms are not merely participants in the digital economy but powerful catalysts for innovation and growth. As we continue to navigate the evolving terrain of the digital era, platform business models stand as a testament to the profound impact of connectivity and collaboration in shaping the future of commerce and human interaction.

2.10 REIMAGINING TRADITION: THE DIGITAL TRANSFORMATION OF ESTABLISHED BUSINESS MODELS

The digital age has compelled traditional businesses to undergo profound transformations, adapting their established practices to keep pace with rapid technological advancements. This transformation is not merely a technological upgrade but a strategic overhaul that redefines how organisations operate, interact with customers, and compete in a digitally driven market. In this section, we delve into the compelling journey of traditional businesses embracing digital transformation, examining real-world examples, the challenges they face, and the strategic approaches that have proven successful in navigating this complex transition.

One of the most striking illustrations of digital transformation is the evolution of the entertainment industry. The advent of streaming platforms such as Netflix revolutionised the way content is consumed, shifting the landscape from physical movie rentals to a digital subscription-based model that offers instant access to a vast library of films and series. This shift not only disrupted traditional business models but also set a new standard for consumer expectations, making convenience and accessibility the hallmarks of modern entertainment consumption.

The retail sector has also experienced a seismic shift, with long-established giants like Walmart integrating e-commerce into their operations. What began as an online extension of their brick-and-mortar stores has evolved into a sophisticated digital ecosystem, enabling seamless shopping experiences that blend physical and digital channels. This transformation has expanded their market reach and redefined customer engagement, illustrating how digital adoption can invigorate traditional business models and open up new avenues for growth (Figure 2.1).

While the potential benefits of digital transformation are substantial, the journey is fraught with challenges. Legacy systems, ingrained organisational cultures, and the intricate process of integrating new technologies can pose significant obstacles. Resistance to change is a common hurdle, as employees and stakeholders may be reluctant to abandon familiar processes for unproven digital solutions. Moreover, the financial and logistical complexities involved in overhauling existing infrastructures can be daunting, particularly for businesses with extensive, deeply entrenched operations.

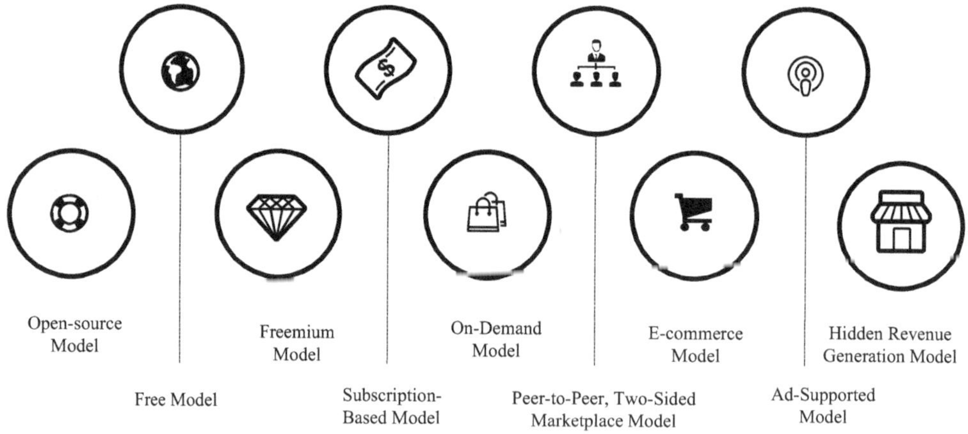

FIGURE 2.1 Digital Business Models

Yet, these challenges are accompanied by immense opportunities. Digital transformation offers businesses the chance to streamline operations, enhance customer engagement, and enter previously inaccessible markets. It enables organisations to leverage data analytics for more informed decision-making, optimise supply chains for greater efficiency, and personalise marketing efforts to resonate more deeply with consumers. In essence, digital transformation can empower traditional businesses to reinvent themselves, remaining relevant and competitive in an increasingly digital marketplace.

For a successful transformation, a meticulously crafted strategy is essential, one that aligns technological adoption with overarching business objectives. This process begins with a comprehensive evaluation of the organisation's current state, identifying areas ripe for digitalisation and potential barriers to change. Leadership plays a pivotal role, as executive commitment is crucial to fostering a culture that embraces innovation and supports the necessary shifts in mindset and operations.

Cross-departmental collaboration is another cornerstone of effective digital transformation. By encouraging communication and cooperation between different areas of the organisation, businesses can ensure a cohesive and integrated approach to implementing new technologies. Agile methodologies and iterative development practices also prove invaluable, allowing businesses to pilot new initiatives, learn from failures, and continuously refine their digital strategies. This flexible approach mitigates risks and maximises the chances of successful adoption, enabling organisations to adapt quickly to evolving market conditions.

Investing in the workforce is equally important. As technology reshapes business operations, employees must be equipped with the skills and knowledge to leverage digital tools effectively. Comprehensive training and upskilling programmes are vital to empowering staff to embrace new technologies and thrive in a transformed workplace. This investment not only facilitates a smoother transition but also fosters a culture of continuous learning and innovation.

In the ever-evolving digital landscape, traditional businesses have a unique opportunity to transcend their conventional limitations and thrive. By learning from the experiences of those who have successfully navigated the digital transformation journey, organisations can identify best practices, anticipate challenges, and confidently chart their course towards sustainable growth. As we explore the convergence of tradition and technology, we uncover the strategies that unlock the true potential of digital transformation, enabling businesses to not only survive but flourish in an increasingly digital world.

2.11 HYBRID BUSINESS MODELS: MERGING TRADITION WITH INNOVATION

In a rapidly evolving commercial landscape where digital transformation intersects with established practices, hybrid business models have emerged as a powerful approach, combining the strengths of both traditional and digital strategies to create new pathways for success. This fusion of time-honoured methods and innovative technologies allows businesses to harness the stability and trust inherent in conventional practices while simultaneously embracing the flexibility and expansive reach of digital platforms.

The essence of hybrid business models lies in their ability to integrate traditional and digital elements into a cohesive and dynamic framework. For instance, a brick-and-mortar retailer might adopt an e-commerce platform, enabling it to reach customers far beyond its physical location. This blend of physical and digital channels not only expands the market presence of the business but also offers customers a seamless and unified shopping experience, where they can move effortlessly between online and offline environments. By maintaining the tangible aspects of traditional business, such as face-to-face interactions and physical product engagement, alongside the convenience and accessibility of digital tools, organisations can cater to a broad spectrum of customer preferences and behaviours.

Achieving synergy in hybrid models is more than just merging traditional and digital components—it's about creating a system where these elements amplify each other's strengths, producing outcomes greater than the sum of their parts. When executed effectively, hybrid models can transform the customer journey, blending the tactile appeal of physical interactions with the immediacy and customisation of digital experiences. This synthesis not only enhances customer satisfaction but also drives operational efficiency, allowing businesses to streamline processes, optimise resource allocation, and respond swiftly to market changes.

For instance, a traditional consultancy firm might incorporate digital platforms to deliver virtual consultations and workshops, expanding its reach and accessibility while still offering in-person services for clients who value direct engagement. Similarly, a restaurant may employ digital tools for online reservations, takeaway orders, and delivery services, complementing the ambience and personal touch of its dine-in experience. These hybrid approaches enable businesses to diversify revenue streams, engage with a broader audience, and adapt to shifting market dynamics without sacrificing their core identity.

The strategic integration of hybrid business models requires careful planning and execution. Organisations must identify which aspects of their traditional operations can be enhanced or supplemented by digital tools, and vice versa. This process involves understanding customer needs, anticipating market trends, and leveraging technology in ways that add genuine value. It also demands a cultural shift within the organisation, where innovation and tradition are not seen as oppositional forces but as complementary elements of a unified strategy.

Hybrid business models embody a forward-thinking approach that recognises the enduring value of traditional practices while embracing the transformative potential of digital innovation. They offer a flexible and resilient framework for navigating the complexities of today's business environment, enabling organisations to stay relevant and competitive in an era of rapid change. By skilfully combining the best of both worlds, businesses can forge a path that honours their heritage while pioneering new avenues for growth and success.

BOX 2.1

Case Studies of Successful Hybrid Models: Pioneering the Path

Real-world examples demonstrate hybrid models' revolutionary potential. Starbucks, a well-known coffeehouse business, connects its mobile app with actual locations, allowing consumers to place orders and pay digitally while still enjoying the ambience of a traditional café. Similarly, automakers have adopted hybrid sales strategies that allow buyers to explore vehicles online and in showrooms, bridging the gap between digital ease and tactile encounters.

Furthermore, hybrid models have been seen in action in the education industry, with colleges offering blended learning experiences that combine in-person instruction with online resources. These examples demonstrate the adaptability of hybrid models across industries, where the intentional integration of analogue and digital components increases consumer engagement and operational effectiveness.

We discover a tapestry fashioned from the threads of tradition and innovation as we travel through the terrain of hybrid company models. Organisations construct value propositions that appeal to modern consumers while honouring existing practices by strategically combining these factors. The path to successful hybrid models necessitates a thorough awareness of client requirements, mastery of digital tools, and an unshakable commitment to adaptability.

In the dynamic interplay of the tangible and the digital, hybrid models provide a compelling avenue for organisations to develop a distinct identity, increase their reach, and prosper in an ever-changing industry. Organisations may transcend conventional boundaries and follow a harmonic route towards ongoing growth and relevance by mastering the art of synergy and embracing the fluidity of change.

2.12 DATA MONETISATION MODELS: TRANSFORMING INFORMATION INTO STRATEGIC VALUE

In the digital age, data have emerged as a vital asset, driving innovation and strategic decision-making across various industries. Once regarded merely as a by-product of business operations, data are now recognised for its intrinsic value, capable of generating significant revenue streams and providing critical insights. This section explores the diverse ways in which organisations can harness data to create value, highlighting the strategic potential, revenue opportunities, and ethical considerations involved in data monetisation.

As businesses increasingly acknowledge the strategic importance of data, they are discovering new ways to leverage this resource beyond traditional analytics. The vast quantities of information generated through customer interactions, operational processes, and digital footprints can be transformed into actionable insights that refine products and services, enhance customer experiences, and drive innovation. For example, by analysing consumer behaviour and preferences, companies can personalise their offerings, optimise marketing strategies, and even predict future trends. This shift in perception—from viewing data as a mere operational output to recognising it as a cornerstone of business strategy—has paved the way for innovative data monetisation models that go beyond internal use.

One of the most significant developments in this area is the transformation of data into a direct source of revenue. Organisations are increasingly adopting models that allow them to capitalise on the insights derived from their data. By offering data-driven products and services, such as advanced analytics or real-time reporting, businesses can provide clients with valuable tools to inform their decision-making processes. Additionally, data-sharing partnerships and collaborative agreements enable companies to monetise their data through exchange or sale to third parties, creating new revenue streams and fostering industry-wide innovation. These practices demonstrate how businesses can not only use data to enhance their own operations but also to generate income by addressing the informational needs of other organisations.

However, the monetisation of data brings with it a host of ethical challenges. As organisations strive to unlock the full potential of their data assets, they must navigate complex issues related to privacy, security, and governance. The use of personal data, in particular, requires a careful balance between innovation and responsibility. Businesses must ensure that their data practices comply with legal regulations and societal expectations, safeguarding user privacy and maintaining transparency in data usage. Effective data governance frameworks and robust security measures are essential to building trust and ensuring that data is used ethically and responsibly. By prioritising ethical considerations, organisations can foster a culture of data integrity that supports sustainable growth and innovation.

Beyond the immediate business implications, data monetisation has broader societal impacts that necessitate a collective approach to data ethics. The increasing reliance on data-driven decision-making in various sectors—ranging from healthcare to finance—underscores the need for a framework that protects user rights and privacy. As organisations explore new ways to monetise data, they must also consider the long-term effects of their practices on individuals and communities. By promoting transparency, accountability, and fairness in their data strategies, businesses can align their commercial objectives with public values, ensuring that the benefits of data-driven innovation are shared equitably.

Data monetisation represents a transformative approach to business in the digital era, offering organisations the opportunity to generate new revenue streams while driving strategic growth. By recognising data as a strategic asset and exploring innovative models of monetisation, businesses can unlock significant value. However, the journey towards effective data monetisation requires not only a deep understanding of data's potential but also a commitment to ethical practices and responsible stewardship. As we delve into the complexities of this evolving landscape, we uncover the potential of data to shape the future of business, fostering sustainable growth, consumer trust, and enduring relevance in an increasingly data-centric world.

2.13 STRATEGIC BUSINESS MODEL SELECTION: CRAFTING A PATH TO SUSTAINABLE SUCCESS

Navigating the digital business landscape is akin to charting a course through shifting tides and unpredictable currents. In this complex environment, choosing the right business model is a pivotal decision that can define an organisation's trajectory. This section explores the intricate process of evaluating and selecting a business model that aligns with an organisation's strategic goals, market conditions, and long-term growth ambitions.

Selecting an effective business model begins with a comprehensive assessment of various factors that collectively form the foundation of the organisation's strategy. Key considerations include the company's inherent strengths, the specific needs of its target customer segments, the uniqueness of its value propositions, and the structure of its revenue streams and costs. Each of these elements plays a crucial role in shaping the strategic blueprint that determines how the business will operate, compete, and grow. A thorough understanding of these factors allows organisations to evaluate the suitability of different business models and choose one that best fits their unique circumstances and objectives.

To make an informed choice, businesses must engage in rigorous market research and analysis. In an era where data drives decision-making, understanding customer preferences, competitive dynamics, and emerging industry trends is essential. Effective market research provides valuable insights into consumer behaviour, identifies gaps in the market, and highlights potential opportunities for innovation and differentiation. This analytical approach enables organisations to make decisions grounded in evidence rather than assumptions, ensuring that the chosen business model is not only relevant but also has the potential to thrive in a competitive environment.

The long-term success of any business model depends not just on its current performance but also on its ability to scale and remain viable over time. Scalability is a critical consideration, particularly in the digital realm, where rapid growth can quickly outpace a company's infrastructure and resources. A robust business model should be designed to support expansion, adapt to evolving market conditions, and withstand external disruptions. This requires foresight and flexibility as well as mechanisms for continual reassessment and refinement. By prioritising scalability and resilience, organisations can ensure that their business model is not just effective today but capable of sustaining success in the future.

The process of selecting the right business model is inherently complex and strategic. It involves a delicate balancing act between leveraging organisational strengths, interpreting market signals, and anticipating future trends. This requires not only analytical rigour but also a clear vision of where the organisation is headed and how it intends to get there. A successful business model is one that integrates these diverse elements into a cohesive strategy, enabling the organisation to navigate uncertainty, capitalise on opportunities, and drive sustained growth and innovation.

As organisations embark on this journey, they must be prepared to adapt and evolve. The digital economy is characterised by rapid change and constant disruption, making it essential for businesses to remain agile and responsive. This means continuously monitoring the effectiveness of their chosen model, staying attuned to shifts in the market, and being willing to pivot or transform as needed. By maintaining a flexible approach and a commitment to strategic clarity, organisations can build a business model that not only aligns with their current objectives but also positions them for long-term success in a dynamic and unpredictable environment.

Ultimately, the art of choosing the right business model lies in the ability to synthesise a deep understanding of market dynamics with a forward-looking vision for growth.

It requires a blend of analytical expertise and strategic insight to craft a model that serves as a living framework for development, innovation, and profitability. This chapter provides a comprehensive guide to navigating the complexities of business model selection, equipping organisations with the knowledge and tools to make informed decisions that shape their future in the ever-evolving digital landscape.

2.14 NAVIGATING THE FUTURE OF DIGITAL BUSINESS MODELS: EXPLORING NEW FRONTIERS

The future of digital business models is an ever-evolving landscape characterised by rapid innovation, transformative disruption, and constant change. As technology continues to advance at an unprecedented pace, businesses must stay ahead of the curve to remain competitive and relevant. This section delves into the emerging trends, revolutionary innovations, and transformative forces shaping the next generation of digital business models, offering a glimpse into the future of the digital economy.

The evolution of digital business models is fuelled by a diverse array of emerging trends and technological advancements poised to redefine how businesses operate. Innovations such as blockchain technology, with its potential to revolutionise supply chains and secure transactions, and augmented reality, which is creating new avenues for immersive customer experiences, are just the beginning. These breakthroughs are not confined to specific industries; they span across sectors, challenging traditional paradigms and presenting opportunities for businesses to reimagine their products, services, and customer interactions. As these technologies mature and become more widely adopted, they will inevitably reshape the commercial landscape, introducing novel ways of creating and capturing value.

Artificial intelligence and automation stand at the forefront of this transformation, heralding a new era in digital business. AI's capacity to analyse vast datasets, generate predictive insights, and automate complex processes is revolutionising business operations across the board. From enhancing customer service through intelligent chatbots to optimising supply chain logistics with predictive analytics, AI is enabling unprecedented levels of efficiency and innovation. Automation is not merely a tool for cost reduction; it is a catalyst for redefining business processes, allowing organisations to focus on strategic, high-value activities. This transformative potential of AI and automation is compelling businesses to rethink their models, leveraging these technologies to streamline operations, enhance decision-making, and create new value propositions that were previously unimaginable.

Looking ahead, the evolution of digital business models will be guided by the convergence of technological innovation and shifting market dynamics. Hybrid models, which seamlessly blend physical and digital domains, are likely to become more prevalent as businesses strive to offer integrated and holistic experiences to their customers. Data monetisation will continue to gain prominence, as organisations increasingly recognise the intrinsic value of data as a strategic asset. These emerging models will not only redefine how businesses generate revenue but also how they interact with stakeholders, foster innovation, and sustain growth in an ever-changing environment.

The future of digital business models is a dynamic interplay of technology, market forces, and human creativity. Organisations must embrace a forward-looking mindset, continually exploring new technologies and business strategies to stay ahead of the curve. By anticipating and adapting to emerging trends, businesses can unlock new opportunities for innovation and growth, positioning themselves to thrive in the digital age. The potential for transformation is immense, and those who are willing to experiment, innovate, and evolve will be best positioned to capitalise on the opportunities that lie ahead.

As businesses navigate this uncharted terrain, they must also be mindful of the broader implications of these changes. The integration of advanced technologies such as AI and blockchain into business models raises important questions about ethics, privacy, and societal impact. Responsible innovation, guided by a commitment to ethical principles and social responsibility, will be essential to ensure that the benefits of digital transformation are realised in a way that is inclusive and sustainable.

In conclusion, the future of digital business models is a vast and vibrant landscape of possibilities. With a keen eye on emerging trends, a strategic approach to innovation, and a commitment to ethical practices, businesses can chart a course through this dynamic environment, harnessing the transformative power of technology to achieve sustainable growth and lasting relevance. As organisations look to the future, they must be prepared to embrace change, experiment with new ideas, and reimagine their business models in response to the evolving digital frontier.

2.15 CHAPTER SUMMARY

This chapter delved into the diverse landscape of digital business models, exploring how they drove innovation and reshaped traditional commerce. It began by highlighting the strategic significance of business models in the digital economy and transitioned into the intricacies of e-commerce, revealing the dynamics that underpinned online retail. The sharing economy was examined next, showcasing how collaborative models redefined ownership and access. Subscription-based models were explored for their role in cultivating continuous customer engagement, while the freemium approach balanced free and premium offerings to attract a broader user base.

Ad-based revenue models were analysed for their complexities in digital advertising, and on-demand service models were noted for revolutionising access and efficiency across various sectors. The chapter then addressed platform business models, illustrating their ability to create expansive ecosystems. The digital transformation of traditional business models and the emergence of hybrid models were discussed, highlighting the blend of legacy and innovation. Data monetisation strategies were presented as a means to leverage information for strategic value, followed by a framework for selecting the right business model. The chapter concluded by navigating future trends, offering a comprehensive view of how digital business models were poised to evolve and shape the digital economy.

Key Questions for Discussion

1. How can businesses strategically choose the most suitable digital business model to remain competitive in the rapidly evolving digital economy? What factors should they consider when making this decision?
2. How has the rise of sharing economy platforms (e.g., Uber, Airbnb) disrupted traditional industries? Do you think the sharing economy is sustainable in the long term, and why?
3. What are the key advantages and challenges of using a freemium model in digital business? How can companies effectively convert free users into paying customers?
4. In the age of big data, how can businesses ethically and strategically use data monetisation to generate revenue while maintaining consumer trust and privacy?
5. How can businesses successfully integrate traditional and innovative digital business models to create a hybrid approach? Can you think of examples where this integration has led to significant success?

BIBLIOGRAPHY

Aagaard, A. (Ed.). (2019). *Digital Business Models: Driving Transformation and Innovation*. Springer.

Bagnoli, C., Albarelli, A. and Biazzo, S. (2022). *Digital Business Models for Industry 4.0: How Innovation and Technology Shape the Future of Companies*. Springer.

Gassmann, O., Frankenberger, K. and Csik, M. (2014). *The Business Model Navigator: 55 Models that Will Revolutionise Your Business*. Pearson.

Osterwalder, A. and Pigneur, Y. (2010). *Business Model Generation: A Handbook for Visionaries, Game Changers, and Challengers*. Wiley.

Parker, G.G., Van Alstyne, M.W. and Choudary, S.P. (2016). *Platform Revolution: How Networked Markets Are Transforming the Economy and How to Make Them Work for You*. W.W. Norton & Company.

Ries, E. (2011). *The Lean Startup: How Today's Entrepreneurs Use Continuous Innovation to Create Radically Successful Businesses*. Crown Business.

Ronteau, S., Muzellec, L., Saxena, D. and Trabucchi, D. (2022). *Digital Business Models: The New Value Creation and Capture Mechanisms of the 21st Century*. De Gruyter.

Siebel, T.M. (2019). *Digital Transformation: Survive and Thrive in an Era of Mass Extinction*. RosettaBooks.

Vaz, N. (2021). *Digital Business Transformation: How Established Companies Sustain Competitive Advantage from Now to Next*. Wiley.

Wirtz, B.W. (2019). *Digital Business Models: Concepts, Models, and the Alphabet Case Study*. Springer.

CHAPTER 3

Digital Transformation and Innovation

Learning Outcomes

By the end of this chapter, you will be able to:

1. Recognise the forces driving digital change and how organisations can embrace and leverage these forces to remain competitive in the modern economy.
2. Gain practical knowledge of various frameworks and models to guide the digital transformation process within organisations.
3. Learn how to integrate innovation into the digital transformation journey and understand the essential role of leadership in managing and guiding transformation efforts effectively.

3.1 INTRODUCTION

Digital transformation has become a driving force behind organisational change and innovation in the 21st century, reshaping industries, markets, and economies worldwide. In this era of rapid technological advancement, organisations are increasingly compelled to embrace digital transformation not only to remain competitive but also to harness the opportunities that come with it. At its core, digital transformation is more than the adoption of new technologies; it represents a fundamental shift in how businesses operate, deliver value, and interact with their customers.

The journey of digital transformation is far from straightforward. It requires a strategic approach that encompasses both technological integration and a change in organisational culture. Businesses must navigate a myriad of forces driving digital change, such as disruptive technologies, shifting consumer expectations, and the increasing need for data-driven decision-making. At the same time, innovation becomes an essential ingredient, allowing organisations to capitalise on new opportunities while remaining agile in an ever-evolving landscape.

This chapter explores the critical components of digital transformation, focusing on the frameworks and models that guide organisations through this complex process. By dissecting

DOI: 10.4324/9781032672458-3

the strategic pillars that underpin successful transformation, the role of leadership, and the ethical considerations that arise, we aim to provide a comprehensive understanding of how businesses can navigate the challenges and opportunities of the digital age. Ultimately, this chapter offers insights into how organisations can not only survive but thrive in a future shaped by constant technological disruption and innovation.

3.2 NAVIGATING DIGITAL TRANSFORMATION: EMBRACING CHANGE IN THE MODERN ECONOMY

In an era defined by rapid technological advancements, businesses must adapt to the ever-evolving digital landscape to remain competitive and relevant. The emergence of the "Digital Economy" has transformed digital transformation from a mere option into an essential strategic imperative across all industries. This chapter delves into the fundamental concepts of digital transformation, exploring its definition, scope, and the critical reasons for its adoption.

Digital transformation extends far beyond the simple implementation of new technologies; it represents a comprehensive and profound shift in how organisations operate, deliver value, and engage with stakeholders. At its core, it involves leveraging digital tools and processes to enhance operational efficiency, improve customer experiences, and drive overall business performance. This transformation is not limited to a single department or function; it permeates every facet of an organisation's ecosystem, from internal workflows to customer interactions and external partnerships. Consequently, a successful digital transformation demands a strategic and integrated approach that aligns technological initiatives with broader organisational objectives (Figure 3.1).

In today's digital economy, the urgency for digital transformation is unmistakable. Businesses operate in an environment characterised by heightened connectivity and data-driven decision-making, where failure to adapt can lead to diminished market relevance and even existential threats. Consumer expectations have evolved dramatically, with demands for seamless digital experiences, personalised services, and instant responses becoming the norm. Furthermore, traditional business models are under constant threat from agile, digital-native competitors who are adept at exploiting these new expectations.

Survival and success in this landscape are not merely about maintaining competitiveness but embracing innovation and resilience. This was starkly evident during the COVID-19 pandemic, where companies with robust digital capabilities were better equipped to navigate unprecedented disruptions and pivot their operations. Digital transformation, therefore, is not just a strategy for growth but a lifeline in turbulent times.

A successful digital transformation journey requires a meticulously crafted strategy that aligns technological innovation with organisational goals. Key elements of this strategy include strong leadership commitment, the acquisition and nurturing of digital talent, fostering a culture open to change, making data-driven decisions, and adopting relevant technologies. Throughout this chapter, we will explore these critical components, providing best practices and real-world case studies to illustrate their significance in driving digital transformation success. By understanding these complexities and strategies, organisations can position themselves to thrive in the digital economy, embracing change as a catalyst for sustained growth and innovation.

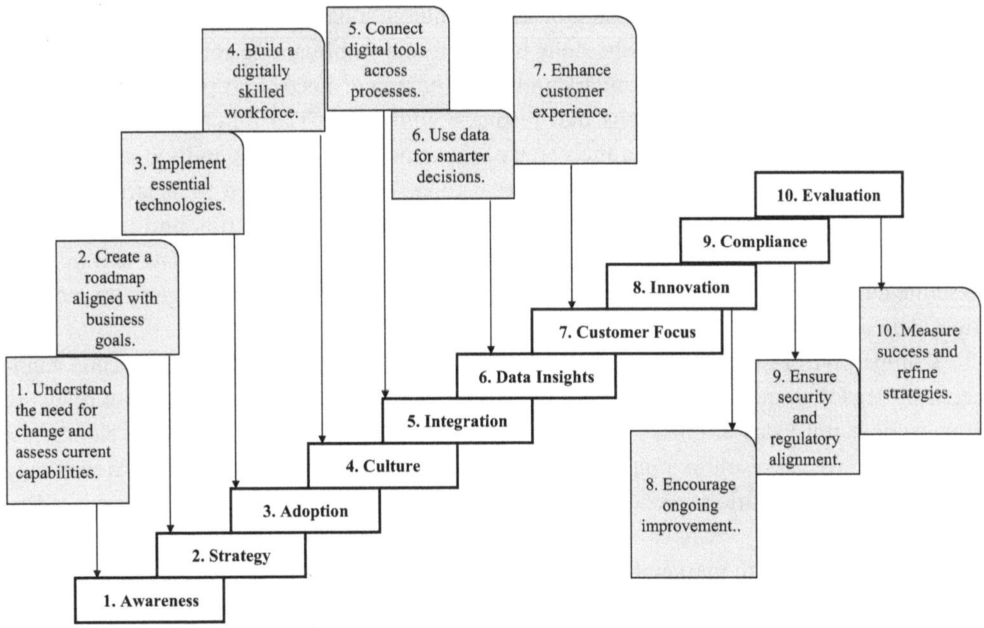

FIGURE 3.1 Digital Transformation Journey for Businesses

3.3 CATALYSTS OF DIGITAL TRANSFORMATION: NAVIGATING FORCES OF CHANGE

Digital transformation is not a phenomenon that occurs in isolation but is driven by a confluence of internal and external factors that compel organisations to adopt and integrate digital technologies. This section delves into the primary forces propelling the surge in digital transformation initiatives, focusing on technological advancements and disruptions, shifting customer expectations and behaviours, and the relentless competitive pressures alongside evolving industry trends.

The rapid pace of technological innovation lies at the heart of digital transformation. Advances in cloud computing, artificial intelligence (AI), big data analytics, the Internet of Things (IoT), and blockchain technology have revolutionised the business landscape, providing organisations with unprecedented opportunities to streamline operations, enhance decision-making, and develop innovative products and services. These technologies serve as the foundation upon which companies can build agile, data-driven operations and dynamic customer experiences. However, technological progress is a double-edged sword; while it opens up new avenues for those willing to embrace change, it poses existential risks for those unable or unwilling to adapt. Established industry leaders have found themselves overtaken by nimble startups that leverage disruptive technologies to redefine traditional business models. This reality compels organisations to continuously innovate and remain vigilant in exploring and adopting emerging technological trends to maintain their relevance and competitiveness.

Equally transformative are the evolving expectations and behaviours of today's consumers, who are more digitally savvy and discerning than ever before. Modern consumers demand seamless, personalised, and convenient interactions with brands across all touchpoints. This shift in consumer behaviour has profound implications for businesses across industries, necessitating a deep understanding of customer needs and preferences and the ability to deliver tailored solutions that resonate with them. The influence of digital and social media has further amplified the voice of the consumer, enabling individuals to praise or criticise brands to a global audience in real time. This heightened transparency exerts tremendous pressure on organisations to prioritise customer satisfaction and uphold their brand reputation. Through digital transformation, companies can harness data and insights to refine customer experiences, foster loyalty, and sustain a competitive edge in an increasingly demanding market.

Competitive pressures in the digital age are unrelenting, with new entrants often unencumbered by legacy systems and processes, disrupting established markets. To remain relevant, organisations must stay attuned to industry trends and the latest technological developments. Failure to do so can result in a rapid loss of market share and relevance. Industry trends may vary widely, but they often revolve around themes such as sustainability, data privacy, cybersecurity, and regulatory changes. Addressing these challenges proactively requires innovative solutions that align with market dynamics and compliance requirements.

Moreover, the importance of strategic partnerships and collaborations has grown in the digital era. Organisations are increasingly joining forces to pool resources, share expertise, and drive collective innovation. Such collaborations can accelerate digital transformation efforts, fostering industry-wide shifts and enabling businesses to tackle complex challenges more effectively.

In navigating the forces of change, organisations must recognise that digital transformation is not merely a technological upgrade but a holistic reimagining of how they operate, compete, and deliver value in a rapidly evolving world. By embracing these driving forces with agility and foresight, businesses can position themselves to thrive amidst the ongoing digital revolution.

3.4 DIGITAL TRANSFORMATION FRAMEWORKS AND MODELS

Organisations frequently resort to established frameworks and models to guide their efforts in the pursuit of successful digital transformation. These organised techniques offer a roadmap and methodology for managing the complexity of digital transformation. In this part, we will look at three popular models: McKinsey's Three Horizons Model, Kotter's 8-Step Process for Leading Change, and the ADKAR Model for Individual Change Management.

3.4.1 McKinsey's Three Horizons Model

The Three Horizons Model from McKinsey & Company is a strategy framework that assists organisations in balancing the requirement for short-term success with the imperative of long-term innovation. It splits the innovation landscape into three "horizons," each with its own time frame and set of goals (Table 3.1).

This table encapsulates McKinsey's Three Horizons Model, outlining the strategic focus and objectives for each horizon, thus providing a balanced approach to immediate success and future growth through innovation.

3.4.2 Kotter's 8-Step Process for Leading Change

John Kotter's 8-Step Process for Leading Change is a widely adopted model for managing organisational change, including digital transformation. It provides a structured approach to guiding organisations through change management challenges (Table 3.2). The eight steps are as follows:

TABLE 3.1 McKinsey's Three Horizons Model for Strategic Innovation

Horizon	Focus Area	Objectives	Characteristics
Horizon 1	Core Business	Optimising and enhancing existing processes, products, and services to deliver short-term results.	Incremental innovations, efficiency gains, and sustaining current business operations.
Horizon 2	Adjacent Business	Exploring new opportunities and markets related to the core business.	Developing new products or services to tap into emerging market trends and address evolving customer needs.
Horizon 3	Transformational Business	Pursuing disruptive innovations and creating entirely new business models that will shape the future.	Focusing on transformational changes that redefine the industry, involving high-risk, high-reward innovations.

TABLE 3.2 Kotter's 8-Step Process for Leading Organisational Change

Step	Description	Key Focus
1. Create a Sense of Urgency	Communicate the necessity of change and create a compelling reason for employees to engage with the transformation process.	Building awareness and motivation for change.
2. Build a Guiding Coalition	Form a team of influential leaders who will advocate for the change and provide guidance throughout the process.	Leadership alignment and commitment.
3. Form a Strategic Vision and Initiatives	Develop a clear vision for the future and outline specific actions to achieve it, providing direction and focus for the organisation.	Vision creation and strategic planning.
4. Enlist a Volunteer Army	Engage a wide range of employees to support the change effort, encouraging them to take ownership and actively participate in implementing the initiatives.	Broad-based employee engagement and support.

(*Continued*)

TABLE 3.2 (Continued)

Step	Description	Key Focus
5. Enable Action by Removing Barriers	Identify and remove obstacles that impede progress, such as outdated procedures or resistance to new technology, to empower employees to take action.	Eliminating obstacles and empowering action.
6. Generate Short-Term Wins	Achieve and celebrate early successes to build momentum, reinforce the value of the change, and encourage continued effort.	Demonstrating success and building momentum.
7. Sustain Acceleration	Maintain the momentum by continually promoting change, reinforcing new behaviours, and preventing regression to old habits.	Ongoing support and reinforcement.
8. Institute Change	Embed the changes into the organisational culture, making them a part of the company's standard practices, policies, and values to ensure long-term adoption.	Cultural integration and institutionalisation.

TABLE 3.3 The ADKAR Model for Individual Change Management

Stage	Description	Focus Area
Awareness	Individuals become aware of the need for change and understand why the change is necessary.	Understanding the need for change.
Desire	Individuals develop the motivation and desire to support and engage with the change initiative.	Building motivation and willingness to change.
Knowledge	Individuals acquire the knowledge and skills required to effectively implement and adapt to the change.	Providing the necessary training and information.
Ability	Individuals gain the capability to demonstrate the new behaviours and perform the tasks associated with the change.	Developing the capacity to enact change.
Reinforcement	Individuals receive ongoing support and reinforcement to sustain the change, ensuring it becomes embedded in the culture.	Strengthening and maintaining new behaviours.

This table provides a concise overview of Kotter's 8-Step Process for Leading Change, highlighting the steps involved in managing and sustaining organisational transformation effectively.

Kotter's model emphasises the importance of strong leadership, clear communication, and employee involvement in driving successful change initiatives.

3.4.3 The ADKAR Model for Individual Change Management

The ADKAR Model, developed by Prosci, is a framework designed to facilitate individual change management. It focuses on the people aspect of change and addresses the stages individuals go through when adapting to new processes or technologies (Table 3.3). ADKAR stands for:

The ADKAR Model recognises that successful digital transformation relies on the willingness and capability of individuals to embrace and adapt to the changes. It provides a structured approach to addressing the human side of transformation.

Incorporating these frameworks and models into a digital transformation strategy can provide organisations with a structured approach to navigate the complexities of change, aligning their efforts with strategic goals and maximising the likelihood of success.

3.5 STRATEGIC PILLARS OF DIGITAL TRANSFORMATION

Successful digital transformation is built upon a foundation of strong leadership, a customer-centric approach, data-driven decision-making, and agile operations. These elements work in tandem to guide organisations through the complexities of the digital landscape, fostering innovation and maintaining competitiveness.

Establishing a digital-first culture is a crucial starting point. This involves more than just adopting digital tools—it requires embedding a mindset that embraces change, innovation, and technology as essential to the organisation's core values. Leadership plays a pivotal role in this transformation by articulating a clear vision and demonstrating commitment to the digital agenda. Effective leaders communicate the significance of digital transformation, linking it to the organisation's long-term objectives, and engage employees at all levels. They promote continuous learning, ensuring that staff are equipped with the necessary skills to thrive in a rapidly evolving technological environment. Encouraging innovation and a willingness to take risks are also key aspects of a digital-first culture. By fostering an environment where experimentation is supported, organisations can harness creative ideas and turn them into valuable opportunities.

Customer-centricity is another pillar that underpins digital transformation. Understanding customer needs, preferences, and pain points is critical for crafting digital strategies that resonate with target audiences. Organisations must leverage customer data to gain insights and develop tailored solutions. Techniques like design thinking and customer journey mapping are invaluable for visualising the entire customer experience and identifying areas for improvement. The advent of digital technologies enables personalisation and customisation at an unprecedented level, allowing businesses to provide unique experiences that foster loyalty and enhance customer satisfaction.

Data-driven decision-making is the third pillar and serves as the backbone of digital transformation efforts. Data, when harnessed effectively, offer profound insights into customer behaviour, operational efficiency, and market trends. Organisations must prioritise robust data governance to ensure accuracy, security, and compliance with regulatory standards. Privacy considerations are paramount, as transparency in data handling builds trust with customers and stakeholders. Advanced analytics and machine learning (ML) can be employed to uncover patterns and trends that inform strategic decision-making, enabling organisations to act with agility and precision.

Agile and flexible operations form the final pillar, ensuring that organisations can respond swiftly to market changes and emerging opportunities. Embracing agile methodologies allows for iterative development and close collaboration across teams, resulting in digital solutions that are finely tuned to customer and business needs. Scalability is also crucial, as digital transformation often requires the ability to expand operations seamlessly in response to growth. Cloud computing and virtualisation provide the flexibility needed to scale resources efficiently. Organisations must also focus on streamlining processes to enhance efficiency and reduce waste. Lean principles, adapted from manufacturing, can be applied to digital operations to optimise workflows and eliminate unnecessary tasks, ultimately driving productivity and innovation.

These four strategic pillars—leadership and culture, customer-centricity and experience, data-driven decision-making, and agile operations—form a comprehensive framework for navigating the digital transformation journey. Together, they empower organisations to not only adapt to but also thrive in a dynamic and ever-evolving digital world.

3.6 NAVIGATING THE COMPLEXITIES OF DIGITAL TRANSFORMATION

Digital transformation is fraught with challenges that can impede an organisation's progress. Successfully navigating these obstacles requires strategic foresight, adaptability, and a clear vision. One of the primary hurdles lies in managing legacy systems and technology debt. Many organisations are anchored by outdated technological infrastructures and software that struggle to support modern digital requirements. These legacy systems not only limit responsiveness to new trends but also carry a burden of technical debt, making them cumbersome to maintain, upgrade, or integrate with contemporary solutions. Addressing this issue necessitates a multi-faceted strategy that begins with a comprehensive evaluation of existing systems to determine their relevance and potential for replacement or integration. Modernisation efforts should focus on critical yet outdated systems, whether by replacing components, migrating to cloud-based platforms, or refactoring existing code. Integration solutions are essential to ensure seamless data and process flow between legacy systems and new digital technologies, while meticulous data migration preserves data integrity and accessibility.

Employee resistance to change presents another significant challenge. Workers accustomed to established procedures may find it difficult to embrace new technologies and processes. Overcoming this resistance is vital for the success of digital transformation initiatives. Effective communication is the cornerstone of this effort, ensuring that employees understand the rationale behind changes, the benefits they will bring, and how these align with the organisation's strategic objectives. Engaging employees in the planning and decision-making stages fosters a sense of ownership and reduces apprehension. Providing comprehensive training and support builds confidence in using new tools and systems. Identifying and empowering change champions within the organisation can further enhance buy-in, as these individuals can inspire and guide their peers through the transformation process.

The issue of integration and data silos also poses a considerable barrier. Many organisations struggle with data that are compartmentalised across various departments and platforms, hindering data-driven decision-making and disrupting efforts to deliver a cohesive customer experience. Breaking down these silos requires a well-defined data strategy that establishes governance, standards, and protocols for data integration. Investing in modern integration platforms facilitates the smooth exchange of information between disparate systems and applications, while cross-functional teams can play a pivotal role in ensuring data consistency and collaboration across the organisation.

Cybersecurity and risk management emerge as critical concerns in the digital transformation landscape. As organisations embrace digital tools and platforms, they also become more exposed to cyber threats. Balancing robust cybersecurity measures with the agility needed for digital transformation is a delicate task. Implementing a comprehensive cybersecurity framework is essential, incorporating regular assessments, vulnerability scanning, and proactive threat detection. Educating employees on cybersecurity best practices and their role in safeguarding digital assets is equally important. A well-defined incident response plan enables swift action in the event of a security breach, while a thorough assessment of third-party vendors and partners ensures that they adhere to stringent security standards.

Digital transformation, while offering immense opportunities, presents several challenges that require a strategic and cohesive approach. By viewing these challenges as catalysts for growth, organisations can not only overcome them but also position themselves to thrive in an increasingly digital world.

3.7 FOSTERING INNOVATION IN DIGITAL TRANSFORMATION

Innovation is the driving force behind successful digital transformation. To thrive in the constantly evolving digital landscape, organisations must not only embrace innovation but also understand its diverse forms and foster a culture that nurtures and supports it. This involves a nuanced approach, recognising the distinct types of innovation, cultivating an environment conducive to creativity, and leveraging the power of open innovation and collaboration.

A comprehensive understanding of innovation begins with distinguishing between incremental and disruptive types. Incremental innovation focuses on refining and enhancing existing products, services, or processes. It involves making gradual improvements that optimise efficiency and meet evolving customer expectations. Although incremental innovation may not result in revolutionary changes, it is vital for maintaining competitiveness. In digital transformation, incremental innovation is often seen in regular software updates, feature enhancements, and improvements to user interfaces, all of which contribute to keeping digital products and services relevant and competitive.

On the other hand, disruptive innovation creates entirely new products, services, or business models that challenge established markets or industries. These innovations often begin in niche markets but can grow to disrupt entire sectors, as seen in the cases of Uber and Airbnb, which transformed the taxi and hospitality industries through innovative digital platforms. In the context of digital transformation, disruptive innovation is crucial for organisations looking to outpace competitors and seize new opportunities. While incremental innovation ensures ongoing improvement, disruptive innovation enables organisations to lead change and redefine industry standards.

For an organisation to sustain innovation, it must cultivate a culture that actively encourages creative thinking and experimentation. Leadership plays a pivotal role in this process. Leaders must articulate a clear vision for innovation and model the behaviours they wish to see, such as championing new ideas and embracing change. An environment where employees feel empowered to experiment and take calculated risks is essential. Empowerment means encouraging contributions from all levels of the organisation, fostering cross-functional collaboration, and allowing employees the autonomy to explore new ideas, experiment, and learn from both successes and failures.

Allocating dedicated resources, including time and funding, to support innovation initiatives is equally important. Organisations should establish innovation labs, specialised teams, or projects to explore new technologies and ideas. This commitment demonstrates that innovation is not a peripheral activity but a core priority. Recognising and rewarding innovative efforts further reinforces this culture, motivating individuals to continue contributing creatively and inspiring others to do the same.

The concept of open innovation expands the boundaries of traditional innovation by actively seeking input and collaboration from external partners such as start-ups, universities, research institutions, and even customers. This approach recognises that valuable ideas and technologies do not solely originate within the organisation. Open innovation is particularly relevant in the digital era, where the rapid pace of change demands access to a broader pool of knowledge and expertise. By engaging with external partners, organisations can accelerate their innovation processes, access cutting-edge developments, and gain new perspectives that keep them at the forefront of their industries.

Collaboration is a fundamental aspect of open innovation and digital transformation. Effective collaboration requires the formation of both formal and informal partnerships that facilitate the exchange of ideas, resources, and capabilities. Cross-industry collaborations, for instance, have led to groundbreaking innovations, such as the integration of digital health solutions in the healthcare sector through partnerships with technology companies. These collaborations not only drive innovation but also contribute to reshaping industries and enhancing the quality of products and services.

In conclusion, innovation is the cornerstone of digital transformation. For organisations to thrive in the digital age, they must strategically harness both incremental and disruptive innovations. Cultivating an innovative culture through strong leadership, employee empowerment, resource allocation, and recognition is crucial for fostering sustained innovation. Furthermore, embracing open innovation and collaboration with external partners can significantly accelerate the pace of digital transformation, ensuring that organisations remain agile, competitive, and well-positioned to navigate the complexities of the digital world.

3.8 HARNESSING EMERGING TECHNOLOGIES FOR DIGITAL TRANSFORMATION

Emerging technologies are fundamentally reshaping how organisations operate, engage with customers, and innovate in the rapidly evolving landscape of digital transformation. Central to this transformation are three pivotal technologies: AI and ML, the IoT and Connected Devices, and Blockchain and Distributed Ledger Technology (DLT), each of which offers unique capabilities and challenges that organisations must navigate to remain competitive.

AI and ML are at the forefront of digital transformation, revolutionising the way systems learn, adapt, and make decisions based on data. These technologies enable systems to process and analyse vast amounts of information, uncovering insights and patterns that would be impossible for humans to discern. Their applications span numerous industries, from enhancing customer interactions to optimising internal operations. AI-driven chatbots and virtual assistants, for instance, are transforming customer service by offering instant, personalised support, powered by Natural Language Processing that allows these systems to understand and respond to customer queries with a high degree of accuracy. Moreover, ML models empower organisations to make data-driven decisions, predict customer behaviour, optimise supply chains, and identify new business opportunities.

AI is also playing a significant role in automating routine business processes, reducing manual effort, and increasing efficiency. Robotic Process Automation and AI-powered workflow management systems are streamlining everything from data entry to complex decision-making tasks. However, as AI and ML continue to advance, they bring with them significant challenges, particularly concerning data privacy, algorithmic bias, and the potential for job displacement due to automation. Organisations must therefore adopt responsible AI practices, ensuring that these technologies are used ethically and transparently.

The IoT represents another transformative force, connecting physical devices, sensors, and objects through the internet to collect and share data. This interconnected ecosystem is revolutionising industries by providing real-time data and insights that facilitate better decision-making. In urban environments, smart city initiatives are leveraging IoT to monitor traffic, optimise energy use, and enhance public services, thereby creating more sustainable and efficient cities. In industrial settings, the Industrial IoT (IIoT) is driving operational efficiency through predictive maintenance and enhanced product quality. By equipping machinery and equipment with sensors that transmit data for analysis, organisations can anticipate maintenance needs, minimise downtime, and improve overall productivity.

Consumer IoT devices, such as smart thermostats and wearable fitness trackers, are becoming increasingly integrated into everyday life, collecting data that can be used to personalise experiences and promote health and well-being. However, the proliferation of connected devices also brings significant security and privacy challenges. With each device serving as a potential entry point for cyberattacks, organisations must prioritise robust security measures and ensure data privacy as they deploy IoT solutions.

Blockchain and DLT offer yet another dimension of digital transformation. As a decentralised and tamper-resistant ledger, blockchain provides a secure and transparent way to record transactions across multiple computers, eliminating the need for intermediaries. This technology is transforming supply chains by offering end-to-end visibility and traceability, allowing companies to track the journey of products from raw materials to end consumers. This transparency not only reduces fraud but also ensures product authenticity.

In addition to supply chain applications, blockchain is revolutionising digital identity and authentication. Blockchain-based digital identity solutions give individuals control over their personal data while enabling organisations to securely verify identities without relying on centralised authorities. Smart contracts, another key feature of blockchain, automate agreements by embedding contractual terms directly into code. These self-executing contracts streamline transactions and processes, reducing the need for intermediaries and minimising the potential for disputes.

Despite its potential, blockchain faces challenges that must be addressed for broader adoption, including issues of scalability, energy consumption, and regulatory compliance. Overcoming these obstacles is essential for organisations seeking to leverage blockchain as a part of their digital transformation strategy.

Emerging technologies like AI, IoT, and blockchain are not just tools for digital transformation—they are the driving forces reshaping business models, enhancing customer experiences, and improving operational efficiency. However, as organisations integrate these technologies into their operations, they must also be mindful of the associated challenges, including ethical considerations, security risks, and the need for scalable solutions. By addressing these issues proactively, organisations can harness the full potential of these technologies and navigate the complexities of the digital landscape with confidence and agility.

CASE STUDY 3

General Electric's Industrial Internet — Transforming Traditional Industries

General Electric (GE), a global leader in industrial manufacturing, undertook a significant digital transformation through its Industrial Internet Initiative. Recognising the growing impact of digital technologies on industrial operations, GE sought to integrate data analytics, ML, and the IoT into its equipment. This move aimed to revolutionise how businesses manage operations, maintenance, and efficiency. By connecting machinery to real-time data analysis, GE aimed to optimise performance, reduce costly downtime, and improve productivity across key industries, including aviation, healthcare, power, and manufacturing.

GE faced the challenge of modernising traditional industrial operations in a world increasingly shaped by digital capabilities. Industrial equipment historically operated in silos, lacked real-time monitoring, and was prone to inefficiencies due to high maintenance costs and unexpected failures. Without predictive insights, businesses often relied on reactive maintenance, addressing faults only after they had occurred, leading to significant downtime and financial losses. GE needed a data-driven solution to enhance operational efficiency and reduce downtime in mission-critical industries.

To address these challenges, GE developed Predix, a cloud-based IIoT platform designed to connect machines, collect real-time operational data, and provide predictive analytics. By embedding digital sensors into industrial equipment, GE enabled businesses to monitor asset performance, predict failures before they happened, and make data-driven maintenance decisions. This predictive approach allowed companies to shift from reactive to proactive maintenance, significantly reducing unexpected breakdowns and improving operational efficiency.

In addition to IoT, GE leveraged big data analytics, AI, and digital twin technology. By creating virtual replicas of machines, engineers could simulate various operational scenarios, test system behaviours, and enhance decision-making. This combination of digital tools provided industries with real-time insights, ensuring that maintenance and operational strategies were optimised for maximum efficiency.

The implementation of the Industrial Internet Initiative led to significant improvements in operational efficiency, cost reduction, and overall productivity. Downtime was reduced by up to 20% through predictive maintenance and early failure detection. Asset performance improved, as real-time data analysis enabled better decision-making. Fuel efficiency in aviation was enhanced, with IoT solutions integrated into jet engines, saving airlines millions in fuel costs. Power plant operations became more efficient, reducing energy waste and improving environmental sustainability. GE's transformation demonstrated the power of digital integration in industrial operations, proving that data and analytics could drive operational excellence and reshape business strategies.

The success of GE's Industrial Internet Initiative highlights the power of data-driven decision-making, where leveraging IoT and AI enhances efficiency, reduces costs, and provides real-time operational insights. Predictive maintenance emerged as a major competitive advantage, allowing businesses to minimise equipment failures, improve productivity, and extend asset lifespan. The adoption of cloud-based platforms such as Predix facilitated seamless data integration and analysis, driving efficiency at scale. The case of GE also underlines the necessity of adaptability in the digital age, as even long-established industrial giants must embrace digital transformation to remain competitive and future-proof their operations in a rapidly evolving business landscape. GE's journey serves as a compelling example of how traditional industries can thrive by integrating digital innovation, data analytics, and IoT technologies into their core operations.

Discussion Questions for Students (with Indicative Answers)

1. **How did GE's Industrial Internet Initiative contribute to the digital transformation of traditional industries?**
   Indicative Answer: By integrating IoT, AI, and cloud computing into industrial equipment, GE enabled real-time data analysis and predictive maintenance, reducing costs and improving efficiency.

2. **What were the key benefits of predictive maintenance in GE's transformation strategy?**
   Indicative Answer: Predictive maintenance helped reduce equipment downtime, minimise unexpected failures, improve asset performance, and enhance safety standards.
3. **What challenges might companies face when implementing an Industrial Internet strategy like GE's?**
   Indicative Answer: Challenges include high implementation costs, cybersecurity risks, workforce reskilling needs, and integration complexities with existing infrastructure.
4. **How does cloud computing enhance digital transformation in industrial businesses?**
   Indicative Answer: Cloud platforms like Predix allow companies to store, analyse, and process vast amounts of machine data, enabling scalable and efficient decision-making.
5. **What lessons can other industries learn from GE's digital transformation journey?**
   Indicative Answer: Companies should prioritise data analytics, automation, and digital innovation to remain competitive, improve efficiency, and future-proof operations.

3.9 EVALUATING THE IMPACT OF DIGITAL TRANSFORMATION

Assessing the success of digital transformation is pivotal for organisations to ensure that they are not only achieving their strategic goals but also adding substantial value. This process involves the careful selection of Key Performance Indicators (KPIs), maintaining a balance between immediate gains and long-term ambitions, and fostering a culture of iterative improvement and continuous learning.

A fundamental step in measuring the impact of digital transformation is the identification and definition of relevant KPIs that align with the organisation's specific goals and objectives. These indicators serve as the benchmarks against which progress can be gauged. Customer satisfaction is a crucial metric, often measured through surveys, feedback, and Net Promoter Scores to assess the impact of digital initiatives on customer experience. Revenue growth is another key indicator, reflecting the financial benefits of digital strategies through increased sales, the development of new revenue streams, and cost savings. Operational efficiency, tracked through metrics such as reduced process cycle times and lower operational costs, highlights how digital transformation is enhancing the organisation's processes. Innovation metrics, such as the number of new products launched, patents filed, or ideas generated, provide insight into how digital transformation is influencing the organisation's culture and fostering creativity. Additionally, monitoring digital adoption rates among employees and customers reveals how well new digital tools and platforms are being integrated and utilised across the organisation.

For effective measurement and evaluation, organisations must employ data analytics and reporting tools that offer real-time insights into these KPIs, enabling the identification of trends, opportunities, and areas that require improvement. Benchmarking against industry peers or competitors provides a valuable context for assessing digital transformation success, allowing organisations to understand their relative performance in terms of customer satisfaction, innovation, and operational efficiency.

While short-term wins are vital for building momentum and maintaining confidence in the digital transformation journey, they must be carefully aligned with long-term strategic objectives. Early successes inspire employees and leaders to embrace further change, but they should not undermine the sustainability or overarching vision of the transformation. Striking the right balance between immediate gains and broader goals is essential for maintaining strategic coherence throughout the transformation process.

An iterative approach, where digital transformation is broken down into manageable phases or projects, is key to sustaining progress. Each phase builds upon the successes and lessons learnt from the previous ones, allowing for continuous adaptation and refinement. This method not only fosters steady development but also provides the flexibility to respond to new challenges and opportunities as they arise.

Embracing iterative improvement and continuous learning is crucial for navigating the complexities of digital transformation. Organisations must cultivate a mindset that views failures not as setbacks but as opportunities for growth and learning. Analysing what went wrong and understanding the reasons behind it enables organisations to make necessary adjustments and refine their strategies. Piloting new digital initiatives on a smaller scale before expanding them across the organisation is a prudent approach, as it helps identify potential challenges and areas for enhancement while collecting valuable feedback from a select group of users.

Fostering an agile and adaptive organisational culture is essential for sustaining momentum and achieving long-term digital transformation success. Such a culture encourages experimentation, values employee input, and is responsive to change, making it more likely that the organisation will navigate the transformation process successfully. Establishing robust feedback loops with employees, customers, and stakeholders is critical for maintaining alignment with evolving needs and expectations. Regular feedback enables organisations to make informed decisions, refine their strategies, and ensure that digital initiatives continue to meet the demands of the dynamic digital landscape.

In sum, measuring and evaluating the success of digital transformation is a complex and ongoing process that requires a comprehensive approach. It involves defining meaningful KPIs, leveraging data for informed decision-making, balancing short-term achievements with long-term goals, and fostering a culture of continuous learning and adaptation. By committing to these principles, organisations can effectively track their progress, remain agile in the face of change, and realise their vision of a digitally transformed future.

3.10 NAVIGATING ETHICAL DIMENSIONS IN DIGITAL TRANSFORMATION

As organisations embark on their digital transformation journeys, they must conscientiously address the ethical implications of their technological advancements to ensure that these changes benefit society, employees, and customers alike. Upholding principles such as fairness, transparency, and respect for human rights is essential to creating a digital ecosystem that serves the common good. This exploration of ethical dimensions in digital transformation considers the responsible use of data and technology, the need for transparency and accountability in AI and automation, and the importance of adopting a human-centric approach.

The ethical use of data and technology is paramount, as digital transformation often necessitates the collection and analysis of extensive datasets. Organisations have a duty to prioritise data privacy and security, safeguarding sensitive information and complying with regulations like the General Data Protection Regulation. This responsibility involves securing informed consent for data collection, enforcing stringent security protocols, and ensuring that data are utilised solely for legitimate purposes. Furthermore, ML algorithms and AI systems, despite their transformative potential, can unintentionally perpetuate biases inherent in the data used to train them. To counteract this, organisations must employ strategies to mitigate bias and ensure that these systems do not discriminate against individuals or groups based on race, gender, or socio-economic status. Regular audits and reviews of AI systems are necessary to detect and rectify any biases that may emerge. Additionally, AI-driven decision-making poses ethical challenges, particularly in sensitive areas such as hiring, lending, and criminal justice. Establishing clear guidelines and maintaining a balance between automation and human oversight is crucial to prevent technology from causing harm or exacerbating existing inequalities.

Transparency and accountability in the deployment of AI and automation are critical for building trust and ensuring responsible use. As AI systems become increasingly complex, the demand for explainable AI grows. Organisations must strive to develop models and algorithms that provide clear, understandable explanations of their decision-making processes. This transparency not only fosters trust but also allows users to comprehend the rationale behind specific decisions. Furthermore, organisations must take responsibility for the outcomes of their AI and automation systems. This includes actively monitoring for unintended consequences, such as algorithmic bias, and promptly addressing any issues that arise. Clear lines of responsibility and accountability must be established within the organisation to ensure that these technologies are used ethically and responsibly. The ethical deployment of automation is also a concern, particularly when it comes to its impact on the workforce. Rather than displacing jobs entirely, automation should be used to augment human capabilities. Efforts must be made to reskill and upskill employees, enabling them to transition into new roles created by technological advancements.

Adopting a human-centric approach to digital transformation is essential for creating a workplace culture that prioritises the well-being and empowerment of employees. This involves actively engaging employees in the transformation process, providing opportunities for upskilling, and fostering a collaborative environment that values their input. A user-centred design approach is also crucial when developing digital products and services. Understanding users' needs, preferences, and pain points, and incorporating their feedback into the design process, leads to solutions that are both ethical and user-friendly. Regular user testing and iterative design help refine these products, ensuring they meet the highest standards of usability and ethical integrity. Furthermore, organisations must be mindful of the potential impact of digital transformation on mental health. The increasing digitisation of work and life can lead to digital overload and burnout. Providing resources and support for maintaining a healthy work-life balance is a vital component of a human-centric strategy. Organisations should also consider the broader social impact of their digital activities, including their environmental footprint and contributions to community well-being. Acting as responsible corporate citizens requires a commitment to sustainable practices and a conscious effort to contribute positively to society.

Ultimately, ethical considerations are indispensable to the success and sustainability of digital transformation initiatives. By prioritising data privacy, AI fairness, technological transparency, and a human-centric approach that empowers employees and benefits society, organisations can achieve their technological ambitions while fostering a more just, equitable, and sustainable digital future. Integrating ethical principles into every facet of digital transformation ensures that technological progress is aligned with the values of integrity and social responsibility.

3.11 LEADING THE CHARGE: THE CRUCIAL ROLE OF LEADERSHIP IN DIGITAL TRANSFORMATION

Digital transformation is far more than a mere technological shift; it requires strong, visionary leadership to steer the organisation through the complexities of change. Leaders are responsible not only for setting the strategic direction but also for nurturing a culture that embraces innovation, collaboration, and resilience. They must empower digital leaders and change agents, foster cross-functional collaboration, and articulate a compelling vision that inspires and engages all stakeholders.

Empowering digital leaders and change agents is essential for driving transformation. Identifying individuals who possess both a deep understanding of digital trends and a passion for innovation can be a catalyst for change. These leaders are not simply technology experts but also strategic thinkers who can bridge the gap between technological possibilities and the organisation's goals. They play a pivotal role in translating the vision into actionable initiatives that resonate across various levels of the organisation. Similarly, change agents, who are often embedded within different teams, serve as champions of transformation. Their influence extends beyond their immediate roles, helping to translate the strategic vision into daily practices. To support these leaders and change agents, organisations must invest in robust training and development programmes that cover not only emerging technologies but also essential leadership and change management skills. This commitment to continuous learning ensures that leaders and their teams remain agile and equipped to navigate the evolving digital landscape.

Effective leadership in digital transformation also involves breaking down silos and fostering cross-functional collaboration. The barriers that exist between departments and teams can stymie progress and lead to conflicting objectives. Leaders must actively dismantle these silos, creating an environment where knowledge flows freely and collaboration is the norm. One effective strategy is the formation of cross-functional teams dedicated to digital transformation. These teams, composed of individuals with diverse skills and perspectives, are better equipped to tackle complex challenges and ensure that various viewpoints are considered in decision-making processes. Aligning these collaborative efforts with the organisation's broader business objectives is crucial. This alignment not only ensures that resources are utilised effectively but also helps to avoid fragmented initiatives that lack strategic coherence.

Communicating the vision and benefits of digital transformation is another fundamental responsibility of leadership. A clear and compelling vision serves as a roadmap, guiding the organisation towards its digital future. Leaders must articulate this vision in a way that resonates with all stakeholders, highlighting the strategic goals and the anticipated benefits of transformation. Effective communication goes beyond simply broadcasting messages; it involves engaging in a continuous dialogue with employees at all levels. This two-way communication fosters transparency, builds trust, and provides a platform for addressing concerns and gathering feedback. Leaders should also make a point of celebrating successes and milestones along the way. Recognising the efforts of teams and individuals, showcasing tangible outcomes, and continually reinforcing the benefits of transformation contribute to a positive and motivated organisational culture.

Change management is an integral aspect of leading digital transformation. Resistance to change is a natural human response, and leaders must be adept at managing this resistance constructively. Understanding the emotional and psychological stages of change enables leaders to provide the right support and guidance at each phase. This might include addressing fears and uncertainties, offering reassurance, and helping employees to see how they fit into the transformed organisation. Flexibility and adaptability are also essential traits for leaders in this context. As digital transformation is an ongoing process, leaders must be prepared to refine and adjust their strategies in response to new information, technological advancements, and shifting business priorities. This willingness to pivot and evolve is key to maintaining momentum and ensuring long-term success.

In essence, effective leadership is the cornerstone of successful digital transformation. By empowering digital leaders and change agents, fostering cross-functional collaboration, and communicating a compelling and inclusive vision, leaders can guide their organisations through the complexities of transformation. Cultivating a culture of innovation, collaboration, and adaptability will position organisations to thrive in an ever-changing digital landscape, ensuring they remain competitive and resilient in the face of future challenges.

3.12 FUTURE-PROOFING ORGANISATIONS: NAVIGATING DISRUPTIONS IN A DYNAMIC WORLD

In an age defined by rapid technological advances and unpredictable global events, organisations must be equipped to navigate disruptions and prepare for an uncertain future. This requires a strategic approach that involves not only recognising and responding to emerging trends but also fostering an organisational culture that is agile, resilient, and open to continuous innovation.

To effectively anticipate and respond to industry trends and market shifts, organisations must engage in continuous monitoring and analysis of their external environment. This involves keeping a close watch on the evolution of technologies, competitor activities, regulatory developments, and changes in consumer behaviour. Staying informed allows businesses to identify emerging opportunities and potential threats early, enabling them to make informed strategic decisions. One effective method for navigating such uncertainty is scenario planning. By crafting hypothetical scenarios that explore a variety of potential futures, organisations can better prepare for different possibilities. This process involves not only identifying potential disruptions but also evaluating their likely impacts on business operations. The insights gained from scenario planning enable leaders to develop proactive strategies that can be quickly adapted as circumstances evolve.

Environmental scanning is another critical component of future-proofing an organisation. This systematic process of gathering and analysing information about the external environment helps to identify early signals of change and disruption. By maintaining a vigilant watch on news, industry reports, and social trends, organisations can gain valuable foresight into shifting dynamics and adjust their strategies accordingly. This proactive stance is essential in a world where rapid change has become the norm rather than the exception.

Agility and resilience are fundamental qualities for organisations operating in today's unpredictable landscape. Agile methodologies, originally developed for software development, have proven highly effective when applied to broader organisational processes. These principles, which include iterative development and flexibility, enable organisations to respond rapidly to changing conditions. By fostering a mindset of continuous improvement and adaptability, businesses can remain nimble and responsive to emerging challenges.

In addition to agility, resilience is a key attribute that allows organisations to withstand and recover from shocks and disruptions. Building resilience involves creating robust crisis management and business continuity plans that outline clear steps for maintaining operations during adverse events. These plans should cover communication protocols, resource allocation, and recovery strategies to ensure the organisation can continue to function effectively in the face of unexpected challenges. Strengthening resilience also requires diversifying supply chains, implementing reliable backup systems, and cultivating a culture of problem-solving and adaptability across all levels of the organisation.

Embracing a growth mindset is another essential aspect of preparing for the future. A growth mindset is characterised by the belief that abilities and intelligence can be developed through dedication and effort. Encouraging this mindset within the organisation helps employees to view challenges as opportunities for growth and to approach setbacks as learning experiences rather than failures. This cultural shift fosters a more dynamic and innovative work environment, where individuals are motivated to explore new ideas and continuously seek improvement.

For innovation to thrive, it must be established as a core value embedded in the organisation's culture. This involves more than just encouraging creative thinking; it requires providing the necessary resources and support for employees to experiment with new ideas and initiatives. By promoting a culture where innovation is valued and rewarded, organisations can drive continuous improvement and maintain a competitive edge.

Collaborative learning is another vital component of fostering an innovative and adaptive organisation. By facilitating the exchange of knowledge and insights across teams and departments, organisations can harness the collective expertise of their workforce to solve complex problems and identify new opportunities. Cross-functional collaboration and the sharing of best practices help to break down silos and enable the organisation to respond more effectively to emerging challenges.

Leadership plays a pivotal role in navigating disruptions and preparing for the future. Adaptive leaders are those who are open to change, embrace innovative ideas, and cultivate a culture of experimentation and exploration. Such leaders not only inspire their teams to think creatively but also provide the support and guidance necessary to turn innovative ideas into actionable strategies. Empowering employees to take initiative and adapt to changing conditions is essential for building a resilient organisation capable of thriving in a rapidly evolving environment.

In conclusion, preparing for future disruptions requires a comprehensive approach that encompasses continuous environmental scanning, fostering agility and resilience, and cultivating a growth mindset that supports ongoing innovation. Organisations that are proactive in recognising and responding to emerging trends, that prioritise resilience and adaptability, and that nurture a culture of innovation are well-positioned to succeed in an increasingly dynamic and uncertain world. By embedding these principles into their strategic framework, organisations can not only weather the storms of disruption but also emerge stronger and more competitive in the ever-changing landscape of the future.

3.13 CHAPTER SUMMARY

In this chapter, we explored the multifaceted aspects of digital transformation and innovation, highlighting how businesses adapted to the evolving demands of the digital economy. We examined the various forces that catalysed digital transformation, including technological advancements and market dynamics, and how organisations responded to these changes. Different frameworks and models were presented to guide organisations in strategically aligning their digital initiatives with overall business objectives.

The chapter emphasised the key strategic pillars that supported successful digital transformation, such as agility, data-driven approaches, and a focus on customer needs. The role of fostering innovation was thoroughly discussed, showing how a culture of continuous improvement and creative thinking enabled organisations to maintain a competitive edge. We also explored how emerging technologies such as AI and IoT were harnessed to reshape operational processes and deliver value.

Ethical considerations around the responsible use of technology were reviewed, along with the pivotal role of leadership in steering organisations through the complexities of digital transformation. Finally, the chapter looked at how organisations prepared themselves for future disruptions, offering strategies to ensure resilience in a constantly changing world.

Through this journey, we underscored that digital transformation was not just about adopting new technologies but also about creating a mindset and culture of ongoing adaptation and innovation.

Key Questions for Discussion

1. What are the primary internal and external catalysts driving digital transformation in modern businesses? Can you think of an example where one of these forces has significantly shaped a company's success or failure?
2. What are the key strategic pillars that organisations must focus on to ensure successful digital transformation? How can they balance technological advancements with cultural and organisational change?
3. How can organisations foster a culture of innovation to thrive during digital transformation? Are there specific strategies or practices that businesses can adopt to encourage innovative thinking among employees?
4. What ethical considerations arise during digital transformation, such as data privacy, AI bias, or workforce displacement? How can organisations address these challenges while pursuing technological advancements?
5. How can businesses future-proof themselves in a world of constant digital disruption? What role does leadership play in ensuring long-term adaptability and resilience during digital transformation?

BIBLIOGRAPHY

DalleMule, L. and Davenport, T.H. (2023). *What's Your Data Strategy?* Harvard Business Review Press.

Davenport, T.H. and Redman, T.C. (2023). *Digital Transformation Comes Down to Talent in Four Key Areas*. Harvard Business Review Press.

Fuller, J.B., Wallenstein, J.K., Raman, M. and de Chalendar, A. (2023). *Your Workforce Is More Adaptable Than You Think*. Harvard Business Review Press.

Fountaine, T., McCarthy, B. and Saleh, T. (2023). *Building the AI-Powered Organization*. Harvard Business Review Press.

Furr, N. and Shipilov, A. (2023). *Digital Doesn't Have to Be Disruptive*. Harvard Business Review Press.

Iansiti, M. and Lakhani, K.R. (2023). *Competing in the Age of AI*. Harvard Business Review Press.

Ismail, S., Malone, M.S. and van Geest, Y. (2023). *Exponential Organizations: Why New Organizations Are Ten Times Better, Faster, and Cheaper than Yours (and What to Do About It)*. Diversion Books.

Kavadias, S., Ladas, K. and Loch, C. (2023). *The Transformative Business Model*. Harvard Business Review Press.

McGrath, R. and McManus, R. (2023). *Discovery-Driven Digital Transformation*. Harvard Business Review Press.

McKinsey & Company (2023). *Rewired: A Manual for Digital Transformations That Work*. McKinsey & Company.

Podolny, J.M. and Hansen, M.T. (2023). *How Apple Is Organized for Innovation*. Harvard Business Review Press.

Porter, M.E. and Heppelmann, J.E. (2023). *How Smart, Connected Products Are Transforming Companies*. Harvard Business Review Press.

Rogers, D.L. (2023). *The Digital Transformation Playbook: Rethink Your Business for the Digital Age*. Columbia Business School Publishing.

Siggelkow, N. and Terwiesch, C. (2023). *The Age of Continuous Connection*. Harvard Business Review Press.

Wessel, M., Levie, A. and Siegel, R. (2023). *The Problem with Legacy Ecosystems*. Harvard Business Review Press.

Westerman, G., Bonnet, D. and McAfee, A. (2023). *Leading Digital: Turning Technology into Business Transformation*. Harvard Business Review Press.

CHAPTER **4**

Building a Digital Business Strategy

Learning Outcomes

By the end of this chapter, you will be able to:

1. Understand how to create a digital business strategy that is focused on customer needs and integrates digital channels effectively to enhance customer experience.
2. Learn how to leverage data analytics to inform and refine digital business decisions, ensuring a more precise and targeted approach.
3. Gain the skills to design and execute an e-commerce strategy that aligns with broader business goals and enhances digital sales success.

4.1 INTRODUCTION

The digital landscape is transforming how businesses operate, compete, and engage with their audiences. The acceleration of technology and the growing dominance of digital platforms have redefined traditional business models, making it imperative for organisations to rethink their strategic approaches. In this chapter, we will explore the critical elements required to build an effective digital business strategy, focusing on how businesses can navigate the complexities of the digital economy. Crafting a successful digital strategy involves more than adopting the latest technologies; it demands a deep understanding of the market, an agile approach to setting objectives, and a commitment to customer centricity. Businesses today must assess their internal capabilities, understand their competitive environment, and align their goals with the realities of the digital era. A key pillar of any digital strategy is the thoughtful selection and integration of digital channels, ensuring a consistent and compelling brand presence. Additionally, we delve into the need for a unified content strategy, particularly in a landscape where attention is fragmented across numerous platforms. In an era where e-commerce continues to surge, businesses must also focus on creating robust sales strategies. Finally, the ability to harness data-driven insights will be the linchpin of a dynamic, continuously evolving digital strategy, ensuring businesses stay agile and competitive as they navigate the digital marketplace. By the end of this chapter, readers will have a solid understanding of the

DOI: 10.4324/9781032672458-4

essential elements required to build a comprehensive and resilient digital business strategy, well-suited for today's fast-paced and ever-changing digital environment.

4.2 CRAFTING AN EFFECTIVE DIGITAL BUSINESS STRATEGY: NAVIGATING THE DIGITAL ECONOMY

In today's fast-paced digital era, marked by rapid technological advancements and constantly evolving consumer expectations, a well-structured digital business strategy is no longer a luxury but a necessity. As organisations manoeuvre through the complexities of the digital landscape, it is essential to grasp the key elements required to craft and implement a strategy that not only keeps pace with change but also drives innovation and sustains long-term growth. This section explores the core aspects of a digital business strategy, delving into its definition, importance, and the key components that contribute to its success.

A digital business strategy, at its heart, represents a comprehensive blueprint that outlines how an organisation will harness the power of digital technologies to meet its overarching business objectives. Unlike the mere adoption of new tools or platforms, it requires a holistic and strategic approach to integrating digital resources in a way that fosters innovation, enhances customer experiences, and secures a sustainable competitive advantage. As digital disruption continues to reshape industries across the board, the importance of such a strategy cannot be overstated. Organisations that neglect to embed a digital mindset risk stagnation or even failure in the face of rapidly shifting market conditions. A well-crafted digital strategy allows businesses to adapt quickly, seize emerging opportunities, and mitigate risks, acting as a guiding compass in an increasingly digital-first world.

In the dynamic digital economy, where the flow of information and technological change happens at unprecedented speeds, the role of strategy becomes the foundation of sustainable success. No longer is competition solely centred on the quality of products or services, but it is based on how effectively organisations can leverage data, embrace continuous innovation, and maintain meaningful engagement with their audience. A digital business strategy, in this context, serves as a vital roadmap. It enables organisations to navigate the shifting digital terrain with agility, ensuring they remain responsive to emerging trends and relevant in an intensely competitive environment.

The development of a successful digital business strategy hinges on a few key components that form the backbone of effective decision-making and execution. To begin with, a thorough assessment of the organisation's current state, encompassing its strengths, weaknesses, opportunities, and threats, is essential. This analysis sets the stage for strategic alignment by ensuring that any digital initiatives undertaken resonate with the organisation's internal capabilities and external market realities. A clear understanding of the business landscape allows leaders to make informed choices about which digital innovations will provide the most value.

The next critical aspect involves defining clear and measurable goals. Utilising the Specific, Measurable, Achievable, Relevant, and Time-bound (SMART) framework enables organisations to set objectives that are not only attainable but also strategically aligned with broader business ambitions. These well-defined goals ensure that the digital journey remains purposeful and focused on outcomes that drive progress.

Finally, the establishment of key performance indicators (KPIs) is crucial for measuring the success of digital initiatives. KPIs provide the quantitative metrics needed to assess whether the strategy is delivering tangible results, whether that involves increasing online visibility, boosting customer engagement, or enhancing conversion rates. With these measurable benchmarks in place, organisations can continuously evaluate and refine their approach, adapting swiftly to evolving digital landscapes.

In sum, a digital business strategy is far more than a response to technological trends; it is a critical driver of organisational success in the digital age. By strategically aligning technology with business objectives, assessing capabilities, setting clear goals, and measuring impact through KPIs, organisations can position themselves to thrive in an ever-evolving digital economy.

4.3 COMPREHENSIVE BUSINESS EVALUATION FOR DIGITAL STRATEGY

In the rapidly evolving landscape of the digital economy, the foundation of any successful digital strategy lies in a thorough and detailed assessment of the business itself. This critical evaluation process, which considers both internal and external factors, is essential for positioning an organisation effectively within its market. The process allows the business to identify its capabilities, challenges, opportunities, and threats, providing a clear direction for the development of a robust digital strategy.

At the heart of this evaluation is the use of a SWOT analysis—an enduring strategic tool that helps organisations understand their current state. The SWOT framework involves examining the business's internal strengths and weaknesses, as well as the external opportunities and threats that it faces. Strengths encompass the business's inherent capabilities and advantages, such as a reputable brand, a highly skilled workforce, or unique technological assets. These strengths form the building blocks of a strategy designed to leverage existing resources and advantages in the market.

In contrast, weaknesses represent internal limitations that could impede the organisation's performance. These might include outdated technology, inefficient processes, or skills shortages. Identifying and addressing these weaknesses is vital to strengthening the organisation's resilience and competitiveness. Meanwhile, opportunities are external factors that present possibilities for growth, such as emerging market trends, technological innovations, or evolving consumer behaviours. Recognising and aligning strategies with these opportunities allows the business to exploit favourable market conditions, facilitating expansion and innovation.

On the other hand, threats refer to external challenges that could hinder the organisation's success. These may include increased competition, regulatory shifts, or economic uncertainties. Understanding and preparing for such risks ensures that the business can mitigate potential disruptions and craft strategies that are both proactive and defensive.

Conducting this analysis requires an in-depth, honest evaluation of the organisation's internal and external environment. This includes engaging with key stakeholders, gathering data, and facilitating open discussions to gain a comprehensive view of the organisation's strengths, weaknesses, opportunities, and threats. Strengths and weaknesses, being internal, require a careful examination of the organisation's processes, performance, and capabilities. Discussions with team members and analysis of historical data are essential to identifying areas of improvement and leveraging internal resources effectively. This introspective phase sets the stage for making informed, strategic decisions that align with the organisation's capabilities and its broader goals.

Meanwhile, opportunities and threats, being external, demand an acute awareness of the business landscape. Continuous monitoring of industry trends, technological developments, and regulatory changes allows the organisation to remain adaptable and forward-thinking. These external factors, while beyond the organisation's direct control, have a significant impact on its future trajectory. Recognising market opportunities, whether in the form of unmet consumer demands, gaps in the competitive landscape, or favourable trends, is crucial to maintaining a strategic edge in a dynamic and fast-moving environment (Table 4.1).

In this context, understanding market opportunities becomes synonymous with innovation and growth. Continuous analysis of market dynamics—such as evolving consumer preferences, advancements in technology, and shifts in competitive positioning—enables the business to capitalise on new trends before they become mainstream. Opportunities for growth and expansion often present themselves in the form of emerging markets, unmet consumer needs, or areas where the organisation's strengths can meet market demands. Identifying these opportunities and aligning them with the business's strengths can drive innovation, product development, and market expansion.

As we proceed to the following sections, the insights gleaned from this assessment will underpin the development of strategic goals and objectives. The balanced interplay between internal strengths and weaknesses, alongside the recognition of external opportunities and threats, will guide the organisation's digital business strategy, ensuring that it remains aligned with both the internal realities of the organisation and the external demands of the business environment. This comprehensive assessment process is crucial to shaping a digital strategy that is responsive, adaptable, and equipped to thrive in the ever-changing digital economy.

TABLE 4.1 SWOT Analysis Framework for Business Evaluation

SWOT Component	Description	Examples
Strengths	Inherent capabilities and advantages that set a business apart.	Strong brand reputation, skilled workforce, and proprietary technologies.
Weaknesses	Internal limitations that could hinder the organisation's performance.	Outdated technology infrastructure, inefficient processes, and skill gaps.
Opportunities	External factors that can be capitalised on to fuel growth and expansion.	Emerging market trends, technological advancements, and shifts in consumer behaviour.
Threats	External factors posing risks to the organisation's success.	Increased competition, regulatory changes, and economic downturns.

4.4 STRATEGIC GOAL DEFINITION IN THE DIGITAL BUSINESS LANDSCAPE

Following a thorough assessment of the business environment, the next critical stage in shaping an effective digital business strategy lies in clearly defining the goals and objectives. This involves an integrated approach that includes strategic goal-setting, ensuring alignment with digital transformation, and establishing KPIs for tracking progress and success.

The process of setting goals is not merely a matter of ambition but requires precision and clarity. The SMART framework provides the foundation for formulating objectives that are both meaningful and attainable. Specificity is key; goals should be clearly defined and leave no room for ambiguity. For instance, rather than vaguely aiming to "improve digital presence," a more targeted objective would be to "increase website traffic by 20% within the next quarter." This sharp focus provides direction for tangible action (Table 4.2).

Equally important is the need for measurability. Goals must be linked to quantifiable metrics, such as sales figures, conversion rates, or customer engagement statistics, so that progress can be tracked objectively. Measuring success allows the organisation to assess the effectiveness of its strategies in real time, adapting where necessary to stay on course.

However, goals must also be realistic and achievable, considering available resources and constraints. While ambition is important, unattainable goals can undermine progress and demotivate teams. Achievable goals foster a sense of accomplishment and maintain momentum throughout the implementation process. They also need to be relevant, aligning with the organisation's broader mission and long-term vision, ensuring that each objective contributes

TABLE 4.2 SMART Goal-Setting Criteria

SMART Criteria	Description	Example
Specific	Goals should be well-defined and clear, eliminating ambiguity. They must focus on a precise objective.	Instead of "improve online presence," a specific goal would be "increase website traffic by 20% within the next quarter."
Measurable	Goals must allow for tangible assessment and progress tracking through quantifiable metrics.	Use metrics such as sales figures, customer engagement rates, or conversion rates to measure success.
Achievable	Goals must be realistic and attainable, considering available resources and constraints, ensuring motivation and progress.	Setting goals that are within reach, ensuring the team remains motivated to achieve them.
Relevant	Goals must align with the organisation's mission, vision, and broader business strategy, contributing meaningfully to long term objectives.	The goal should harmonise with the company's core values and overall strategy.
Time-bound	Goals must have a defined timeline, creating a sense of urgency and helping to prioritise tasks to ensure timely completion.	A clear deadline for achieving the goal, e.g., "within the next quarter," prevents tasks from dragging indefinitely.

meaningfully to the overall strategy. Relevance ensures that every effort is in harmony with the company's core values, promoting synergy between digital initiatives and overarching business objectives.

Finally, goals must be time-bound, with a defined timeline for completion. Having a clear timeframe not only adds urgency to the process but also enables effective prioritisation of tasks. Without a deadline, even the best-formulated goals can lose momentum, and progress may stall.

In today's digital era, aligning strategic goals with digital transformation is critical. Digital transformation goes beyond simple technological upgrades—it requires a fundamental rethinking of how the business operates, engages with its customers, and creates value. Goals aligned with digital transformation reflect an organisation's commitment to integrating digital tools and technologies into its core business processes. Whether enhancing customer interactions through digital platforms, streamlining workflows with automation, or adopting cutting-edge innovations to maintain competitiveness, these objectives signal a future-ready, tech-centric mindset.

This alignment with digital transformation ensures that the organisation's vision remains forward-looking, embracing the trends that are shaping the future of business. It also allows companies to harness the full potential of technological advancements, which are key to driving innovation, improving operational efficiency, and building resilience in an ever-evolving market landscape.

The establishment of KPIs is essential once these goals are set. KPIs serve as measurable indicators that provide clear benchmarks for evaluating the success of a digital strategy. They offer quantifiable metrics that make it possible to monitor progress and make data-driven adjustments as needed. For instance, if the goal is to enhance customer engagement through digital channels, KPIs might include metrics such as website traffic, social media engagement rates, or conversion rates. In cases where the focus is on operational efficiency, KPIs could include measures such as process cycle times, error reduction, or resource optimisation.

Selecting the right KPIs is vital. They must align with specific objectives and provide clear insights into the effectiveness of the strategy. Regular monitoring of KPIs not only ensures that goals are being met but also allows for agility in decision-making, enabling organisations to adapt quickly to changing circumstances or performance gaps. This data-driven approach ensures that the strategy remains dynamic and responsive.

Thus, the process of defining goals and objectives is foundational to the success of a digital business strategy. By employing SMART goal-setting principles, ensuring alignment with digital transformation, and establishing relevant KPIs, businesses can create a roadmap that is both aspirational and practical, setting the stage for successful execution and measurable outcomes.

4.5 CRAFTING A CUSTOMER-CENTRIC STRATEGY FOR THE DIGITAL ERA

In today's rapidly evolving digital landscape, where consumers have unprecedented influence and countless options, creating a customer-centric strategy is essential. Understanding the needs, preferences, and behaviours of target audiences forms the foundation of this approach.

A successful customer-centric strategy begins with a thorough analysis of target customer segments, followed by the development of detailed customer personas, and is completed through the mapping of the customer journey to ensure a seamless and engaging experience across all touchpoints.

Understanding the different customer segments is the cornerstone of any customer-focused approach. In the past, businesses could rely on a more generalised understanding of their audience, but the digital age demands a far more refined strategy. Market segmentation divides a broad target audience into smaller, more manageable segments based on shared characteristics such as demographics, psychographics, behaviour patterns, or even geographic location. By doing so, companies can craft strategies that resonate with the specific needs of each group. For example, an e-commerce platform might distinguish between customers seeking high-end luxury goods and those more interested in practical, affordable items. This allows them to create personalised marketing campaigns, product offerings, and customer experiences that directly address the needs of each segment, increasing the likelihood of customer engagement and brand loyalty.

To further refine this understanding, businesses often create detailed customer personas, which serve as semi-fictional representations of ideal customers within a particular segment. These personas go beyond basic demographic information, exploring motivations, goals, challenges, and personal preferences. Building these personas requires a combination of market research, customer surveys, and data analysis. For instance, a streaming service might develop a persona such as "Avid Movie Buff Molly," who enjoys independent films, binge-watches series on weekends, and prefers personalised recommendations. By humanising customer segments in this way, businesses can make their marketing strategies more targeted and effective. These personas guide decisions across the organisation, from product development to marketing campaigns, ensuring that every initiative resonates with the audience's specific preferences and needs.

Mapping the customer journey is the next critical step in delivering a customer-centric strategy. This journey represents the various stages a customer goes through when interacting with a business, from initial awareness to post-purchase engagement. Understanding the customer journey involves identifying every potential touchpoint, such as social media interactions, website visits, or customer support, and ensuring that each of these moments delivers a seamless and positive experience. For example, when a customer first encounters a product via a social media ad, the following steps, including browsing the website, exploring the product, and completing the purchase, should all be intuitive and engaging. Post-purchase communication, such as customer support or feedback opportunities, should be equally seamless and accessible.

Digital tools and data analytics are indispensable in mapping and refining the customer journey. By collecting data on customer interactions, preferences, and behaviours, businesses can gain valuable insights into the effectiveness of each touchpoint. This process not only highlights areas that need improvement but also helps ensure that the customer-centric strategy remains flexible and responsive to changing customer expectations. Ultimately, mapping the customer journey allows businesses to identify and address pain points, enhancing customer satisfaction and fostering long-term loyalty.

In sum, a customer-centric strategy requires much more than traditional marketing methods. It demands an immersive, dynamic approach that begins with understanding distinct customer segments, moves through the creation of detailed personas, and culminates in a comprehensive mapping of the customer journey. By consistently placing the customer at the heart of every decision, businesses are better equipped to build lasting connections, inspire loyalty, and thrive in the digital marketplace.

CASE STUDY 4

Starbucks' Digital Loyalty Programme

Starbucks, one of the world's leading coffeehouse chains, implemented a digital transformation strategy to enhance customer engagement and streamline operations. With the rise of mobile technology and changing consumer expectations, Starbucks saw an opportunity to leverage digital tools to improve the customer experience and increase brand loyalty. The company recognised that modern consumers sought convenience, personalised interactions, and seamless digital payment options. However, Starbucks faced the challenge of ensuring that its digital strategy effectively met these evolving demands while maintaining operational efficiency and a strong customer connection.

To address this, Starbucks launched a mobile app featuring an integrated loyalty programme, mobile ordering, and digital payment options. The Starbucks Rewards programme allowed customers to earn points, or "Stars," for every purchase, which could then be redeemed for free drinks and food. By incorporating personalised offers based on purchase history, Starbucks strengthened customer engagement and retention. Mobile ordering and payment functionality enabled customers to place orders in advance and collect them in-store without waiting in line, significantly improving service efficiency. The app also provided real-time store information, including location details and estimated wait times, ensuring a smooth and convenient experience.

The introduction of this digital strategy delivered impressive results. Starbucks witnessed a substantial increase in customer engagement, with millions of users actively participating in the Rewards programme. The company reported a significant rise in revenue, driven by repeat purchases and personalised promotions that encouraged customer spending. Mobile ordering accounted for a growing share of total sales, reducing congestion in stores and improving service speed. Additionally, by leveraging data from the app, Starbucks gained valuable insights into customer preferences, enabling more targeted marketing and inventory management. The integration of digital payments further streamlined transactions, reducing cash-handling costs and enhancing security.

The Starbucks case illustrates the impact of a well-executed digital business strategy. By leveraging technology to personalise customer interactions, the company strengthened brand loyalty and optimised operational efficiency. The success of the Starbucks Rewards programme highlights the importance of integrating digital tools into business models to enhance customer experience. Furthermore, the use of data analytics to understand consumer behaviour underscores the significance of data-driven decision-making in modern digital business strategies. The case also demonstrates the growing importance of mobile commerce and the need for businesses to adapt to changing consumer habits by embracing innovative digital solutions.

Discussion Questions for Students (with Indicative Answers)

1. **How did Starbucks use digital technology to enhance customer engagement and brand loyalty?**
   Indicative Answer: Starbucks leveraged a mobile app with an integrated loyalty programme, mobile ordering, and digital payments. By offering personalised rewards and a seamless ordering experience, the company encouraged repeat purchases and strengthened customer loyalty.
2. **What operational benefits did Starbucks gain from its mobile ordering and payment system?**
   Indicative Answer: Mobile ordering reduced in-store congestion and improved service speed, leading to increased efficiency. Digital payments streamlined transactions, minimised cash-handling costs, and enhanced security.
3. **How did data analytics contribute to Starbucks' digital strategy?**
   Indicative Answer: The app collected customer data on purchasing behaviour, allowing Starbucks to offer targeted promotions, improve inventory management, and refine its marketing strategies.
4. **What lessons can other businesses learn from Starbucks' approach to digital transformation?**
   Indicative Answer: Businesses should integrate digital tools to enhance customer experience, use data analytics for decision-making, and adapt to consumer preferences through mobile commerce and personalised marketing.
5. **What potential challenges might arise from implementing a similar digital strategy, and how could businesses address them?**
   Indicative Answer: Challenges include high implementation costs, data privacy concerns, and potential technical issues. Businesses can mitigate these by investing in cybersecurity, ensuring compliance with data protection laws, and continuously improving the user experience through feedback and innovation.

4.6 STRATEGIC SELECTION AND INTEGRATION OF DIGITAL CHANNELS IN BUSINESS

In the modern digital age, the selection of appropriate digital channels is crucial for the success of any business strategy. The vast and dynamic online landscape offers a multitude of opportunities, yet the key to unlocking this potential lies in strategically choosing the channels that align with a business's unique objectives. Understanding the various digital marketing channels, strategically selecting them based on business goals, and ensuring the seamless integration of online and offline efforts are the essential components of this approach.

Digital marketing channels are the lifeblood of customer engagement, enabling businesses to connect with their audience, increase brand visibility, and drive conversions. Among the most prominent channels are social media platforms, which offer unparalleled access to different demographics and communities. Platforms such as Facebook, Instagram, Twitter, and LinkedIn are dynamic arenas for engagement, visibility, and targeted advertising, with each platform serving distinct purposes depending on the audience. Complementing social media efforts, search engine optimisation (SEO) is fundamental in ensuring online visibility. Through optimising website content and structure, businesses can rank higher in search engine results, making it easier for potential customers to discover their products or services when they are searching for them.

Email marketing remains a time-tested method of direct communication. It provides businesses with the means to send personalised messages, product updates, and promotions to their audience. Through automation, email marketing can deliver tailored content to specific customer segments, ensuring timely outreach with relevant information. Content marketing, another critical channel, involves creating valuable, informative, and engaging material such as blog posts, videos, and infographics. This content not only helps in establishing authority within an industry but also attracts potential customers and builds long-term brand loyalty. Finally, pay-per-click advertising, on platforms like Google Ads and Bing Ads, is a highly cost-effective way to drive traffic by bidding on specific keywords and paying only when users click on the ads.

The selection of digital channels must be closely aligned with a business's overarching goals. There is no universal solution; the channels chosen should reflect the specific outcomes a business is seeking. For companies prioritising brand awareness, social media platforms and display advertising are particularly effective. These channels offer an expansive reach, ideal for businesses looking to introduce their brand to a wider audience. If lead generation is the primary goal, businesses might focus on search engine marketing, both through organic SEO efforts and paid advertising, along with content marketing and strategies that encourage potential customers to engage, such as gated content.

When the objective shifts towards conversion and sales, a more targeted approach is necessary. Social media advertising, tailored to specific demographics, combined with retargeting ads and email marketing, can guide prospects through the sales funnel. By delivering the right message at each stage of the customer journey, businesses can turn leads into loyal customers. Meanwhile, for businesses focused on retaining existing customers, email marketing and content that provides value post-purchase are critical. Personalised engagement on social media also fosters a sense of connection and encourages customers to remain loyal to the brand over time (Figure 4.1).

The key components of a digital strategy are:

1. **SEO (Search Engine Optimisation)**: Enhancing your website's visibility on search engines to attract organic traffic.
2. **Social Media Marketing**: Leveraging platforms like Facebook, Instagram, LinkedIn, and Twitter to engage with your audience and promote your brand.
3. **Google Ads**: Utilising paid search advertising to drive targeted traffic to your website.
4. **Content Marketing**: Creating and distributing valuable, relevant content to attract and retain a clearly defined audience.
5. **Media Buying**: Purchasing advertising space on various platforms to reach a broader audience.
6. **Data Analysis**: Continuously analysing data to measure the effectiveness of your digital efforts and make informed decisions.
7. **Email Marketing**: Using email campaigns to nurture leads, engage customers, and drive conversions.
8. **Online Advertising**: Running ads on various digital platforms to increase brand awareness and drive traffic.
9. **Web Development**: Ensuring your website is user-friendly, responsive, and optimised for conversions.

Digital strategy focuses on using technology to improve business performance, whether that means creating new products or reimagining current processes. It specifies the direction an organisation will take to create new competitive advantages with technology, as well as the tactics it will use to achieve these changes.

FIGURE 4.1 Digital Strategy

An effective digital strategy doesn't stop at selecting the right online channels—it also involves the integration of online and offline channels to create a unified experience. While the digital world offers immense opportunities, offline interactions still play a crucial role, particularly in industries where physical touchpoints remain essential. A seamless customer experience across both online and offline touchpoints is vital for maintaining a consistent brand image. From the language used in communications to the level of customer service, customers should experience the same brand values regardless of the channel they engage with.

Cross-channel marketing strategies offer another dimension to this integration. For instance, a retail business might leverage its online presence to promote in-store events, driving foot traffic through digital promotions. This synergy between digital and physical experiences creates a holistic marketing approach that maximises customer engagement across multiple touchpoints. Furthermore, integrating data from both online and offline sources provides a more comprehensive view of customer behaviour. This holistic view allows businesses to tailor their strategies, personalising offerings and improving customer experiences based on insights derived from a complete understanding of the customer's journey across all platforms.

The strategic selection of digital channels is not a static process but rather an ongoing, dynamic effort. It requires a deep understanding of business goals, the ever-changing digital landscape, and the unique characteristics of each available channel. By carefully selecting the most suitable channels and integrating them seamlessly with offline efforts, businesses can create a cohesive and comprehensive strategy that engages customers at every touchpoint. This approach not only enhances brand visibility and engagement but also fosters customer loyalty and drives long-term success in the increasingly competitive digital marketplace.

4.7 CRAFTING A UNIFIED CONTENT STRATEGY FOR DIGITAL SUCCESS

In the ever-evolving digital landscape, where attention is fleeting and consumer expectations are higher than ever, a well-executed content strategy and a unified approach to branding are indispensable for building a successful online presence. These intertwined elements are critical for creating a lasting impression, fostering audience engagement, and cultivating brand loyalty. The art of crafting engaging content, maintaining consistent branding across all digital channels, and using the power of storytelling to deepen emotional connections form the bedrock of an effective digital strategy.

At the heart of digital engagement is the creation of compelling content. Content is much more than just information; it is the medium through which businesses communicate their value, connect with their audience, and foster long-term relationships. The key to creating content that truly resonates begins with a deep understanding of the audience's needs and preferences. Conducting thorough audience research, analysing consumer behaviour, and staying informed about current trends are essential to ensuring that the content is relevant and addresses the specific challenges or desires of the target market. By aligning content with the interests of the audience, businesses can create a meaningful connection that transcends simple transactions.

Furthermore, the format in which content is delivered plays a vital role in its impact. Different audiences engage with content in varying ways, and embracing a diverse range of formats ensures that the message reaches the widest possible audience. Whether through blog posts, videos, podcasts, or interactive infographics, the chosen format should not only reflect the nature of the message but also suit the consumption habits of the intended audience. Providing educational resources, entertaining materials, or thought-provoking articles adds value to the consumer's life and positions the brand as a trustworthy and credible source of information.

Consistency in content creation is equally important. Establishing a regular schedule for content delivery through a well-structured content calendar helps maintain the audience's engagement and keeps the brand fresh in their minds. Whether it's weekly blog posts or monthly video updates, consistently delivering high-quality content fosters anticipation and loyalty among the audience. Over time, this regular engagement builds a strong digital presence that reinforces the brand's authority in its industry.

Equally significant in the digital world is the need for consistent branding across all digital touchpoints. Consistency in branding not only reinforces the brand's identity but also creates a seamless experience for customers, regardless of where they encounter the brand. Visual identity is paramount in this process—ensuring that logos, colour schemes, and design elements remain uniform across platforms strengthens the recognisability of the brand. Whether a customer visits the company's website, follows its social media pages, or receives an email campaign, the visual cohesion should immediately signal familiarity and trustworthiness.

The brand's voice and messaging are also integral to a consistent digital presence. The tone in which a brand communicates, whether formal or conversational, and the language it employs should remain consistent across all channels. Whether drafting a tweet, composing a marketing email, or writing website copy, the messaging should reflect the brand's core values and personality. This unified voice not only enhances the brand's authenticity but also ensures that the audience experiences a coherent and immersive brand identity at every interaction.

A seamless user experience is essential for maintaining positive brand perceptions. Navigational elements, interactive features, and the overall design aesthetic should align perfectly across all digital platforms, creating a harmonious journey for users as they move between different touchpoints. For example, a customer's experience on a mobile app should feel as intuitive and visually cohesive as it does on the website. This integration of platforms guarantees that no matter how or where customers engage, they will experience the same level of professionalism and quality.

Storytelling, the ancient art of creating emotional resonance, is perhaps one of the most powerful tools available to brands in the digital age. Amidst the endless stream of information and content online, stories stand out as a way to make meaningful connections with consumers. Through storytelling, a brand can transcend its products or services and engage its audience on a more profound level. Stories humanise the brand, allowing customers to see the people behind the business, understand its journey, and connect with its values. These narratives foster a sense of authenticity and relatability that numbers and statistics alone cannot achieve.

When stories evoke emotions—be it joy, inspiration, empathy, or hope—they leave a lasting impression on the audience. Emotional connections make the brand more memorable and encourage long-term loyalty. Sharing the brand's origin story or the values that drive its mission helps customers understand what the brand stands for. In an age where consumers increasingly choose to support companies whose values align with their own, storytelling becomes a key vehicle for communicating these values.

The inclusion of interactive storytelling can further enhance engagement. By encouraging the audience to participate in the brand's narrative through quizzes, polls, or user-generated content, businesses can involve customers in a more dynamic way. These interactive experiences allow consumers to become active participants in the brand's journey, rather than passive observers, fostering a deeper sense of connection and co-creation.

A robust content strategy intertwined with consistent branding and compelling storytelling lays the groundwork for an effective digital business strategy. By delivering content that adds value to the audience, maintaining a unified brand presence across all platforms, and harnessing the emotional power of storytelling, businesses can create a strong, memorable, and engaging brand presence. As the digital landscape continues to evolve, these foundational elements will remain critical in shaping how brands are perceived and how they connect with their audience.

4.8 BUILDING A ROBUST E-COMMERCE AND SALES STRATEGY FOR DIGITAL SUCCESS

In the fast-paced world of digital commerce, developing an effective e-commerce and sales strategy is essential for businesses looking to seize the opportunities offered by online transactions. Success in this realm requires more than simply having products or services to sell; it demands a thorough understanding of the digital landscape and a clear strategy for navigating its complexities. From determining e-commerce readiness to selecting the right platform and optimising the sales funnel, each step plays a crucial role in driving conversions and ensuring long-term growth.

The first step in establishing a successful e-commerce strategy is to evaluate the business's readiness to handle the demands of online sales. This goes far beyond the basics of having a product or service that is in demand. It requires a deep dive into how well-suited the offerings are to the digital marketplace. Understanding the target audience and their online behaviours is critical. The success of an e-commerce venture hinges on ensuring that the products or services align with the needs and preferences of the online consumer. Market research, competitor analysis, and feedback from potential customers all play a part in shaping a viable online offering.

A well-prepared digital infrastructure is another key element in determining e-commerce readiness. A business must ensure that its website is capable of delivering a seamless and secure browsing and shopping experience. This includes robust security measures, a scalable platform that can grow with the business, and a layout that is intuitive for users. As online sales increase, the infrastructure must be able to accommodate this growth without compromising performance or security.

Logistics and fulfilment are equally crucial in meeting customer expectations. Efficient systems for managing inventory, processing orders, and ensuring prompt, reliable delivery are fundamental. Without strong logistics in place, even the most attractive online store will struggle to retain customers. Coupled with this is the need for secure, trustworthy payment gateways. The rise of e-commerce has made consumers more conscious of data security. By implementing secure payment processes, businesses can build the trust required to encourage online transactions.

In addition to these technical and logistical aspects, a successful e-commerce strategy must include strong customer support. In an online setting, where direct, in-person interaction is absent, the role of customer support becomes even more critical. Businesses must be equipped to handle pre-purchase enquiries, post-purchase concerns, and any issues that arise during the customer journey. A responsive and accessible support system helps build confidence and can be a decisive factor in whether a potential customer completes a purchase.

The choice of an e-commerce platform is another crucial decision that directly impacts the efficiency and success of an online store. The platform must be capable of scaling as the business grows, accommodating changes in product offerings and enabling the addition of new features without causing major disruptions. Flexibility and adaptability are essential to ensure that the platform evolves alongside the business's needs. An intuitive and user-friendly interface is equally important, both for customers browsing the online store and for the business's own management of the back-end processes. A well-designed platform simplifies the administration of product listings, order processing, and customer data management, which is critical for smooth operations.

Integration with other business systems, such as payment gateways, marketing tools, and inventory management software, also needs to be considered. Seamless integration enhances the efficiency of daily operations and provides a cohesive experience for both the business and its customers. Additionally, with the increasing dominance of mobile commerce, it is vital that the chosen platform is mobile responsive. A mobile-friendly website broadens the reach of the business by catering to customers who shop on their smartphones or tablets. In today's marketplace, businesses that neglect mobile responsiveness risk alienating a significant portion of their audience.

Security remains a top priority when selecting an e-commerce platform. Safeguarding customer data is paramount, and this requires stringent security protocols such as SSL encryption and PCI compliance. As cyber threats become more sophisticated, businesses must stay ahead by continuously updating their security measures to protect customer information and maintain trust.

Once the platform is in place, the focus shifts to optimising the sales funnel to ensure that customers move smoothly from product discovery to purchase. A streamlined, intuitive navigation system is essential in guiding users through this journey. A well-organised website that makes it easy to find products and complete purchases minimises friction and increases the likelihood of conversions. Providing clear, comprehensive product information is another key factor. Detailed descriptions, high-quality images, and clear specifications help customers make informed decisions, thereby boosting their confidence and encouraging them to finalise purchases.

Transparency in pricing and policies also plays a significant role in building trust. Hidden fees or unclear return policies are common reasons for abandoned shopping carts. By clearly communicating shipping costs, delivery times, and return policies upfront, businesses can foster a sense of reliability and openness, which is critical for customer retention.

Calls-to-action (CTAs) should be strategically placed throughout the website to guide customers through the sales funnel. These CTAs, whether urging users to explore a product page or complete a purchase, need to be visually prominent and easy to act upon. A well-designed CTA can make the difference between a user leaving the site and completing a purchase.

Personalisation can further enhance the user experience and improve conversions. By analysing customer behaviour and purchase history, businesses can offer personalised recommendations that encourage upselling and cross-selling. These targeted suggestions not only increase the value of each transaction but also enhance the overall shopping experience by offering customers products that align with their preferences.

Addressing abandoned carts is another crucial aspect of optimising the sales funnel. Many potential customers add items to their cart but leave before completing the purchase. Businesses can re-engage these users by implementing automated follow-up emails, offering personalised discounts, or sending timely reminders to encourage them to return and finalise their purchase.

A well-executed e-commerce and sales strategy is essential for thriving in the competitive digital marketplace. From ensuring readiness through infrastructure and support to choosing the right platform and optimising the customer journey, every element must be carefully considered and continually refined. By focusing on these key areas, businesses can not only capture new customers but also foster long-term loyalty, positioning themselves for sustained success in the online marketplace. This comprehensive approach forms the foundation for navigating the complexities of e-commerce and integrating it seamlessly into the broader digital business strategy.

4.9 HARNESSING THE POWER OF DATA-DRIVEN DECISION-MAKING IN DIGITAL STRATEGY

In today's digital environment, where information flows in abundance and the landscape is constantly shifting, the ability to harness data effectively is critical for making informed and strategic decisions. Businesses that can tap into data analytics, engage in experimentation through A/B testing, and consistently measure key metrics are better positioned to adapt and thrive in the competitive digital marketplace. This approach to data-driven decision-making allows organisations to refine their strategies continuously, ensuring they remain relevant and optimised in a fast-evolving digital world.

Central to the process of data-driven decision-making is the strategic use of data analytics. By analysing vast amounts of data from various digital touchpoints, businesses can gain deep insights into customer behaviour, market trends, and the overall effectiveness of their digital efforts. Understanding how customers interact with a company's online platforms—be it a website, mobile app, or social media channels—is essential to enhancing user experiences. Patterns in website visits, clicks, navigation paths, and engagement with content provide a clearer picture of what resonates with customers and what does not. Armed with this knowledge, businesses can make informed decisions about content placement, website design, and personalised customer interactions.

Beyond individual customer behaviour, data analytics allows organisations to stay on top of market trends and gain a competitive edge. By monitoring industry data and analysing competitor strategies, businesses can better understand the broader market context and consumer sentiment. This enables them to make real-time adjustments to their digital strategies, ensuring they remain competitive and relevant as market conditions evolve. The ability to adapt quickly, based on data, often separates thriving businesses from those that struggle to keep pace with industry changes.

Moreover, tracking the performance of digital campaigns through key metrics, such as conversion rates and engagement levels, provides valuable feedback on how well specific initiatives are performing. By continuously monitoring these indicators, businesses can make agile decisions, reallocating resources or adjusting strategies where necessary to improve effectiveness. Predictive analytics takes this one step further, allowing businesses to forecast future trends and behaviours based on historical data. This forward-looking approach ensures that organisations can plan strategically, anticipate shifts in the market, and be proactive in adapting to changing dynamics.

In addition to data analytics, A/B testing—also known as split testing—provides a systematic method for refining digital strategies through controlled experimentation. This approach is invaluable for optimising various elements of a company's digital presence, from website design to email marketing and digital advertising. By testing two variations of a digital asset—whether it's a webpage, an email, or an advertisement—businesses can compare performance and identify the most effective version. For instance, testing different headlines, layouts, or CTA buttons on a website can reveal which combination drives higher engagement and conversion rates. These insights can then be applied to optimise the overall user experience and improve business outcomes.

A/B testing is not confined to websites alone. It can also be employed in email marketing campaigns, where experimenting with subject lines, content variations, or send times helps businesses fine-tune their messaging to increase open rates and click-through rates. Similarly, in the realm of digital advertising, split testing of ad copy, visuals, and targeting parameters helps refine campaigns for maximum impact. This iterative process of experimentation and refinement ensures that digital assets are continually optimised for better performance, leading to improved return on investment (ROI) and customer engagement.

For e-commerce businesses, A/B testing can also be applied to product pages. By experimenting with different product descriptions, images, or pricing strategies, companies can determine which elements are most effective in driving conversions. This kind of data-driven optimisation enhances the shopping experience and directly impacts sales.

The effectiveness of any data-driven strategy ultimately depends on the accurate measurement and analysis of KPIs. These metrics serve as a compass, guiding businesses in their digital strategy and helping them gauge success. One of the most fundamental metrics is the conversion rate, which measures the percentage of website visitors who take a desired action, such as making a purchase or signing up for a newsletter. By analysing conversion rates, businesses can gain insights into the effectiveness of their sales funnels and the persuasiveness of their digital assets, identifying areas for improvement in the customer journey.

Another vital metric is the customer acquisition cost, which measures the cost of acquiring a new customer. When analysed in conjunction with the customer lifetime value, this metric provides businesses with a clear understanding of the sustainability and efficiency of their customer acquisition strategies. The goal is to ensure that the cost of acquiring a customer is justified by their long-term value to the business, enabling more strategic resource allocation.

ROI is another essential metric, quantifying the profitability of digital campaigns and initiatives. By measuring ROI across various marketing channels, businesses can determine which efforts yield the highest returns and focus their resources accordingly. This data-driven approach to marketing ensures that businesses are investing in the right areas to maximise profitability and growth.

Finally, user engagement metrics such as bounce rate, time on page, and social media interactions provide valuable insights into how effectively businesses are engaging with their audience. These metrics help businesses understand how well their content resonates with users, whether their user experience is compelling, and whether their overall digital engagement strategy is working. By analysing these metrics regularly, businesses can identify weak points and make necessary adjustments to improve user satisfaction and engagement.

Data-driven decision-making is a fundamental pillar of a successful digital business strategy. It allows organisations to navigate the complexities of the digital landscape with precision and adaptability. By leveraging data analytics for actionable insights, conducting A/B testing to refine digital assets, and measuring key metrics to ensure continuous improvement, businesses can make informed, strategic decisions that enhance their digital presence and drive long-term success. As the digital world continues to evolve, the integration of data-driven insights will remain a crucial guiding principle for businesses seeking to remain competitive and agile.

BOX 4.1

Developing a successful digital business strategy involves the careful consideration of several foundational components. Each element plays a vital role in shaping how a business navigates the complexities of the digital landscape, from initial evaluations to leveraging data for ongoing optimisation. Table 4.3 outlines the key elements necessary to build an effective digital strategy, highlighting essential areas such as customer-centric approaches, channel selection, and the integration of e-commerce. By focusing on these aspects, businesses can ensure adaptability, competitiveness, and long-term success in the digital age.

TABLE 4.3 Key Elements for Building a Comprehensive Digital Business Strategy

Key Element	Description
1. Comprehensive Business Evaluation	Assess internal capabilities, resources, market position, and digital readiness.
2. Strategic Goal Definition	Establish clear, measurable objectives (SMART goals) aligned with business aims.
3. Customer-Centric Strategy	Focus on customer needs and behaviours to ensure engagement and satisfaction.
4. Digital Channel Selection & Integration	Choose appropriate digital platforms (social media, SEO, email, etc.) and ensure consistent branding across all.
5. Unified Content Strategy	Develop a cohesive content plan that adds value, engages the audience, and builds trust.
6. E-Commerce & Sales Strategy	Build a seamless digital sales funnel and ensure optimal online shopping experiences.
7. Data-Driven Decision-Making	Leverage data analytics, A/B testing, and key performance metrics for continuous optimisation and adaptation.
8. Agility and Innovation	Foster a culture of agility, innovation, and responsiveness to market and technological changes.

4.10 CHAPTER SUMMARY

As we conclude this chapter, it is vital to reflect on the core insights discussed. This chapter began by examining the essential components of crafting a digital strategy, including conducting SWOT analyses, setting SMART goals, and adopting customer-centric approaches. These foundational steps provided a clear framework for navigating the complexities of the digital landscape, focusing on strategic assessment, goal definition, and the use of data-driven insights. The importance of maintaining a dynamic strategy was also highlighted. In a constantly evolving digital world, static strategies quickly became outdated. Businesses needed to remain agile, adapting to market changes, consumer behaviour, and technological advancements to ensure ongoing relevance and resilience. Finally, this chapter underscored the significance of fostering a culture of digital innovation. Success required more than adopting new technologies; it demanded an organisational mindset open to experimentation, risk, and continuous learning. By encouraging creative problem-solving and embracing both successes and failures, businesses positioned themselves to thrive in a digital future. In sum, this chapter provided a comprehensive guide to building and maintaining a robust digital strategy, essential for long-term success in an ever-changing digital ecosystem.

Key Questions for Discussion

1. In today's fast-changing digital economy, what are the essential components of an effective digital business strategy? How can businesses adapt their strategies to stay competitive in the face of constant technological disruption?
2. Why is conducting a thorough business evaluation critical before building a digital business strategy? What tools or frameworks can organisations use to assess their readiness for digital transformation?
3. What does it mean to create a customer-centric digital business strategy? How can businesses leverage technology and data to deliver personalised experiences and meet customer expectations?
4. How can businesses use data analytics to make informed strategic decisions in the digital era? What challenges might arise when implementing data-driven decision-making processes, and how can they be addressed?
5. With so many digital channels available, how can businesses strategically select and integrate the right channels to achieve their goals? What factors should they consider to maximise customer engagement and ROI?

BIBLIOGRAPHY

Berman, S.J. (2012). *Digital Transformation: Opportunities to Create New Business Models.* IBM Institute for Business Value.

Berman, S.J. and Marshall, A. (2014). The Next Digital Transformation: From an Individual-Centered to an Everyone-to-Everyone Economy. *Strategy & Leadership*, 42(5), pp. 9–17.

Bharadwaj, A., El Sawy, O.A., Pavlou, P.A. and Venkatraman, N. (2013). Digital Business Strategy: Toward a Next Generation of Insights. *MIS Quarterly*, 37(2), pp. 471–482.

Chaffey, D. and Ellis-Chadwick, F. (2022). *Digital Marketing: Strategy, Implementation and Practice.* 8th ed. Pearson.

Fitzgerald, M., Kruschwitz, N., Bonnet, D. and Welch, M. (2014). Embracing Digital Technology: A New Strategic Imperative. *MIT Sloan Management Review*, 55(2), pp. 1–12.Hess, T., Matt, C., Benlian, A. and Wiesböck, F. (2016a). Digital Transformation Strategies. *Business & Information Systems Engineering*, 58(6), pp. 431–440.

Hess, T., Matt, C., Benlian, A. and Wiesböck, F. (2016b). Options for Formulating a Digital Transformation Strategy. *MIS Quarterly Executive*, 15(2), pp. 123–139.

Ismail, S., Malone, M.S. and van Geest, Y. (2014). *Exponential Organizations: Why New Organizations Are Ten Times Better, Faster, and Cheaper Than Yours (and What to Do About It).* Diversion Books.

Kane, G.C., Palmer, D., Phillips, A.N., Kiron, D. and Buckley, N. (2015). *Strategy, Not Technology, Drives Digital Transformation.* MIT Sloan Management Review and Deloitte University Press.

Kavadias, S., Ladas, K. and Loch, C. (2016). The Transformative Business Model. *Harvard Business Review*, 94(10), pp. 91–98.

McGrath, R.G. (2013). *The End of Competitive Advantage: How to Keep Your Strategy Moving as Fast as Your Business.* Harvard Business Review Press.

Rogers, D.L. (2016). *The Digital Transformation Playbook: Rethink Your Business for the Digital Age.* Columbia University Press.

Ross, J.W., Sebastian, I.M. and Beath, C.M. (2019). *Designed for Digital: How to Architect Your Business for Sustained Success*. MIT Press.

Sebastian, I.M., Ross, J.W., Beath, C.M., Mocker, M., Moloney, K.G. and Fonstad, N.O. (2017). How Big Old Companies Navigate Digital Transformation. *MIS Quarterly Executive*, 16(3), pp. 197–213.

Solis, B. (2014). *What's the Future of Business? Changing the Way Businesses Create Experiences*. Wiley.

Wade, M. and Marchant, D. (2014). Are You Prepared for Your Digital Transformation?. IMD International, (1/2014), pp. 1–6.Westerman, G. (2018). Why Digital Transformations Fail: The Surprising Disciplines of How to Take Off and Stay Ahead. MIT Sloan Management Review, 59(4), pp. 14–23.

Westerman, G., Bonnet, D. and McAfee, A. (2014). *Leading Digital: Turning Technology into Business Transformation*. Harvard Business Review Press.

CHAPTER 5

Digital Marketing

Reaching and Engaging Your Target Audience Online

Learning Objectives

By the end of this chapter, you will be able to:

1. Understand the core elements of a successful digital marketing strategy, including SEO, content marketing, PPC, social media, email marketing, and influencer collaborations.
2. Learn how to effectively analyse and engage with target audiences across various digital channels and optimise performance through tools like video marketing, affiliate marketing, and mobile strategies.
3. Gain insights into maintaining compliance with ethical standards in digital marketing while evaluating and optimising marketing efforts for sustained business success.

5.1 INTRODUCTION

The rapid rise of the digital age has fundamentally transformed the way businesses operate and communicate with their audiences. In the past, traditional marketing methods such as television, print, and radio dominated the advertising landscape. However, the emergence of digital marketing has revolutionised the interaction between businesses and consumers, allowing for more personalised, targeted, and measurable campaigns. Digital marketing offers businesses unprecedented opportunities to engage with their audiences through a range of online platforms, from social media to search engines, and beyond. This shift has given businesses a competitive edge, enabling them to adapt to changing consumer behaviours and expectations. As digital marketing evolves, so too does the importance of understanding the various tactics, tools, and platforms available for reaching a target audience online.

This chapter delves into the multifaceted world of digital marketing, beginning with an exploration of its role in today's business landscape. It then examines the consumer's digital journey, from awareness to purchase, providing insights into audience segmentation and

DOI: 10.4324/9781032672458-5

behavioural patterns. As businesses increasingly adopt digital marketing strategies, it is crucial to master content marketing, search engine optimisation (SEO), pay-per-click (PPC), and social media to create impactful, data-driven campaigns. Additionally, we will explore the growing influence of email, influencer, and video marketing, as well as ethical standards and compliance regulations that guide modern marketing practices. By the end of this chapter, readers will be equipped with the knowledge and strategies required to reach and engage their target audience effectively online.

5.2 THE ROLE OF DIGITAL MARKETING IN THE MODERN BUSINESS LANDSCAPE

Digital marketing has fundamentally transformed the way businesses engage with their audiences, shaping the modern commercial environment. It represents the strategic use of online platforms and technologies to promote products, services, and brands, creating a broader and more dynamic range of promotional opportunities than ever before. By embracing tools such as SEO, social media marketing (SMM), email campaigns, content creation, and paid digital advertising, businesses are able to connect with a global audience almost instantaneously. This chapter explores the core principles of digital marketing, its significance, and the interplay between digital and traditional strategies.

At its core, digital marketing refers to the deployment of digital channels to reach consumers, allowing businesses to engage with a diverse and widespread audience in ways that were previously impossible. Its importance is grounded in the rapid shift of consumer behaviour towards the digital world. In an era where most consumers are connected online, companies must cultivate a strong digital presence to remain relevant. This allows businesses to interact with their target market in real-time, respond quickly to feedback, analyse data instantly, and adjust marketing strategies to meet evolving customer demands.

The shift towards digital marketing is part of the broader evolution of marketing in the digital age, driven by both technological advancements and changing consumer expectations. Where traditional marketing once dominated through print media, radio, and television, the rise of the internet has ushered in a new era. The online world has radically altered how consumers interact with brands, requiring businesses to adopt more interactive and personalised approaches to maintain customer interest and loyalty. Today, digital marketing isn't just a tool but an essential part of the entire marketing strategy, reflecting the shift towards a more engaged and responsive relationship between brands and consumers.

Despite the growing dominance of digital platforms, the integration of traditional and digital marketing strategies remains an essential approach for many businesses. Traditional methods, such as print advertising, television spots, and direct mail campaigns, still hold value in particular contexts, especially where specific demographics or industries continue to rely on them. Combining these methods with digital channels provides a more comprehensive and impactful marketing strategy. For instance, a television campaign may be amplified through digital channels such as social media or online ads, extending its reach and effectiveness. Similarly, traditional print materials can be integrated into the digital ecosystem through the use of QR codes or links that direct customers to online content, creating a seamless bridge between offline and online worlds. This fusion of traditional and digital strategies creates a more unified brand experience, ensuring that businesses can effectively engage with their audiences across multiple platforms and touchpoints.

5.3 NAVIGATING THE DIGITAL CONSUMER JOURNEY

In today's digital age, understanding the consumer journey is essential for businesses seeking to convert online interactions into long-lasting customer relationships. This journey encompasses a series of interactions across various digital touchpoints, from initial awareness to final conversion. Grasping each stage of this process is crucial for developing strategies that guide potential customers seamlessly through their decision-making, ultimately fostering both sales and loyalty.

The journey begins with the awareness stage, where businesses aim to capture the attention of individuals who may be unfamiliar with their products or services. At this point, consumers are often passively browsing, unaware of what a brand offers. To stand out in this crowded digital space, businesses utilise various methods to generate interest. Content marketing plays a pivotal role by delivering relevant, informative, and engaging material that addresses the needs or pain points of the target audience. SEO is equally critical, as it ensures that the business's content is easily discoverable when consumers search for solutions or products related to their interests. Social media platforms are another key asset, where brands can deploy targeted advertisements and organic content to attract potential customers.

As consumers move into the consideration stage, their awareness has piqued enough interest to explore options. They now actively seek more detailed information to help them evaluate and compare their choices. At this point, businesses need to shift their strategy towards providing more in-depth and insightful content. Articles, whitepapers, and case studies are highly valuable here, as they help demonstrate the brand's expertise and position it as a thought leader in its industry. This stage also presents an opportunity to build relationships through email marketing, offering personalised content, exclusive insights, and promotions that nurture leads further. Remarketing campaigns, where targeted ads remind users of their previous engagement with the brand, are particularly effective in keeping the brand front of mind as consumers deliberate over their options.

The final phase of the journey is the decision stage, where the potential customer is ready to make a purchase. At this crucial juncture, businesses must employ focused strategies to drive conversions. Personalised offers, limited-time discounts, and persuasive calls to action (CTA) can tip the scales in the brand's favour. Equally important is the quality of the user experience (UX) on the brand's website—smooth navigation, clear product information, and an easy purchasing process all enhance the likelihood of a successful conversion. Paid advertising, particularly PPC campaigns, can help direct prospects to the most relevant product pages or promotional offers. Additionally, the inclusion of customer testimonials, reviews, and other forms of social proof are vital in instilling confidence and validating the consumer's decision to purchase.

Understanding the nuances of the digital consumer journey is fundamental for any business aiming to thrive in the online marketplace. By employing a strategic, customer-centric approach that effectively addresses the needs and concerns at each stage—awareness, consideration, and decision—businesses not only increase the likelihood of conversion but also lay the groundwork for fostering long-term customer loyalty. This comprehensive and thoughtful approach ensures that customers receive a positive, engaging experience throughout their journey, from initial interest to the final purchase, and beyond.

5.4 CRAFTING A COMPREHENSIVE UNDERSTANDING OF YOUR TARGET AUDIENCE

In the ever-evolving landscape of digital marketing, precision is not just advantageous—it's essential. The success of any marketing campaign is heavily reliant on how well you define and understand your target audience. This process involves a detailed exploration of market segmentation, the creation of customer personas, identifying pain points, and conducting ongoing market research to keep pace with shifting consumer preferences.

The first crucial step is market segmentation. This is the strategic division of a larger target market into smaller, distinct groups that share common characteristics (see Figure 5.1). By breaking down a broad audience into more defined categories, marketers can tailor their messages to resonate deeply with specific subsets. Each segment represents a unique set of needs, preferences, and behaviours, allowing for more targeted and effective communication. From these segmented groups, businesses then craft detailed customer personas—fictional representations of their ideal customers. These personas are designed to reflect not only demographic information but also psychographics and behavioural patterns. For instance, a software company might develop personas such as "Tech-Savvy Sarah" or "Corporate Claire," each requiring a distinct approach in terms of marketing messages, tone, and channel.

However, understanding who your audience is only gets you halfway. To truly connect, businesses must delve deeper into the challenges and frustrations faced by their customers. Identifying customer pain points and needs is a critical component of audience definition, as

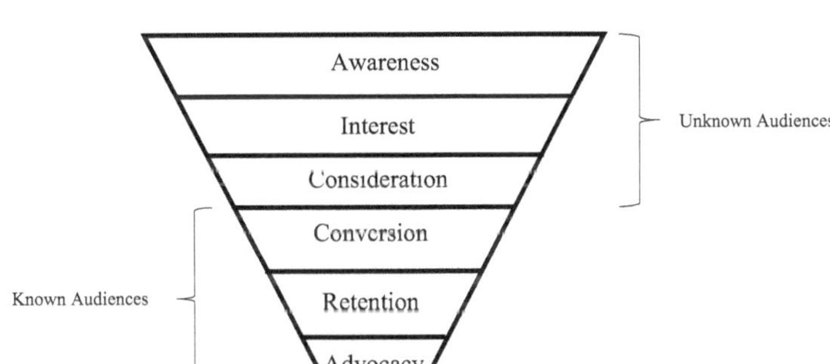

FIGURE 5.1 Target audience analysis: Everything digital marketers

it uncovers the problems that your products or services aim to solve. This requires empathy—understanding what drives and motivates your audience, what holds them back, and what solutions they are actively seeking. Whether through surveys, feedback forms, or social media monitoring, businesses can gather invaluable insights into the daily struggles of their customers. For instance, a fitness brand might discover that its target audience struggles with time management and is looking for quick, effective workout routines. This knowledge enables the brand to create content and products that specifically address these concerns, ensuring a more relevant and impactful marketing strategy.

Conducting thorough and continuous market research further sharpens this understanding of your audience. The digital landscape is fluid, and consumer preferences are in constant flux, making ongoing research essential for staying relevant. Market research helps businesses remain attuned to industry trends, competitor movements, and shifts in consumer behaviour. By leveraging digital tools like analytics platforms, social media metrics, and keyword research, companies can uncover new opportunities or emerging challenges. For instance, an online retailer might detect a growing demand for sustainable products, prompting an adjustment in both its inventory and marketing messages to align with consumer values.

Ultimately, defining your target audience is a multifaceted process that goes beyond simple demographic data. It requires a deep and evolving understanding of who your audience is, what their core challenges are, and how your products or services can provide meaningful solutions. Through methodical segmentation, persona development, pain point analysis, and continuous market research, businesses can forge more authentic, lasting connections with their customers, fostering loyalty and engagement that extend well beyond a single transaction.

5.5 CRAFTING A COMPREHENSIVE CONTENT MARKETING STRATEGY

In the vast digital landscape where information is readily available, a carefully devised content marketing strategy is crucial for connecting with your audience in a meaningful way. Content marketing goes beyond the mere production of materials; it demands a thoughtful approach to creating, distributing, and diversifying content to achieve maximum impact. The success of a strategy depends not only on the quality of the content but also on how effectively it reaches the intended audience and the varied formats used to engage them.

The cornerstone of any effective content marketing strategy is the creation of valuable and relevant content. This means producing materials that directly address the needs, challenges, and interests of your target audience, offering them solutions, insights, or entertainment. Content must go beyond mere information; it should be tailored to resonate deeply with the audience's particular context. Whether it's through blog posts, videos, articles, or infographics, the content needs to provide tangible value. By positioning your brand as a trusted authority that understands and responds to audience pain points, you build long-term credibility and foster loyalty.

However, simply creating content is not enough. Once content is developed, its strategic distribution and promotion are paramount to ensure it reaches the desired audience. This involves disseminating content across multiple platforms where your target audience is most active—whether through social media, email newsletters, or industry forums. Social media plays an especially powerful role in this regard, as it provides a space for real-time interaction, sharing, and engagement. By crafting shareable and interactive posts, you increase the likelihood that your content will spread organically, amplifying its reach. Email marketing offers a more personalised approach, allowing businesses to send tailored updates, promotions, and articles directly to their subscribers. Additionally, collaborations with influencers or thought leaders can substantially broaden the reach of your content. These individuals bring their established follower base into the fold, boosting the credibility of your brand and extending its visibility.

To further enhance the effectiveness of content marketing, it is crucial to offer a variety of content types that cater to different audience preferences and consumption habits. Not everyone consumes information in the same way, so a diverse mix ensures you reach a broader spectrum of potential customers. Blog posts remain a foundational component of content marketing, offering detailed, SEO-optimised content that can drive traffic and build authority. Videos, meanwhile, tap into visual and auditory engagement, offering a dynamic and often more engaging medium for storytelling, product demonstrations, or tutorials. Infographics serve as a highly effective way to condense complex information into an easily digestible format, perfect for presenting data, statistics, or processes in a visually compelling manner. Beyond these, podcasts, webinars, and interactive elements such as polls or quizzes provide further opportunities for audience interaction and engagement. By understanding your audience's content consumption habits, you can tailor your approach and ensure your content resonates on multiple levels.

In conclusion, an effective content marketing strategy is built on three pillars: creating valuable and relevant content, strategically distributing it across multiple channels, and leveraging a diverse range of content types to appeal to different audience preferences. By doing so, businesses can not only capture their audience's attention but also foster engagement, loyalty, and long-term relationships. A well-executed content marketing strategy ultimately positions a brand as a leader in its industry, continuously delivering value to its audience in the ever-competitive digital space.

5.6 MASTERING SEO FOR DIGITAL SUCCESS

In today's highly competitive digital landscape, achieving visibility is crucial for online success, and mastering SEO is a fundamental component in establishing a strong online presence. SEO is no longer a mere technical exercise; it is a comprehensive strategy that requires a deep understanding of both search engine algorithms and user behaviour. From the foundational concepts to advanced on-page and off-page techniques, the integration of SEO best practices ensures that businesses remain visible, relevant, and competitive in the vast expanse of the internet.

At its core, SEO is the process of optimising content and websites to align with the algorithms used by search engines like Google. These algorithms are designed to evaluate the relevance and authority of web pages in relation to specific search queries. Understanding the basics of SEO begins with keyword research—identifying the words and phrases that potential customers are likely to use when searching for information related to your products or services. By incorporating these keywords strategically throughout the website's content, meta tags, headers, and descriptions, businesses increase the chances of being discovered by search engines and, consequently, by their target audience. The ultimate aim is to ensure that the website ranks higher in search engine results pages (SERPs), as higher visibility generally translates into increased traffic, leads, and conversions.

Effective SEO, however, extends beyond basic keyword optimisation. It encompasses a combination of on-page and off-page strategies that work in concert to improve a website's performance in SERPs. On-page SEO refers to optimising elements within the website itself. This involves ensuring that content is rich with relevant keywords, structured with appropriate header tags, and enhanced with engaging meta descriptions. Additionally, factors such as page loading speed, UX, and mobile responsiveness are crucial to on-page success. Websites that load quickly, are easy to navigate, and offer a seamless mobile experience not only perform better in search rankings but also provide a superior UX, which search engines like Google increasingly reward.

On the other hand, off-page SEO focuses on external factors that influence a website's authority and credibility. A key component of off-page SEO is building backlinks—gaining links from reputable, authoritative websites that point to your content. Search engines interpret these backlinks as endorsements of the quality and relevance of your content, boosting its authority and search ranking. Additionally, a robust presence on social media, along with positive online reviews and mentions in respected publications, strengthens your website's visibility and credibility. These off-page factors work in conjunction with on-page efforts to form a holistic SEO strategy that enhances a website's standing in the digital ecosystem.

Adhering to SEO best practices is essential for sustained success. Regularly updating and expanding content signals to search engines that the website is active, relevant, and worth promoting. High-quality content that is not only keyword-optimised but also addresses the specific needs and intent of users is more likely to earn favourable rankings. This approach ensures that search engines see your website as a valuable resource that answers users' queries effectively.

Technical SEO also plays a pivotal role in improving a website's ranking potential. A well-optimised site structure, fast page load times, and secure HTTPS protocols contribute to better SEO performance. Technical enhancements, such as the inclusion of an XML sitemap and a well-organised robots.txt file, ensure that search engines can easily crawl and index the site. This level of optimisation supports the smooth functioning of the website from a technical perspective, further improving its chances of ranking higher.

Ongoing analysis is critical to refining and improving SEO efforts. Tools like Google Analytics and Google Search Console provide invaluable insights into user behaviour, keyword performance, and any potential issues affecting visibility. These insights enable businesses to continuously refine their SEO strategies, adapting to algorithm updates and changing user trends.

Finally, the integration of UX into SEO has become increasingly important. Search engines prioritise websites that offer a positive, intuitive UX, rewarding those that provide clear navigation, visually appealing designs, and seamless mobile functionality. Optimising UX not only aligns with search engine priorities but also enhances user satisfaction, leading to longer site visits, lower bounce rates, and higher conversion rates.

In summary, SEO is a multifaceted discipline that requires a well-rounded approach, incorporating everything from basic keyword research to advanced technical and off-page strategies. By understanding the fundamentals, implementing on-page and off-page techniques, and adhering to SEO best practices, businesses can achieve higher search rankings and maintain a strong, competitive online presence. This comprehensive strategy not only positions a website for visibility but also ensures long-term digital success in an increasingly crowded marketplace.

5.7 MAXIMISING THE POWER OF PPC ADVERTISING

In the expansive world of digital marketing, PPC advertising has emerged as one of the most effective methods for attracting highly targeted audiences and driving conversions. Unlike organic traffic, PPC allows businesses to bid on specific keywords and secure prime advertising positions on search engines and other digital platforms, ensuring immediate visibility to potential customers. The success of PPC campaigns hinges on understanding key platforms such as Google Ads and Bing Ads, crafting precise campaigns, and optimising ad copy and landing pages to convert clicks into valuable actions.

PPC campaigns are most commonly associated with two giants in the search engine market: Google Ads and Bing Ads. Google Ads, due to its dominance in global search traffic, offers unparalleled reach and flexibility. With Google Ads, businesses can create a variety of ads, including text, display, video, and even app ads, all targeted at users based on specific keywords, demographics, and browsing behaviour. This extensive targeting ensures that ads reach precisely the right audience at the right moment. Moreover, Google's powerful analytics tools allow advertisers to continually refine their campaigns by offering insights into performance and areas for improvement.

Though often overshadowed by Google, Bing Ads, run by Microsoft, also holds significant value, especially for businesses looking for cost-effective opportunities in less saturated markets. While its reach is smaller, Bing Ads offers a less competitive landscape where businesses can often achieve a higher return on investment (ROI) for their advertising spend. Like Google, Bing Ads provides comprehensive targeting features and customisation options, allowing advertisers to define their audience by age, gender, location, and even specific interests. For businesses that aim to diversify their PPC strategies, combining both platforms can offer broader exposure and untapped potential.

The foundation of a successful PPC campaign lies in meticulous planning. Effective PPC campaigns are built on thorough keyword research. The selection of the right keywords ensures that ads appear in front of users who are actively searching for relevant products or services. Tools like Google's Keyword Planner aid businesses in discovering high-performing keywords that can increase ad relevance and visibility. This stage also involves defining the target audience with precision, narrowing down by demographics, location, and user interests to ensure that ads resonate with those most likely to convert. Tailoring campaigns to specific segments of the audience ensures that the advertising message speaks directly to their needs and desires.

At the core of every PPC campaign is compelling ad copy. Effective ads need to be concise, persuasive, and armed with a clear CTA. By focusing on the unique selling propositions of a product or service, businesses can create ad copy that captures the attention of users scrolling through search results or web pages. The ad must entice users to click while communicating value and urgency. Managing the budget of PPC campaigns is equally crucial. Advertisers need to set clear budget limits that align with their goals and regularly adjust this allocation based on campaign performance. A careful balance between budget management and targeted spending ensures that resources are used efficiently to maximise returns.

Optimisation is an ongoing process, and nowhere is this more critical than in refining ad copy and landing pages. After the initial launch of a PPC campaign, continuous A/B testing of different ad variations becomes essential. Experimenting with different headlines, descriptions, and CTA helps identify which combination resonates best with the target audience. The ability to make data-driven adjustments is a powerful advantage in ensuring the longevity and effectiveness of PPC efforts. Additionally, ad extensions, which provide supplementary information such as phone numbers, additional links, or product details, can further enhance the visibility and appeal of an ad.

The ultimate goal of any PPC campaign is to guide users to a landing page where conversions occur. Optimising these landing pages is pivotal to turning clicks into tangible outcomes. The landing page must align with the promises made in the ad, offering users a seamless and relevant experience. Pages that are user-friendly, load quickly, and feature clear, prominent CTA are more likely to lead to conversions. Whether it's a purchase, a form submission, or a sign-up, the landing page needs to be optimised for engagement, keeping user behaviour and intent in mind. Strategic placement of forms, appealing visuals, and persuasive copy all contribute to an effective landing page that converts traffic into meaningful actions.

To measure the success of these efforts, implementing conversion tracking is crucial. By setting up tracking mechanisms—whether for product purchases, form submissions, or other desired actions—businesses can analyse the performance of both their ads and landing pages. These data provide insights into what's working and where improvements can be made. As PPC advertising operates in a dynamic and competitive environment, businesses must continually monitor their campaigns, making necessary adjustments to stay ahead of trends and competitor activities.

In conclusion, PPC advertising is a powerful tool for driving targeted traffic and conversions, particularly on platforms like Google Ads and Bing Ads. However, the key to success lies in careful planning, diligent optimisation, and an unwavering commitment to refining both ad copy and landing pages. By combining data-driven insights with creativity and strategic budget management, businesses can leverage PPC to not only reach their target audience but also achieve significant returns on their investment in the ever-evolving world of digital marketing.

5.8 HARNESSING THE POWER OF SMM

In today's digital-first world, SMM has become an essential tool for businesses seeking to build meaningful connections with their audiences, strengthen brand identity, and foster engagement. The rapid evolution of social media platforms has transformed how businesses interact with consumers, offering unique opportunities to engage in dialogue, promote services, and create a sense of community around their brand. A successful social media strategy hinges on selecting the right platforms, producing compelling content, and leveraging advertising and influencer marketing to maximise reach and impact.

With the sheer variety of social media platforms available, choosing the right one is crucial for delivering your message effectively. Each platform caters to different audiences and types of content, so aligning your business with the most appropriate platforms is a strategic decision that can greatly influence the success of your campaigns. Facebook, with its extensive user base and versatile content formats, remains a popular choice for businesses looking to build awareness and create communities. It offers the flexibility to post everything from text updates to video content, making it suitable for a broad range of industries.

Instagram, on the other hand, is the go-to platform for visually driven brands. Its emphasis on beautiful imagery and short, snappy videos makes it ideal for industries such as fashion, lifestyle, and art, where aesthetics are central to the brand message. For businesses seeking real-time engagement and conversations, Twitter offers a platform where timely updates, trending topics, and quick interactions can take centre stage, proving particularly effective for news-driven or fast-moving industries.

LinkedIn serves a different purpose as a professional network, making it perfect for business-to-business marketing and professional networking. Thought leadership, industry insights, and company updates thrive here, especially when businesses seek to connect with professionals or position themselves as authorities in their field. Meanwhile, Pinterest, though smaller in scope, is a treasure trove for businesses in the lifestyle, DIY, and e-commerce sectors, with its visually inspiring content tailored to audiences looking for ideas and creativity.

Understanding the nuances of each platform and how your target audience engages with them is vital. Rather than spreading resources too thin across all available platforms, an effective social media strategy focuses on those that align with your business goals and the preferences of your audience. This often involves a carefully curated mix of platforms, each serving a different function in the broader strategy.

Once the platforms are chosen, the heart of a social media strategy lies in creating engaging and relevant content. Social media is a crowded space where brands are competing for attention, so standing out requires a thoughtful approach to content creation. Visual appeal is one of the most powerful tools in this environment. High-quality images, engaging videos, and visually cohesive posts grab attention as users scroll through their feeds. Investing in well-designed visuals that reflect the essence of your brand helps establish a strong presence and entice potential customers.

Storytelling, too, plays an important role in connecting with your audience. Social media offers an opportunity to humanise your brand, allowing you to share behind-the-scenes moments, customer success stories, and real-world applications of your products or services. This type of authentic content helps foster trust and encourages a deeper emotional connection between your brand and its followers. Whether through heartfelt anecdotes or a glimpse into the day-to-day workings of your company, storytelling helps transform your brand from a faceless entity into one that people can relate to and engage with on a personal level.

In addition to visual appeal and storytelling, consistency and variety are critical elements of a successful content strategy. Posting regularly keeps your brand at the forefront of your audience's mind, but varying the content format prevents your feed from becoming monotonous. Engaging content such as polls, infographics, videos, and interactive posts can all be used to create a more dynamic and diverse social media presence, tailored to the strengths and audience expectations of each platform.

Alongside organic content, social media advertising offers businesses a powerful way to reach even more users. Paid advertising on platforms like Facebook and Instagram allows businesses to target specific demographics, behaviours, and interests, providing an avenue for more personalised engagement. Sponsored posts, video ads, and carousel ads can be tailored to meet your advertising goals, whether you are aiming for brand awareness, website traffic, or conversions. These advertising tools also offer detailed analytics that track engagement, conversions, and overall campaign effectiveness, helping businesses refine their strategy as they go.

Influencer marketing has also risen to prominence in recent years as a key element of SMM. By collaborating with influencers—individuals who have a substantial and loyal following—businesses can tap into existing communities that trust the influencer's recommendations. When done authentically, influencer partnerships can significantly expand brand visibility and provide a stamp of credibility that traditional advertising may not achieve. Whether through product placements, reviews, or sponsored content, influencers help brands reach new audiences in a way that feels more organic and genuine. However, as with any marketing strategy, success depends on choosing influencers whose values align with your brand and whose audience mirrors your target market.

Understanding your audience is fundamental to both social media advertising and influencer marketing. By tailoring your ads to resonate with specific demographics and ensuring that influencer collaborations are well-aligned with your brand message, businesses can maximise the impact of their campaigns. Tracking metrics and analysing results through social media analytics tools further ensures that your efforts remain on course, enabling adjustments for optimal performance and sustained engagement.

In essence, SMM is a multi-faceted approach that requires a combination of careful platform selection, thoughtful content creation, and smart use of paid advertising and influencer collaborations. By crafting a cohesive strategy that speaks to the right audience in the right places, businesses can unlock the full potential of social media to build brand loyalty, drive engagement, and ultimately, achieve their marketing goals. As social media continues to evolve, staying attuned to emerging trends and audience behaviours will be essential for maintaining relevance and success in this fast-moving digital landscape.

CASE STUDY 5

Nike's Digital Marketing Strategy—Strengthening Brand Presence and Customer Loyalty

Nike, one of the world's most recognisable sportswear brands, has mastered the art of digital marketing to maintain its dominance in the industry. As consumer behaviour shifted towards online engagement, Nike recognised the need to enhance its digital presence and connect with customers on a deeper level. The company faced the challenge of standing out in a highly competitive market while catering to digitally savvy consumers who expected personalised and interactive brand experiences. Traditional marketing approaches alone were no longer sufficient in an era where social media, e-commerce, and digital storytelling played a crucial role in shaping brand perception and customer loyalty.

To address this, Nike implemented a comprehensive digital marketing strategy focused on social media engagement, personalised content, and e-commerce integration. The company leveraged platforms such as Instagram, Twitter, and TikTok to engage with audiences through visually compelling content, interactive campaigns, and collaborations with influencers and athletes. Nike's campaigns often incorporated strong storytelling, as seen in its "You Can't Stop Us" campaign, which resonated globally with themes of resilience and unity. In addition, Nike developed the Nike+ ecosystem, which includes mobile apps such as Nike Training Club and Nike Run Club, offering personalised fitness plans, challenges, and community engagement. By integrating data analytics and AI-driven personalisation, Nike provided tailored product recommendations and exclusive content to customers based on their preferences and activity history. The brand also strengthened its e-commerce strategy by enhancing its website and direct-to-consumer sales channels, allowing customers to shop seamlessly across multiple digital touchpoints.

Nike's digital marketing initiatives yielded impressive results. The company saw increased customer engagement, with millions actively participating in digital campaigns and mobile app experiences. Nike's social media presence significantly boosted brand awareness, leading to a surge in online sales and direct-to-consumer revenue. The Nike+ apps fostered a sense of community among fitness enthusiasts, strengthening brand loyalty and encouraging repeat purchases. Additionally, data-driven personalisation improved customer satisfaction and conversion rates, as users received relevant product recommendations tailored to their interests. Nike's ability to combine storytelling with data-driven marketing cemented its position as a leader in digital engagement.

Nike's digital marketing success highlights several key lessons. The strategic use of social media can enhance brand awareness and create authentic connections with consumers. Personalisation, powered by data analytics and AI, improves customer engagement and increases sales by delivering relevant content and product recommendations. A seamless e-commerce experience strengthens direct-to-consumer relationships, reducing reliance on third-party retailers. Finally, digital marketing is most effective when combined with strong brand storytelling, reinforcing a brand's identity and values in a way that resonates with audiences.

Discussion Questions for Students (with Indicative Answers)

1. **How has Nike used digital marketing to enhance its brand presence and customer loyalty?**
   Indicative Answer: Nike leverages social media, personalised content, and e-commerce to engage with customers. Its campaigns incorporate storytelling and interactive digital experiences, strengthening brand loyalty.
2. **Why is social media engagement crucial for brands like Nike in today's digital landscape?**
   Indicative Answer: Social media allows brands to connect with consumers in real time, share compelling content, and build a community around their products, increasing brand awareness and customer engagement.
3. **What role does personalisation play in Nike's digital marketing strategy?**
   Indicative Answer: Personalisation, powered by AI and data analytics, enables Nike to tailor product recommendations, fitness challenges, and exclusive content to individual users, improving customer satisfaction and retention.
4. **How does Nike's direct-to-consumer e-commerce strategy benefit the company?**
   Indicative Answer: By focusing on direct-to-consumer sales, Nike gains greater control over pricing, branding, and customer relationships, reducing reliance on third-party retailers and increasing profit margins.
5. **What lessons can other businesses learn from Nike's approach to digital marketing?**
   Indicative Answer: Businesses should invest in social media engagement, use data-driven personalisation, integrate e-commerce seamlessly, and leverage storytelling to create meaningful connections with their audiences.

5.9 MASTERING EMAIL MARKETING AND AUTOMATION FOR LASTING CONNECTIONS

In the ever-expanding world of digital marketing, email continues to prove its resilience and relevance as a crucial means of establishing meaningful connections with an audience. While many new technologies and platforms have emerged over the years, email remains a highly effective and reliable method of communicating with potential and existing customers. Mastering the art of email marketing and automation involves understanding how to build a quality email list, segmenting subscribers for more personalised engagement, crafting compelling campaigns, and leveraging automation to streamline processes and improve outcomes.

The foundation of any successful email marketing strategy begins with building a robust and engaged email list. This requires encouraging visitors to your website, social media followers, and existing customers to subscribe to your emails. Using sign-up forms in prominent areas of your website, pop-ups, and CTA on social media can entice potential subscribers to join. Offering exclusive content, promotional discounts, or early access to products and services serves as a powerful incentive to capture email addresses. A well-crafted value proposition is often enough to convince visitors to join your list, knowing they will gain something of worth by subscribing.

However, simply building an email list is not enough. The real strength of email marketing lies in how you communicate with your subscribers. Segmentation is essential to tailoring your messages to specific groups within your list, ensuring that the content you deliver is both relevant and engaging. By dividing your audience based on demographics, behaviours, or interests, you can send more targeted messages that align with each recipient's preferences. For example, an e-commerce store might segment its audience based on purchase history, sending tailored promotions to loyal customers or re-engagement emails to those who haven't made a purchase in a while. This strategic segmentation allows you to meet your subscribers where they are in their customer journey, creating a more personalised experience that fosters stronger relationships.

Once the list has been built and segmented, the next step is to create engaging email campaigns that capture attention and drive action. One of the first challenges in email marketing is ensuring that your emails are opened. Subject lines and preview text are your first opportunity to make an impression. A well-crafted subject line should be attention-grabbing, concise, and evoke a sense of urgency or curiosity. Adding a personalised touch, such as addressing the recipient by name, often increases the likelihood of the email being opened.

Once the email has been opened, the content itself must deliver on the promise of the subject line. The information within should be valuable, whether it's providing educational insights, exclusive offers, or updates on new products or services. It's essential to keep the content concise and engaging, as overly long emails can quickly lose a reader's attention. Visual appeal is also key—using high-quality images, clean designs, and easy-to-read formatting helps make the email more digestible. Whether promoting a product or offering educational content, each email should have a clear and compelling CTA that directs recipients towards the next step. Whether it's clicking through to a landing page, downloading a resource, or making a purchase, the CTA must be both visible and persuasive.

In today's mobile-centric world, it's equally important to ensure that your emails are optimised for mobile devices. With a significant percentage of emails being opened on mobile, failing to design emails that are mobile-friendly can lead to a poor UX and a loss of potential engagement. Text must be easy to read, images should scale properly, and the overall layout should adjust seamlessly to fit smaller screens. Ensuring that your emails are fully responsive across all devices improves their chances of being read and acted upon.

Beyond manual email campaigns, the power of automation enables marketers to engage with their audience in a more timely and efficient manner. Automation workflows allow businesses to send emails triggered by specific actions or behaviours, creating a personalised experience at scale. A welcome series is often the first step in nurturing new subscribers. By automating a series of introductory emails that introduce your brand, share valuable information, and guide new subscribers towards making their first purchase or engaging with your services, you begin to build a relationship from the outset.

Segmented campaigns can also be automated to target specific groups within your email list based on their past behaviours or expressed preferences. For example, if a subscriber has recently shown interest in a particular product category, you can automate a campaign that highlights products related to that interest or provides exclusive discounts to encourage a purchase. These highly targeted emails improve the likelihood of conversion by offering content that directly addresses the subscriber's needs and desires.

Another key area where automation shines is in recovering abandoned sales. Abandoned cart emails are a powerful tool for encouraging potential customers to complete their purchase. By automatically sending a reminder email when a customer leaves items in their cart without completing the transaction, you create an opportunity to re-engage them and gently prompt them towards making the purchase. Offering incentives, such as free shipping or a small discount, can further increase the likelihood of conversion.

Drip campaigns are another popular form of automation, where a series of emails is sent over time to nurture leads or guide subscribers through a specific customer journey. This could involve gradually providing more information about your products and services, educating subscribers on the benefits, and offering exclusive promotions to move them towards making a purchase or engaging further with your brand.

Automation, when done right, not only saves time and resources but also enhances the overall experience for your subscribers. It allows for personalised communication at scale, ensuring that each subscriber receives the right message at the right time based on their individual interactions with your brand. Furthermore, tracking the performance of these automated workflows and campaigns through analytics helps refine and improve the approach over time, ensuring continued relevance and effectiveness.

In essence, email marketing and automation stand as integral components of any comprehensive digital marketing strategy. By strategically building and segmenting your email list, crafting engaging campaigns, and implementing automated workflows, businesses can forge lasting connections with their audience, drive conversions, and enhance customer satisfaction. Continual refinement, informed by analytics and subscriber feedback, ensures that email marketing efforts remain adaptive and effective in an ever-evolving digital landscape.

5.10 STRENGTHENING YOUR DIGITAL PRESENCE: ONLINE PR AND REPUTATION MANAGEMENT

In today's fast-paced digital environment, where information can spread globally in an instant, online PR and reputation management have become essential to maintaining a strong and positive brand image. The way a brand is perceived online can significantly influence its success or failure, making it imperative for businesses to strategically manage their reputation and actively engage with the online community. This section explores the key elements involved in monitoring brand perception, engaging meaningfully with online forums and communities, and addressing negative publicity through effective crisis management.

At the core of any successful online reputation management strategy is the ability to monitor brand mentions across various digital platforms. Brands need to stay aware of how they are being discussed in social media spaces, on review websites, in blog posts, and within news articles. Employing tools that track these mentions in real-time allows businesses to stay ahead of both praise and criticism, providing opportunities to engage with satisfied customers and address any issues before they escalate. Monitoring brand sentiment helps businesses to not only manage immediate concerns but also to assess long-term trends in customer satisfaction and public perception.

Positive brand advocacy plays an equally important role in shaping a favourable online reputation. Encouraging loyal customers to share their experiences and feedback online can serve as powerful social proof, helping to bolster a brand's credibility. By featuring customer testimonials, reviews, and other user-generated content, businesses can showcase their successes and foster a community of advocates who willingly share their positive experiences. This organic promotion of the brand can serve as a buffer against any negative feedback that may arise, creating a balanced and more authentic online presence.

Consistency in brand messaging is another crucial aspect of managing perception. The voice, values, and message of the brand must remain uniform across all online channels—whether in official posts, responses to reviews, or content shared by employees. Consistent messaging ensures that the brand's narrative remains strong and clear, which reinforces a positive image and builds trust with the audience. Whether you are sharing your company's mission or responding to a customer's concern, the tone and substance should align with the brand's core values.

Engaging directly with online communities and forums offers businesses a valuable opportunity to build relationships and increase their visibility in an organic, non-promotional way. Identifying the platforms most relevant to your industry or target audience—whether it be specific social media groups, industry-specific forums, or niche communities—enables you to become part of the ongoing conversation. Participating genuinely, without overtly promoting your products or services, helps build credibility and trust. By contributing meaningful insights, answering questions, and sharing your expertise, you not only elevate your brand's authority but also demonstrate that your business cares about its industry and its customers.

It is equally important to respond to feedback in these spaces, both positive and negative. Acknowledging positive feedback reinforces customer loyalty, while addressing negative comments professionally and transparently can prevent issues from escalating. Timely responses show that your business is attentive, engaged, and committed to customer satisfaction. In particular, handling negative feedback with tact, professionalism, and a clear path to resolution is key to maintaining a positive image. Customers and audiences respect brands that take responsibility and are proactive in seeking solutions.

When negative publicity arises, it is critical to respond swiftly and thoughtfully. A delayed response can exacerbate the situation, while a well-timed and carefully crafted reply can help contain the spread of harmful narratives. Acknowledge the issue directly, express empathy for those affected, and provide a clear outline of how the situation is being addressed. Quick action demonstrates accountability, which can go a long way in minimising reputational damage. Taking ownership of the issue and clearly communicating the steps taken shows your audience that the business values transparency and is committed to resolving the matter.

Throughout any crisis, honesty and transparency are key. Attempting to downplay or mislead stakeholders about the severity of a situation can have lasting repercussions. Clear, honest communication helps build and maintain trust, even in difficult times. This approach reassures your audience that the business is not only willing to admit fault but is also prepared to take responsibility and make things right. An open, honest dialogue with customers, employees, and stakeholders solidifies your reputation as a trustworthy brand, even during moments of crisis.

Crises should also be viewed as opportunities for growth and improvement. After managing a difficult situation, businesses should take the time to evaluate the root cause of the issue and determine the necessary steps to prevent future occurrences. Conducting a post-crisis analysis enables businesses to refine their processes and improve their overall resilience. Sharing the corrective actions taken with the public further demonstrates a commitment to learning and growing from the experience, which can help to restore faith in the brand.

Proactively planning for crises is another vital part of reputation management. While not all situations can be predicted, having a comprehensive crisis management plan in place prepares businesses to respond quickly and effectively when problems arise. Identifying potential vulnerabilities and establishing clear communication protocols are important steps in ensuring that the business can maintain control over the narrative during a crisis. Designating key team members to handle specific aspects of the response, from social media to internal communications, ensures that everyone knows their role in addressing the issue.

In conclusion, managing online PR and reputation is a continuous, multi-faceted process that requires vigilance, responsiveness, and a commitment to transparent communication. By actively monitoring online conversations, engaging with relevant communities, and being prepared to address negative publicity in an honest and timely manner, businesses can build and protect their brand's image. In the rapidly evolving digital landscape, a strong online reputation not only differentiates your business from competitors but also fosters lasting trust and loyalty among your audience.

5.11 EXPANDING REACH THROUGH AFFILIATE MARKETING AND STRATEGIC PARTNERSHIPS

In today's competitive digital marketplace, affiliate marketing and strategic partnerships have proven to be vital tools for businesses seeking to expand their reach and drive sales. By leveraging the influence of affiliates, businesses can increase brand visibility, generate leads, and ultimately enhance their bottom line. This section explores the intricacies of affiliate marketing programmes, including how to identify and engage the right affiliates and the importance of tracking and measuring performance to ensure a sustainable and effective strategy.

At the heart of affiliate marketing is a performance-based structure that rewards affiliates for promoting products or services and driving sales or leads. Affiliates, who are often influencers, bloggers, or businesses themselves, use their platforms to market a brand's offerings, earning a commission for every successful transaction or lead they generate. The commission is typically earned when a customer completes a desired action through the affiliate's unique link. These actions might range from making a purchase (pay-per-sale), completing a sign-up form (pay per lead), or merely clicking on a link PPC, with pay per sale being the most prevalent model. This structure ensures that affiliates are incentivised to effectively market the brand, as their earnings are directly tied to their promotional success.

An effective affiliate marketing programme begins with the strategic identification of suitable affiliates who can authentically represent the brand. Businesses must carefully research and target potential affiliates whose audience aligns with their own target market. Affiliates with an established online presence in the same industry or related niches are ideal, as they are likely to have a following that is already interested in the products or services being offered. For example, a fitness brand might look to collaborate with health bloggers, wellness influencers, or complementary businesses in the health sector. This synergy not only increases the likelihood of success but also builds credibility, as the affiliate's audience is more inclined to trust their recommendations.

Engaging potential affiliates requires a compelling value proposition that outlines the benefits of joining the programme. Offering competitive commission rates, providing access to high-quality promotional materials, and offering additional incentives such as bonuses or exclusive offers can attract top-tier affiliates. It is also important to emphasise the uniqueness of the brand or product, ensuring that affiliates feel aligned with the values and offerings they will be promoting. Personalised outreach is crucial in this process; it's not just about sending mass invitations but rather about building genuine connections with affiliates, clearly communicating how the partnership will be mutually beneficial, and providing them with all the tools they need to promote the brand effectively.

Once affiliates are on board, tracking and measuring their performance becomes the cornerstone of a successful affiliate marketing strategy. Robust tracking technology and tools are necessary to monitor affiliate activities and accurately attribute conversions to specific partners. Many businesses use affiliate software or third-party networks to automate this process, making it easier to track conversions, clicks, and overall affiliate engagement. This level of tracking ensures that businesses can not only monitor the performance of individual affiliates but also evaluate the overall success of their programme.

To gain deeper insights into the effectiveness of the programme, it's essential to establish key performance indicators (KPIs) that measure various aspects of affiliate marketing success. Metrics such as conversion rates, click-through rates, and total revenue generated are commonly used to assess the performance of affiliates and the programme as a whole. Analysing this data allows businesses to identify their top-performing affiliates, areas for improvement, and potential changes needed to maximise the programme's efficiency.

Open communication with affiliates is essential to maintaining strong, productive relationships. By regularly updating affiliates on new products, special promotions, or changes within the programme, businesses ensure that their partners are well-informed and equipped to continue promoting the brand effectively. Support is also key; providing affiliates with high-quality marketing materials and promptly addressing any questions or concerns will help them succeed in their promotional efforts. A well-supported affiliate is likely to perform better, resulting in increased sales and a stronger overall partnership.

Incentivising affiliates for exceptional performance is another strategy that can help maintain enthusiasm and drive better results. Offering tiered commission structures, performance-based bonuses, or early access to new products or promotions can motivate affiliates to go above and beyond in their efforts. Publicly recognising top performers, whether through social media shout-outs or affiliate leaderboards, reinforces the importance of their contributions and strengthens the sense of partnership between the business and its affiliates.

In conclusion, affiliate marketing and partnerships provide a powerful means for businesses to expand their marketing reach, tap into new customer bases, and achieve significant sales growth. A deep understanding of affiliate marketing programmes, from structuring commissions to identifying the right partners, is essential for success. Equally important is the ability to track performance, provide support, and incentivise affiliates, ensuring that the programme not only delivers results but also fosters long-term, fruitful relationships. By continuously refining their approach based on data and affiliate feedback, businesses can harness the full potential of affiliate marketing and strategic partnerships to enhance their digital presence and achieve their marketing objectives.

5.12 CRAFTING A SUCCESSFUL INFLUENCER MARKETING STRATEGY

Influencer marketing has evolved into a fundamental element of modern digital strategies, offering businesses a highly effective means of engaging with their target audiences. A well-executed influencer marketing strategy can elevate brand visibility, foster consumer trust, and drive conversions. Achieving these outcomes requires a thoughtful approach, encompassing the identification of relevant influencers, the cultivation of genuine relationships, and the accurate measurement of campaign success.

The starting point of any influencer marketing strategy is to clearly define your target audience. Without a thorough understanding of the demographics and psychographics of the people you want to reach, finding the right influencers becomes a shot in the dark. Knowing whether you are targeting young professionals, health-conscious millennials, or industry experts allows you to align with influencers who have a direct connection with these groups. It's not just about follower numbers but about aligning with individuals who create content that speaks to the interests, values, and preferences of your intended audience.

To facilitate this, various influencer platforms and tools can be employed. Using platforms like AspireIQ or Traackr enables businesses to identify potential influencers across different industries, offering insight into critical metrics such as engagement rates, follower demographics, and even the influencer's history of collaborations. This kind of data-driven approach streamlines the selection process, helping to ensure that you partner with influencers whose reach and relevance align perfectly with your brand's objectives. However, it's crucial not to rely on numbers alone—authenticity is equally essential. Audiences respond most positively to influencers who genuinely live and breathe the values they promote. Collaborating with those who align authentically with your brand can have a significant and lasting impact, as their followers are more likely to trust their recommendations.

Once the right influencers have been identified, the next step involves building authentic and sustainable relationships with them. The outreach process should be personalised, reflecting a genuine appreciation for the influencer's work. Simply sending a generic proposal risks coming across as insincere, reducing the likelihood of a meaningful partnership. Instead, engaging with influencers on a personal level, acknowledging their unique content, and explaining how a collaboration could benefit both parties sets the stage for a more productive relationship.

Clear and transparent communication is key to ensuring successful collaboration. Being upfront about campaign expectations, goals, and compensation will establish trust from the outset. It is equally important to discuss the creative freedom the influencer will have in shaping the campaign, ensuring that their voice and style remain authentic. This authenticity is what resonates most with audiences, and a genuine, unscripted campaign can greatly enhance the effectiveness of the collaboration. Moreover, businesses should consider the long-term benefits of building ongoing relationships with influencers rather than focusing solely on one-off campaigns. A long-term partnership gives influencers the opportunity to become intimately familiar with the brand, which can lead to more thoughtful, consistent, and impactful content. Over time, this approach fosters a deeper connection between the influencer and the brand's audience.

As with any marketing strategy, measuring the impact of influencer campaigns is crucial for determining success and refining future efforts. Setting clear and measurable objectives before the campaign begins is essential. Whether the aim is to boost brand awareness, engagement, or conversions, having these goals defined enables more effective evaluation of the campaign's outcomes. Engagement metrics are one of the most common indicators of campaign success. By tracking likes, comments, shares, and other forms of interaction, businesses can assess how well the content resonates with the influencer's audience. High engagement often translates to greater visibility and reach, amplifying the brand's presence within the market.

For campaigns aimed at driving sales or lead generation, conversion tracking becomes particularly important. This can be achieved through the use of unique tracking links or promo codes that enable businesses to directly attribute sales or leads to the influencer's efforts. Analysing conversion rates provides valuable insight into the campaign's financial return on investment and helps identify which influencers are most effective in driving desired outcomes.

Beyond quantitative metrics, the qualitative impact of an influencer campaign should not be overlooked. Monitoring brand sentiment and perception in the aftermath of an influencer collaboration can provide a fuller picture of the campaign's effectiveness. Tools such as social listening platforms and sentiment analysis can help gauge the audience's response and provide valuable feedback on the overall perception of the brand. If the campaign has had a positive influence on brand sentiment, it can further solidify the business's reputation and foster greater trust among consumers.

Finally, conducting a post-campaign analysis is essential for drawing actionable insights from influencer collaborations. This involves not only comparing performance data against the set objectives but also considering qualitative feedback and overall return on investment. Through careful analysis of what worked and what didn't, businesses can refine their influencer marketing strategies, making them more targeted and effective in future campaigns.

Ultimately, a successful influencer marketing strategy hinges on a combination of carefully selected partners, authentic relationships, and data-driven insights. By working with influencers who resonate with your target audience and allowing their creativity to shine through in campaigns, businesses can build stronger, more credible connections with consumers. Moreover, the continuous refinement of strategies, based on comprehensive analysis, ensures that influencer marketing remains a dynamic and integral part of the broader marketing mix, driving tangible results and fostering long-term brand growth.

5.13 HARNESSING THE POWER OF VIDEO MARKETING AND LIVE STREAMING

In the ever-evolving world of digital marketing, video marketing and live streaming have emerged as powerful tools for engaging audiences, communicating brand messages, and fostering meaningful real-time interaction. These dynamic strategies enable brands to captivate and connect with their target markets in ways that traditional forms of media often cannot match. By crafting visually engaging content, telling compelling stories, and capitalising on the immediacy of live interaction, businesses can elevate their marketing efforts and strengthen brand loyalty.

The versatility of video content makes it a highly effective medium for various marketing objectives. Whether demonstrating a product, offering tutorials, sharing testimonials, or telling a brand's story, video content can capture and hold attention like few other formats. The rich combination of visuals, sound, and motion appeals to diverse audience preferences and can be adapted for a multitude of platforms. Whether embedded in websites, shared across social media, or integrated into email campaigns, video content significantly enhances brand visibility and audience engagement. Importantly, search engines now prioritise video content, which can improve a website's ranking on SERPs, thus contributing to better SEO outcomes. By optimising video titles, descriptions, and tags with relevant keywords, businesses can maximise the visibility of their content and improve organic traffic.

Social media platforms, such as Instagram, Facebook, and TikTok, have increasingly become video-centric, favouring video content in their algorithms and making it more likely to reach larger, more engaged audiences. This trend underscores the importance of video as a key component of any social media strategy. By integrating video content into these platforms, businesses can not only engage with their audience but also encourage shareability, expanding their reach and visibility further.

A critical aspect of successful video marketing is the art of storytelling. Rather than simply promoting products or services, businesses should aim to create compelling narratives that resonate emotionally with viewers. Stories are powerful vehicles for connecting with audiences, adding depth to a brand and making it more relatable. Whether sharing a company's origins, customer success stories, or offering behind-the-scenes insights, storytelling brings a human element to the marketing message, allowing viewers to form stronger connections with the brand. High-quality visuals that align with the brand's identity also play a pivotal role in creating a cohesive and memorable visual experience. Consistency in branding, such as using specific colour schemes, logos, and fonts, ensures that the video content reinforces brand recognition and leaves a lasting impression on the audience.

To enhance engagement, businesses can incorporate interactive elements into their videos. Features such as polls, quizzes, or clickable links encourage viewers to actively participate, transforming passive viewing into an engaging experience. This not only increases viewer retention but also provides valuable insights into audience preferences and behaviours. Additionally, every video should include a clear CTA to guide viewers towards a desired response, whether that's visiting a website, subscribing to a channel, or making a purchase. Strategically placed CTAs can dramatically improve the impact of video marketing campaigns, turning engagement into tangible results.

In addition to pre-recorded content, live streaming has emerged as a potent tool for real-time engagement. Live streaming enables businesses to create authentic, spontaneous interactions with their audiences, offering a unique level of immediacy and personal connection. Whether hosting live Q&A sessions, product launches, or offering behind-the-scenes looks at the brand, live streaming fosters a sense of urgency and exclusivity that can't be replicated through other mediums. The live format allows businesses to connect with their audience on a personal level, humanising the brand and creating a sense of community.

One of the significant advantages of live streaming is the opportunity for real-time feedback and interaction. As viewers comment and ask questions, businesses can respond immediately, creating a dynamic feedback loop that deepens engagement. This level of responsiveness enhances the sense of inclusivity and involvement, making audiences feel more connected to the brand. Moreover, live streaming is an excellent tool for amplifying events. Conferences, workshops, or product launches can be broadcast to a global audience, allowing businesses to extend the reach of their events far beyond physical attendees. Live streaming not only increases visibility but also creates additional opportunities for interaction, with virtual audiences participating in real-time from anywhere in the world.

To maximise the impact of live streaming, businesses should explore cross-platform integration, broadcasting on multiple channels simultaneously. Platforms such as Facebook Live, YouTube Live, and Instagram Live each cater to different audience demographics, so streaming across multiple platforms ensures that the content reaches a diverse and widespread audience. This multi-channel approach enhances exposure and drives higher levels of engagement, ensuring that the live stream captures the attention of as many potential customers as possible.

In conclusion, video marketing and live streaming are indispensable components of any modern digital marketing strategy. By leveraging the versatility of video, incorporating compelling storytelling techniques, and embracing the real-time interaction made possible through live streaming, businesses can significantly enhance brand visibility and foster deeper connections with their audiences. Continuously refining these strategies based on audience feedback and staying attuned to emerging trends will ensure that businesses fully harness the potential of video and live content, driving meaningful engagement and achieving long-term marketing success.

5.14 MAXIMISING ENGAGEMENT THROUGH MOBILE MARKETING AND LOCATION-BASED STRATEGIES

In an age where smartphones have become integral to daily life, mobile marketing and location-based strategies offer businesses unparalleled opportunities to engage their audiences in real time, delivering tailored experiences that are both immediate and highly relevant. With mobile users constituting a substantial portion of internet traffic, ensuring a seamless mobile experience, coupled with targeted communication and strategic geo-marketing, is crucial for any brand looking to build lasting relationships with its consumers.

The foundation of any successful mobile marketing strategy begins with a well-optimised mobile presence. Websites must be designed with responsive technology, ensuring they adapt effortlessly to various screen sizes and resolutions. A mobile-friendly interface not only enhances the UX but also reduces bounce rates and significantly improves search engine rankings. A smooth, visually appealing mobile experience is vital for retaining visitors and encouraging deeper engagement. For brands with a dedicated customer base, developing a user-friendly mobile app can deepen the relationship further. These apps should prioritise intuitive navigation, exclusive content, and features that offer value beyond what the website might provide. From streamlined purchasing processes to personalised content, apps encourage repeat usage and build loyalty through convenience. Speed is another critical factor in the mobile UX. Compressing images, eliminating unnecessary code, and ensuring pages load quickly can significantly enhance user satisfaction while also improving search engine visibility.

Beyond an optimised mobile presence, direct communication via SMS marketing and push notifications presents a highly effective means of engaging with audiences. SMS marketing boasts an impressive open rate, making it ideal for time-sensitive promotions, event reminders, or limited-time offers. Push notifications sent through apps serve a similar function, offering users instant updates that can drive immediate action. The real strength of both SMS and push notifications lies in their ability to deliver personalised messages based on user preferences, behaviours, or even location. Tailoring these communications increases their relevance and makes users more likely to engage with the content. Crucially, businesses must ensure they respect user preferences by implementing clear opt-in and opt-out mechanisms. Giving users control over their subscription to these services fosters trust and prevents the brand from appearing intrusive or spammy.

Geo-targeting and location-based advertising take mobile marketing a step further, offering businesses the ability to deliver highly relevant content based on a user's geographical location. This level of precision enables companies to tailor their marketing efforts to specific regions or even down to neighbourhoods, ensuring that promotional messages resonate with the local audience. For instance, a retail business could send a targeted offer to users when they are in proximity to their store, increasing the likelihood of an immediate visit. Contextual relevance is a key advantage of location-based marketing. Users are more likely to respond to content that speaks to their immediate surroundings or needs. This real-time interaction can be particularly effective in driving foot traffic to physical stores or encouraging on-the-spot purchases.

Emerging technologies like beacons also offer exciting possibilities for hyper-local marketing. Beacon technology, which utilises Bluetooth Low Energy (BLE), enables businesses to send notifications or offers to customers' smartphones as they enter or navigate a physical space, such as a shop or a specific area within it. This form of marketing enhances the in-store experience, driving customer engagement by delivering highly personalised and timely content. Social media also plays a pivotal role in location-based strategies. Encouraging users to tag their location when sharing content related to your business can amplify the reach of your brand and serve as valuable word-of-mouth marketing. User-generated content with geographical context not only boosts your brand's visibility but also adds an authentic, peer-recommended quality to your marketing efforts.

Incorporating mobile marketing and location-based strategies into a broader digital marketing approach is no longer a luxury but a necessity. These tactics offer businesses the ability to create more personalised, immediate, and relevant interactions with their audiences. From mobile-optimised websites and apps to tailored SMS messages and precise geo-targeting, these strategies are integral to delivering superior UXs and driving engagement. As the technological landscape continues to evolve, businesses must remain agile and responsive, leveraging these tools to stay ahead in an increasingly mobile-first world.

5.15 EVALUATING AND OPTIMISING DIGITAL MARKETING PERFORMANCE

In today's rapidly evolving digital landscape, the ability to accurately measure marketing performance is essential for sustained success. A comprehensive evaluation process not only reveals how effectively strategies are working but also highlights areas for improvement. This is achieved through a thorough understanding of KPIs, the use of advanced web analytics, and a commitment to data-driven decision-making, all of which combine to create a responsive and continuously optimised marketing approach.

The foundation of effective measurement lies in the establishment of clear and relevant KPIs. These metrics must align directly with broader business goals, whether the aim is to increase brand visibility, boost lead generation, improve conversion rates, or enhance customer retention. KPIs should be specific and measurable, allowing businesses to track performance with clarity and precision. Vague targets like "increase traffic" are unhelpful, but specifying a goal such as "boost organic traffic by 20% over the next three months" provides a tangible benchmark for success. As each marketing channel serves different purposes, KPIs must be tailored accordingly. For instance, social media may be evaluated on engagement and follower growth, while email marketing's effectiveness could be measured by open and click-through rates. This differentiation ensures that all digital marketing efforts are being accurately gauged in alignment with their specific roles.

In addition to setting and monitoring KPIs, web analytics and conversion tracking play pivotal roles in evaluating performance. Web analytics tools, like Google Analytics, offer businesses a wealth of information, from traffic volumes and user behaviours to bounce rates and time spent on pages. These insights reveal the effectiveness of various marketing efforts, indicating which channels are driving traffic and which are falling short. Conversion tracking, in particular, is indispensable for assessing how well digital marketing initiatives are meeting their goals. Whether the target is a completed purchase, a form submission, or a newsletter sign-up, tracking conversions provides a clear indication of success and reveals the effectiveness of each step in the customer journey.

Furthermore, attribution models provide essential insights into which marketing touchpoints contribute most significantly to conversions. These models—whether first-touch, last-touch, or multi-touch—allow marketers to understand which interactions are the most influential. This understanding is invaluable for optimising resource allocation and refining future strategies, ensuring that the right channels receive the right level of investment.

The final component of an effective digital marketing evaluation process is a commitment to data-driven decision-making and ongoing optimisation. Performance data must be continuously monitored to identify trends, opportunities, and underperforming areas. This proactive approach to analysis allows businesses to make timely adjustments, keeping campaigns relevant and aligned with evolving market conditions. A/B testing serves as a critical tool in this process, enabling marketers to experiment with different variables—whether content, design, or placement—before committing to a final strategy. By comparing the performance of these variations, businesses can determine which elements resonate most with their audience and adjust their strategies accordingly.

Ultimately, optimisation is not a one-off event but a continuous process that evolves in response to the data gathered. Insights gained from both web analytics and testing should be applied iteratively, driving constant improvements to campaigns, UX, and overall strategy. This agility ensures that businesses remain competitive, responsive to customer behaviour, and able to adapt to the ever-shifting digital environment.

In essence, measuring digital marketing performance is an ongoing, multi-dimensional process. By defining relevant KPIs, using web analytics and conversion tracking effectively, and embracing a data-driven mindset, businesses can fine-tune their strategies and maximise their return on investment. This iterative approach empowers companies to stay at the forefront of digital marketing, ensuring long-term success and resilience in a competitive landscape.

5.16 NAVIGATING COMPLIANCE AND ETHICAL STANDARDS IN DIGITAL MARKETING

As digital marketing continues to expand in reach and sophistication, the need to prioritise compliance and ethical standards has become increasingly significant. A successful and reputable business must navigate the complexities of privacy regulations, maintain transparency in its marketing practices, and adhere to ethical principles that foster trust and long-term loyalty.

Privacy and data protection regulations lie at the heart of responsible digital marketing. With laws such as the General Data Protection Regulation in Europe and the California Consumer Privacy Act in the United States, businesses must stay informed and compliant with the specific legal frameworks governing the regions in which they operate. Compliance not only serves to avoid legal penalties but also plays a crucial role in earning and maintaining consumer trust. It is essential to be transparent in the collection and use of personal data. Users should be informed about what information is being gathered, how it will be utilised, and be given the opportunity to grant explicit consent. Equally important is the responsibility to ensure secure handling of data by implementing robust security measures, such as encryption and regular updates, to prevent unauthorised access or data breaches.

In addition to regulatory compliance, digital marketers must adhere to industry guidelines and best practices. This begins with a commitment to honesty and accuracy. Marketing content should never mislead or deceive consumers with false claims or exaggerated promises.

Establishing credibility through transparent communication helps build trust, and a brand that is perceived as reliable is more likely to enjoy long-term success. Responsible targeting is another critical aspect, as businesses must avoid exploiting vulnerable groups or employing manipulative tactics. Instead, inclusivity and fairness should guide all marketing efforts, ensuring a respectful and considerate approach to diverse audiences. Furthermore, any disclosures or disclaimers must be easily understood and visible, whether involving sponsored content or terms and conditions, to preserve transparency and avoid confusion or distrust.

Ethical marketing demands authenticity and accountability. A brand's communications should always reflect its values and offerings honestly, without misleading representations or creating unrealistic expectations. Authenticity cultivates consumer trust and positions a brand as one that can be relied upon. Moreover, businesses have an opportunity to demonstrate social responsibility by embracing sustainable practices and highlighting eco-friendly initiatives in their messaging. This not only resonates with ethically minded consumers but also enhances the brand's social standing. It is vital to ensure that terms and conditions related to products or services are communicated clearly, leaving no room for ambiguity or fine-print surprises. Transparency around pricing, return policies, and potential limitations ensures that consumers make informed decisions, which, in turn, reduces dissatisfaction.

Monitoring and responding to consumer feedback is equally important in maintaining a brand's ethical integrity. Engaging with customer concerns, particularly on social media and review platforms, demonstrates a commitment to customer satisfaction and an openness to continuous improvement. By addressing issues promptly and transparently, brands show accountability, which further strengthens their ethical reputation.

In conclusion, compliance with privacy regulations and ethical marketing practices is essential to building a trusted brand in today's digital world. By prioritising transparency, responsible targeting, and authenticity, businesses not only ensure legal compliance but also establish a foundation of trust, loyalty, and long-term success. Ethical marketing is not just about following the rules; it is about creating meaningful, honest connections with consumers in an increasingly competitive landscape.

5.17 CHAPTER SUMMARY

In the ever-evolving digital marketplace, businesses must remain agile and responsive to the rapid changes in consumer behaviour and technological advancements. The strategies and tools explored in this chapter underscore the importance of a holistic approach to digital marketing. Whether it's through effective SEO, the crafting of compelling content, or leveraging the power of social media and PPC advertising, digital marketing offers unparalleled opportunities to connect with a target audience in meaningful and measurable ways. Businesses that are able to harness these tools strategically will not only increase their visibility but also foster lasting relationships with their customers.

As demonstrated in this chapter, the foundation of any successful digital marketing strategy lies in a deep understanding of the consumer journey, careful audience segmentation, and a commitment to delivering value through relevant, engaging content. Moreover, adhering to ethical guidelines and compliance regulations ensures that digital marketing efforts remain responsible and sustainable in the long run. This chapter has also highlighted the importance of integrating multiple platforms and approaches, including video marketing, mobile marketing, and influencer strategies, to achieve maximum reach and engagement. By applying these insights and strategies, businesses can successfully navigate the complexities of the digital landscape and continue to thrive in a competitive environment.

Key Questions for Discussion

1. How has the role of digital marketing evolved in the modern business environment, and why is it critical for businesses to adopt a digital-first approach to reach their target audiences?
2. What tools and techniques can businesses use to gain a deeper understanding of their target audience? How does this knowledge shape the effectiveness of their digital marketing strategies?
3. How can businesses balance SEO and PPC strategies to maximise visibility and digital success? What are the key differences in their application, and when should one be prioritised over the other?
4. How can businesses leverage social media platforms and influencer partnerships to connect with their audience authentically? What challenges and ethical considerations arise in the realm of influencer marketing?
5. What metrics and tools should businesses focus on to evaluate the success of their digital marketing campaigns? How can they ensure continuous improvement and stay aligned with evolving consumer behaviours and market trends?

BIBLIOGRAPHY

Baer, J. (2023). *Hug Your Haters: How to Embrace Complaints and Keep Your Customers*. Penguin.

Barker, M., Barker, D.I., Bormann, N.F. and Neher, K.E. (2023). *Social Media Marketing: A Strategic Approach*. 3rd ed. Cengage Learning.

Berger, J. (2023). *Contagious: How to Build Word of Mouth in the Digital Age*. Simon & Schuster.

Chaffey, D. and Ellis-Chadwick, F. (2022). *Digital Marketing: Strategy, Implementation and Practice*. 8th ed. Pearson.

Charlesworth, A. (2022). *Digital Marketing: A Practical Approach*. 3rd ed. Routledge.

Dodson, I. (2023). *The Art of Digital Marketing: The Definitive Guide to Creating Strategic, Targeted, and Measurable Online Campaigns*. 2nd ed. Wiley.

Fishkin, R. and Wiesenberg, A. (2023). *Lost and Founder: A Painfully Honest Field Guide to the Startup World*. Penguin.

Godin, S. (2023). *This Is Marketing: You Can't Be Seen Until You Learn to See*. Portfolio.

Halligan, B. and Shah, D. (2023). *Inbound Marketing: Attract, Engage, and Delight Customers Online*. 2nd ed. Wiley.

Handley, A. (2022). *Everybody Writes: Your Go-To Guide to Creating Ridiculously Good Content*. 2nd ed. Wiley.

Holiday, R. (2023). *Growth Hacker Marketing: A Primer on the Future of PR, Marketing, and Advertising.* Revised ed. Penguin.
Kingsnorth, S. (2022). *Digital Marketing Strategy: An Integrated Approach to Online Marketing.* 3rd ed. Kogan Page.
Kotler, P., Kartajaya, H. and Setiawan, I. (2023). *Marketing 5.0: Technology for Humanity.* Wiley.
Miller, M. (2023). *B2B Digital Marketing: Using the Web to Market Directly to Businesses.* 2nd ed. Que Publishing.
Patel, N. and Goh, P. (2023). *Hustle: The Power to Charge Your Life with Money, Meaning, and Momentum.* Rodale Books.
Pulizzi, J. (2023). *Content Inc.: Start a Content-First Business, Build a Massive Audience and Become Radically Successful (with Little to No Money).* 2nd ed. McGraw-Hill.
Ryan, D. (2023). *Understanding Digital Marketing: Marketing Strategies for Engaging the Digital Generation.* 5th ed. Kogan Page.
Tuten, T.L. and Solomon, M.R. (2023). *Social Media Marketing.* 4th ed. Sage.

CHAPTER 6

Creating a Strong Online Presence

Website Design and Development

Learning Objectives

By the end of this chapter, you will be able to:

1. Understand the core principles of website design and development, including human-centred design, mobile optimisation, and performance enhancement to create user-friendly and efficient online platforms.
2. Learn the techniques for improving website visibility through SEO strategies and ensuring accessibility for all users by incorporating inclusive web design principles.
3. Gain insights into the importance of website security, user data protection, and post-launch management to maintain a dynamic, secure, and high-performing website.

6.1 INTRODUCTION

In an increasingly digital world, a well-designed website is often the first interaction that potential clients, customers, or audiences have with a business or individual. The necessity of creating a strong online presence has become undeniable, as websites are no longer just an extension of a business—they are integral to its identity and success. This chapter aims to provide a comprehensive understanding of website design and development, beginning with the foundational principles necessary to build a dynamic and effective online presence.

At its core, successful website design and development require a clear understanding of a website's objectives and the alignment of these goals with broader business strategies. Crafting a user-friendly experience is equally crucial, as human-centred design ensures that a website resonates with its audience, engages users, and guides them effortlessly through their online journey. Responsive design, in particular, plays a critical role in ensuring that the website functions optimally across a wide range of devices, while performance and speed optimisation guarantee that the site meets the fast-paced demands of today's users.

As the digital landscape grows increasingly complex, it is vital to ensure that websites are built on solid technological foundations, optimised for search engines, accessible to all users, and secure from cyber threats. This chapter will also delve into the ongoing challenges

DOI: 10.4324/9781032672458-6

of maintaining a dynamic website after launch, providing practical guidance on how to ensure long-term success and relevance in an ever-changing digital environment.

6.2 BUILDING A DYNAMIC ONLINE PRESENCE: THE FUNDAMENTALS OF WEBSITE DESIGN AND DEVELOPMENT

In today's digital age, creating a strong online presence is essential for any business aiming to succeed in an increasingly competitive marketplace. The foundation of this presence lies in the design and development of an effective website that not only draws users in but also reflects the brand's identity and values. This chapter explores the multifaceted aspects of website design and development, examining the profound impact that a well-crafted website can have on a business's overall success. From understanding the significance of an online presence to the essential components that form an effective website, this section provides an in-depth look into how businesses can strategically leverage their websites for growth and engagement.

A company's website is more than a simple digital presence; it is the brand's virtual shopfront, often the first point of interaction for potential customers. As the majority of consumers now turn to the internet for product research, services, and transactions, a robust online presence is a necessity. A well-executed website not only heightens brand visibility but also fosters credibility and trust among users. It acts as a gateway that is accessible at all times, allowing consumers to explore and engage with the brand's offerings on their own terms. Beyond increasing visibility, an effective online presence can significantly enhance customer retention and acquisition, leaving an indelible mark that extends beyond the virtual sphere.

The role of website design within digital business cannot be understated. It is the cornerstone of any successful digital strategy, influencing not only the user's experience but also shaping how a brand is perceived. Effective website design is not merely about visual aesthetics; it takes into account the entire user journey. With seamless navigation, an intuitive user interface (UI), and a focus on user experience (UX), a well-designed website ensures that visitors interact with the brand in a meaningful and engaging way. This strategic element of digital marketing extends beyond simply showcasing the brand, as it directly supports business objectives, such as increasing conversions and driving sales. Integrating features like e-commerce capabilities, ensuring responsiveness across devices, and optimising for search engines are crucial in delivering a design that positively affects the business's performance.

To build a successful website, careful consideration must be given to several key components, which collectively determine the site's effectiveness. At the forefront is a user-centric design. Prioritising the needs and preferences of the target audience ensures that visitors can navigate easily, find information effortlessly, and complete desired actions seamlessly. The design should also be responsive, meaning it must adapt to a variety of screen sizes and resolutions, given the ubiquity of mobile devices. This responsiveness is critical to maintaining an optimal UX and reaching a broader audience (Figure 6.1).

FIGURE 6.1 Key Steps to Establishing a Strong Online Presence

Content remains the backbone of any website, as it provides value to visitors while supporting search engine optimisation (SEO) efforts. Engaging and relevant content encourages users to spend more time on the site and keeps them coming back. In cases where e-commerce functionality is involved, such as online stores, integrating secure payment gateways and user-friendly shopping experiences is essential. Lastly, no website is complete without proper SEO implementation, which ensures that the site ranks well in search results, driving organic traffic and improving its overall discoverability.

In conclusion, the design and development of a website form the bedrock of a strong online presence. By understanding the critical role a website plays in digital business and implementing key elements such as user-focused design, responsiveness, compelling content, e-commerce integration, and SEO optimisation, businesses can position themselves for success. These strategies enable businesses not only to captivate their audience but also to thrive in the competitive digital marketplace. A well-designed website does far more than act as a marketing tool—it becomes a powerful asset that drives growth, engagement, and long-term success in the digital era.

6.3 STRATEGIC ALIGNMENT: DEFINING CLEAR WEBSITE GOALS AND OBJECTIVES

In the fast-paced and continuously evolving digital environment, a website's success is inherently dependent on the clarity and precision with which its goals and objectives are outlined. The strategic process of defining these aspects is crucial to ensuring the website not only fulfils its purpose but also aligns with broader business objectives, contributing to overall growth and success. This section delves into the critical steps involved in identifying the website's purpose, establishing clear objectives, and ensuring these are seamlessly integrated with an organisation's wider goals.

Before engaging with the complexities of design and development, it is essential to understand the primary purpose of the website. Whether the aim is to showcase products and services, facilitate lead generation, provide information, or drive e-commerce transactions, a clear understanding of this purpose forms the foundation for all further decisions. The role the website plays varies significantly depending on its purpose. An information-driven site, for example, will likely prioritise content presentation and user education, while an e-commerce platform will focus on seamless navigation, secure payment options, and an intuitive shopping experience. A well-defined purpose ensures that the website is tailored to meet specific user needs and operates in alignment with the business's overarching goals.

Once the purpose has been clearly articulated, the next step involves setting well-defined objectives that provide a measurable pathway to success. Objectives should follow the SMART framework—Specific, Measurable, Achievable, Relevant, and Time-bound—to ensure that they are clear and actionable. For example, if the primary aim of a website is to drive lead generation, one of the objectives could be to increase the number of newsletter sign-ups by a specific percentage over a set period. These objectives must be concrete and offer a way to evaluate the website's effectiveness in meeting its intended outcomes.

In tandem with setting objectives, identifying key performance indicators (KPIs) is crucial. KPIs serve as quantifiable measures that track the progress towards the goals. Metrics such as website traffic, conversion rates, bounce rates, and user engagement offer valuable insights into the performance of the website and provide guidance for further optimisation. Regularly tracking these indicators enables businesses to assess whether their strategies are effective and allows for adjustments to be made where necessary.

For a website to be more than just a digital front and to contribute meaningfully to the organisation's success, its goals must align closely with the broader objectives of the business. This strategic alignment ensures that the website is not an isolated online entity but rather a dynamic asset that supports the overall business mission. For instance, if a business's objective is to increase online sales, the website's goals must focus on enhancing the e-commerce experience, improving conversion rates, and maximising the customer's lifetime value. Furthermore, the alignment extends beyond performance metrics and encompasses the entire UX, ensuring that the website supports the brand narrative and remains consistent with the company's values and long-term aspirations.

Ultimately, the process of defining website goals and objectives goes far beyond aesthetics or basic functionality. It requires a nuanced understanding of both the digital landscape and the business's strategic vision. A successful website is a dynamic tool, with its purpose, objectives, and KPIs meticulously tailored to meet both user needs and organisational aims. By identifying its core purpose, establishing measurable objectives, and aligning these with broader business goals, a website becomes a pivotal element in an organisation's digital strategy. This strategic approach ensures that the website not only performs optimally but also drives the business forward, making it a key differentiator in the competitive digital space.

6.4 HUMAN-CENTRED DESIGN: CRAFTING UX THAT ENGAGE AND DELIGHT

In the world of website design and development, user-centred design (UCD) principles form the bedrock of creating digital experiences that resonate deeply with users. By prioritising the user's needs, behaviours, and expectations at every step of the design journey, UCD fosters meaningful connections between the user and the digital environment. This comprehensive approach considers not only the visual and functional elements of a website but also the emotional and psychological aspects that influence how users interact with digital platforms. Central to this approach are the principles of UX design, user research, and the application of UCD throughout the entire design process.

At the heart of UCD lies the concept of UX design, which extends beyond aesthetics to focus on how users feel when navigating a website. In today's digital age, where attention spans are short and competition is fierce, delivering a positive UX is no longer optional—it is essential. A well-executed UX design creates an intuitive, responsive, and enjoyable experience for users, ensuring they can navigate the site effortlessly, find information with ease, and complete desired tasks seamlessly. It involves crafting a user journey that is not only functional but emotionally satisfying, guiding users smoothly from entry to action. UX design weaves together elements such as ease of navigation, visual clarity, and interaction flow to create a holistic experience that aligns with user expectations and leaves a lasting impression. The ultimate goal of UX is to foster a positive emotional connection between the user and the brand, enhancing engagement and encouraging return visits.

Central to UCD is a deep understanding of the target audience, which is achieved through comprehensive user research. This research is the cornerstone of effective design, as it allows designers to step into the shoes of users, identifying their needs, preferences, and pain points. Employing techniques such as surveys, interviews, and analytics tools, user research provides invaluable insights into how users interact with websites, what frustrates them, and what they find rewarding. Through this research, user personas are developed—fictional representations of different audience segments, embodying the characteristics, goals, and behaviours of real users. These personas are essential tools for guiding design decisions, allowing designers to create tailored experiences that cater to the distinct needs of various user groups. For example, the design for a tech-savvy, time-conscious millennial might prioritise streamlined functionality and quick access to information, while a more experienced professional might require in-depth resources and a more thorough presentation of information.

The application of UCD principles is not confined to the initial stages of design but is an ongoing, iterative process that informs every phase of website development. From early conceptualisation to final implementation, UCD provides a framework that ensures the user remains at the centre of every decision. Wireframing and prototyping play crucial roles in this process, allowing designers to map out the user journey, visualise layout structures, and test the site's functionality before development is fully underway. These early models provide a tangible representation of the website's design and flow, enabling designers to identify potential issues and refine solutions before significant resources are invested.

Usability testing further strengthens the design process by gathering real-world feedback on the effectiveness and intuitiveness of the website. By involving actual users in testing, designers can observe how people interact with the site, identify any pain points, and make necessary adjustments to improve the experience. This iterative process ensures that the final product is not only functional but also optimised to meet user expectations. Equally important is the need for responsive design, a fundamental aspect of UCD that ensures the website adapts seamlessly across various devices and screen sizes. With users accessing websites from an array of devices, from desktop computers to smartphones, a responsive design is crucial for delivering a consistent and engaging experience, regardless of the platform.

Ultimately, UCD is more than just a design methodology—it is a philosophy that champions the user as the focal point of the design process. By integrating user research, personas, iterative design, prototyping, testing, and responsive design, UCD ensures that websites not only function efficiently but also provide a meaningful and satisfying experience for the people who use them. In a digital landscape where user loyalty is earned through exceptional experiences, UCD serves as the guiding principle that enables designers to craft websites that truly resonate with and engage their audience, ensuring long-term success.

CASE STUDY 6

Airbnb's User-Centric Website Design—Enhancing the Digital Experience

Airbnb has revolutionised the hospitality industry by creating a digital platform that connects travellers with hosts offering unique accommodation options. A key factor in the company's success has been its commitment to a seamless, user-centric website design that prioritises intuitive navigation, high-quality visuals, and personalised recommendations. In an increasingly competitive market, Airbnb recognised the need to enhance its online experience to attract more users, increase bookings, and strengthen trust between hosts and guests. The primary challenge was ensuring that both travellers and property owners could easily navigate the platform, find relevant listings, and complete transactions smoothly. Given the global nature of Airbnb's operations, the platform also needed to be scalable, responsive across multiple devices, and capable of handling complex search filters and user-generated content.

To address these challenges, Airbnb implemented a design strategy focused on simplicity, efficiency, and engagement. The company introduced a clean and minimalistic interface that makes it easy for users to search for properties, refine their preferences, and make bookings in just a few clicks. High-quality visuals, including professional photography and immersive virtual tours, were integrated to help travellers make informed decisions. Personalisation became another critical component, with Airbnb using AI and machine learning to analyse user behaviour and provide tailored recommendations based on previous searches and preferences. The platform's review and rating system was also enhanced to build trust, allowing guests to read genuine feedback from past stays. Additionally, Airbnb optimised its website for mobile users, ensuring a seamless experience across devices.

These enhancements produced significant results. Airbnb's website improvements led to higher engagement rates, increased booking conversions, and greater user satisfaction. The intuitive interface reduced friction in the booking process, resulting in faster transactions and lower bounce rates. The use of high-quality visuals and detailed property descriptions helped increase trust among users, encouraging more hosts to list their properties. Furthermore, AI-driven personalisation enhanced the UX by delivering relevant search results and recommendations, making it easier for travellers to find accommodation that suited their needs. The focus on mobile responsiveness also contributed to a higher percentage of bookings being made via smartphones, aligning with changing consumer behaviour.

Airbnb's success in website design highlights several key lessons. A seamless and intuitive interface enhances user engagement and encourages higher conversion rates. High-quality visuals and detailed property information help build trust, which is essential in online marketplaces. Personalisation powered by AI and machine learning improves user satisfaction by delivering tailored experiences. Finally, mobile optimisation is crucial in today's digital landscape, ensuring that businesses cater to the growing number of users who browse and book via smartphones.

Discussion Questions for Students (with Indicative Answers)

1. **How has Airbnb's user-centric website design contributed to its success?**
   Indicative Answer: Airbnb's intuitive navigation, high-quality visuals, and personalised recommendations make it easy for users to find and book accommodations, leading to increased engagement and bookings.
2. **Why is personalisation important in website design, and how does Airbnb use it?**
   Indicative Answer: Personalisation improves the UX by providing relevant recommendations based on browsing history and preferences. Airbnb uses AI and machine learning to tailor search results, making it easier for travellers to find suitable listings.

3. **How do high-quality visuals and reviews enhance trust in Airbnb's platform?**
   Indicative Answer: Professional photos, virtual tours, and guest reviews provide transparency and credibility, helping potential guests make informed decisions and encouraging hosts to maintain high standards.
4. **What role does mobile optimisation play in Airbnb's digital strategy?**
   Indicative Answer: Mobile optimisation ensures a seamless experience for users on smartphones and tablets, leading to higher engagement and conversions, as more travellers book accommodations via mobile devices.
5. **What lessons can other businesses learn from Airbnb's approach to website design?**
   Indicative Answer: Businesses should focus on user-friendly navigation, personalisation, high-quality visuals, and mobile responsiveness to enhance the customer experience and drive conversions in the digital marketplace.

6.5 CRAFTING SEAMLESS DIGITAL EXPERIENCES: THE ESSENTIAL ROLE OF RESPONSIVE WEB DESIGN AND MOBILE OPTIMISATION

In today's fast-paced digital landscape, where users access websites across a multitude of devices, from smartphones and tablets to desktops and laptops, the importance of responsive web design and mobile optimisation cannot be overstated. Ensuring that websites function seamlessly on a range of screen sizes is no longer a luxury but an absolute necessity for any business aiming to remain competitive. This section explores the critical significance of mobile-friendly design, the techniques involved in responsive web development, and the best practices for optimising websites specifically for mobile devices.

As smartphones and tablets become the dominant tools for browsing the internet, having a mobile-friendly website has shifted from a convenience to a strategic imperative. A growing majority of users interact with websites primarily through mobile devices, meaning that businesses must prioritise delivering a consistently positive experience across all platforms. A failure to optimise for mobile use can lead to a host of issues, including sluggish loading times, distorted or inaccessible content, and clunky navigation, all of which can frustrate users and drive them away. In contrast, a mobile-optimised website responds effortlessly to the smaller screens of mobile devices, ensuring a consistent and enjoyable experience that is not only aesthetically pleasing but also highly functional.

The importance of mobile-friendliness goes beyond UX—it plays a crucial role in SEO. Search engines, particularly Google, have made it clear that mobile-friendly websites are prioritised in search rankings. Websites that fail to meet mobile usability standards are often penalised, leading to lower search engine visibility, reduced organic traffic, and a subsequent dip in online success. As such, businesses that invest in mobile optimisation are not only enhancing the UX but also improving their search rankings and digital footprint.

To achieve mobile-friendly websites, responsive design has emerged as the key approach. Responsive web design ensures that websites dynamically adapt to different screen sizes and resolutions, delivering a consistent UX regardless of the device being used. The core of responsive design lies in the flexibility it offers, allowing the same website to look and function optimally on both large desktop screens and smaller mobile devices. A critical element of this adaptability is the use of fluid grids, which enable layouts to resize proportionally according to the screen's dimensions. This ensures that website content remains visually cohesive and accessible, regardless of the device being used.

Equally important is the optimisation of images. By ensuring that images can scale proportionally within their designated spaces, designers prevent distortion and maintain visual clarity. Using CSS techniques, images are made responsive, contributing to the overall fluidity and appeal of the design. Furthermore, media queries play a pivotal role in responsive design, allowing designers to apply different styles based on the device's characteristics. This means that factors such as screen width, resolution, and orientation can be accounted for, enabling designers to customise the UX for each device type.

An increasingly popular method in responsive web design is the mobile-first approach, which prioritises the design and functionality for mobile devices before scaling up to larger screens. This strategy ensures that the core experience is crafted with the mobile user in mind, making it particularly suited to the growing number of users who access the internet primarily through smartphones. By starting with mobile design, developers can focus on the essentials, stripping away unnecessary elements and creating a clean, efficient UX that is then enhanced for larger devices.

Beyond responsive design, mobile optimisation involves fine-tuning various aspects of the website to enhance its performance, functionality, and overall experience on mobile devices. One of the most critical factors in mobile optimisation is loading time. Mobile users are less tolerant of delays, and a slow-loading website can quickly lead to high bounce rates. Optimising images, utilising browser caching, and minimising extraneous scripts are all effective methods to improve page speed and create a more efficient UX.

Another vital consideration is navigation. For mobile users, navigating a website should be intuitive and straightforward, with clear menus and prominent calls to action. Simplifying the structure and content ensures that users can quickly find what they are looking for without unnecessary scrolling or searching. In addition, touch-friendly design is essential. Since mobile devices rely on touchscreens, interactive elements such as buttons and links must be appropriately sized and spaced to accommodate touch gestures. This prevents user frustration and ensures a smooth, fluid interaction with the site.

Finally, for websites that incorporate forms, it is crucial to optimise these for mobile devices. Filling out forms on mobile screens can be a cumbersome process if not properly designed. Reducing the number of required fields, using appropriate input methods, and incorporating features such as auto-complete can greatly enhance the UX during data entry.

In conclusion, responsive web design and mobile optimisation are indispensable components of any successful digital strategy. By recognising the importance of mobile-friendly websites, implementing responsive design techniques, and following best practices for mobile optimisation, businesses can ensure that their websites are accessible, adaptable, and effective across a variety of devices. As the digital world continues to evolve, placing mobile-friendliness at the forefront of web design is not merely a trend but a necessity, offering businesses the opportunity to thrive in an increasingly competitive and device-diverse ecosystem.

6.6 BUILDING THE FOUNDATIONS: WEBSITE DEVELOPMENT AND THE TECHNOLOGIES BEHIND IT

The development phase represents the core of website creation, where every strategic decision regarding platforms, coding languages, and the integration of databases determines the functionality, performance, and long-term success of the final product. This process involves a delicate balance of choosing the right development platform, understanding the intricacies of front-end technologies like HTML, CSS, and JavaScript, and mastering back-end development, which encompasses database integration and server-side technologies. The synergy between these elements forms the foundation of a well-built website, designed to meet both business needs and user expectations.

Selecting the appropriate web development platform is one of the most critical decisions in the entire development process, as it significantly impacts the website's scalability, functionality, and ease of maintenance. Broadly, platforms fall into two categories: content management systems (CMS) and custom development. CMS platforms such as WordPress, Joomla, and Drupal are widely popular for their user-friendly interfaces that simplify content management and ongoing website updates. These platforms come with a variety of themes, templates, and plugins, offering an accessible entry point for businesses focused on content-driven sites. However, while CMS solutions provide quick and cost-effective ways to launch and manage a site, they often come with limitations on customisation. On the other hand, custom development allows for a website to be built entirely from the ground up, tailored to specific business needs. This approach provides unparalleled flexibility, where every detail, feature, and function is designed to meet exact specifications. Custom development is particularly suitable for large-scale enterprises or complex projects with unique requirements. Ultimately, the choice between CMS and custom development depends on factors such as the complexity of the project, the budget, scalability needs, and the level of control desired. Aligning this choice with the long-term goals of the website ensures a sound decision that supports future growth and adaptability.

The front-end development process is where the user-facing aspect of the website is constructed, shaping the visual elements and interactions that users engage with. Hypertext Markup Language (HTML), CSS, and JavaScript form the backbone of front-end development, each playing a vital role in the website's appearance and functionality. HTML is the foundational structure of every webpage, organising content through the use of tags like headings, paragraphs, images, and links. It serves as the scaffolding that browsers rely on to render the various components of a web page. CSS (Cascading Style Sheets) is the styling layer that determines how this HTML content is presented visually. By controlling the layout, colour schemes, typography, and spacing, CSS ensures that the website is not only aesthetically pleasing but also responsive and functional across different devices. It allows developers to create consistent, polished designs that maintain their integrity, whether viewed on a desktop or a mobile device. JavaScript adds another layer of functionality to the front-end, bringing interactivity and dynamic behaviour to websites. As a versatile scripting language, it allows developers to incorporate features such as real-time updates, animations, and client-side form validation. JavaScript frameworks and libraries, like React, Angular, and Vue.js, have become central to modern web development, empowering developers to create more complex and seamless UX. The combined power of HTML, CSS, and JavaScript enables the creation of responsive and visually engaging websites that meet design specifications while ensuring an intuitive and enjoyable UX.

While front-end development concerns itself with the elements users see and interact with, back-end development handles the hidden, server-side functionalities that support the website's logic, data storage, and complex operations. Database integration is a critical component of the back-end, allowing websites to store, retrieve, and manage data efficiently. Popular databases like MySQL, PostgreSQL, and MongoDB each serve different needs based on the structure and scalability requirements of the application. The choice of database depends largely on the nature of the data being handled and how it needs to be accessed and managed. Alongside database integration, server-side technologies form the backbone of back-end development. Server-side scripting languages such as PHP, Python, Ruby, and Node.js perform a variety of essential functions, including handling requests from users, interacting with databases, and generating dynamic content. These languages enable websites to deliver personalised, data-driven experiences, from e-commerce shopping carts to user authentication systems. To expedite development and provide structure, many developers use frameworks built upon these languages. Frameworks such as Laravel for PHP, Django for Python, and Express.js for Node.js streamline the development process by offering pre-built modules, conventions, and best practices. This not only accelerates development but also ensures that the final product is robust, secure, and scalable. The selection of server-side technologies must take into account the specific requirements of the project, the expertise of the development team, and the need for future scalability.

In essence, website development is a multifaceted journey that requires careful consideration at every step. From the initial decision on which platform to use—whether it be a CMS or custom-built solution—to the mastery of front-end technologies like HTML, CSS, and JavaScript, and the navigation of complex back-end tasks such as database integration and server-side scripting, each decision plays a crucial role in the overall success of the website. As the digital landscape continues to evolve, staying abreast of technological trends and making informed choices ensures that websites remain adaptable, secure, and capable of delivering an exceptional UX. By aligning development strategies with both business goals and user expectations, companies can build websites that are not only functional but also transformative in their ability to engage, convert, and retain users.

6.7 MAXIMISING WEBSITE EFFICIENCY: THE IMPERATIVE OF PERFORMANCE AND SPEED OPTIMISATION

In today's fast-moving digital world, where user expectations are increasingly demanding, the performance and speed of a website are critical determinants of success. A well-optimised site not only boosts user satisfaction but also influences engagement, search rankings, and conversion rates. Understanding the pivotal role of loading speed, employing advanced techniques to enhance performance, and leveraging specialised tools to monitor and analyse speed are key components in building and maintaining a high-performing website.

The speed at which a website loads has become one of the primary factors shaping a user's overall experience. In an environment where users expect immediate access to information, even a few seconds of delay can significantly alter their perception of a brand. A slow-loading site tends to frustrate users, leading to increased bounce rates and a diminished UX. The fast pace at which users expect sites to load directly impacts their patience, with many abandoning pages that fail to load within seconds. Moreover, speed is an essential factor in SEO. Google, for instance, has incorporated website speed into its ranking algorithms, meaning that faster sites are more likely to rank higher in search results. This can result in greater visibility and increased organic traffic. From a business perspective, the connection between speed and conversion rates is undeniable. A fast website ensures a seamless user journey, increasing the likelihood of users completing desired actions, whether that be purchasing products, submitting forms, or engaging with content. The rise of mobile browsing further underscores the importance of speed optimisation. Users accessing websites on mobile devices are often working with slower network speeds, making it even more crucial to ensure that websites are optimised for rapid loading across all devices.

Enhancing website performance requires a strategic approach that addresses various aspects of website architecture, content delivery, and resource management. One of the primary areas of focus is image optimisation. Images, while visually essential, often contribute to slower loading times if not managed correctly. Compressing images, using the right file formats, and employing techniques like lazy loading, where images load only when they are needed, can dramatically improve site speed without sacrificing quality. Another important method is the minification of CSS, JavaScript, and HTML files. By removing unnecessary characters such as spaces and comments from these files, their size is reduced, allowing for quicker downloads and faster page rendering. Browser caching is another powerful technique, enabling commonly accessed resources to be stored locally on users' devices, reducing the need for repeated downloads on subsequent visits. Content delivery networks play a crucial role in reducing latency and enhancing speed by distributing content across servers around the globe. With static content cached on multiple servers, users can access website elements faster, regardless of their location. Optimising server performance also plays a central role in website speed. Selecting a reliable hosting provider, fine-tuning server configurations, and using server-side caching mechanisms all contribute to better server response times. Minimising HTTP requests is another key technique. By reducing the number of elements a browser needs to request to load a page, the site's speed can be significantly improved. This can be achieved by combining CSS and JavaScript files or by using image sprites to reduce the number of image requests.

Measuring and analysing website speed is an essential part of the optimisation process. Several tools provide detailed insights into a website's performance, offering actionable recommendations to improve speed. Google PageSpeed Insights is one of the most popular tools for evaluating performance on both desktop and mobile devices. It provides a performance score based on factors such as image optimisation, server response times, and resource loading, offering clear suggestions for improvement. GTmetrix is another powerful tool that provides an in-depth analysis of page load times, page size, and the number of requests. It also generates specific recommendations for improving performance across various elements of the website. Pingdom, which monitors both website performance and uptime, offers insights into load times and performance grades, identifying potential bottlenecks that slow down the UX. WebPageTest, an open-source tool, allows users to run speed tests from multiple locations and devices, producing a comprehensive report that includes detailed waterfall charts and filmstrip views of the entire loading process. Lighthouse, built into Google Chrome's DevTools, offers a more holistic assessment by measuring not only performance but also accessibility, SEO, and best practices, providing an overall score and tailored recommendations for each area.

Ultimately, optimising website performance and speed is crucial for any business that seeks to deliver a superior UX. Beyond enhancing user satisfaction, fast-loading websites are rewarded with improved search engine rankings and higher conversion rates. Implementing a range of techniques, such as image optimisation, minification, and caching, while regularly utilising tools like PageSpeed Insights and GTmetrix, enables businesses to systematically improve their site's performance. Regular monitoring and fine-tuning ensure that websites remain fast, efficient, and in line with evolving user expectations. In an increasingly competitive digital landscape, the ability to maintain a responsive, high-performing website can be the difference between success and irrelevance.

6.8 MASTERING SEO FOR ENHANCED WEBSITE VISIBILITY

In the highly competitive digital space, SEO serves as a cornerstone for ensuring a website's prominence, discoverability, and relevance within search engine results. It involves a multi-layered approach encompassing on-page elements, content creation, and technical refinements to boost a site's ranking and performance. To thrive in the modern online landscape, it is imperative to understand and apply effective SEO strategies across all aspects of website development.

On-page SEO is one of the most crucial elements in optimising individual pages to enhance their rankings and draw in relevant organic traffic. At the heart of this is keyword optimisation, which involves placing relevant keywords strategically within page titles, headers, meta descriptions, and throughout the content itself. This allows search engines to identify a page's relevance to specific queries. Equally important is the use of meta tags, where concise and compelling meta titles and descriptions can significantly influence click-through rates. These tags not only provide users with a preview of the content but also serve as crucial ranking factors when target keywords are incorporated.

Additionally, well-structured URLs can greatly improve visibility and comprehension for both search engines and users. Short, descriptive, and keyword-rich URLs that reflect the content's hierarchy contribute positively to SEO. Equally significant is the use of header tags, such as H1, H2, and H3, which structure the content logically, making it easier for both users and search engines to navigate. The H1 tag, typically featuring the main title of the page, should be crafted to reflect the page's central theme, aiding in its recognition as the most important element.

Visual content also plays a role in SEO, with image alt text serving a dual purpose: improving accessibility for users with disabilities and providing additional context to search engines. By optimising the alt text with relevant keywords, the SEO value of images increases, complementing the textual content. Internal linking further strengthens the website's architecture by linking relevant pages together, enhancing user navigation, and distributing link equity, which in turn helps improve SEO.

Above all, the quality and relevance of content are paramount. Content must be user-focused, providing valuable, informative, and relevant information that directly addresses user intent. Search engines increasingly prioritise content that satisfies user queries and offers a positive experience, meaning that websites featuring well-structured, high-quality content are likely to perform better in search rankings.

Creating SEO-friendly content involves a deliberate mix of strategic keyword placement, relevancy, and user-focused writing. Conducting thorough keyword research is the first step in identifying terms and phrases that align with the business or industry, providing a roadmap for the content strategy. Integrating these keywords naturally throughout the content signals to search engines the relevance of the page to specific topics. Beyond keywords, the quality of the content itself is crucial. Search engines reward comprehensive, well-researched, and engaging content that thoroughly addresses user queries, thereby contributing to higher rankings.

Readability and proper formatting are also critical. Users are more likely to engage with content that is clear and easy to digest. Well-structured headings, short paragraphs, and concise writing improve the overall readability of a page, keeping users on-site for longer and reducing bounce rates. Furthermore, content that is regularly updated signals to search engines that the website is active and continues to provide relevant information, thereby improving its ranking potential. Incorporating multimedia elements, such as images and videos, also enhances user engagement and provides additional opportunities for optimisation. Properly labelled and optimised multimedia content can increase visibility on search engines, adding to the page's SEO value.

Alongside on-page and content considerations, technical SEO plays a crucial role in ensuring that search engines can efficiently crawl, index, and understand a website's structure. One of the most important technical aspects is the creation of an XML sitemap. This sitemap, submitted directly to search engines, provides them with a blueprint of the website, highlighting the hierarchy and relevance of each page for prioritised indexing. Another vital file is the robots.txt, which instructs search engine bots on which pages they should crawl and which to exclude from indexing. Properly configuring this file ensures that the website's most important pages are visible to search engines while keeping irrelevant or redundant pages hidden.

Website speed and performance are increasingly important technical factors in SEO. Search engines, especially Google, favour fast-loading websites, and performance metrics are taken into account when ranking sites. Optimising images, reducing HTTP requests, and leveraging browser caching all contribute to faster load times, ultimately improving both the UX and search engine rankings. Similarly, mobile-friendly design is now critical as search engines have shifted towards mobile-first indexing. This approach means that the mobile version of a website is prioritised in rankings, making responsive design essential for seamless access across devices.

Another essential technical consideration is Secure Socket Layer (SSL) encryption. Search engines and users alike now expect websites to be secure. Implementing SSL ensures that data exchanged between users and the site remains private, and it has become a recognised ranking factor, with secure websites being favoured in search results. Furthermore, canonical tags help prevent the common issue of duplicate content by identifying the preferred version of a page when multiple URLs contain similar or identical content. This ensures that search engines do not penalise the website for duplicate content and helps maintain strong SEO across the site.

SEO is a complex and ever-evolving discipline that requires a comprehensive approach, blending on-page strategies, content creation, and technical considerations. By continually refining SEO techniques—whether through keyword research, content relevance, or technical adjustments—websites can maintain their visibility in search engine results and stay competitive in the digital space. The dynamic nature of SEO means that staying informed about the latest industry trends and algorithm updates is essential for maintaining a strong online presence.

6.9 INCLUSIVE WEB DESIGN: ENSURING ACCESSIBILITY FOR ALL USERS

In the digital age, where websites serve as essential gateways to information, products, and services, ensuring accessibility and inclusivity in design is not only a legal and ethical obligation but also a crucial aspect of enhancing UX. Every individual, regardless of ability or disability, should have the opportunity to engage with web content seamlessly. By integrating accessibility principles from the outset, websites can accommodate a diverse range of users, including those with visual, auditory, motor, and cognitive impairments.

An inclusive approach begins with the foundation of responsive design, ensuring websites adapt effortlessly to various devices, screen sizes, and user preferences. This flexibility allows users with different abilities to engage with the content comfortably, whether on mobile, tablet, or desktop. Equally essential is intuitive and consistent navigation, which aids users in moving through the website efficiently. Logical menu structures, clear headings, and descriptive link text are particularly beneficial for users with cognitive or motor impairments, ensuring that they can find and access information without confusion or frustration.

For users with visual impairments, incorporating alternative text for images plays a vital role in making content perceivable. Screen readers rely on this descriptive text to convey the meaning of images, transforming visual information into an auditory experience. Equally significant is the consideration of colour contrast. Ensuring adequate contrast between text and background elements enhances readability, particularly for individuals with colour blindness or other visual impairments. This design choice not only improves accessibility but also enhances the general legibility of the website for all users.

Navigational ease extends beyond the visual elements of a website. For users with motor impairments, designing sites that are fully operable through keyboard navigation is crucial. The ability to move through a website using only a keyboard or alternative input methods ensures that users who cannot use a traditional mouse can still interact with content, complete forms, and navigate between pages. Forms, in particular, should be well-structured and clearly labelled, with clear instructions and accessible error messages to assist users who rely on assistive technologies or have cognitive impairments.

For multimedia content, accessibility features such as captions for videos and transcripts for audio files are essential in ensuring that users with hearing impairments can access and comprehend the information presented. These features not only enhance accessibility but also improve user engagement by making multimedia content usable across a broader audience.

Central to accessible web design are the Web Content Accessibility Guidelines (WCAG), developed by the World Wide Web Consortium. These guidelines provide a comprehensive framework for creating web content that is accessible to all users, focusing on four key principles: perceivable, operable, understandable, and robust. The first principle, perceivable, ensures that all users can perceive the information and interface components presented on a website. This includes providing text alternatives for non-text content, such as images, and offering captions and other alternatives for multimedia. Adapting content so it can be presented in different formats without losing meaning is also critical under this principle.

Operability, the second principle, emphasises the need for UI components and navigation to be accessible to everyone. Keyboard accessibility is a prime example, allowing users to interact with the site without relying on a mouse. Providing sufficient time for users to read and respond to content, avoiding seizure-inducing designs, and creating consistent, predictable navigation all contribute to an operable and user-friendly website.

The third principle, understandability, focuses on making both the content and the operation of the website easy to comprehend. Clear and concise text, predictable interactions, and input assistance—such as error prevention techniques—enhance the usability of the site. Users should feel confident in their interactions with the website, knowing that the interface will behave in a logical and predictable manner.

The final principle, robustness, ensures that content is designed in a way that it can be reliably interpreted by a wide variety of user agents, including assistive technologies. This means using standard coding practices and ensuring that the website can adapt to evolving technologies without sacrificing accessibility.

Creating a truly inclusive website requires not only adhering to the WCAG but also engaging in rigorous testing to identify and address potential barriers for users with disabilities. Automated accessibility testing tools, such as WAVE, Axe, and Google Lighthouse, can provide an initial assessment of common accessibility issues, offering specific recommendations for improvement. While these tools are valuable for spotting errors, manual testing remains essential for gaining a true understanding of the UX. Evaluating a website using assistive technologies, such as screen readers, keyboard navigation, and voice recognition software, provides insights that automated tools might miss.

Equally important is involving individuals with disabilities in the testing process. User testing with a diverse group of participants allows designers and developers to uncover challenges that may not be immediately apparent. These real-world insights are invaluable in creating a truly inclusive experience, as they reflect the unique needs and preferences of different users. For a more comprehensive evaluation, third-party accessibility experts can conduct compliance audits, reviewing the website's code, design, and user interactions in detail. These audits provide an objective analysis of a website's accessibility and offer tailored recommendations for improvement.

Accessibility is not a one-time task but an ongoing commitment. Websites should be regularly audited and updated to ensure that new content, features, or design changes do not introduce new barriers. By embedding accessibility into the development process and maintaining regular checks, businesses can ensure their websites remain inclusive and compliant over time.

Incorporating accessibility and inclusivity into web design not only meets legal and ethical obligations but also enhances the overall UX. Websites that prioritise the needs of all users, regardless of their abilities, demonstrate a commitment to inclusivity and create digital spaces that are welcoming, functional, and accessible to everyone.

6.10 SECURING DIGITAL SPACES: PROTECTING WEBSITES AND USER DATA

In an age where cyber threats are ever-present and data breaches can have severe ramifications, ensuring the security of websites and protecting user data has never been more crucial. From safeguarding sensitive information to maintaining website functionality, robust security protocols are vital for preventing unauthorised access and malicious attacks. These measures are not only about protecting the website's integrity but also about fostering trust among users who rely on secure online experiences.

Website security begins with implementing stringent defences across every layer of the website's infrastructure. Regular security audits are an essential part of this process, providing a comprehensive review of potential vulnerabilities and identifying weaknesses before they can be exploited. Such proactive assessments are crucial in detecting issues that might otherwise go unnoticed, offering an opportunity to address them before they develop into serious threats.

Firewalls and Intrusion Detection Systems (IDS) are key components in building these defences, with firewalls acting as the first line of defence against suspicious traffic and IDS actively monitoring for unusual patterns that might indicate a security breach. Together, these systems create a barrier to unauthorised access and alert administrators to potential risks in real time.

Security also relies heavily on secure password practices, which are fundamental to protecting user accounts and administrative access. Enforcing the use of complex passwords, ensuring regular password updates, and incorporating multi-factor authentication (MFA) significantly reduces the risk of unauthorised access. With MFA, users are required to provide multiple verification factors to gain access, adding an extra layer of security that makes it harder for hackers to compromise accounts.

Another vital component of website security is the implementation of a Content Security Policy (CSP). CSP acts as a safeguard against cross-site scripting and other code injection attacks by specifying the sources from which a website can load scripts and other resources. This ensures that malicious scripts, often a gateway for hackers, are blocked from executing on the site.

Maintaining a secure environment also involves keeping software up to date, including the website's CMS and any associated plugins or extensions. Regular updates often include critical security patches that resolve known vulnerabilities. A failure to update software can leave a site exposed to known threats that hackers can easily exploit. Ensuring file upload security is also paramount, as malicious files can be an entry point for malware. Restricting file types, limiting file sizes, and validating input before accepting uploads are essential steps in safeguarding the website from harmful content.

One of the most fundamental elements of website security is the use of SSL certificates and Hypertext Transfer Protocol Secure (HTTPS) encryption. An SSL certificate verifies the authenticity of a website and establishes an encrypted connection between the user's browser and the web server. This encryption ensures that data transmitted between the two is protected from interception by third parties, securing sensitive information like login credentials, personal data, and payment details.

Using HTTPS not only provides encryption but also signals to users that the website is secure, which is particularly important in the context of online transactions or the exchange of personal information. HTTPS is now a standard expectation, and search engines such as Google give preference to HTTPS websites, further enhancing their visibility in search rankings. Some websites also opt for Extended Validation (EV) certificates, which offer the highest level of security and visibly reassure users by displaying a green address bar in their browser, reinforcing trust in the site's legitimacy.

For websites that manage multiple subdomains or domains, wildcard and multi-domain SSL certificates provide a practical solution. These certificates allow website owners to secure several sites under one certificate, streamlining the process while maintaining robust security across all associated web properties.

Protecting user data and ensuring privacy is a critical obligation for any website, especially in an era where data protection regulations like the General Data Protection Regulation govern the handling of personal information. Websites must be transparent about how they collect, store, and process user data. A clear and comprehensive privacy policy not only satisfies legal requirements but also builds user trust by explaining what data is collected, how it is used, and the steps taken to protect it.

In line with privacy principles, websites should adopt a data minimisation approach, collecting only the information necessary for specific purposes. This reduces the risk associated with data breaches, as less sensitive information is stored and thus less is at risk of being compromised. In addition to minimising data collection, explicit user consent must be obtained before gathering or processing any personal data. Implementing opt-in mechanisms ensures that users actively agree to share their information, providing greater transparency and control.

For e-commerce sites, securing payment processing is essential to protect users' financial information. This involves using secure payment gateways and adhering to the Payment Card Industry Data Security Standard, a set of regulations designed to protect credit card data during transactions. Encrypting payment information, both in transit and at rest, adds further security, ensuring that sensitive data are protected from end to end.

Encrypting data at rest, as well as during transmission, ensures that even if an unauthorised party accesses stored information, they will be unable to decipher it. Encryption acts as an additional safeguard, particularly for sensitive user data such as financial details or personal identification information. To further mitigate risks, regular data backups are essential, providing a way to restore website functionality quickly in the event of an attack. Backups allow for the restoration of data to a secure version, ensuring minimal disruption and reducing the impact of any data loss or corruption.

By implementing a robust suite of security measures, securing data transmission through SSL certificates, and prioritising user privacy, websites can build a trustworthy and resilient online presence. In a world where the exchange of sensitive information is a daily occurrence, the responsibility to protect user data and secure digital spaces has never been more important. Ensuring a secure and private environment not only shields users from cyber threats but also strengthens the credibility and reputation of the website itself.

6.11 NAVIGATING THE LAUNCH AND BEYOND: ENSURING A DYNAMIC WEBSITE POST-DEPLOYMENT

Launching a website is a pivotal moment, marking the culmination of development efforts. However, the launch is merely the beginning of an ongoing process that demands careful preparation, performance monitoring, and continuous improvements. A successful launch requires rigorous attention to detail, from the final stages of development to maintaining peak performance and responding to user feedback after the site goes live.

Before a website can be unveiled, thorough testing and quality assurance are essential to ensure that all functions work flawlessly. Every aspect of the site—from its navigation to its forms—must be examined meticulously to catch any remaining bugs or errors. Broken links need to be corrected, all interactive elements validated, and the site should undergo extensive testing across devices and browsers to ensure seamless UX. Once the functionality is confirmed, the focus shifts to content, which must be reviewed one final time to guarantee its accuracy, relevance, and alignment with the intended messaging. Equally important is optimising content for search engines; meta tags, keyword implementation, and proper heading structures must be in place. Creating an XML sitemap and submitting it to search engines further enhances visibility, laying a solid foundation for the site's discoverability.

Security also takes centre stage as launch approaches, particularly with the establishment of backup and recovery systems. These measures safeguard the site from unforeseen technical issues, allowing for rapid restoration in the event of a problem. A clearly defined launch plan is crucial, outlining each step of the deployment process, assigning responsibilities, and preparing the technical and content teams for any potential downtime. Communication plays an integral role here—users, stakeholders, and team members must be notified in advance of the launch date and any associated disruptions. Furthermore, domain configurations should be double-checked, ensuring that domain names are correctly pointed and hosting settings are properly configured. SSL certificates must be active and working, alongside server configurations optimised for a production environment, to provide users with a secure and reliable browsing experience.

Once the website is live, the real work begins in monitoring its performance. Deploying real-time monitoring tools allows for constant observation of server health, response times, and user interaction patterns. This is essential in identifying any bottlenecks or areas of underperformance. Tools like Google Analytics become invaluable in tracking visitor traffic, engagement levels, bounce rates, and conversion metrics, offering deep insights into user behaviour. These analytics reveal how effectively the site is functioning and provide a baseline for measuring its success. Load testing is also critical at this stage, simulating varying levels of user traffic to assess how well the website performs under strain. This stress testing helps identify potential performance issues that could impede scalability, ensuring the site can handle future growth in traffic.

Security audits remain paramount even after the site has launched. The digital landscape is ever-evolving, and new vulnerabilities are constantly emerging. Regularly scheduled audits help to identify and patch any weaknesses before they can be exploited, and ongoing vigilance is needed to respond swiftly to security risks. Equally important is the continuous review of error logs, which can pinpoint issues users may encounter during their interactions with the site. Addressing these errors proactively is key to ensuring the website's long-term stability and preventing future disruptions.

Feedback plays a crucial role in the post-launch phase, guiding the iterative process of website improvement. Offering users clear channels for providing feedback, whether through contact forms, surveys, or dedicated buttons, helps gather actionable insights. Encouraging users to share their experiences reveals areas for refinement while monitoring social media can uncover additional feedback on user sentiment. Comments, reviews, and mentions on social platforms offer unfiltered opinions that can significantly inform future development. Customer support channels are equally valuable in this regard. Listening to users who encounter issues or have specific requests provides an opportunity to address problems quickly and create a more positive UX.

With the influx of data and user input, it becomes possible to prioritise improvements. Website development should follow an iterative cycle, constantly evolving based on user feedback, the latest industry trends, and the changing needs of the business. This agile approach ensures that the site remains dynamic, adaptable, and responsive to its audience's expectations. Regular content updates are also necessary to keep the website relevant and engaging. Fresh content not only enhances UX but also benefits the site's search engine ranking, signalling to search engines that the website is active and well-maintained.

Performance optimisation must continue after the initial launch, fine-tuning code and addressing any issues identified during monitoring. Image compression, code minification, and server-side enhancements can all improve loading speeds and overall site efficiency. Security patching is another critical aspect of maintaining a site's resilience. The underlying technologies of the website, such as plugins and third-party software, should be kept up to date to prevent the exploitation of known vulnerabilities. Failure to patch promptly can expose the site to significant risks, making regular updates essential to a secure online presence.

The post-launch phase is not the conclusion of a project but rather the beginning of a new stage in the website's lifecycle. With careful preparation for deployment, rigorous performance monitoring, and an ongoing commitment to user feedback and iterative improvements, developers and stakeholders can ensure that their website evolves alongside user expectations.

A successful website is never static; it requires consistent optimisation, security vigilance, and content updates to remain relevant and effective in the constantly shifting digital landscape.

6.12 CHAPTER SUMMARY

Building and maintaining a strong online presence through effective website design and development is no longer a luxury but a necessity for any business or individual seeking to succeed in today's digital landscape. This chapter has outlined the key principles and strategic approaches essential for creating a website that is not only visually appealing but also functional, responsive, and user-centred. From setting clear objectives and aligning them with broader organisational goals to ensuring the website remains accessible and inclusive to all users, each element plays a critical role in the overall success of a website.

As highlighted, performance optimisation, security, and search engine visibility are fundamental to a website's long-term viability. Moreover, responsive design is imperative in an era where users access content across a multitude of devices, ensuring that UX are consistent and seamless. This chapter also emphasised the importance of ongoing monitoring and post-launch maintenance, as the digital landscape is in a constant state of flux. Regular updates, feedback-driven improvements, and vigilant security measures ensure that the website remains relevant, resilient, and capable of evolving with user needs and technological advancements.

Ultimately, building a strong online presence is an ongoing journey, one that demands both a strategic and technical approach. By following the principles and practices outlined in this chapter, individuals and organisations can create and sustain websites that not only meet their immediate needs but also adapt to the future demands of the digital world.

Key Questions for Discussion

1. How can businesses ensure their website goals align with their overall digital strategy? What are some examples of measurable objectives that can guide the development of a successful website?
2. Why is human-centred design critical for creating engaging UX? How do responsive web design and mobile optimisation enhance the overall digital experience, particularly in today's mobile-first world?
3. What are some emerging technologies shaping website development today? How can businesses decide which technologies to adopt for building efficient, modern websites?
4. How can businesses prioritise inclusivity in web design to ensure accessibility for all users, including those with disabilities? What measures can they take to safeguard websites and user data in an increasingly risky digital landscape?
5. After launching a website, what key steps should businesses take to maintain its relevance, performance, and security? How can they continuously evaluate and optimise the website to keep up with changing user needs and digital trends?

BIBLIOGRAPHY

Beaird, J. and George, J. (2023). *The Principles of Beautiful Web Design*. 4th ed. SitePoint.
Cederholm, D. (2023). *Sass for Web Designers*. 2nd ed. A Book Apart.
Duckett, J. (2024a). *HTML and CSS: Design and Build Websites*. 1st ed. Wiley.
Duckett, J. (2024b). *JavaScript and JQuery: Interactive Front-End Web Development*. 2nd ed. Wiley.
Frain, B. (2023). *Responsive Web Design with HTML5 and CSS*. 3rd ed. Packt Publishing.
Haverbeke, M. (2024). *Eloquent JavaScript*. 4th ed. No Starch Press.
Keith, J. (2023a). *DOM Scripting: Web Design with JavaScript and the Document Object Model*. 2nd ed. Apress.
Keith, J. (2023b). *HTML5 for Web Designers*. 2nd ed. A Book Apart.
Marcotte, E. (2023). *Responsive Web Design*. 2nd ed. A Book Apart.
Meyer, E. (2023). *CSS: The Definitive Guide*. 5th ed. O'Reilly Media.
Wroblewski, L. (2023). *Mobile First*. 2nd ed. A Book Apart.
Zeldman, J. (2023). *Designing with Web Standards*. 4th ed. New Riders.

CHAPTER 7

E-commerce

Selling Online and Maximising Sales

> **Learning Outcomes**
>
> By the end of this chapter, you will be able to:
>
> 1. Learn how to select the most suitable E-commerce platform and optimise your online store to drive sales and enhance customer experience.
> 2. Gain the skills to craft comprehensive marketing strategies that attract, engage, and convert online customers, ensuring business success.
> 3. Understand the key strategies for safeguarding E-commerce transactions, preventing fraud, and building trust with customers to ensure long-term growth.

7.1 INTRODUCTION

In today's fast-paced digital age, E-commerce has become a dominant force reshaping how businesses connect with consumers. What started as a novel way to reach customers via the internet has evolved into a thriving ecosystem, where businesses of all sizes—from small start-ups to global conglomerates—engage in selling products and services online. The growth of E-commerce is fuelled by ever-evolving technologies, mobile accessibility, and shifting consumer behaviour that favours convenience, efficiency, and accessibility. As the digital marketplace continues to expand, it brings with it both incredible opportunities and substantial challenges. For businesses, it is not enough to simply establish an online presence; there is a growing need to optimise every element of the E-commerce journey to remain competitive and maximise sales. From selecting the optimal platform to creating an engaging and functional website, ensuring secure payment infrastructure, and crafting targeted marketing strategies, E-commerce demands a comprehensive, multi-faceted approach to success. This chapter will guide you through the essential components of building and managing a successful online business, addressing the complexities and intricacies that are often overlooked. Whether you are starting a new venture or looking to enhance an existing E-commerce operation, this chapter provides actionable insights into the evolving world of online retail (Figure 7.1).

DOI: 10.4324/9781032672458-7

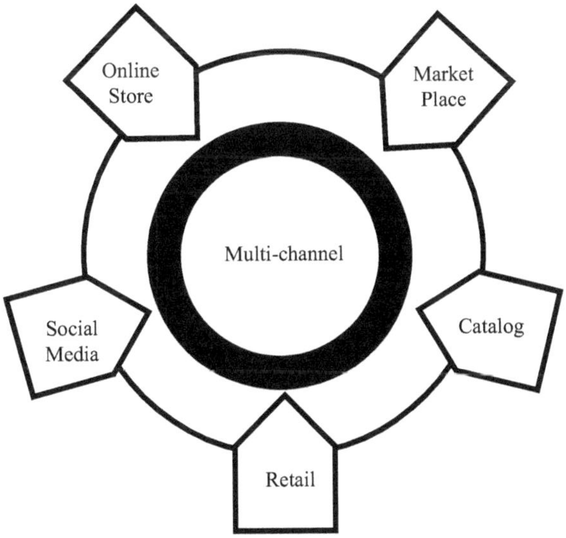

FIGURE 7.1 What Is eCommerce? Everything You Need to Know

7.2 THE EVOLUTION OF E-COMMERCE IN THE DIGITAL AGE

E-commerce has radically transformed the commercial landscape, ushering in a new era where businesses are no longer confined by physical locations. The growth of online commerce has revolutionised the way products and services are bought and sold, fundamentally altering the fabric of the digital economy. This shift has been driven by the increasing preference of consumers for the convenience of online shopping, a trend accelerated by technological innovations and the widespread availability of high-speed internet. As more businesses migrate from traditional brick-and-mortar establishments to online platforms, E-commerce has firmly established itself as a cornerstone of modern life, offering unprecedented access to a vast array of goods and services at the click of a button.

The benefits of selling online are multifaceted, providing significant advantages for both businesses and consumers alike. For companies, the ability to reach a global audience without the geographical limitations of a physical store is transformative. Businesses can now connect with customers across the world, broadening their potential market and opening up new avenues for revenue growth. The financial advantages are also notable: E-commerce eliminates the need for the high overhead costs associated with maintaining a physical storefront, such as rent, utilities, and in-store staffing. This reduced operational cost often translates into higher profit margins, allowing businesses to offer more competitive pricing while retaining profitability. Furthermore, the ability to automate key processes, such as inventory management and order fulfilment, optimises operational efficiency, streamlining the overall business workflow.

For consumers, the appeal of E-commerce lies in its unparalleled convenience. Shopping can be done from the comfort of home, with stores available 24/7, erasing the constraints of time and location. Customers can easily compare products and prices, gaining access to an expansive selection that allows for more informed purchasing decisions. This sense of empowerment, paired with the ease of browsing and buying, makes online shopping an increasingly attractive option for today's digital consumer.

To navigate the E-commerce landscape effectively, businesses must first understand the various business models available, each tailored to different needs and market conditions. The most widely recognised model is Business-to-Consumer (B2C), where businesses sell directly to consumers. This is the model most consumers interact with, as seen with platforms like Amazon or ASOS. The B2C model is often transactional, involving either one-off purchases, digital downloads, or ongoing subscriptions. Alternatively, the Business-to-Business (B2B) model is designed for transactions between businesses, often involving wholesale suppliers or manufacturers. Platforms like Alibaba facilitate these bulk transactions, and the relationships within B2B are often long-term and involve greater quantities of goods.

Another prominent model is Consumer-to-Consumer, in which individual consumers sell products or services to one another. Platforms such as eBay and Gumtree exemplify this model, relying on user-generated listings and peer-to-peer transactions. In contrast, the Consumer-to-Business model allows individuals to sell their products, services, or skills to businesses. Freelance platforms like Upwork illustrate this, where professionals offer their services for businesses to purchase, often creating a dynamic and flexible relationship between buyers and sellers. Direct-to-Consumer is another model that has gained traction in recent years, as brands seek to bypass traditional retail channels and sell directly to customers. This allows brands to exert greater control over the customer experience, as well as collect valuable consumer data that can inform future business decisions.

A more recent innovation within E-commerce is the subscription model, where customers sign up for recurring delivery of a product or service. Companies like Netflix and Dollar Shave Club operate on this model, creating consistent revenue streams through continuous engagement with their customer base. Each E-commerce model presents unique challenges and opportunities, and businesses must carefully select the model that aligns with their products, audience, and overall goals.

As this chapter continues, we will explore the crucial aspects of E-commerce that contribute to building a successful online business. Subsequent sections will delve into the essential components of website design, the strategic implementation of marketing initiatives, and the importance of optimising customer engagement. These elements, when combined with a solid understanding of E-commerce business models, will empower businesses to thrive in the competitive online marketplace, maximising their sales and driving long-term success.

7.3 SELECTING THE OPTIMAL E-COMMERCE PLATFORM FOR BUSINESS SUCCESS

Choosing the right E-commerce platform is one of the most critical decisions for any business entering the digital marketplace. The platform forms the backbone of an online store, influencing not only the user experience (UX) but also the efficiency of operations, scalability, and growth potential. With a wide array of options available, businesses must undertake a thorough evaluation to ensure the chosen platform aligns with their unique requirements, goals, and long-term aspirations.

The variety of E-commerce platforms ranges from fully hosted solutions like Shopify and BigCommerce to open-source options such as Magento and WooCommerce. Shopify is particularly popular for its user-friendly interface and comprehensive tools, making it a go-to choice for small and medium-sized enterprises. It simplifies the entire E-commerce process, offering built-in features for website building, inventory management, and marketing. Similarly, BigCommerce provides an all-in-one hosted solution that is designed to accommodate growing businesses with multi-channel selling and built-in analytics, making it an attractive option for companies looking to expand their reach.

For businesses with more complex needs, platforms like Magento offer unmatched customisation and scalability. As an open-source solution, Magento allows businesses to fully control their E-commerce environment, tailoring it to their precise specifications. This makes it ideal for those with larger product catalogues or intricate product configurations. However, it requires technical expertise, as businesses opting for a self-hosted platform like Magento must manage their own server maintenance, security updates, and infrastructure needs. WooCommerce, a plugin for WordPress, is another flexible option that seamlessly integrates with existing WordPress websites. It provides extensive customisation through a vast array of extensions, allowing businesses to expand functionalities as required.

Other notable platforms include Wix and Squarespace, both of which are highly regarded for their ease of use and visually stunning templates. Wix offers a drag-and-drop interface, making it an appealing choice for small businesses or those without technical expertise. Squarespace, renowned for its design-centric approach, enables businesses to create beautifully designed websites with built-in E-commerce features, ideal for brands that prioritise aesthetic appeal. For businesses seeking a lightweight and efficient solution, OpenCart stands out with its simplicity and range of extensions, though it is more suitable for moderate-sized product catalogues.

Beyond evaluating specific platforms, businesses must also decide between hosted and self-hosted solutions. Hosted platforms like Shopify and BigCommerce handle all the technical aspects—such as server maintenance, security, and regular updates—offering a hassle-free solution for businesses looking to minimise their IT involvement. These platforms often operate on a subscription model, providing convenience but potentially limiting customisation. In contrast, self-hosted platforms like Magento and WooCommerce offer complete control, enabling businesses to customise their online store to the smallest detail. However, with this freedom comes the responsibility of managing server infrastructure and security, which may require dedicated IT resources.

Scalability is another vital factor to consider when choosing an E-commerce platform, particularly for businesses with long term growth aspirations. Hosted platforms usually handle scalability seamlessly, adjusting resources as traffic increases. In contrast, self-hosted solutions may require businesses to invest in additional infrastructure as their operations grow, ensuring that their platform can support increasing demand.

Equally important is the level of customisation required by the business. Hosted platforms offer user-friendly templates and predefined functionalities, making them ideal for businesses that prefer a streamlined setup. However, companies with specific design or operational needs might find self-hosted platforms more suitable, as these provide limitless customisation options. Integration capabilities should also be factored in, as the ability to integrate with third-party tools—such as payment gateways, shipping carriers, and marketing platforms—is crucial for creating a seamless online ecosystem. Furthermore, businesses should evaluate the available support and community resources for their chosen platform. Platforms with robust customer support and an active user community can be invaluable, providing guidance, troubleshooting assistance, and insights into best practices.

Ultimately, selecting the right E-commerce platform is a pivotal step that lays the foundation for a successful online business. By carefully considering platform options, weighing the benefits of hosted versus self-hosted solutions, and ensuring scalability and customisation align with business objectives, companies can build a solid, future-proof E-commerce presence.

7.4 BUILDING THE FOUNDATION OF YOUR E-COMMERCE STORE

Establishing a successful E-commerce store begins with several foundational steps that are crucial in creating a seamless and engaging shopping experience. From selecting a domain and reliable hosting to designing an appealing storefront and configuring product management systems, each step contributes to the store's overall performance and user satisfaction.

The first step in setting up an E-commerce store is securing a domain and choosing suitable website hosting. The domain name functions as the unique web address of the store, forming a key part of the business's online identity. A well-chosen domain name should reflect the brand, be memorable, and be easy for customers to recall. Once selected, businesses must register the domain, thereby staking their claim to a distinct presence in the crowded online marketplace. Simultaneously, selecting the right website hosting is critical. The hosting provider influences the speed, reliability, and security of the online store, all of which affect customer experience. Hosted E-commerce platforms like Shopify typically include hosting within their services, easing this process for businesses. However, self-hosted solutions require the business to choose a reliable hosting provider that aligns with their needs, particularly concerning traffic capacity, security protocols, and scalability. A fast, secure, and scalable hosting environment is essential to offer customers a smooth and safe online shopping experience.

Once the domain and hosting are in place, attention must shift to the design of the storefront. The visual appearance of the website is the first point of interaction with customers and has a profound influence on their perception of the brand. Most E-commerce platforms offer a variety of themes or templates that businesses can use as the foundation for their website's appearance. However, while these themes provide structure, they should be customised to align with the unique brand identity of the business. Colours, typography, layouts, logos, banners, and promotional graphics must all reflect the essence of the brand and ensure consistency across the platform. Beyond aesthetics, the UX should be carefully considered during this phase. Intuitive navigation, easy-to-locate product categories, and prominent calls to action all help streamline the user journey. Additionally, with an increasing number of customers shopping on mobile devices, ensuring that the storefront is fully responsive across all devices—from desktops to smartphones—is non-negotiable. A well-designed, mobile-friendly website is key to capturing a broader audience and ensuring a positive customer experience regardless of how users access the site.

An equally important aspect of setting up the store is the effective configuration of product categories and inventory management. The way products are organised can make or break the customer's ability to find what they are looking for. Products should be grouped into logical categories and subcategories, simplifying navigation and enhancing the overall browsing experience. Well-structured product categories create a sense of order, enabling customers to explore the store more easily and increasing the likelihood of conversions.

Inventory management is another cornerstone of running a successful E-commerce store. Maintaining accurate stock levels ensures that customers are not left disappointed by out-of-stock items. E-commerce platforms often provide tools that allow businesses to automate inventory tracking, set low-stock alerts, and manage reordering. By having a real-time understanding of inventory, businesses can prevent overselling and streamline the fulfilment process, thereby enhancing customer trust and satisfaction.

Moreover, a well-organised product catalogue should be supported by clear, comprehensive product information. High-quality images, detailed descriptions, and accurate specifications not only provide customers with all the information they need to make purchasing decisions but also reduce the likelihood of post-purchase enquiries and returns. Robust product information management systems can be instrumental in achieving this, ensuring that each product page offers the level of detail needed to inspire confidence in the customer.

For businesses offering products with multiple variations—such as different sizes, colours, or configurations—ensuring that these options are clearly presented and easy to navigate is equally important. When customers can quickly find and select the specific variant they want, it increases the likelihood of a sale and reduces frustration.

In essence, the process of setting up an E-commerce store requires attention to detail across multiple facets—securing the right domain and hosting, designing a visually compelling and user-friendly website, and ensuring a well-organised and accurately managed product catalogue. By investing time and resources into these areas, businesses can create a strong foundation that not only attracts customers but also encourages repeat visits and builds long-term success in the competitive world of online retail.

7.5 OPTIMISING THE CHECKOUT EXPERIENCE FOR ENHANCED CONVERSIONS

The checkout process is the critical juncture where a customer's intention to purchase is finalised, and it can significantly impact the overall success of an E-commerce venture. Ensuring that this phase is as smooth and efficient as possible is crucial for maximising conversions and reducing cart abandonment. A well optimised checkout experience is key to creating a seamless journey from the shopping cart to order confirmation, helping to foster customer satisfaction and repeat business.

At the heart of optimising the checkout process is the need to simplify it. A lengthy or complicated checkout flow can quickly deter customers, causing them to abandon their purchase out of frustration or impatience. By reducing the number of steps required to complete a transaction, businesses can improve UX and increase the likelihood of conversion. The fewer pages and form fields involved, the better. Clear and concise prompts, with minimal distractions, allow customers to focus on completing their purchase without unnecessary obstacles.

To further enhance transparency, progress indicators should be integrated, offering customers a visual guide of how far they've advanced through the process. This not only provides a sense of control but also minimises uncertainty, reassuring customers that they are nearing completion.

For an even more streamlined experience, businesses might consider offering a one-page checkout. This approach consolidates all required information—billing, shipping, and payment details—into a single page, minimising clicks and reducing the time it takes to finalise a purchase. One-page checkouts are particularly effective for customers who prioritise speed and efficiency, offering them a hassle-free solution that caters to modern shopping habits.

Another pivotal feature in the checkout process is the availability of a guest checkout option. Forcing customers to create an account before completing their purchase can be a significant barrier, particularly for first-time buyers who may wish to make a quick, uncomplicated transaction. Implementing a guest checkout option allows customers to proceed without the need to register, thus reducing friction and making the purchasing experience smoother. However, account creation can still offer significant benefits, such as tracking past orders, simplifying future purchases, and offering personalised recommendations. To balance these advantages without creating obstacles, businesses should consider incentivising account registration. Offering perks such as discounts for registered users or the option to save personal and payment details for future use can encourage customers to sign up voluntarily rather than feeling compelled.

Security is another non-negotiable aspect of the checkout process. Customers need to feel confident that their sensitive information, including payment details, is protected. Implementing secure socket layer (SSL) certificates is a fundamental step in ensuring that all data transmitted between the customer's browser and the website's server is encrypted and secure. The presence of SSL certificates, often indicated by a padlock icon in the browser's address bar, provides a visual cue that reassures customers of the website's commitment to security. Beyond visual trust signals, businesses must select payment gateways that prioritise security and compliance. Reputable payment processors typically include built-in fraud detection and prevention features, offering an additional layer of protection for both the business and its customers.

To maintain this high level of security, it's essential to regularly update the E-commerce platform and payment systems, addressing any emerging vulnerabilities or threats. By keeping the infrastructure current, businesses can safeguard against potential breaches and protect customer information. Alongside these technical measures, clear communication around security is key. Businesses should be transparent about the protective protocols in place, informing customers of the steps taken to secure their data. Simple, straightforward messaging around encryption, secure payment gateways, and data handling builds trust and encourages customers to complete their transactions without hesitation.

In summary, streamlining the checkout process requires thoughtful planning and careful consideration of the UX. By simplifying the flow, offering guest checkout options, and ensuring that security is a top priority through SSL encryption and robust payment systems, businesses can create an efficient and trustworthy environment for their customers. The final stage of the purchasing journey is not merely a formality; it is a vital point that shapes customer perceptions and loyalty. A well-optimised and secure checkout process ensures that customers complete their transactions with confidence, leaving them satisfied and more likely to return for future purchases.

7.6 BUILDING A ROBUST PAYMENT INFRASTRUCTURE FOR E-COMMERCE SUCCESS

The choice of payment gateways is one of the most crucial decisions in setting up an E-commerce platform, as it has a direct impact on both the ease of transaction and the overall customer experience. Payment gateways serve as the secure intermediaries between an online store and financial institutions, facilitating transactions and ensuring that payments are processed smoothly. Businesses must carefully evaluate the payment gateway options available to them, considering factors that align with their operational needs, technical infrastructure, and, most importantly, the preferences of their customers.

When selecting a payment gateway, the first step is to ensure compatibility with the existing E-commerce platform. Many widely-used platforms integrate with multiple payment providers, allowing businesses to choose the solution that best suits their requirements. It is essential to assess key factors such as transaction fees, processing times, and how easily the payment gateway integrates with the overall system. The goal is to find a balance between cost efficiency and functional performance, ensuring that the payment process runs smoothly without imposing significant overhead costs.

Security is an indispensable consideration in the selection process. Payment gateways must adhere to the highest industry standards, such as Payment Card Industry Data Security Standard (PCI DSS), to ensure the protection of sensitive customer information during transactions. Customers must feel confident that their financial data is secure, and businesses must take every possible precaution to build and maintain that trust. Gateways offering features like tokenisation and encryption provide an added layer of security, ensuring that even in the event of a breach, sensitive information remains protected. By selecting secure, compliant payment processors, businesses can create a shopping environment that prioritises customer safety.

The geographical reach of a payment gateway is another critical factor. Businesses that aim to operate internationally must ensure their chosen payment provider can accommodate transactions in multiple currencies and serve various regions. Not all gateways offer comprehensive international coverage, and certain payment methods may be restricted to specific countries. For businesses with global ambitions, prioritising a gateway that supports international currencies, local payment methods, and multi-currency transactions is essential to providing a seamless shopping experience to customers regardless of their location.

In addition to selecting a suitable gateway, offering a diverse range of payment methods is key to enhancing customer satisfaction and expanding market reach. Shoppers today expect convenience and flexibility, and one way to cater to their needs is by supporting multiple payment options. While credit and debit cards remain popular, digital wallets such as PayPal, Apple Pay, and Google Pay are rapidly gaining traction. Integrating these options into the checkout process offers customers familiar, trusted alternatives and streamlines the payment experience. Region-specific payment solutions can also be a valuable addition, helping businesses cater to local preferences and ensuring that customers from diverse regions feel included.

The checkout experience itself plays a pivotal role in how customers perceive the payment process. It must be designed to accommodate multiple payment methods effortlessly, ensuring that users can easily select their preferred option without confusion or inconvenience. By clearly communicating the available payment choices and providing a user-friendly interface, businesses can create a checkout process that is both seamless and enjoyable. In a competitive E-commerce landscape, offering payment flexibility can set a business apart, fostering customer loyalty and encouraging repeat transactions.

For businesses with an international customer base, handling multi-currency transactions effectively is vital to streamlining the purchasing process. Payment gateways that support multiple currencies allow customers to view prices in their local currency, providing a more transparent and user-friendly shopping experience. Real-time currency conversion capabilities ensure that prices are accurately reflected, helping customers avoid any confusion or hesitation during checkout. Clear communication regarding currency conversion rates and any associated fees also helps to manage customer expectations, building trust and reducing the likelihood of abandoned carts.

Regulatory compliance is another important consideration for businesses dealing with cross-border transactions. Each country may have its own financial regulations and legal requirements, and businesses must ensure they are fully compliant with these local rules. Failing to comply can result in fines, legal complications, or disrupted service, all of which can negatively impact business operations. Selecting a payment gateway that is well-versed in international regulations and equipped to handle the complexities of cross-border payments is essential for long-term success in the global marketplace.

In conclusion, the process of selecting and integrating payment gateways is far from trivial. It requires careful consideration of various factors, including compatibility with the E-commerce platform, the security measures provided, and the geographical reach of the payment provider. By offering a diverse range of payment options and ensuring a smooth, secure, and transparent transaction process, businesses can enhance customer satisfaction and establish a strong foundation for growth. In a competitive global market, a reliable and efficient payment infrastructure is not just a convenience; it is a critical driver of success.

CASE STUDY 7

B&Q's Integration of "Dark Stores"—Enhancing E-commerce Efficiency

B&Q, a leading home improvement and garden retailer in the UK, faced a significant challenge in adapting to the rapid rise of e-commerce. With online shopping becoming the preferred choice for many customers, the company needed to improve its fulfilment capabilities to meet growing demand while still leveraging its extensive network of physical stores. The challenge lay in optimising inventory management and ensuring that online customers receive their orders quickly and efficiently. Traditional retail stores were not designed to function as fulfilment centres, leading to logistical bottlenecks, inefficiencies in space utilisation, and delays in order processing. B&Q recognised that a more innovative approach was required to bridge the gap between its physical stores and its digital sales strategy.

To address this, B&Q implemented the concept of "dark stores"—dedicated fulfilment spaces within existing retail locations that operated as mini-distribution centres. By repurposing parts of their physical stores, B&Q were able to store and process online orders more efficiently, significantly reducing delivery times. These dark stores acted as hybrid spaces, allowing for faster order picking, packing, and dispatching, ultimately enhancing the online shopping experience. Additionally, they facilitated a more seamless click-and-collect service, enabling customers to pick up their purchases from nearby stores without delay. The integration of advanced inventory management systems further optimised stock distribution, ensuring that products were always available at the right locations to meet online demand.

The results of this strategy were impressive. B&Q saw a significant reduction in order fulfilment times, leading to improved customer satisfaction and a rise in online sales. The implementation of dark stores enhanced operational efficiency by making better use of physical retail spaces while reducing reliance on large, centralised warehouses. This approach also strengthened B&Q's omnichannel strategy, allowing the company to merge its physical and digital operations effectively. The ability to fulfil online orders faster helped B&Q remain competitive in an increasingly digital retail landscape.

This case highlights key takeaways for businesses navigating the digital economy. Firstly, integrating physical and digital operations can enhance efficiency and improve the customer experience. Secondly, repurposing existing retail spaces for e-commerce fulfilment can be a cost-effective alternative to building new distribution centres. Thirdly, efficient inventory management and strategic stock placement play a crucial role in optimising supply chains. Lastly, businesses that embrace innovation in response to market trends can sustain long-term growth and competitiveness.

Discussion Questions for Students (with Indicative Answers)

1. **How did B&Q's implementation of dark stores improve its e-commerce capabilities?**
   Indicative Answer: By converting parts of physical stores into fulfilment centres, B&Q reduced order processing times, improved delivery efficiency, and enhanced the customer experience.
2. **Why is integrating physical and digital operations beneficial for retailers?**
   Indicative Answer: It allows businesses to optimise space usage, streamline logistics, and provide faster service to customers through hybrid fulfilment strategies.

3. **What are the advantages of using dark stores compared to traditional warehouses?**
   Indicative Answer: Dark stores enable quicker order processing, reduce reliance on large distribution centres, and allow businesses to fulfil online orders closer to customers.
4. **How does efficient inventory management contribute to the success of e-commerce strategies?**
   Indicative Answer: It ensures that products are stocked in the right locations, minimises delays, reduces costs, and enhances the overall efficiency of fulfilment operations.
5. **What lessons can other retailers learn from B&Q's approach to e-commerce fulfilment?**
   Indicative Answer: Businesses can benefit from repurposing retail spaces, integrating online and offline operations, and investing in innovative fulfilment solutions to remain competitive in the digital economy.

7.7 CRAFTING A COMPREHENSIVE E-COMMERCE MARKETING STRATEGY FOR SUCCESS

In the dynamic and competitive realm of E-commerce, a well-rounded marketing strategy is crucial for attracting customers, fostering engagement, and driving long-term growth. To stand out in a crowded marketplace, businesses must leverage a variety of digital marketing channels, optimise their online presence through search engine optimisation (SEO), and build meaningful relationships with customers through content and email marketing. By integrating these diverse tactics, E-commerce ventures can craft a powerful approach to promoting their brand and driving sustained success.

One of the most effective ways to reach potential customers is by harnessing the power of digital marketing channels. Social media, pay-per-click (PPC) advertising, and influencer partnerships offer businesses the opportunity to engage with audiences and direct traffic to their online stores. Social media platforms such as Facebook, Instagram, and Pinterest serve as vital tools for creating brand awareness and promoting products in a visually appealing and engaging manner. Businesses can build communities around their brand by sharing creative content, running targeted advertising campaigns, and fostering meaningful interactions with users. The ability to reach specific audiences based on their interests and behaviours allows for personalised marketing that resonates with potential buyers and encourages them to explore the brand further.

PPC advertising, particularly through platforms like Google Ads, enables businesses to display highly targeted ads to individuals actively searching for products or services. By bidding on carefully chosen keywords, businesses can place their ads in front of the right audience at the right moment. Crafting compelling ad copy, selecting high-quality visuals, and using data-driven insights to continually refine campaign strategies are key to maximising the effectiveness of PPC advertising. By monitoring metrics such as click-through rates and conversions, businesses can adjust their approach to optimise their return on investment and capture the attention of prospective customers.

Influencer marketing has become a significant force in modern E-commerce strategies. Partnering with influencers, who have already cultivated a large following within a particular niche, offers businesses the opportunity to tap into new markets. The authenticity that influencers bring to their endorsements resonates with their audiences, making this form of marketing particularly effective in building trust and expanding brand visibility. By carefully selecting influencers whose values align with the business, brands can create impactful campaigns that generate genuine interest in their products and services.

Beyond paid advertising and social media engagement, SEO and content marketing are indispensable tools for enhancing a brand's discoverability and authority. E-commerce SEO focuses on improving the visibility of product pages and other relevant content in search engine results. This begins with thorough keyword research to identify search terms customers use when looking for products. Integrating these keywords into product titles, descriptions, and meta tags can significantly improve a store's ranking on search engines. Additionally, optimising images with descriptive alt text, ensuring fast loading times, and maintaining a mobile-friendly website all contribute to higher search engine rankings and an improved UX.

Content marketing plays a complementary role to SEO, providing valuable information to customers while enhancing search engine performance. Blog posts, tutorials, product guides, and how-to articles not only serve as educational resources for potential buyers but also present opportunities to naturally incorporate keywords, thereby driving organic traffic. By positioning the brand as a thought leader or expert within its industry, businesses can attract more visitors and create meaningful connections with their audience. Customer reviews and testimonials also serve as vital user-generated content that can enhance SEO efforts. This fresh, authentic material signals to search engines that the website is regularly updated and relevant to users.

Another critical component of an E-commerce marketing strategy is email marketing, a powerful tool for fostering customer retention and encouraging repeat purchases. Building and segmenting an email list allows businesses to communicate directly with customers, providing personalised offers, product recommendations, and updates that cater to their individual preferences and buying behaviour. Automated email sequences, such as welcome emails for new customers or abandoned cart reminders for those who leave items unpurchased, are particularly effective in nurturing customer relationships and encouraging conversions. Sending post-purchase follow-ups, including product care tips or suggestions for complementary products, can further enhance customer engagement and satisfaction.

Email marketing also plays a central role in long-term customer retention. By offering exclusive discounts, early access to new products, or membership to loyalty programmes, businesses can incentivise repeat purchases and strengthen brand loyalty. Personalised emails based on customer preferences or purchase history create a tailored experience that resonates with recipients, increasing the likelihood of continued engagement. Analysing performance metrics such as open rates and click-through rates helps businesses refine their email strategies, ensuring they remain relevant and impactful without overwhelming the customer.

Together, these marketing approaches form a comprehensive and cohesive strategy for driving success in the competitive world of E-commerce. By leveraging the power of digital marketing channels, optimising for search engines, producing valuable content, and nurturing customer relationships through email, businesses can create a compelling and lasting online presence. A holistic approach to marketing that adapts to customer preferences and industry trends will ensure long-term growth, enhanced customer loyalty, and a competitive edge in the marketplace.

7.8 HARNESSING E-COMMERCE ANALYTICS FOR STRATEGIC GROWTH

In the ever-evolving world of E-commerce, the ability to track and analyse key metrics is fundamental to understanding customer behaviour, optimising sales strategies, and driving long-term success. Effective use of E-commerce analytics not only offers insights into the performance of marketing campaigns and the overall health of the business but also empowers companies to make informed, data-driven decisions. By examining crucial metrics such as conversion rates and average order values (AOVs), businesses can refine their operations, enhance customer experiences, and ultimately improve profitability.

At the heart of E-commerce performance tracking lies the measurement of key metrics. Two of the most significant indicators of success are the conversion rate and the AOV. The conversion rate, which measures the percentage of website visitors who complete a desired action—usually a purchase—serves as a direct indicator of the effectiveness of the UX and the persuasiveness of the website's content. By closely monitoring the conversion rate, businesses can identify potential weaknesses in the sales funnel, such as high exit rates at specific stages of the checkout process, and implement targeted strategies to address these issues.

AOV, on the other hand, provides insight into the monetary value of each transaction. A higher AOV suggests that customers are either purchasing more products or opting for higher-priced items, both of which positively impact revenue. By analysing AOV, businesses can identify opportunities to encourage larger purchases through upselling, cross-selling, or strategic discounts and promotions. This deeper understanding of customer purchasing behaviour allows businesses to fine-tune their pricing strategies and promotions to maximise revenue per transaction.

Beyond these fundamental metrics, understanding customer behaviour and shopping patterns plays a crucial role in the success of any E-commerce strategy. By employing powerful tools such as Google Analytics, businesses can track user interactions across their websites, revealing detailed insights into how customers navigate and engage with different pages. This data provides a comprehensive view of user journeys, enabling businesses to identify popular entry points, key navigation paths, and areas where customers may drop off before completing a purchase.

Visual tools like heatmaps and session recordings offer an additional layer of insight, showcasing where users are clicking, scrolling, and spending the most time on a page. These visual representations help businesses pinpoint areas where the UX can be improved—whether by simplifying navigation, adjusting the placement of key calls to action, or streamlining the checkout process to reduce friction.

Moreover, analysing shopping patterns reveals critical trends that can inform broader business strategies. By identifying peak times for website traffic and understanding seasonal fluctuations in demand, businesses can tailor their marketing efforts, inventory management, and staffing to meet the needs of their customers effectively. Insights into purchase trends can also inform decisions about product development, helping businesses to anticipate shifts in consumer preferences and adjust their offerings accordingly.

E-commerce analytics also serve as a foundation for data-driven decision-making, enabling businesses to move beyond intuition and gut feelings when it comes to making strategic choices. With the aid of robust analytics tools, companies can experiment with various approaches through techniques like A/B testing. This method involves testing different website layouts, promotional offers, or product presentations to measure the impact on key metrics such as conversion rates or AOVs. By systematically comparing the results of these tests, businesses gain concrete, quantitative insights into what resonates best with their target audience.

Data-driven decision-making extends beyond optimising the website experience. Analytics play a crucial role in assessing the effectiveness of marketing campaigns across various digital channels. By tracking performance metrics, businesses can determine which marketing efforts—whether through paid search, social media, or email campaigns—are driving the most significant results. Attribution models help businesses understand the role of each marketing touchpoint in the customer journey, allowing for more informed decisions regarding budget allocation and resource distribution. With this knowledge, businesses can direct their marketing efforts towards the channels and tactics that generate the highest return on investment.

Ultimately, the integration of E-commerce analytics into a company's decision-making process is essential for staying competitive in an increasingly data-driven marketplace. By consistently measuring key performance indicators, analysing customer behaviour, and leveraging insights to optimise strategies, businesses can not only improve their day-to-day operations but also gain a significant advantage over their competitors. The ability to track and interpret data in real time allows businesses to adapt to changes in consumer behaviour, respond to emerging trends, and make informed decisions that contribute to their long-term growth.

As the digital marketplace continues to evolve, those businesses that prioritise analytics and performance tracking will be best positioned to thrive. In a landscape where agility and responsiveness are critical to success, the strategic use of data is no longer a luxury but a necessity for any E-commerce venture seeking to remain competitive and achieve sustained success. Through a combination of robust analytics tools, an understanding of key metrics, and a commitment to data-driven decision-making, businesses can unlock new opportunities for growth, optimise their customer experience, and solidify their position as leaders in the ever-changing world of E-commerce.

7.9 SAFEGUARDING E-COMMERCE: SECURITY AND FRAUD PREVENTION STRATEGIES

In the increasingly digital world of E-commerce, ensuring the security of online transactions is not only a priority but a necessity. To cultivate customer trust and protect sensitive information, businesses must employ a robust, multi-layered approach to security and fraud prevention. This approach spans the entire transaction process, safeguarding data from the moment a customer engages with the website to the point of completing a payment. Implementing comprehensive security measures, protecting customer data, and utilising advanced fraud detection systems are essential for maintaining the integrity and reputation of any E-commerce platform.

One of the fundamental pillars of online transaction security is the use of SSL encryption. SSL technology plays a crucial role in protecting the flow of information between the customer's browser and the E-commerce platform. By encrypting sensitive data, such as personal details and payment information, SSL ensures that the information transmitted during transactions remains shielded from malicious actors who might attempt to intercept or manipulate it. This encryption not only protects the data itself but also instils confidence in customers by demonstrating that the website prioritises their security.

Partnering with reputable and secure payment gateways further enhances the protection of online transactions. Payment processors that comply with industry standards, particularly the PCI DSS, offer robust safeguards for handling sensitive payment data. One critical aspect of this protection is the use of tokenisation, a method that replaces sensitive information with unique tokens. These tokens can be used in place of actual payment details during transactions, significantly reducing the exposure of critical customer data and minimising the risk of theft or fraud.

The protection of customer data extends far beyond the transactional process. E-commerce businesses must implement comprehensive strategies that address both the technical and organisational aspects of data protection. This begins with ensuring the secure storage of customer information, particularly through data encryption, which keeps details confidential during both storage and transmission. Restricting access to sensitive data by enforcing strong authentication processes for internal systems is another essential step in preventing unauthorised access.

Regular security audits and vulnerability assessments are indispensable tools in maintaining the integrity of an E-commerce system. By conducting routine evaluations of the website's code, databases, and any third-party integrations, businesses can proactively identify and address potential weaknesses before they can be exploited by cybercriminals. These assessments also help businesses remain compliant with evolving security standards and best practices. Equally important is the role of employee awareness. Training staff on security protocols and potential threats fosters a culture of vigilance and responsibility, further reducing the risk of internal breaches.

Beyond data protection, E-commerce businesses face the ongoing challenge of identifying and preventing fraudulent activities such as unauthorised transactions and identity theft. In an era where fraudsters continually adapt their tactics, businesses must remain agile and use advanced technology to stay ahead of threats. One of the most effective tools in combating fraud is the implementation of machine learning algorithms and artificial intelligence (AI). These technologies are capable of processing vast amounts of data, from user behaviour and transaction history to device fingerprints, and can detect patterns that deviate from normal activity, flagging suspicious transactions in real time.

Multi-factor authentication (MFA) is another critical element of a robust security framework. By requiring users to provide multiple forms of verification—such as a password and a one-time code sent to their mobile device—MFA significantly reduces the likelihood of unauthorised access. This added layer of protection serves as a deterrent to fraudsters attempting to exploit weak passwords or other common vulnerabilities.

Collaboration with fraud prevention services is another vital aspect of a proactive approach to E-commerce security. These services, which often integrate geolocation data into their assessments, can help identify transactions that deviate from typical geographical patterns, such as purchases made from unusual locations. By flagging these transactions for further review, businesses can minimise the risk of fraudulent activity while also reducing the potential for false positives. Furthermore, monitoring chargeback rates and collaborating with payment processors to identify instances of friendly fraud—where a legitimate customer disputes a transaction—are essential strategies for mitigating financial losses.

In an age where cyber threats are continually evolving, businesses must remain diligent and forward-thinking in their approach to security. The key to safeguarding the integrity of E-commerce operations lies in a proactive, multi-layered approach. By employing robust security measures for online transactions, protecting customer data with comprehensive strategies, and deploying advanced fraud detection systems, businesses can create a secure, trustworthy environment for their customers. As technology continues to advance, E-commerce businesses must stay abreast of emerging threats and adapt their security protocols accordingly, ensuring that they not only protect their customers but also preserve their reputation and competitiveness in the digital marketplace.

7.10 CHAPTER SUMMARY

The ever-changing landscape of E-commerce offers both exciting opportunities and unique challenges for businesses aiming to thrive in the digital world. As this chapter has highlighted, success in E-commerce requires more than simply launching an online store. Businesses must adopt a holistic approach that considers everything from platform selection and website optimisation to creating a seamless checkout process that maximises conversions. Furthermore, building a secure and reliable payment infrastructure is vital, ensuring customers feel confident when making purchases. Marketing plays an integral role in driving traffic and fostering customer engagement, and a robust E-commerce strategy is incomplete without data-driven insights gained through analytics. Analysing customer behaviour, sales trends, and marketing effectiveness enables businesses to make informed decisions and continuously refine their operations for long-term growth. Finally, the importance of safeguarding customer data through stringent security measures and fraud prevention cannot be understated, as it protects both the reputation and financial well-being of the business. Ultimately, E-commerce success is achieved through an interconnected web of strategy, innovation, and vigilance. By focusing on every aspect of the online selling process, businesses are better positioned to maximise sales, build customer loyalty, and stay competitive in the ever-expanding digital marketplace.

Key Questions for Discussion

1. How has the evolution of e-commerce transformed consumer behaviour and business practices? What are some key trends shaping the future of e-commerce?
2. What factors should businesses consider when choosing an e-commerce platform, and how do these choices impact long-term success? Are there specific features that are now non-negotiable for modern e-commerce platforms?
3. What are the most common challenges businesses face in the checkout process, and how can they address them to boost conversions? Additionally, how can businesses build a secure and user-friendly payment infrastructure to enhance customer trust?
4. In a highly competitive digital marketplace, what are the most effective strategies for marketing an e-commerce store? How can businesses use personalised marketing techniques to increase customer engagement and loyalty?
5. How can businesses leverage e-commerce analytics to drive strategic growth and improve performance? What proactive measures should they take to safeguard their platforms against security breaches and fraud?

BIBLIOGRAPHY

Chaffey, D. (2024). *Digital Marketing: Strategy, Implementation and Practice.* 8th ed. Pearson.
Chaffey, D. and Ellis-Chadwick, F. (2023). *Digital Marketing: Strategy, Implementation and Practice.* 7th ed. Pearson.
Charlesworth, A. (2023). *Digital Marketing: A Practical Approach.* 3rd ed. Routledge.
Evans, D. (2023). *Social Media Marketing: An Hour a Day.* 3rd ed. Wiley.
Green, D. (2023). *The E-commerce Book: Building the E-empire.* 3rd ed. Springer.
Grewal, D. and Levy, M. (2023). *Marketing.* 8th ed. McGraw-Hill Education.
Laudon, K.C. and Traver, C.G. (2024). *E-commerce 2024: Business, Technology, Society.* 17th ed. Pearson.
Leeflang, P.S.H., Verhoef, P.C., Dahlström, P. and Freundt, T. (2023). *Digital Marketing & Analytics: A Practical Introduction.* 1st ed. Routledge.
Khosrow-Pour, M. (2023). *Encyclopedia of E-Commerce Development, Implementation, and Management.* 2nd ed. IGI Global.
King, D. (2023). *E-commerce Essentials.* 2nd ed. Pearson.
Kotler, P., Kartajaya, H. and Setiawan, I. (2023). *Marketing 5.0: Technology for Humanity.* 1st ed. Wiley
Ryan, D. (2023). *Understanding Digital Marketing: Marketing Strategies for Engaging the Digital Generation.* 5th ed. Kogan Page.
Smith, P.R. and Zook, Z. (2023). *Marketing Communications: Offline and Online Integration, Engagement and Analytics.* 7th ed. Kogan Page.
Strauss, J. and Frost, R. (2023). *E-marketing.* 8th ed. Routledge.
Yadav, M.S. and Pavlou, P.A. (2023). *E-commerce and the Digital Economy.* 1st ed. Routledge.

CHAPTER 8

Data-Driven Decision-Making

Analytics and Insights for Digital Business

Learning Outcomes

By the end of this chapter, you will be able to:

1. Understand how data-driven decision-making can improve business performance and drive strategic outcomes in the digital business landscape.
2. Learn how to apply key technologies such as predictive analytics and machine learning, as well as techniques like profiling and segmentation, to optimise customer experiences and sales conversions.
3. Gain insights into the ethical imperatives of data collection and management, with a focus on privacy, transparency, and fairness in the context of data-driven business strategies.

8.1 INTRODUCTION

In the digital age, data have become an indispensable asset for businesses, driving decisions and shaping strategies across all sectors. The advent of digital technologies has given rise to an unprecedented amount of data, offering companies invaluable insights into customer behaviour, market trends, and operational efficiencies. This growing reliance on data has ushered in the era of data-driven decision-making, where data are no longer simply a byproduct of operations but a strategic resource that can determine business success or failure.

This chapter explores the power and potential of data-driven decision-making within the context of digital businesses. As the world becomes increasingly digital, the ability to collect, analyse, and derive meaningful insights from vast datasets has become a cornerstone of competitive advantage. Whether it is understanding customer preferences, optimising sales and conversion rates, or forecasting market trends, data analytics provides the foundation for making informed, real-time decisions that can elevate a business to new heights. Yet, navigating the complexities of data management, including issues surrounding

DOI: 10.4324/9781032672458-8

data quality, security, and privacy, requires a sophisticated approach. This chapter addresses these challenges and introduces key technologies that enable businesses to harness the full potential of their data.

From web analytics to customer profiling and predictive modelling, the subsequent sections delve deep into the tools and techniques that modern digital businesses must master. This chapter not only explores how data can be used to drive business growth but also highlights the ethical considerations and responsibilities that accompany this shift towards data-centric strategies.

8.2 THE POWER OF DATA-DRIVEN DECISION-MAKING IN DIGITAL BUSINESS

In the rapidly evolving world of digital business, the integration of data-driven decision-making has become a pivotal element of success. Data analytics, at its core, involves the methodical examination of extensive datasets to derive actionable insights, ultimately informing strategic choices. Within the digital landscape, companies gather a wealth of information from various channels, including customer behaviour, website performance metrics, and broader market trends. Recognising the role of data analytics is akin to harnessing a vital tool that grants businesses a profound understanding of customer preferences, market shifts, and operational effectiveness.

The adoption of data analytics enables organisations to transcend decisions based on instinct or limited information, allowing for evidence-based and more accurate decision-making. Through comprehensive analysis, businesses can detect underlying patterns, identify emerging trends, and uncover correlations that would otherwise go unnoticed. This heightened awareness not only increases the precision of decisions but also allows companies to respond swiftly and effectively to evolving market conditions and consumer demands.

The advantages of data-driven decision-making are substantial and permeate every aspect of digital business operations. One of the most significant benefits is the enhancement of strategic planning and goal setting. With precise and timely data, companies can formulate realistic objectives grounded in the actualities of the market and consumer behaviour. This data-backed approach ensures that strategic initiatives are not only well-informed but also more likely to succeed, improving overall resource allocation and financial planning.

Data-driven strategies also foster a deeper connection with customers. By analysing consumer interactions and preferences, businesses can create highly personalised products, services, and marketing efforts that resonate with individual expectations. This level of personalisation nurtures stronger relationships between the brand and its customers, thereby strengthening brand loyalty and positioning the company more competitively within its sector. Moreover, such an approach enhances customer satisfaction, leading to higher retention rates and long-term success.

Operational efficiency is another key advantage afforded by data-driven decision-making. Businesses that utilise data to scrutinise their internal processes can readily identify inefficiencies, bottlenecks, or redundancies within workflows. By addressing these issues, companies can streamline their operations, reduce costs, and optimise the use of their resources. This not only improves day-to-day functioning but also creates long-term sustainability and profitability.

The process of data analytics itself is a structured journey, beginning with data collection and culminating in actionable insights. It starts by identifying relevant data sources, which may include customer interactions, website activity, social media engagement, and broader market research. Companies may employ a variety of data collection techniques, from using digital tools and analytics software to conducting surveys or integrating third-party data.

Once data have been collected, they must be cleaned and pre-processed to ensure accuracy and consistency. This step involves addressing any gaps or missing data, removing outliers, and standardising formats to create a dataset that is ready for analysis. Without this crucial step, data could provide misleading or incomplete insights, rendering the decision-making process ineffective.

The analysis phase forms the core of the data analytics process. By applying statistical models and machine learning algorithms, businesses can extract meaningful patterns and correlations from the data. The process may involve several types of analysis: descriptive analytics to assess past performance, diagnostic analytics to understand why certain trends occurred, predictive analytics to forecast future outcomes, and prescriptive analytics to recommend the best courses of action (Figure 8.1).

The final stage is translating the analysis into insights that guide decision-making. Through the use of visualisations, reports, and dashboards, the findings are presented in a clear and comprehensible manner, enabling stakeholders to make informed and strategic decisions. It's important to remember that the data analytics process is iterative, continuously feeding back into itself as new data are collected and analysed, refining strategies and adjusting to emerging trends.

In essence, data-driven decision-making stands at the heart of digital business success. It offers not only the tools to gain a competitive edge but also the capacity to make precise, informed choices. By embracing the full spectrum of data analytics and understanding its advantages, businesses can harness the transformative potential of data, driving innovation, growth, and sustainability in the ever-evolving digital economy.

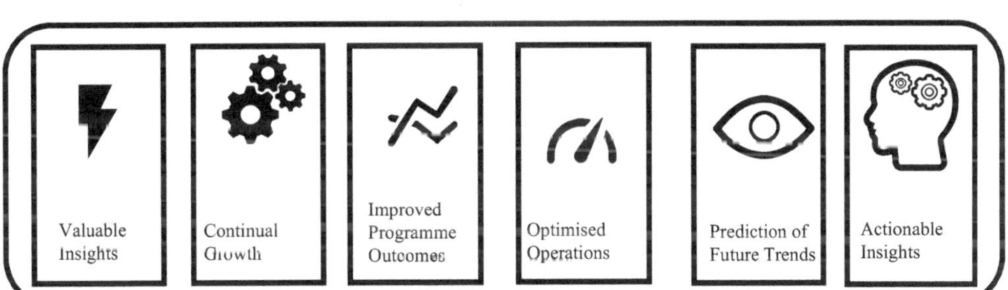

FIGURE 8.1 Data-Driven Decision-making: Accelerating Business Growth in the Digital Age

8.3 NAVIGATING THE COMPLEXITIES OF DATA IN DIGITAL BUSINESS

In the expansive world of digital business, data present themselves in many forms, and understanding these distinctions is critical to unlocking its full potential. Data can be broadly classified into structured and unstructured types, each offering unique opportunities and challenges for analysis and interpretation. Structured data refers to highly organised information that follows a predefined format, often residing in databases. Common examples include customer profiles, transaction histories, and product inventories. These forms of data are easily searchable, quantifiable, and lend themselves well to traditional analysis techniques using relational database systems. In contrast, unstructured data are less organised and lack a set structure. They can include text, images, audio, video, and other forms of content, such as social media posts or customer reviews. While more challenging to analyse, unstructured data hold valuable insights into consumer behaviour, preferences, and trends, which can be critical for digital businesses seeking to stay ahead of the competition.

In addition to understanding the form data take, it is important for digital businesses to distinguish between internal and external data sources. Internal data stem directly from an organisation's own operations, encompassing everything from sales figures and customer interactions to employee performance metrics and internal process data. These data offer businesses a detailed, intimate view of their day-to-day operations and how they engage with their customers. However, external data—sourced from outside the organisation—broadens this perspective. External data might include competitor insights, market trends, industry benchmarks, and macroeconomic indicators. By integrating both internal and external data, businesses can better contextualise their own performance, understanding where they stand within the larger market landscape. This holistic approach enables more informed decision-making, providing businesses with the insight needed to adjust their strategies in response to external pressures and opportunities.

The method of processing data is another key consideration for businesses in the digital age, particularly in choosing between real-time and batch data processing. Real-time data processing analyses information as it is generated, allowing businesses to act on insights immediately. This capability is especially crucial in situations that require rapid responses, such as detecting fraud or monitoring customer behaviour during an ongoing marketing campaign. The ability to make real-time adjustments can significantly enhance a business's agility and responsiveness. Conversely, batch data processing involves collecting data over a designated period and then analysing it in bulk. This method is well-suited to tasks that do not demand immediate insights, such as generating regular financial reports, conducting historical trend analysis, or performing large-scale computations. The decision between real-time and batch processing is largely dictated by the specific needs of the business, with each method offering advantages depending on the urgency and scale of the task at hand.

A nuanced understanding of these data distinctions—structured versus unstructured, internal versus external, and real-time versus batch processing—equips businesses with the insight necessary to master data management. By leveraging the appropriate types of data and processing techniques, businesses can unlock valuable insights that fuel smarter decision-making, enhance their competitive positioning, and drive innovation. As data continue to be the lifeblood of digital business, mastering its complexities is essential for sustained success in an increasingly data-driven world.

8.4 HARNESSING KEY TECHNOLOGIES FOR DATA ANALYTICS IN DIGITAL BUSINESS

In today's digital landscape, the ability to effectively harness data analytics technologies and tools is fundamental to the success of any business. At the heart of this process are advanced data analytics platforms, business intelligence (BI) tools, and powerful data visualisation capabilities that work together to convert raw data into actionable insights.

Data analytics platforms like Google Analytics and Adobe Analytics serve as the foundational technology for collecting, processing, and interpreting vast amounts of data. Google Analytics, one of the most widely used tools in the industry, allows businesses to analyse website traffic, track user behaviour, and measure conversion rates. It offers detailed insights into user demographics, browsing patterns, and the overall effectiveness of marketing campaigns. Adobe Analytics extends beyond traditional website analytics, offering a more comprehensive view of customer interactions across a range of digital platforms. Together, these platforms provide a clear and comprehensive understanding of how users engage with a business, empowering organisations to make data-driven decisions that improve performance and customer engagement.

Complementing these platforms are BI tools, which play a crucial role in transforming raw data into clear, actionable insights. Tools such as Tableau, Microsoft Power BI, and Qlik enable businesses to extract meaningful patterns from large datasets, making it easier to interpret complex information. Tableau, for instance, is renowned for its powerful data visualisation features, allowing users to create highly interactive charts, graphs, and dashboards. Microsoft Power BI stands out for its seamless integration with a wide array of data sources, giving users the ability to analyse and share insights across departments. Meanwhile, Qlik's associative analytics capabilities allow businesses to uncover hidden relationships in their data, fostering a deeper understanding of the dynamics at play. By using these BI tools, organisations can visualise trends, monitor performance, and effectively communicate insights to stakeholders across all levels.

The ability to communicate data insights visually is a vital aspect of modern business, and tools designed for data visualisation and dashboard creation are critical in achieving this. Platforms such as D3.js, Plotly, and Chart.js enable businesses to convert complex datasets into visually engaging formats. D3.js, for example, is a JavaScript library that offers an unparalleled level of customisation, enabling the creation of bespoke visualisations tailored to the specific needs of a business. Plotly provides a range of dynamic visualisation options and a user-friendly interface, making it particularly useful for businesses needing to present data in clear and engaging formats. Similarly, Chart.js is valued for its simplicity and versatility, offering an ideal solution for organisations seeking quick and effective visualisation options.

Dashboards play an equally significant role in presenting key insights. Tools like Klipfolio, Tableau, and Microsoft Power BI excel at creating intuitive, real-time dashboards that allow businesses to track and monitor key performance indicators (KPIs) in a single interface. Klipfolio's cloud-based platform enables businesses to build customisable dashboards, integrating data from a variety of sources to create a unified view of business performance. Tableau's dashboard capabilities allow users to combine multiple visualisations into interactive, cohesive displays that provide an at-a-glance view of critical metrics. Microsoft Power BI, with its powerful integration capabilities, provides highly customisable dashboards tailored to the specific needs of different business units, ensuring that each department can track the metrics most relevant to its operations.

These technologies collectively form the backbone of data-driven decision-making in digital business. By integrating platforms like Google Analytics and Adobe Analytics with BI tools such as Tableau and Power BI and enhancing data interpretation through visualisation tools like D3.js and Plotly, businesses can unlock valuable insights hidden in their data. These insights not only help organisations make informed decisions but also foster a culture of data-driven innovation. With the right combination of data analytics technologies, digital businesses are well-equipped to navigate the increasingly complex and competitive landscape, ensuring sustained growth and success in the digital age.

8.5 COMPREHENSIVE DATA COLLECTION AND MANAGEMENT FOR DIGITAL BUSINESS SUCCESS

The success of any data-driven decision-making strategy is deeply rooted in the ability to efficiently collect and manage high-quality data. In the digital business landscape, this requires the establishment of effective data collection mechanisms, maintaining rigorous data quality standards, and adhering to essential data governance and privacy regulations.

To begin with, setting up reliable and comprehensive data collection systems is critical. For a digital business to derive meaningful insights, it must first gather accurate and relevant data from various touchpoints. Tools such as Google Analytics, Mixpanel, and Segment offer advanced capabilities to track and collect data. Google Analytics, for instance, provides businesses with a detailed understanding of website traffic, user behaviour, and conversion performance. Mixpanel focuses on event-based tracking, enabling businesses to understand user actions within web and mobile applications, providing invaluable insights into customer journeys. Segment acts as a central hub for managing customer data, allowing businesses to seamlessly collect, unify, and transmit data across various marketing and analytics platforms. However, effective data collection extends beyond the tools themselves—it requires a strategic approach. Businesses must define clear objectives and KPIs to ensure the data collected aligns with the overarching business goals, whether it's improving customer experiences, refining marketing strategies, or optimising product development.

Once data are collected, maintaining its quality is of paramount importance. The analytics process can only be as effective as the quality of the data being analysed. With the multitude of data sources that businesses interact with daily, ensuring the accuracy, completeness, and consistency of data becomes a complex but necessary task. Data cleansing, the process of detecting and rectifying errors and inconsistencies, is essential to safeguard the integrity of the information. Automated tools like Trifacta and OpenRefine simplify this process, making it easier for businesses to clean and prepare data for analysis. Trifacta, leveraging machine learning, identifies patterns and anomalies within datasets, automating much of the error detection process. OpenRefine, a powerful yet user-friendly tool, enables businesses to explore and clean datasets, ensuring consistency by addressing issues like missing values or duplicate entries. Establishing data quality standards, coupled with routine validation checks during the data collection phase, helps prevent potential errors from contaminating the dataset. Conducting regular data audits ensures the continuous accuracy and reliability of information, ultimately improving the confidence with which businesses can base their decisions on the data.

Beyond collection and quality control, digital businesses must navigate the increasingly complex terrain of data governance and privacy. Effective data governance entails developing and enforcing policies and standards to manage and protect data assets. These policies must define clear roles, responsibilities, and access controls to ensure that data are used responsibly. Additionally, compliance with major privacy regulations like the General Data Protection Regulation (GDPR) and the California Consumer Privacy Act (CCPA) is a non-negotiable aspect of data management. These laws emphasise the need for transparent data practices, user consent, and the protection of sensitive information. Businesses must adopt practical steps such as implementing consent management tools to obtain and manage user permissions and anonymising or pseudonymising personally identifiable information to protect individual privacy. Furthermore, robust data security measures must be put in place to protect data during transmission. Encryption techniques and secure transmission protocols, such as secure sockets layer or Transport Layer Security, ensure that data remain confidential and inaccessible to unauthorised parties during its journey across the internet.

In sum, the collection and management of data within a digital business are multifaceted processes that demand a careful blend of technological solutions and strategic planning. Employing tools like Google Analytics, Mixpanel, and Segment streamlines the data collection process, while platforms like Trifacta and OpenRefine ensure that data quality is maintained. Moreover, by establishing sound data governance practices and adhering to global privacy regulations, businesses safeguard their data and build trust with their customers. By taking a comprehensive approach to managing the entire data lifecycle, digital businesses position themselves to extract meaningful insights and make informed, strategic decisions that can drive growth and success in today's competitive digital environment.

8.6 UNDERSTANDING WEB ANALYTICS AND USER BEHAVIOUR: MAXIMISING ONLINE INTERACTIONS

Web analytics and user behaviour tracking are essential for digital businesses aiming to enhance user experience and optimise their online strategies. By closely monitoring website visitors and their interactions, businesses can gain critical insights into how users navigate through their websites, what content engages them, and what actions they take. One of the most widely used tools in this domain is Google Analytics, which provides detailed information about visitor demographics, traffic sources, and the paths users take through the site. Through the implementation of tracking codes, businesses can observe user interactions, including clicks, form submissions, and time spent on various pages. These data serve as the foundation for improving the user experience, identifying which aspects of a site work well, and where improvements can be made.

In addition to basic visitor tracking, the analysis of user behaviour has evolved to offer a more detailed understanding of how users engage with a website. Tools such as Hotjar and Crazy Egg allow businesses to visualise user behaviour through heatmaps, session recordings, and user feedback. Heatmaps, in particular, are instrumental in showing where users are clicking, scrolling, and moving on a page, giving businesses a clear picture of high-engagement areas or potential friction points. This visual information can inform decisions about content placement, page layout, and user interface design, ensuring that a website is as intuitive and user-friendly as possible.

The analysis of website traffic provides further valuable insight, allowing businesses to understand not only how many visitors are coming to the site but also where they are coming from and how they are interacting once they arrive. Web analytics tools like Google Analytics offer detailed traffic reports that break down this information into categories such as new versus returning visitors, geographic location, and device type. These insights help businesses tailor their marketing strategies, refine content, and ensure their website caters to the needs of their target audience. Understanding the conversion funnel is an essential aspect of this process, as it maps the journey users take from their initial visit to completing a desired action, such as making a purchase or signing up for a service. Analysing this funnel can reveal where users are dropping off or encountering obstacles, allowing businesses to address issues and optimise the journey at each stage. Google Analytics, in particular, provides comprehensive conversion tracking features that enable businesses to measure and optimise KPIs throughout the funnel, ultimately improving conversion rates.

Beyond traditional traffic metrics, heatmaps and clickstream analysis offer a deeper understanding of user interactions. Heatmaps visually represent the intensity of user activity on a webpage, highlighting the areas where users are most engaged and where they might be experiencing difficulty. Tools like Crazy Egg generate these heatmaps, providing insights into how users click, move, and scroll on a webpage. These data are vital for optimising website design, improving layout, and making sure that the most important information is readily accessible to users. In addition to heatmaps, clickstream analysis tracks the specific sequence of clicks and interactions a user makes during their visit. Tools such as Mixpanel and Kissmetrics allow businesses to map out these paths, showing which routes through the site are most popular and where users tend to focus their attention. By identifying common navigation routes and potential bottlenecks, businesses can further refine the user journey, ensuring that it aligns with their objectives and improves the overall user experience.

Incorporating these advanced tools and analyses into a digital strategy equips businesses with a holistic understanding of user behaviour. By tracking visitor interactions, analysing traffic patterns, and leveraging the detailed insights provided by heatmaps and clickstream analysis, businesses can optimise their websites to meet user needs more effectively. The data gathered through these methods forms the foundation for continuous improvement, allowing businesses to make informed, data-driven decisions that enhance user satisfaction, boost engagement, and ultimately lead to the achievement of their digital goals. This comprehensive approach to understanding and managing user behaviour is indispensable for businesses seeking success in the fast-paced and ever-evolving digital landscape.

CASE STUDY 8

Amazon's Recommendation Engine — Harnessing Data for Personalised Customer Experiences

Amazon, the global e-commerce giant, has built its success on leveraging data to enhance customer experiences and drive sales. One of its most powerful tools is its recommendation engine, which utilises big data analytics and machine learning to analyse customer behaviour and deliver personalised product suggestions. As online retail competition intensified, Amazon needed a way to improve customer engagement, boost sales, and differentiate itself from other digital marketplaces. The challenge was to develop a system that could understand individual customer preferences, predict future purchases, and provide relevant recommendations in real time. Given the vast number of products available on its platform, Amazon required an advanced approach to data-driven decision-making to ensure that customers could easily discover products suited to their needs.

To address this, Amazon developed a sophisticated recommendation engine that collects and analyses vast amounts of data, including browsing history, past purchases, product reviews, and items in customers' shopping carts. Using collaborative filtering and deep learning algorithms, the system identifies patterns in user behaviour and suggests products tailored to individual preferences. The recommendation engine works across multiple touchpoints, from personalised homepage suggestions to targeted emails and dynamic advertisements. Amazon also integrates real-time data streams, allowing the engine to refine recommendations based on current trends and seasonal shopping patterns. The system continuously learns and adapts, ensuring that the recommendations become more accurate over time.

The results of Amazon's recommendation engine have been transformative. Approximately 35% of Amazon's total sales are attributed to its personalised recommendations, demonstrating the effectiveness of data-driven decision-making. The system has significantly improved customer engagement, as personalised suggestions lead to increased time spent on the platform and higher conversion rates. Additionally, the recommendation engine has enhanced customer satisfaction by making shopping experiences more intuitive and relevant. Amazon's data-driven approach not only boosts its revenue but also fosters customer loyalty, as users return to the platform expecting a tailored shopping experience.

This case study highlights several key lessons in data-driven decision-making. First, personalisation is a powerful tool in digital business, allowing companies to increase engagement and sales by catering to individual customer preferences. Second, businesses can leverage big data analytics to enhance user experiences and improve operational efficiency. Third, continuous learning and adaptation are essential for maintaining a competitive edge, as data-driven systems must evolve with changing consumer behaviours. Lastly, integrating analytics into multiple business functions can drive long-term success, demonstrating how data-driven strategies can become a core pillar of business growth.

Discussion Questions for Students (with Indicative Answers)

1. **How does Amazon's recommendation engine enhance the customer shopping experience?**
   Indicative Answer: By analysing customer data, Amazon provides personalised product recommendations that help customers discover relevant items, improving engagement and satisfaction.
2. **Why is data-driven decision-making important for e-commerce businesses?**
   Indicative Answer: It enables businesses to optimise operations, personalise customer interactions, and increase sales through insights derived from user behaviour.
3. **What technologies and methods does Amazon use in its recommendation engine?**
   Indicative Answer: Amazon employs collaborative filtering, deep learning, and real-time data analytics to refine and personalise recommendations.
4. **What are the key benefits of using a recommendation engine for an online retailer?**
   Indicative Answer: It increases customer engagement, boosts sales, enhances user experience, and fosters customer loyalty.
5. **What lessons can other businesses learn from Amazon's use of big data analytics?**
   Indicative Answer: Companies should prioritise data-driven strategies, personalise customer experiences, and continuously adapt their systems to remain competitive in the digital economy.

8.7 HARNESSING CUSTOMER DATA: PROFILING, SEGMENTATION, AND PERSONALISATION IN DIGITAL BUSINESS

In the competitive world of digital business, understanding your customers beyond surface-level interactions is crucial. This is where customer profiling, segmentation, and personalisation play pivotal roles in shaping strategies that align with customer needs and preferences. Customer profiling is the first step in this process, where businesses develop detailed portraits of their audience based on demographic data, behavioural patterns, and personal preferences. By leveraging tools such as Salesforce or HubSpot CRM, businesses are able to centralise and manage vast amounts of customer data. These tools help build comprehensive profiles that serve as the cornerstone of targeted marketing campaigns and customer outreach, ensuring that each communication is more relevant and engaging.

Segmentation strategies refine this customer profiling by categorising individuals into specific groups based on shared characteristics. These segmentation strategies are highly nuanced and may involve several key approaches. Geographic segmentation, for example, focuses on where customers are located, while demographic segmentation delves into aspects such as age, gender, and income level. Psychographic segmentation explores deeper elements like lifestyle choices, values, and personality traits, whereas behavioural segmentation centres on how customers interact with a business or brand. Each of these methods allows businesses to further tailor their messaging, promotions, and product offerings to better suit the needs of distinct customer groups. By dividing the customer base in this way, companies can deliver more targeted experiences, ensuring that marketing efforts resonate with the unique preferences and behaviours of different segments.

Beyond simply categorising customers, businesses today are taking advantage of customer data to deliver highly personalised experiences. Personalisation, a strategy that involves adjusting content, recommendations, and communication based on individual preferences and past interactions, has become essential in digital commerce. Leading companies like Amazon set the benchmark in personalisation by using advanced algorithms to suggest products that align with each customer's browsing history and purchase patterns. This data-driven approach ensures that customers are continuously offered relevant and appealing options, fostering a deeper sense of connection between the business and its clientele.

Customisation takes this a step further by giving customers the ability to directly shape their own experience. E-commerce platforms, for instance, frequently allow customers to modify product configurations, select their preferred delivery options, or adjust their subscription preferences. Whether it's tailoring the type of emails they receive or customising product choices, giving users control over their interactions makes them feel valued and understood. Collecting and analysing customer data underpins both personalisation and customisation efforts. It ensures that the experiences businesses create are not only relevant but also responsive to individual needs, fostering increased customer satisfaction and loyalty.

An equally important aspect of customer data analysis is customer lifetime value (CLV). This metric measures the total revenue a business can expect from a customer throughout their relationship. Understanding CLV helps businesses prioritise high-value customers, allowing them to focus resources on those most likely to generate long term profit. By examining key factors such as purchase frequency, average transaction value, and customer retention rates, businesses can develop a more accurate picture of which customers are worth greater investment. Tools like Kissmetrics and Google Analytics assist in tracking and calculating CLV, offering insights into which marketing channels are most effective for acquiring valuable customers and how retention efforts contribute to overall profitability. These insights enable businesses to make smarter decisions about where to invest their marketing and customer service efforts, leading to optimised strategies for both acquisition and retention.

In the fast-paced, ever-changing digital landscape, customer data is the foundation of success. Profiling, segmentation, personalisation, and CLV analysis are all interconnected strategies that allow businesses to build deeper, more meaningful relationships with their customers. By creating tailored experiences that meet the specific needs and preferences of distinct customer segments, businesses not only enhance customer satisfaction but also increase loyalty and long-term profitability. Through the strategic use of customer data, companies can navigate the complexities of digital business with greater precision, driving sustainable growth and securing a competitive edge in the marketplace.

8.8 MAXIMISING SALES AND CONVERSION SUCCESS THROUGH DATA ANALYTICS

In the competitive digital marketplace, data analytics is an invaluable asset for businesses seeking to optimise sales performance and conversion rates. Analysing sales data and funnel efficiency provides a comprehensive understanding of the customer journey, from the first point of interaction through to final conversion. Platforms such as Salesforce and HubSpot Sales Hub are crucial in this process, enabling businesses to meticulously track sales activities, monitor pipeline progress, and analyse deal closures. These tools offer sales teams the ability to identify winning strategies, streamline sales processes, and even forecast future sales based on historical data. With such insights, businesses are better equipped to implement data-driven decisions that directly impact growth and profitability.

Examining the sales funnel is a critical aspect of understanding how potential customers move through different stages of engagement before making a purchase. The sales funnel is a visual representation of this journey, and tools like Google Analytics and Mixpanel are instrumental in helping businesses analyse each step of the process. These platforms allow businesses to track user progression through the funnel, identifying key drop-off points or bottlenecks that may hinder conversions. By analysing these inefficiencies, companies can develop and implement targeted strategies to enhance the user experience, making the path to conversion smoother and more efficient. This approach ensures that potential leads are nurtured effectively and are less likely to abandon the journey before completing a transaction.

Conversion rate optimisation (CRO) is a data-centric approach designed to maximise the percentage of website visitors who take a desired action, such as completing a purchase or submitting a form. CRO techniques utilise valuable data insights to refine the user experience, ensuring that every interaction on the website encourages desired behaviours. Tools like Crazy Egg and Hotjar provide visual heatmaps, which highlight areas of high user engagement on a webpage. These heatmaps enable businesses to optimise critical elements such as page layout, call-to-action placement, and overall design for greater impact. By focusing on the most active areas of user interaction, businesses can refine their websites to make them more user-friendly and increase the likelihood of conversions.

User journey analysis further deepens the understanding of how customers navigate a website before completing an action. Platforms like Google Analytics and Kissmetrics facilitate this analysis, allowing businesses to track the paths users take and how they engage with different elements on the site. This knowledge is invaluable for aligning website structure and content with user expectations, ensuring that the overall experience is seamless and intuitive. When customers can easily find the information or products they are seeking, they are more likely to convert, making a well-optimised user journey an essential component of digital success.

A/B testing and multivariate testing are critical tools in the CRO process, enabling businesses to experiment with different elements on their websites and identify the most effective combinations for driving conversions. A/B testing involves comparing two different versions of a webpage or specific element, such as headlines, images, or call-to-action buttons, to determine which version performs better. Tools like Optimizely and Visual Website Optimiser make this process straightforward, splitting traffic between the two variations and providing detailed statistical analysis of the results. The insights gained from A/B testing allow businesses to make informed decisions about which design or content variations resonate most with their audience.

Multivariate testing, on the other hand, takes this approach to a more sophisticated level by testing multiple variations of several elements simultaneously. While A/B testing is useful for testing one change at a time, multivariate testing is ideal when businesses want to explore the combined effects of multiple changes on user behaviour. This method allows for a deeper understanding of how different elements work together to influence conversions. The ability to experiment with multiple variables at once ensures that businesses can fine-tune their websites to achieve the optimal combination of design, messaging, and functionality.

In the fast-evolving digital landscape, leveraging data analytics to enhance sales and conversion rates is not just a strategy but a necessity. By closely analysing sales performance and refining funnel efficiency, businesses gain valuable insights that enable them to optimise their sales processes and develop more effective strategies. CRO techniques, including the use of heatmaps, user journey analysis, and rigorous testing methods like A/B and multivariate testing, empower businesses to continuously improve the user experience and increase the likelihood of conversions. In an increasingly competitive online environment, the ability to extract meaningful insights from data and apply them to optimise sales and conversions is a defining factor for success.

8.9 HARNESSING PREDICTIVE ANALYTICS AND MACHINE LEARNING FOR STRATEGIC ADVANTAGE

Predictive analytics and machine learning are revolutionising the way businesses navigate the digital landscape, offering powerful tools to anticipate trends, optimise decision-making, and foster growth. At the heart of predictive analytics lies the ability to use historical data to forecast future events, uncover patterns, and make informed decisions with precision and foresight. Key models such as regression analysis, time series forecasting, and machine learning algorithms are instrumental in extracting valuable insights that drive business strategies.

Regression analysis plays a pivotal role in understanding the relationship between variables, enabling businesses to predict outcomes based on historical trends. For example, regression models can help forecast sales figures by analysing past performance in relation to marketing spend, seasonality, and market conditions. Time series forecasting, in contrast, focuses on predicting outcomes over time, making it particularly valuable in industries where patterns evolve cyclically, such as retail, finance, or supply chain management. Through time series forecasting, businesses can anticipate demand shifts, plan inventory, and prepare for peak seasons with greater accuracy.

Machine learning algorithms elevate predictive analytics by providing deeper, more intricate analyses of data. These algorithms, such as decision trees, support vector machines, and neural networks, have the ability to process vast datasets, identify non-obvious relationships, and predict outcomes with a high degree of accuracy. By leveraging machine learning, businesses can go beyond simple correlations and uncover hidden insights within their data, enabling them to make smarter, data-driven decisions.

The implementation of machine learning algorithms is a complex yet rewarding endeavour, requiring the selection of the appropriate model for the task at hand, training the model with historical data, and fine-tuning it for optimal performance. Platforms such as TensorFlow and scikit-learn offer robust frameworks that allow businesses to experiment with various algorithms and fine-tune models to meet specific business objectives. For instance, classification algorithms are commonly used to predict discrete outcomes such as customer churn, where businesses can proactively identify customers at risk of leaving and intervene with retention strategies. Regression algorithms, such as random forests, are frequently used to predict continuous outcomes like future revenue or demand. Clustering algorithms, like k-means, are invaluable in identifying patterns or segmenting customers into distinct groups, enabling more personalised and effective marketing strategies.

Predictive analytics is transforming numerous sectors within digital business, delivering meaningful applications across a variety of domains. In e-commerce, businesses harness predictive models to analyse customer behaviour, forecast purchasing patterns, and offer personalised product recommendations. By integrating machine learning, these platforms can dynamically adjust pricing strategies based on real-time data, such as customer demand, competitor pricing, and even external market conditions. This level of pricing optimisation not only increases revenue but also enhances customer satisfaction by delivering the right product at the right price.

In digital marketing, predictive analytics is reshaping how businesses target their audiences. By identifying high-value customer segments through predictive modelling, marketers can personalise campaigns, ensuring the right messages reach the right people at the right time. This data-driven approach significantly increases engagement and conversion rates, as well as improves the return on marketing investment. Additionally, predictive analytics helps marketers to forecast which channels—be it email, social media, or pay per click—will perform best for specific campaigns, allowing businesses to allocate resources more efficiently and achieve better results.

Financial services, particularly in the areas of fraud detection and risk management, also benefit from predictive analytics. By continuously monitoring transaction data, machine learning algorithms can detect suspicious patterns or anomalies that may indicate fraudulent activity. These models evolve alongside the tactics employed by fraudsters, providing a dynamic and proactive defence mechanism that enhances both security and customer trust. Similarly, in healthcare, predictive analytics is employed to improve patient outcomes by identifying individuals at risk of developing certain conditions. By analysing patient data, healthcare providers can intervene earlier, personalise treatment plans, and ultimately improve patient care while reducing operational costs.

The field of human resources is not immune to the advantages of predictive analytics, particularly in talent acquisition and retention. Machine learning models can assess candidates' potential by analysing resumes and comparing them to historical employee data, predicting which applicants are likely to be successful. Additionally, predictive models can identify factors that contribute to employee turnover, allowing HR teams to implement targeted retention strategies, improve employee satisfaction, and reduce the costs associated with recruitment and onboarding.

The integration of predictive analytics and machine learning into digital business practices offers a transformative edge, allowing companies to make proactive, informed decisions. Whether in e-commerce, marketing, finance, healthcare, or human resources, the ability to anticipate trends, optimise operations, and tailor strategies based on predictive insights is a significant differentiator in today's competitive marketplace. By mastering these tools, businesses not only unlock the potential of their data but also position themselves to thrive in an ever-evolving digital world.

8.10 ETHICAL IMPERATIVES IN DATA ANALYTICS: PRIVACY, TRANSPARENCY, AND FAIRNESS

In an era where data analytics profoundly influences business strategies and decision-making, ethical considerations have become a critical dimension of responsible data usage. The growing prevalence of data-driven practices requires that businesses not only maximise the utility of data but also uphold the rights and protections of individuals whose information is being analysed. Central to this ethical obligation is a commitment to safeguarding data privacy, ensuring transparency in data collection, and eliminating bias in data analysis, all of which are essential in fostering trust and integrity within the digital ecosystem.

The concept of data privacy lies at the heart of ethical data analytics. As businesses increasingly rely on personal information to inform their operations, they must navigate complex regulatory frameworks such as the GDPR in Europe and the CCPA in the United States. These regulations are designed to protect individuals from the misuse of their data, demanding that organisations handle personal information with the utmost care and integrity. For businesses, this means ensuring that personal data are collected and used only for legitimate purposes and that the highest standards of security are in place to prevent unauthorised access and potential data breaches. Privacy-enhancing technologies, such as differential privacy, offer innovative ways to protect individual identities while still enabling businesses to perform valuable analyses on datasets. However, these technologies must be coupled with ethical data governance frameworks that prioritise individual rights over commercial gain.

Equally essential is the need for transparency and consent in data collection practices. Users should never be left in the dark regarding how their personal information will be gathered, processed, or stored. Transparency means clearly communicating the types of data being collected, the purposes for which it is being used, and the duration for which it will be retained. This level of openness fosters trust and demonstrates a commitment to ethical behaviour. Businesses must go beyond perfunctory privacy policies filled with legal jargon, instead crafting clear, accessible, and user-friendly explanations of their data practices. Consent, too, must be an active and informed process. This entails offering users granular control over what data they are willing to share, using opt-in mechanisms that give individuals the ability to make meaningful choices about their personal information.

This principle of transparency and consent becomes even more crucial as new technologies such as the Internet of Things and wearable devices begin to play an increasingly prominent role in everyday life. These technologies often collect vast quantities of personal data, sometimes passively, including sensitive information about users' behaviours, preferences, and health. Ethical data practices demand that businesses collecting data through such devices communicate their intentions clearly and secure explicit consent from users. Failing to do so risks serious breaches of trust and can lead to unintended privacy violations.

Beyond privacy and transparency, another pressing ethical challenge in data analytics is the prevention of bias and discrimination. Data, while seemingly objective, often reflects the biases present in its collection, whether these biases stem from societal inequalities, historical disparities, or flawed methodologies. When data is used to train machine learning models, these biases can become embedded in algorithms, potentially leading to unfair outcomes or even systemic discrimination. For example, if a model is trained on data that overrepresent one demographic group while underrepresenting others, the resulting analysis may favour the dominant group at the expense of minorities. This has significant implications in areas such as hiring, lending, and healthcare, where biased algorithms can perpetuate inequality.

Addressing this issue requires a proactive and multifaceted approach. Businesses must critically assess their data sources, ensuring diverse representation in the datasets they use and regularly auditing their algorithms to identify and rectify any potential biases. This also involves fostering a culture of awareness about bias within data science teams, encouraging scrutiny of data collection methods and interpretation of results. Fairness-aware machine learning techniques, which aim to build models that reduce biased outcomes, offer promising solutions to these challenges. However, they must be deployed with diligence, as even the most sophisticated algorithms cannot fully eliminate bias without human oversight and intervention.

Ethical data analysis also calls for an acknowledgement of historical biases embedded in many datasets. These biases may reflect long-standing societal prejudices, which, if left unchecked, can skew the results of data-driven decisions. To counter this, businesses should undertake a critical examination of the historical context of their data and implement corrective actions where necessary. This is not simply a technical exercise but an ethical commitment to promoting inclusivity and fairness in the insights that data analytics produces. Encouraging diversity within data science teams can further support these efforts, as diverse perspectives help ensure a more equitable and comprehensive approach to data analysis.

In the ever-evolving digital world, ethical data analytics is no longer just a regulatory requirement but a moral obligation. Upholding the principles of data privacy and protection, ensuring transparency in data collection, and actively working to avoid bias in data analysis are all essential components of responsible data practices. As businesses increasingly rely on data to inform decisions, they must remain vigilant in maintaining these ethical standards. By doing so, they can foster trust with their users, build more inclusive systems, and ultimately, harness the power of data in ways that benefit both individuals and society at large.

8.11 MAXIMISING THE ROI AND BUSINESS IMPACT OF DATA ANALYTICS

Measuring the return on investment (ROI) and business impact of data analytics initiatives is critical for organisations aiming to assess the true value derived from their analytics efforts. To gauge the effectiveness of these initiatives, businesses must establish KPIs that align with their overarching objectives and the specific goals set for each analytics project. These KPIs provide a clear and structured way to measure progress and determine whether data-driven strategies are delivering on their intended promises.

In the context of data analytics, KPIs vary significantly depending on the focus of the project and the industry in which it is applied. For example, marketing analytics might prioritise KPIs such as customer acquisition cost, conversion rates, and CLV, as these metrics reflect the success of targeted campaigns and customer engagement strategies. In contrast, for operations-focused analytics, KPIs may centre around metrics like efficiency gains, cost reductions, and supply chain optimisation, all of which directly impact a company's ability to streamline operations and cut unnecessary costs. Regardless of the specific KPIs selected, they must be closely tailored to the unique objectives of each project to ensure that they effectively measure progress toward the desired business outcomes.

While tracking KPIs provides an immediate sense of performance, evaluating the ROI of data analytics initiatives offers a more comprehensive view of their financial impact. ROI is a key metric for businesses looking to justify their investments in analytics and technology infrastructure. To calculate ROI, organisations typically use the formula: [(Net Benefit / Cost) * 100], where the net benefit represents the increase in revenue or reduction in costs directly attributable to the data analytics initiative. For instance, if a data-driven approach leads to improved decision-making that enhances sales or optimises operational processes, these gains are considered part of the net benefit. On the other hand, the costs factor in technology expenses, including the procurement of analytics tools, maintenance of infrastructure, and recruitment of specialised talent.

ROI evaluation is not a one-time task but an ongoing process that requires continuous monitoring and adjustment. As the data landscape evolves and analytics technologies advance, organisations must adapt their strategies and refine their investments to maximise value. This often involves re-evaluating both the costs and benefits associated with a particular initiative, as well as updating KPIs to reflect shifting business priorities or market conditions. Moreover, an effective evaluation of ROI requires a deep understanding of the specific goals the data initiative seeks to achieve and the strategic role that analytics plays in overall business decision-making.

Another crucial aspect of maximising the impact of data analytics is the ability to communicate data insights effectively to key stakeholders. Data analytics, while immensely powerful, often yields complex results that are not easily understood by all members of an organisation. Executives, department heads, and frontline employees may all require tailored communication approaches to fully grasp the relevance and implications of analytics findings. To bridge this gap, businesses must focus on presenting data in an accessible and compelling manner that aligns with the needs and concerns of various stakeholders.

Data visualisation tools play a central role in this process, transforming raw data into clear, easily interpretable visuals. Dashboards, charts, and interactive reports help stakeholders understand trends, correlations, and patterns within the data. Tools such as Tableau, Power BI, and Google Data Studio enable organisations to create dynamic, visually appealing representations of their data that allow for deeper exploration and insight generation. These visualisations are particularly effective in simplifying complex datasets, making it easier for non-technical stakeholders to engage with and act upon the insights provided.

In addition to visualisation, communicating data insights effectively requires the use of storytelling techniques. The ability to frame data in a narrative context helps to humanise the information and connect it to real-world business challenges. Storytelling not only makes the data more relatable but also emphasises the actionable steps that stakeholders can take based on the insights gleaned from the analysis. By integrating data into a broader narrative, businesses can foster a sense of urgency and purpose, encouraging stakeholders to use the information to drive informed decision-making.

To support this, regular communication across multiple channels is essential. Whether through team meetings, executive presentations, or internal newsletters, the continuous dissemination of data insights ensures that analytics become a routine part of the decision-making process at all levels of the organisation. Moreover, fostering a data-driven culture is key to ensuring that the insights generated by analytics are fully integrated into the organisation's daily operations. When employees at every level of the organisation are empowered to use data in their roles, the potential for achieving meaningful, analytics-driven business impact is significantly enhanced.

In conclusion, measuring the ROI and business impact of data analytics requires a comprehensive approach that incorporates KPIs, ROI assessment, and strategic communication. By aligning analytics initiatives with carefully chosen KPIs, businesses can track performance against specific goals and ensure that their efforts are delivering value. Regularly evaluating ROI provides a quantitative measure of the success of these investments, while effective communication ensures that data insights are accessible, actionable, and integrated into the organisation's decision-making processes. Ultimately, it is through this blend of measurement, evaluation, and communication that businesses can harness the full power of data analytics to drive sustained success in today's competitive marketplace.

8.12 CHAPTER SUMMARY

Data-driven decision-making is not just a trend in the digital business world—it is a necessity. In a landscape where customer expectations are rapidly evolving, competition is fierce, and markets are in constant flux, the ability to collect, analyse, and act upon data is what sets successful businesses apart. This chapter has explored the multifaceted nature of data analytics in digital business, providing a comprehensive overview of how companies can harness data for strategic advantage.

From the foundational aspects of data collection and management to more advanced applications like predictive analytics and machine learning, this chapter has highlighted the importance of a holistic approach to data. Web analytics and customer profiling offer a window into consumer behaviour, while segmentation and personalisation allow businesses to tailor their offerings for maximum impact. Yet, as organisations become more data-driven, they must also be mindful of the ethical implications of their practices. Transparency, privacy, and fairness are not only legal obligations but are also crucial for maintaining customer trust and loyalty.

The final takeaway from this chapter is that data analytics is not just about technology—it's about creating a culture where insights are valued, and decisions are driven by evidence rather than intuition. By fostering this mindset and investing in the right tools and practices, digital businesses can unlock new levels of efficiency, profitability, and long-term success.

Key Questions for Discussion

1. How does data-driven decision-making give businesses a competitive edge in the digital economy? Can you provide examples of companies that have successfully leveraged data analytics to transform their operations?
2. What are the primary challenges businesses face when collecting, managing, and analysing data? How can organisations overcome these challenges to ensure data quality and reliability?
3. How can businesses use predictive analytics and machine learning to forecast trends and make proactive decisions? What industries have seen the most success with these technologies, and why?
4. As businesses increasingly rely on data analytics, what ethical considerations should they prioritise to protect privacy, ensure transparency, and promote fairness? How do regulations like GDPR shape these considerations?
5. How can organisations measure the ROI of their data analytics efforts, and what strategies can they use to maximise the business impact of their insights?

BIBLIOGRAPHY

Baesens, B. (2014). *Analytics in a Big Data World: The Essential Guide to Data Science and its Applications*. Wiley.

Camm, J.D., Cochran, J.J., Fry, M.J., Ohlmann, J.W. and Anderson, D.R. (2020). *Business Analytics*. Cengage Learning.

Chen, H., Chiang, R.H.L. and Storey, V.C. (2012). Business Intelligence and Analytics: From Big Data to Big Impact. *MIS Quarterly*, 36(4), pp. 1165–1188.

Davenport, T.H. and Harris, J.G. (2017). *Competing on Analytics: The New Science of Winning.* Harvard Business Review Press.

De Langhe, B. and Puntoni, S. (2024). *Decision-Driven Analytics: Leveraging Human Intelligence to Unlock the Power of Data*. MIT Press.

Kelleher, J.D. and Tierney, B. (2018). Data Science. MIT Press.

Marr, B. (2018). *Data-Driven HR: How to Use Analytics and Metrics to Drive Performance.* Kogan Page.

McAfee, A. and Brynjolfsson, E. (2017). *Machine, Platform, Crowd: Harnessing Our Digital Future.* W.W. Norton & Company.

Provost, F. and Fawcett, T. (2013). *Data Science for Business: What You Need to Know About Data Mining and Data-Analytic Thinking.* O'Reilly Media.

Sharda, R., Delen, D. and Turban, E. (2020). Analytics, Data Science, & Artificial Intelligence: Systems for Decision Support. Pearson.

Siegel, E. (2016). *Predictive Analytics: The Power to Predict Who Will Click*, Buy, Lie, or Die. Wiley.

Singh, S., Rajest, S.S. and Hadoussa, S. (2023). *Data-Driven Decision Making for Long-Term Business Success*. Springer.

Szukits, Á. and Móricz, P. (2023). Towards Data-Driven Decision Making: The Role of Analytical Culture and Centralization Efforts. *Review of Managerial Science*, 18, pp. 2849–2887.

Waller, M.A. and Fawcett, S.E. (2013). *Data Science, Predictive Analytics, and Big Data: A Revolution that Will Transform Supply Chain Design and Management*. Pearson FT Press.

CHAPTER 9

Business Sustainability

Learning Outcomes

By the end of this chapter, you will be able to:

1. Understand the strategic, financial, and environmental importance of sustainable business practices and their role in long-term resilience.
2. Learn how businesses can implement sustainable supply chain management, energy efficiency, green technologies, and environmental, social, and governance integration to drive responsible growth.
3. Examine emerging trends, global sustainability efforts, and the impact of digi tal transformation on shaping a more sustainable and climate-resilient business landscape.

9.1 INTRODUCTION

Business sustainability has transitioned from a peripheral concern to a strategic necessity in the modern corporate landscape. Companies across industries are increasingly recognising the need to integrate sustainability at the core of their operations, not only as a moral obligation but as a driver of long-term success and resilience. This chapter offers a comprehensive exploration of business sustainability, underpinned by the understanding that sustainable practices are no longer optional—they are imperative for survival in an era defined by environmental degradation, resource scarcity, and increasing societal expectations.

This chapter begins by presenting a holistic understanding of sustainability, providing insights into why businesses must adopt sustainable practices from both an ethical and financial perspective. It explores how sustainability is now a strategic and financial imperative that drives competitive advantage, operational efficiency, and risk mitigation. From the strategic integration of sustainable business practices to innovative approaches in supply chain management, energy use, and corporate responsibility, this chapter seeks to provide a thorough guide for businesses aiming to embed sustainability into their DNA.

DOI: 10.4324/9781032672458-9

As businesses are also key drivers of technological and social innovation, this chapter highlights how pioneering sustainable strategies and the embrace of green technologies can catalyse change. Through these discussions, this chapter positions business sustainability not merely as a reaction to current challenges but as a forward-thinking approach to shaping a resilient and responsible future.

9.2 A HOLISTIC UNDERSTANDING OF BUSINESS SUSTAINABILITY

Business sustainability has become a cornerstone of modern corporate strategy, reflecting a commitment to balancing economic growth with environmental stewardship and social responsibility. At its core, sustainability in business is about meeting the needs of the present without compromising the ability of future generations to meet theirs. This principle recognises the intricate link between economic success, environmental protection, and societal well-being. Sustainable business practices are not just about adhering to regulations; they represent a deeper, proactive engagement with the world, ensuring that operations today do not deplete or degrade the resources of tomorrow.

In practice, sustainability involves making informed decisions that minimise harm to the environment and society while also securing economic stability. Companies are increasingly looking beyond short-term financial gains and are assessing the long-term consequences of their activities. This forward-thinking approach ensures that environmental damage is mitigated, social inequality is addressed, and economic stability is preserved for future generations.

The rise of the digital economy has amplified the importance of sustainability. As businesses increasingly operate in an interconnected, digital world, they face new challenges and responsibilities. The digital transformation offers vast potential for innovation, efficiency, and global connectivity, but it also raises pressing concerns about the environmental impact of technology and the ethical use of data. Companies must now grapple with issues such as electronic waste, energy consumption, and resource depletion, alongside data privacy and social inclusivity. These concerns demand that sustainability is integrated into the very heart of digital business strategies.

Sustainability in the digital era is not limited to environmental considerations. It also encompasses inclusivity and accessibility, ensuring that technological advances benefit all, rather than deepening the digital divide. Addressing social inequalities, promoting digital literacy, and ensuring broad access to technological innovations are critical components of sustainable practices in the digital economy. As businesses adopt new technologies, they must do so in ways that uplift society as a whole, creating opportunities and fostering equality (Figure 9.1).

A fundamental framework that encapsulates the essence of sustainability is the Triple Bottom Line (TBL), which focuses on three interrelated pillars: People, Planet, and Profit. This model expands the traditional notion of business success, moving beyond profit alone to include social and environmental considerations.

The "People" aspect of the TBL highlights the social responsibilities that businesses carry. This includes the treatment of employees, respect for human rights, and engagement

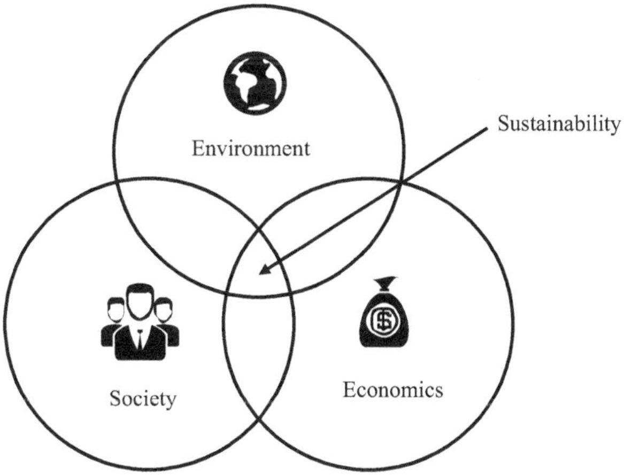

FIGURE 9.1 What Is a Sustainable Business?

with local communities. Sustainable businesses prioritise fair wages, ethical labour practices, diversity, and inclusion, and they seek to create positive impacts on the communities they touch. Ensuring the well-being of employees and stakeholders is not only a moral imperative but also a key driver of long-term business success.

The "Planet" dimension addresses the need for environmental sustainability. Companies are expected to reduce their ecological footprints through practices such as lowering carbon emissions, conserving natural resources, and adopting eco-friendly technologies. Initiatives like energy conservation, waste minimisation, and sustainable sourcing demonstrate a commitment to preserving the environment for future generations. As environmental challenges become more acute, businesses that fail to adopt sustainable practices risk not only reputational damage but also long-term viability.

The final pillar, "Profit," remains central to business operations but is redefined within the TBL framework. Profit is no longer viewed solely as an end goal; rather, it is a means to support ongoing investments in sustainable practices. Financial success enables businesses to make a greater impact on social and environmental fronts, creating a virtuous cycle where profitability fuels sustainable development.

The TBL reinforces the interdependence of economic, social, and environmental factors. It calls for a holistic approach to business where success is measured not just by financial returns but by the positive contributions to people and the planet. By embracing this comprehensive approach, businesses can achieve long-term sustainability and resilience while making meaningful contributions to society and the environment.

In summary, business sustainability is a multifaceted concept that extends beyond profit to encompass responsibility towards society and the environment. The growing importance of sustainability in the digital age underscores the need for businesses to adopt practices that are not only innovative but also ethically and environmentally sound. The TBL offers a framework through which businesses can align their economic goals with the broader aim of creating a sustainable and equitable future for all.

9.3 THE STRATEGIC AND FINANCIAL IMPERATIVE OF SUSTAINABLE BUSINESS PRACTICES

Sustainability in business is not merely an ethical obligation but a vital strategy that delivers tangible benefits across multiple dimensions. Organisations that embed sustainability into their operations and long-term strategies find themselves better equipped to navigate today's dynamic global landscape. One of the foremost advantages is the mitigation of risks. By proactively addressing environmental, social, and regulatory challenges, businesses are able to safeguard themselves from potential crises and reputational damage. This foresight enables companies to remain resilient in the face of increasingly stringent regulations and shifting market conditions.

Incorporating sustainable practices also serves as a catalyst for innovation. Companies that prioritise sustainability often lead the way in technological and operational advancements. Whether it's harnessing renewable energy sources, developing environmentally friendly products, or implementing circular economy models, these organisations unlock new realms of creativity and maintain a competitive edge. This innovation not only drives growth but also opens new revenue streams, positioning businesses as forward-thinking leaders within their respective industries. Sustainable innovations not only attract new markets but also strengthen a company's reputation as an industry leader committed to a progressive future.

Brand reputation and customer loyalty are other significant outcomes of a commitment to sustainability. Today's consumers are increasingly selective, gravitating towards brands that align with their own values, particularly regarding environmental and social issues. Companies that demonstrate genuine dedication to sustainability cultivate trust and build a loyal customer base. A strong narrative around sustainability differentiates brands in crowded marketplaces, enabling businesses to stand out and draw in customers who prioritise ethical choices in their purchasing decisions.

Furthermore, transparency in sustainability efforts amplifies this positive effect. By openly communicating the progress of their initiatives, businesses foster a deeper connection with their customers, making them partners in their sustainability journey. This participatory approach not only enhances customer engagement but also instils a sense of shared responsibility for broader environmental and social goals. As customers increasingly seek brands they can trust, those that visibly commit to sustainability find themselves benefiting from heightened loyalty and sustained consumer support.

Contrary to the misconception that sustainability is a costly endeavour, adopting environmentally responsible practices often leads to significant financial savings and operational efficiency. By investing in energy-efficient technologies and renewable energy sources, such as solar and wind power, businesses can reduce long-term energy costs. Sustainable supply chain practices, which include sourcing raw materials responsibly and optimising transportation routes, further reduce operational expenses while enhancing efficiency. Initiatives to reduce waste and implement recycling programmes not only minimise environmental impact but also lower disposal costs, creating a win-win situation for both the business and the planet.

Moreover, sustainability boosts a company's appeal to investors, especially those focused on environmental, social, and governance (ESG) factors. In today's financial landscape, investors are increasingly placing value on long-term resilience and responsible business conduct. Companies that embrace sustainability are perceived as low-risk, forward-thinking, and well-prepared for future challenges. This makes them more attractive to investors who are seeking sustainable, growth-oriented opportunities.

Ultimately, the case for sustainability in business is clear. By adopting sustainable practices, organisations reduce risks, drive innovation, enhance brand reputation, foster customer loyalty, and achieve cost savings and efficiency gains. In a world where the global business landscape is increasingly intertwined with environmental and social concerns, sustainability is no longer optional but a strategic necessity. Companies that embed it into their core operations are not only securing their own future but also contributing to the development of a more responsible and sustainable global economy.

9.4 PIONEERING SUSTAINABLE BUSINESS STRATEGIES FOR A RESILIENT FUTURE

In the modern business landscape, the integration of sustainability is not simply a peripheral concern; it has become a central driver of long-term success. Leading the way in sustainable business strategy are globally recognised frameworks and innovative models that encourage organisations to operate responsibly while contributing to the welfare of society and the planet. Among these are the United Nations Sustainable Development Goals (SDGs), the Circular Economy model, and the Cradle to Cradle (C2C) design approach, each offering a blueprint for businesses to align their practices with broader environmental and social imperatives.

The United Nations SDGs stand as a globally recognised framework that provides businesses with a comprehensive set of objectives to support a sustainable future. With 17 interconnected goals addressing a wide array of global challenges, from climate action to reducing inequality, the SDGs offer a strategic foundation for companies to align their activities with wider societal goals. By adopting these goals, businesses can drive impactful changes within their industries while contributing to positive social and environmental outcomes. The SDGs encourage businesses to re-evaluate their roles not just as economic entities but as partners in global development. Companies across various sectors are increasingly tailoring their objectives to reflect specific SDGs. For instance, a food company might focus on eradicating hunger (SDG 2) by promoting sustainable agricultural practices, while a technology firm could support affordable and clean energy initiatives (SDG 7). Beyond these direct contributions, embracing the SDGs strengthens a business's reputation, fosters better relationships with stakeholders, and positions companies as leaders in responsible corporate citizenship.

Another transformative framework shaping sustainable business strategies is the circular economy model, which challenges the conventional linear model of production and consumption. Unlike the traditional "take, make, and dispose" approach, the circular economy promotes a regenerative system where resources are used more efficiently, and waste is minimised. This model emphasises the continual use of materials, encouraging businesses to rethink how they design, manufacture, and distribute products. In adopting this approach, businesses focus on designing products that are durable, reusable, and recyclable. Products and materials are no longer destined for landfills but instead re-enter the production cycle as valuable resources. The potential benefits of the circular economy extend far beyond environmental sustainability. Businesses adopting this model often discover new economic opportunities by creating additional revenue streams from recycled materials and refurbished products. They also reduce their dependency on finite resources, ensuring greater resilience in a world where natural resource scarcity is becoming increasingly pressing. The shift to a circular model allows companies to unlock greater value from their products while contributing to a sustainable and resource-efficient economy.

The C2C design approach builds on the principles of the Circular Economy by fostering a complete rethinking of how products are designed and produced. This approach, conceptualised by William McDonough and Michael Braungart, seeks to create products that, at the end of their useful life, can be recycled without any negative impact on the environment or repurposed as biological nutrients. The C2C philosophy is not about simply reducing harm; it aims to create a net positive effect on the planet and society. Businesses that embrace the C2C model are encouraged to innovate by developing products that can be part of a continuous, closed-loop cycle. Such products are designed with non-toxic materials that can either be recycled endlessly or naturally decompose back into the ecosystem, thus eliminating waste altogether. The C2C approach evaluates products across several quality dimensions, including material health, material reutilisation, renewable energy, water stewardship, and social fairness. By adopting these principles, businesses set new standards for environmental responsibility, ensuring that their products not only minimise harm but contribute positively to ecological systems.

These sustainable business strategies, underpinned by frameworks such as the SDGs, the circular economy, and the C2C design approach, are reshaping the way companies operate in the 21st century. By incorporating these forward-thinking models into their core practices, businesses are not only advancing their own resilience and profitability but are also playing a crucial role in driving global sustainability efforts. These strategies provide a clear path for companies to address economic, environmental, and social challenges in an integrated manner, positioning them for success in an increasingly complex and interconnected world.

CASE STUDY 9

Patagonia's Commitment to Environmental Sustainability—Aligning Business with Responsibility

Patagonia, a global leader in outdoor apparel, has built its brand around environmental sustainability, demonstrating that businesses can be both profitable and socially responsible. In an era of increasing consumer awareness about climate change and ethical consumption, Patagonia recognised the need to rethink traditional business models to align with sustainable practices. The company faced the challenge of maintaining growth while reducing its environmental impact, particularly in an industry known for excessive resource consumption and waste. Fast fashion and mass production contribute significantly to environmental degradation, and Patagonia sought to position itself as a brand that prioritised the planet without compromising on product quality or profitability.

To address this challenge, Patagonia implemented a range of sustainable initiatives across its operations. The company prioritised the use of eco-friendly materials such as organic cotton, recycled polyester, and wool sourced from responsible suppliers. It also introduced the *Worn Wear* programme, which encourages customers to repair, reuse, and recycle their clothing rather than discard it. By offering repair services and resale options, Patagonia extended the lifecycle of its products, reducing textile waste and promoting circular economy principles. Additionally, Patagonia has remained an outspoken advocate for environmental protection, donating 1% of its sales to grassroots environmental initiatives through its *1% for the Planet* commitment. The company has also made bold political and legal moves, such as suing the U.S. government over policies that threatened national parks and advocating for stricter environmental regulations.

These sustainability efforts have led to impressive results for Patagonia. The company's sales have steadily grown, proving that a commitment to sustainability can drive financial success rather than hinder it. By fostering brand loyalty among environmentally conscious consumers, Patagonia has created a dedicated customer base willing to pay a premium for ethically produced products. Additionally, the *Worn Wear* initiative has reduced waste and encouraged responsible consumption, strengthening the brand's reputation as a leader in sustainable business practices. The company's activism has also enhanced its credibility, positioning it as a brand that not only sells products but also actively works to protect the environment.

Patagonia's approach offers key lessons for businesses navigating the intersection of sustainability and profitability. First, integrating sustainable practices into a business model can enhance brand value, consumer loyalty, and long-term financial success. Second, transparency and ethical sourcing play a crucial role in gaining consumer trust. Third, companies that actively advocate for sustainability beyond their own operations can become powerful forces for environmental change. Finally, circular economy principles, such as repair and reuse, can be leveraged to minimise waste while maintaining a strong revenue stream. Patagonia's case illustrates that sustainability is not just an ethical obligation but also a viable business strategy in the modern marketplace.

Discussion Questions for Students (with Indicative Answers)

1. **How has Patagonia integrated sustainability into its business model?**
   Indicative Answer: Patagonia uses eco-friendly materials, promotes product repair and reuse, and donates 1% of sales to environmental initiatives.
2. **Why is the Worn Wear programme an example of a circular economy approach?**
   Indicative Answer: It encourages customers to repair and reuse clothing instead of discarding it, reducing waste and extending product life cycles.
3. **How does Patagonia balance sustainability with profitability?**
   Indicative Answer: By fostering consumer loyalty, charging premium prices for sustainable products, and differentiating itself as an ethical brand.
4. **What role does corporate activism play in Patagonia's brand identity?**
   Indicative Answer: Patagonia actively supports environmental causes, challenges harmful policies, and aligns its brand with sustainability-driven advocacy.
5. **What lessons can other businesses learn from Patagonia's sustainability strategy?**
   Indicative Answer: Companies can achieve financial success while prioritising sustainability by adopting ethical sourcing, circular economy principles, and corporate activism.

9.5 ADVANCING SUSTAINABLE SUPPLY CHAIN MANAGEMENT FOR A RESPONSIBLE FUTURE

Integrating sustainability into supply chain management is an essential priority for businesses striving to reduce their environmental footprint while promoting social responsibility and ethical practices. This approach requires a holistic evaluation of every aspect of the supply chain, from the sourcing of raw materials through to production and distribution, to ensure that both environmental and social impacts are minimised. Sustainable supply chain management has become a strategic imperative, offering companies an opportunity to align with global conservation efforts, meet stakeholder expectations, and gain a competitive edge in an increasingly conscientious marketplace.

A critical step in advancing sustainability within the supply chain is assessing and mitigating environmental impact. This involves a thorough examination of all processes, from material extraction to the end product's journey to consumers. In this comprehensive evaluation, businesses can identify areas where they can reduce resource consumption, decrease waste, and limit emissions. For instance, by adopting energy-efficient technologies, optimising transport routes, and implementing circular economy principles, businesses can cut down on carbon emissions and resource wastage. However, achieving significant reductions in environmental impact requires not only internal changes but also active collaboration with suppliers. By working closely with partners who share the same environmental values and practices, businesses can build an eco-friendly supply chain that contributes to the preservation of natural resources and the fight against climate change.

In addition to environmental considerations, ethical sourcing plays a vital role in sustainable supply chain management. Ethical sourcing focuses on ensuring that all materials and services within the supply chain are obtained in a manner that upholds human rights and social justice. This commitment goes beyond compliance with labour laws and extends to the fair treatment of workers, ensuring they receive fair wages and work in safe conditions. As part of ethical sourcing, businesses must actively engage with their suppliers, fostering a culture of responsibility and transparency. Establishing clear ethical guidelines, conducting audits, and collaborating on social sustainability initiatives are vital steps in this process. By nurturing strong relationships with suppliers and demanding the highest ethical standards, businesses can ensure that their supply chains not only meet legal obligations but also contribute positively to society, addressing issues like modern slavery, unsafe working conditions, and unequal pay.

The final piece of the puzzle in sustainable supply chain management is ensuring transparency and traceability. In an era where consumers demand greater accountability from the brands they support, visibility into a company's supply chain has become a key differentiator. Transparency enables businesses to offer stakeholders insight into the sourcing, production, and distribution processes, giving consumers confidence in the ethical and environmental integrity of the products they purchase. To achieve this, many companies are leveraging technology to increase transparency. Blockchain, for instance, allows for the secure, immutable tracking of products from their origin to the end consumer. This ensures that each step in the supply chain adheres to sustainability standards and reduces the likelihood of unethical practices going unnoticed. In addition to transparency, traceability allows businesses to pinpoint exactly where materials and goods come from, offering a detailed view of every stage in the supply chain. By having this level of insight, companies can quickly identify and address issues such as environmental breaches, unethical labour practices, or inefficiencies in the supply network. In this way, traceability becomes a tool not only for risk management but also for fostering trust and building a resilient, sustainable supply chain.

The integration of sustainability into supply chain management is far more than a trend; it is a strategic necessity for businesses that wish to thrive in today's ethically conscious market. By addressing environmental impact, ethical sourcing, and supply chain transparency and traceability, companies can create supply chains that are both responsible and robust. As consumers and stakeholders increasingly expect businesses to operate with integrity and sustainability at their core, supply chain management has become a critical area where sustainability can be both demonstrated and measured. In adopting these practices, businesses are not only contributing to a more equitable and sustainable global economy but are also positioning themselves for success in a rapidly evolving world.

9.6 ADVANCING SUSTAINABILITY THROUGH ENERGY AND RESOURCE MANAGEMENT

The pursuit of sustainable energy and resource management is integral to responsible business practices in the modern world, where addressing environmental challenges is no longer optional. By adopting renewable energy sources, improving energy efficiency, and optimising the use of resources such as water, businesses not only reduce their environmental impact but also ensure their long-term resilience in an increasingly resource-conscious global market. These strategies form the foundation of a sustainable and forward-thinking business model that aligns with global environmental goals and responds to the growing demand for corporate responsibility.

A critical element of this transition lies in the adoption of renewable energy sources. Moving away from reliance on fossil fuels towards sustainable alternatives is a fundamental step in reducing a company's carbon footprint and environmental impact. Renewable energy, drawn from sources such as solar, wind, hydro, and geothermal, offers businesses an opportunity to power their operations cleanly and efficiently. By investing in renewable energy infrastructure—whether through solar panels, wind turbines, or hydroelectric systems—businesses not only contribute to the decarbonisation of the energy grid but also reduce their dependency on finite resources. This shift places companies at the forefront of the transition to a low-carbon economy, where they become industry leaders in environmental stewardship. Many businesses have already committed to achieving carbon neutrality by integrating significant proportions of renewable energy into their energy portfolios, thereby aligning their operations with broader sustainability objectives. Beyond the environmental benefits, renewable energy adoption enhances a company's reputation and market competitiveness in a world that increasingly values green innovation.

Alongside renewable energy adoption, businesses must also prioritise energy efficiency and conservation. While renewable energy represents a shift in the source of power, energy efficiency focuses on the intelligent use of that power, ensuring that energy is utilised as effectively as possible. By upgrading outdated equipment, retrofitting buildings with energy-saving technologies, and integrating smart systems that monitor and regulate energy use, businesses can significantly reduce their overall energy consumption. Conducting thorough energy audits allows companies to identify inefficiencies in their operations and implement targeted solutions to optimise energy use. This commitment to efficiency not only minimises a company's environmental impact but also results in substantial financial savings through reduced energy costs. The role of energy conservation is equally important, involving the cultivation of a culture of responsible energy use within the organisation. This may be achieved through initiatives such as staff training, installing smart lighting systems, and adopting energy-efficient practices across all departments. These efforts contribute to the broader goal of sustainable operations, simultaneously driving down operational expenses and environmental costs.

Another crucial aspect of sustainable resource management involves the careful stewardship of water and other essential resources. Water, being one of the most precious and increasingly scarce natural resources, demands particular attention in sustainable business strategies. Businesses are expected to scrutinise their water usage, reducing consumption through the introduction of water-efficient technologies, such as low-flow fixtures and smart irrigation systems, and finding ways to recycle or reuse water where feasible. Reducing water waste not only contributes to the conservation of natural ecosystems but also ensures that businesses maintain access to this vital resource in the future, thereby safeguarding their operations from water scarcity risks.

In addition to water, businesses must manage their use of other natural resources more efficiently, adopting a holistic approach to sustainability that extends beyond energy and water to encompass the responsible sourcing and consumption of raw materials. This often involves implementing circular economy principles, where materials are reused, recycled, or repurposed to create a closed-loop system that minimises waste and maximises the value of resources. Businesses that integrate circular systems into their supply chains benefit from reduced waste disposal costs and enhanced resource efficiency while simultaneously contributing to environmental conservation. Sustainable sourcing practices ensure that materials are sourced responsibly, avoiding over-exploitation of natural resources and reducing the ecological footprint of business operations. Waste reduction initiatives, such as recycling programmes and the use of recycled materials in production processes, further amplify these efforts, ensuring that the life cycle of materials is extended and their environmental impact minimised.

Sustainable energy and resource management are essential pillars in the foundation of a responsible business. By embracing renewable energy sources, improving energy efficiency, and adopting comprehensive resource management strategies, businesses not only contribute to the preservation of the environment but also enhance their own operational efficiency and long-term viability. As the global focus on sustainability sharpens, businesses that lead in these areas position themselves as pioneers of responsible resource stewardship. In doing so, they not only align with the growing societal demand for environmental action but also secure their place in the economy of the future, where sustainability is not only a corporate responsibility but a competitive advantage.

9.7 CULTIVATING A CORPORATE CULTURE OF SUSTAINABILITY AND RESPONSIBILITY

Creating a sustainable corporate culture is an evolving process that requires embedding sustainability and responsibility into the core values, behaviours, and decision-making frameworks of an organisation. This cultural transformation is most effective when led from the top, with senior management committing to make sustainability a defining feature of the company's identity. Leadership plays a vital role in setting the tone, ensuring that sustainability is not an afterthought but a central consideration in all business operations. Clear and consistent communication from leadership about the importance of environmental and social responsibility, combined with a commitment to lead by example, helps foster a culture where sustainable practices become second nature. When sustainability is woven into the organisational DNA, it permeates all levels of the company, encouraging employees to integrate these principles into their everyday work.

A key aspect of building this culture is the creation of dedicated sustainability committees or task forces that oversee the incorporation of responsible practices into all facets of the business. These bodies act as catalysts for change, helping to embed sustainability into operational processes, from supply chain management to workplace habits. By establishing open channels for dialogue and feedback, businesses create a space where employees feel empowered to contribute to the development and evolution of the company's sustainability efforts. This sense of ownership fosters an environment where everyone, regardless of role, sees themselves as responsible for the organisation's environmental and social footprint.

Education and training are essential components in nurturing this culture of sustainability. Employees need to be equipped with the knowledge and skills to make informed decisions that align with the company's sustainability objectives. Comprehensive training programmes, which may cover topics such as resource efficiency, waste reduction, ethical sourcing, and social responsibility, enable staff to understand how their actions directly impact the organisation's sustainability goals. Through this training, individuals gain a deeper appreciation of how small changes in their daily routines can contribute to larger environmental and social outcomes.

Continuous learning is also crucial in maintaining engagement and keeping pace with the ever-evolving landscape of sustainability. Organisations might employ a range of educational tools, such as e-learning platforms, workshops, and seminars, to ensure their workforce stays informed about the latest trends and innovations in sustainability. Regular updates on emerging best practices not only keep employees engaged but also signal the company's commitment to leading in sustainability.

Engagement is another critical factor in solidifying a sustainable corporate culture. Encouraging employees to participate actively in sustainability initiatives instils a sense of collective responsibility and pride in the company's environmental and social performance. When employees are involved in shaping and implementing sustainability strategies, they feel more invested in the success of these efforts. Whether through direct involvement in decision-making processes related to sustainability, participation in volunteer activities, or taking part in internal sustainability challenges, employees who are engaged in these efforts feel a stronger connection to the organisation's mission.

Many businesses recognise the value of creating internal sustainability networks or resource groups, providing a platform for employees who are passionate about these issues to collaborate and contribute ideas. These networks often become incubators for innovative sustainability initiatives, enabling companies to benefit from the creativity and enthusiasm of their workforce. Recognition and reward schemes for employees who demonstrate leadership in sustainability further reinforce this engagement, encouraging others to contribute ideas and take ownership of sustainability goals.

Developing a sustainable corporate culture is not a one-time project but an ongoing commitment that requires leadership, education, and active participation from every level of the organisation. As businesses increasingly recognise the strategic importance of sustainability for long-term success and resilience, fostering a culture that reflects these values becomes essential. A workplace where sustainability is deeply ingrained in the corporate ethos—where employees are continuously educated and actively engaged—sets the foundation for responsible, ethical practices that define the company's identity and position it as a leader in sustainability. Through this approach, companies not only contribute to a better world but also ensure their future viability in a market that increasingly values sustainability as a core principle.

9.8 PIONEERING SUSTAINABLE INNOVATION AND GREEN TECHNOLOGIES

The drive towards a more sustainable and environmentally conscious business landscape demands a bold commitment to sustainable innovation. This begins with strategic investment in research and development (R&D), ensuring that the pursuit of sustainability is central to a company's growth and operational practices. By channelling resources into sustainable R&D, businesses not only fulfil their environmental and social responsibilities but also position themselves as leaders at the forefront of their respective industries. Such innovation plays a crucial role in developing products and solutions that reduce environmental impact while addressing some of the most urgent global challenges.

Businesses committed to sustainable innovation frequently establish specialised R&D teams dedicated to the exploration of eco-friendly technologies and processes. These teams engage in the development of alternative materials, energy-efficient practices, and waste reduction strategies that contribute to a greener and more sustainable business model. Encouraging a culture of creativity and experimentation within the organisation creates a continuous feedback loop of innovation, whereby each breakthrough fuels further progress. As a result, businesses are not only able to drive sustainable growth but also contribute positively to broader environmental and societal goals.

Central to this wave of innovation is the exploration and adoption of green technologies. These innovations provide companies with valuable tools to reduce their carbon footprint and implement environmentally friendly practices across their operations. Renewable energy sources, such as solar, wind, and hydroelectric power, represent one of the most significant shifts towards sustainable energy use, allowing businesses to move away from reliance on fossil fuels and cut their greenhouse gas emissions. Energy-efficient technologies, ranging from smart building systems to cutting-edge sustainable manufacturing processes, contribute to the conservation of resources and reduce operational costs in the long run.

Furthermore, embracing the principles of the circular economy allows companies to revolutionise product design and lifecycle management. Products are now being developed with an emphasis on longevity, recyclability, and minimal waste generation. This circular approach not only reduces the environmental impact of the production process but also extends the life of materials, ensuring that they can be reused or repurposed rather than discarded. Such innovations are helping businesses close the loop on resource use, creating a more sustainable product lifecycle that benefits both the environment and the bottom line.

The focus on green technologies is not confined to energy production and product design alone. Forward-thinking businesses are also exploring innovations in supply chain management, seeking to reduce the environmental impact of procurement, production, and distribution. Sustainable sourcing practices ensure that materials are ethically and responsibly obtained while reducing the environmental burden associated with transportation. The integration of smart technologies, particularly Internet of Things (IoT) devices, allows for real-time monitoring and optimisation of resource usage across the supply chain. This not only enhances efficiency but also reduces waste and energy consumption, contributing to the overall sustainability of business operations.

However, no business exists in isolation, and addressing the complexities of sustainability often requires a collaborative approach. Businesses increasingly recognise that tackling large-scale environmental challenges necessitates partnerships with industry peers, research institutions, and government bodies. These collaborative efforts can range from the joint investment in sustainable R&D projects to participation in industry-wide consortia dedicated to advancing green technologies. Such partnerships allow businesses to share best practices, pool resources, and accelerate the pace of innovation, driving the development of transformative eco-friendly solutions.

Open innovation models, which encourage collaboration with external partners, including startups and academic institutions, are particularly effective in generating fresh perspectives on sustainability. By looking beyond their internal resources, businesses can tap into a broader network of expertise and innovation, fostering an environment where ideas flow freely and sustainable solutions are developed more quickly. Cross-industry collaborations are also on the rise, with businesses from different sectors working together to create innovative technologies and processes that have far-reaching environmental benefits. For example, collaborations between the automotive and technology industries have been pivotal in the development of electric vehicles, a breakthrough that is having ripple effects across multiple sectors and reshaping the future of sustainable transportation.

In conclusion, sustainable innovation and green technologies are crucial drivers of a more responsible and environmentally conscious business future. By investing in sustainable R&D, adopting green technologies, and fostering collaborative efforts, businesses can significantly reduce their environmental impact while positioning themselves as pioneers in sustainable practices. In an era where consumer expectations and regulatory pressures increasingly demand sustainable solutions, companies that prioritise and proactively embrace innovation will gain a competitive advantage. More importantly, they will contribute to building a more sustainable and resilient world for future generations.

9.9 BUILDING CLIMATE RESILIENCE: ADAPTING TO A CHANGING WORLD

In the face of escalating climate change, businesses must prioritise adaptation to enhance resilience and mitigate the potentially devastating impacts of a rapidly shifting global environment. Adapting to these changes requires a thorough and strategic approach, beginning with the assessment of climate risks and vulnerabilities that are specific to each business's industry, region, and operational context. This initial phase is essential to understanding the full scope of potential climate-related threats and allows businesses to take proactive steps in safeguarding their operations.

A comprehensive climate risk assessment involves collaboration with climate scientists, environmental specialists, and risk management professionals who can provide invaluable insights into the ways in which climate change may affect key areas of a business, from supply chains to infrastructure. Rising temperatures, more frequent extreme weather events, and the threat of sea-level rise are just a few of the risks that may disrupt business continuity, cause damage to physical assets, and affect the broader ecosystem within which companies operate. These assessments, which are tailored to the specific vulnerabilities of each business, offer a clearer picture of how climate change might impact both short-term operations and long-term sustainability. Armed with this knowledge, businesses are better positioned to implement effective adaptation strategies that mitigate risks before they become reality.

Once vulnerabilities have been identified, the next crucial step is the development and execution of robust climate adaptation and resilience plans. These plans encompass a wide array of strategies, each designed to protect operations, minimise disruptions, and ensure the business remains viable in an increasingly unpredictable climate. One key aspect of these plans is the enhancement of physical infrastructure. This often involves fortifying buildings and facilities to withstand extreme weather events, such as floods or hurricanes, that are becoming more common and severe due to climate change. Beyond infrastructure, adaptation plans frequently call for diversification of supply chains to account for potential disruptions, ensuring that businesses can continue to function even when certain resources or routes are affected by climate-related challenges.

Moreover, these resilience plans often integrate advanced water and resource management practices, addressing both immediate needs and long-term sustainability goals. Energy-efficient technologies are increasingly becoming a staple in climate adaptation, as they not only reduce operational costs but also contribute to lower greenhouse gas emissions, aligning with broader sustainability objectives. Some companies are also turning to nature-based solutions—such as green infrastructure and habitat restoration—that provide additional layers of resilience by working with natural ecosystems rather than against them. These solutions, which include the planting of trees and the creation of wetlands, can mitigate flooding, improve air quality, and support biodiversity, all while benefiting the surrounding community and contributing to overall well-being.

While local climate adaptation efforts are critical, businesses must also recognise their role in supporting global climate action. Climate change is a global issue that transcends borders, and effective solutions require collaboration at an international level. By actively participating in global climate initiatives, companies not only contribute to the larger fight against climate change but also bolster their reputation as leaders in sustainability and social responsibility.

Many businesses are aligning themselves with international frameworks and initiatives such as the Science-Based Targets initiative, which sets clear, measurable goals for reducing greenhouse gas emissions. By adopting science-based targets, companies ensure that their efforts to mitigate climate change are consistent with the overarching aim of limiting global warming to well below 2°C. This not only positions them as responsible corporate citizens but also strengthens their standing in an increasingly climate-conscious marketplace. Such commitments reflect a deep understanding that climate adaptation at the local level must be accompanied by active participation in global solutions if meaningful progress is to be made.

Furthermore, businesses have the opportunity to engage in international dialogues and policy discussions through platforms such as the United Nations Framework Convention on Climate Change. Participation in these forums allows companies to stay informed about emerging climate policies and trends, share best practices with peers, and advocate for stronger climate actions that align with their sustainability goals. Collaborating with non-governmental organisations and other sustainability-focused entities opens additional avenues for businesses to make meaningful contributions to global climate action while enhancing their own climate resilience strategies.

Ultimately, building climate resilience is a multifaceted endeavour that requires businesses to assess their risks, implement comprehensive adaptation plans, and engage actively in the global fight against climate change. Companies that invest in climate resilience not only safeguard their own future operations but also play a crucial role in fostering a more sustainable and resilient global economy. As the world continues to grapple with the realities of climate change, those businesses that embrace adaptation and resilience as strategic imperatives will position themselves as leaders in the global movement towards a more sustainable future, ensuring their long-term success in a rapidly evolving world.

9.10 SUSTAINABLE FINANCE AND ESG INTEGRATION: PAVING THE PATH TO A RESPONSIBLE FUTURE

The evolving landscape of finance has seen the rise of sustainable finance and the integration of ESG factors as powerful mechanisms to foster both financial returns and positive environmental and social outcomes. These practices signify a significant shift in how financial decisions are made, embedding sustainability into the very heart of economic activities. By incorporating ESG considerations into investment strategies, businesses can better align their financial goals with the growing need for ethical, sustainable, and socially responsible practices.

The integration of ESG factors begins with a holistic evaluation of how companies interact with the environment, society, and their own governance structures. Environmental considerations revolve around assessing a company's impact on natural resources, its carbon footprint, and the sustainability of its operations, such as energy use and waste management. The "S" in ESG focuses on the human dimension—how businesses address labour practices, human rights, diversity, and the welfare of the communities they serve. Meanwhile, the governance aspect scrutinises the transparency, ethical conduct, and accountability of a company's leadership and internal decision-making processes. Together, these dimensions form a comprehensive framework that guides investors and financial managers towards decisions that are not only financially viable but also ethically sound and sustainable for the planet.

ESG integration transcends traditional investment areas, affecting equities, fixed-income investments, real estate, and even more novel instruments such as derivatives. By factoring these elements into financial decisions, businesses are better positioned to attract responsible investors who are increasingly interested in supporting companies that demonstrate a commitment to long-term sustainability. This alignment between financial performance and ESG goals is critical in fostering a more responsible and ethical financial ecosystem.

In parallel with ESG integration, green financing has emerged as a crucial avenue for directing capital towards projects that deliver clear environmental and social benefits. Green finance refers to raising capital specifically for initiatives that have a positive environmental impact, such as renewable energy developments, energy-efficient buildings, and sustainable urban infrastructure projects. Through green bonds, loans, and similar financial products, businesses can access the funds required to pursue sustainability projects while contributing to the broader societal push towards environmental responsibility.

Governments, financial institutions, and regulatory bodies are increasingly recognising the importance of green finance and are introducing incentives to encourage businesses to adopt greener practices. This trend is enabling companies to explore opportunities beyond traditional financing avenues, such as venture capital and private equity investments in innovative startups focused on eco-friendly solutions. Impact investing, a model in which financial returns are pursued alongside measurable social and environmental outcomes, is also gaining traction. These sustainable investment opportunities allow businesses to not only meet their financial objectives but also play an active role in advancing the global sustainability agenda.

Engaging with responsible investors has become a central component of sustainable finance, as investors are more likely to consider ESG factors when making their investment choices. Companies that proactively address these considerations stand a better chance of attracting responsible investors, creating stronger, long-term partnerships that are built on shared values and commitments to sustainability. Effective engagement requires transparency in communicating sustainability initiatives, performance metrics, and long-term objectives. By regularly reporting on ESG performance through sustainability reports or other communication channels, companies foster trust and build credibility with their investors. Open, collaborative dialogues with shareholders on sustainability goals not only deepen investor relations but also demonstrate a company's commitment to long-term environmental and social impact.

Many businesses are increasingly seeking to establish partnerships with responsible investors and engage with global sustainability frameworks, such as the Principles for Responsible Investment (PRI) and the Global Reporting Initiative. These platforms promote best practices, transparency, and accountability in ESG reporting and performance, encouraging continuous improvement and innovation. Businesses that align themselves with these frameworks not only enhance their standing among responsible investors but also demonstrate a deep commitment to driving positive change in the global economy.

The rise of sustainable finance and ESG investing marks a fundamental shift in the financial world, where financial success is now seen as inextricably linked to environmental and social responsibility. Companies that embrace ESG principles and integrate sustainability into their financial decision-making processes are positioning themselves at the forefront of this transition. By exploring green financing opportunities, engaging with responsible investors, and aligning with global sustainability frameworks, businesses not only secure their financial futures but also contribute to building a more equitable, ethical, and sustainable global economy. As the demand for responsible investing continues to grow, companies that lead with a commitment to sustainable finance will be well-placed to achieve long-term success while making a positive impact on society and the planet.

9.11 SHAPING A SUSTAINABLE FUTURE: TRENDS, GLOBAL EFFORTS, AND THE ROLE OF DIGITAL TRANSFORMATION

The future of business sustainability is being redefined by the convergence of innovative trends, global development initiatives, and the growing influence of digital technology. As the urgency of environmental and social challenges intensifies, businesses are compelled to adapt, adopt forward-thinking practices, and embrace innovations that not only respond to consumer expectations but also align with the broader sustainability agenda.

Central to this transformation is the growing prominence of the circular economy, an emerging model that prioritises resource efficiency, waste minimisation, and sustainability across product life cycles. Companies are increasingly rethinking how products are designed, manufactured, and disposed of, focusing on reducing waste by reusing materials and ensuring products are easily recyclable. This shift is not just about meeting sustainability targets but about transforming supply chains and business models to respond to the pressing need for responsible resource management. The circular economy reflects a fundamental shift in how businesses perceive their relationship with natural resources, paving the way for long-term sustainability that minimises environmental impact and addresses concerns of resource scarcity.

At the same time, the global transition to renewable energy is gaining speed as a cornerstone of sustainable business practices. As renewable technologies such as solar, wind, and advanced energy storage become more affordable and accessible, companies are shifting towards cleaner energy sources to reduce their reliance on fossil fuels. This decarbonisation movement is driven by both regulatory pressures and corporate ambitions to play a meaningful role in the fight against climate change. By integrating renewable energy into their operations, businesses are making significant strides in reducing their carbon footprints while also contributing to a more sustainable energy landscape. Renewable energy is no longer an alternative but is fast becoming a mainstream solution that businesses are adopting to meet both environmental goals and consumer demands for cleaner, greener operations.

Equally significant is the growing focus on sustainable packaging. The shift towards alternatives to single-use plastics and the adoption of biodegradable and recyclable materials is reshaping how businesses approach packaging design. The environmental burden of packaging waste has become a prominent concern, and businesses are responding by rethinking their packaging strategies, not just to meet regulatory requirements but also to appeal to increasingly eco-conscious consumers. Sustainable packaging is now seen as a key driver of brand reputation, as consumers gravitate towards companies that prioritise reducing the environmental impact of their products.

The future of business sustainability also lies in its alignment with global efforts to address systemic challenges. The United Nations' SDGs provide a roadmap for businesses seeking to contribute to sustainable development on a global scale. These goals encompass a wide range of critical areas, from climate action and clean water to gender equality and poverty alleviation. Businesses are recognising the opportunities that come from aligning their practices with the SDGs, not only as ethical imperatives but also as avenues for demonstrating leadership and driving positive societal change. Moreover, sustainable development offers companies the chance to engage in meaningful collaborations that transcend geographical boundaries, with a focus on promoting economic growth, social equity, and environmental stewardship worldwide. This global context underscores the importance of businesses playing an active role in narrowing the gap between developed and developing regions by fostering shared prosperity and a healthier planet.

In this evolving landscape, digital businesses are poised to become transformative forces in shaping a more sustainable future. The rise of data analytics, artificial intelligence, and the IoT is enabling businesses to optimise their operations with unprecedented precision. These technologies are not just making businesses more efficient but are also enhancing their sustainability performance by enabling real-time monitoring and management of resources. For example, IoT devices can track and reduce energy consumption, streamline supply chain processes, and generate insights that support data-driven decision-making aligned with sustainability goals. By leveraging these technologies, businesses are able to reduce waste, improve energy efficiency, and achieve better sustainability outcomes across their entire value chains.

Moreover, digital platforms such as e-commerce and digital marketplaces are playing an instrumental role in advancing sustainable business practices. By reducing the need for traditional brick-and-mortar spaces and optimising logistics, digital businesses contribute to a more efficient and environmentally friendly way of operating. These platforms also serve as powerful tools for influencing consumer behaviour, as they increasingly integrate sustainability into their offerings by providing transparent information about the environmental and social impact of products. In this way, digital businesses are not just enablers of convenience but are becoming key drivers of sustainable consumption patterns that are reshaping industries.

As businesses continue to adapt to the demands of sustainability, they are not only responding to immediate challenges but also leading the way towards a more equitable and sustainable future. The embrace of circular economy models, renewable energy adoption, and sustainable packaging innovations reflects a deepening commitment to environmental responsibility, while alignment with global sustainability goals signals a broader vision for positive change. Looking ahead, digital businesses will remain at the forefront of this transformation, harnessing technology to drive innovation, enhance sustainability performance, and contribute to a positive impact on the environment, society, and the global economy. The future of business sustainability is, therefore, not just about survival in a changing world but about shaping that world for the better.

9.12 CHAPTER SUMMARY

As this chapter has demonstrated, business sustainability is no longer a niche concept confined to environmentalists or ethical investors. It has become a strategic priority with far-reaching implications for every aspect of corporate operations, from financial performance to stakeholder engagement and global competitiveness. The integration of sustainable practices, coupled with innovative strategies, is essential for businesses to navigate the complexities of a world increasingly shaped by climate change, resource constraints, and shifting consumer expectations.

This chapter has underscored the strategic and financial imperatives that sustainability presents to modern enterprises. By adopting sustainable business practices, companies not only mitigate risks but also position themselves for long-term success in a marketplace that increasingly values responsibility and transparency. Moreover, the adoption of innovative technologies, such as renewable energy and circular economy models, can enhance operational efficiencies and reduce environmental footprints. This chapter also highlights the need for businesses to build resilience in the face of climate change and foster a culture that prioritises sustainability at all levels of the organisation.

Looking ahead, the future of business sustainability lies in the effective integration of ESG principles, the continuous exploration of green innovations, and the embrace of digital transformation to drive sustainable growth. By leading the charge towards a responsible and resilient future, businesses have the opportunity not only to thrive but also to become agents of positive, global change.

Key Questions for Discussion

1. How can businesses integrate sustainability into their core operations while balancing profitability? What are some examples of companies that have successfully achieved this balance?
2. What role does sustainable supply chain management play in reducing a business's environmental impact? How can companies ensure transparency and responsibility throughout their supply chains?
3. How can businesses leverage innovation and green technologies to achieve sustainability goals? What are some emerging green technologies that have the potential to revolutionise industries?
4. In what ways can businesses adapt to the challenges posed by climate change to ensure long-term resilience? How can digital tools and technologies support this adaptation?
5. Why is integrating ESG criteria into financial strategies becoming a priority for businesses? How can businesses use ESG practices to attract investors and improve their long-term prospects?

BIBLIOGRAPHY

Attenborough, D. (2020). *A Life on Our Planet: My Witness Statement and a Vision for the Future.* Ebury Press.

Chhabra, E. (2023). *Working to Restore: Harnessing the Power of Regenerative Business to Heal the World.* Penguin Random House.

Elkington, J. (2020). *Green Swans: The Coming Boom in Regenerative Capitalism.* Fast Company Press.

Gates, B. (2021). *How to Avoid a Climate Disaster: The Solutions We Have and the Breakthroughs We Need.* Knopf.

Leonard, A. (2024). *The Story of Stuff: How Our Obsession with Stuff Is Trashing the Planet, Our Communities, and Our Health.* Free Press.

Lovins, A.B., Lovins, L.H. and Hawken, P. (2020). *Natural Capitalism: Creating the Next Industrial Revolution.* Updated ed. Little, Brown and Company.

McAteer, P. (2024). *Sustainability Is the New Advantage: Leadership, Change, and the Future of Business.* Routledge.

McDonough, W. and Braungart, M. (2024). *Cradle to Cradle: Remaking the Way We Make Things.* Updated ed. North Point Press.

Raworth, K. (2017). *Doughnut Economics: Seven Ways to Think Like a 21st-Century Economist.* Random House Business.

Senge, P.M., Smith, B., Kruschwitz, N., Laur, J. and Schley, S. (2008). *The Necessary Revolution: How Individuals and Organizations Are Working Together to Create a Sustainable World.* Crown Business.

Thunberg, G. (2021). *No One Is Too Small to Make a Difference.* Updated ed. Penguin Books.

Weybrecht, G. (2024). *The Sustainable MBA: A Business Guide to Sustainability.* 3rd ed. Wiley.

CHAPTER 10

Cybersecurity

Protecting Your Digital Business

Learning Outcomes

By the end of this chapter, you will be able to:

1. Analyse the growing importance of cybersecurity, the latest threats, and the need for proactive digital protection in the modern business environment.
2. Learn how to establish a robust cybersecurity foundation, including network security, data protection, encryption, and incident response.
3. Examine the role of leadership, governance, and emerging technologies in strengthening cyber resilience and preparing for future security challenges.

10.1 INTRODUCTION

As digital transformation continues to reshape industries, businesses are more connected than ever before, relying heavily on digital platforms, cloud computing, and the Internet of Things (IoT) to drive innovation and growth. However, with this shift comes an alarming rise in cyber threats that exploit the vulnerabilities inherent in interconnected digital systems. In the digital age, cybersecurity is no longer a niche concern for IT departments but a critical business issue that affects every level of an organisation. From data breaches that jeopardise sensitive information to ransomware attacks that disrupt operations, the consequences of inadequate cybersecurity can be catastrophic, both financially and reputationally.

This chapter provides a comprehensive overview of the essential strategies and best practices for safeguarding your organisation's digital assets. We begin by examining the ever-evolving landscape of cybersecurity threats and the necessity of building a robust cybersecurity foundation. Next, we explore practical approaches to fortifying network security and protecting critical assets, including data protection and encryption. This chapter also emphasises the importance of incident response and crisis management, as well as ongoing monitoring and threat intelligence to stay ahead of potential attacks. Furthermore, secure software development practices are essential in ensuring that security is embedded throughout the lifecycle of digital products and services. Finally, we address the crucial role of leadership and governance

DOI: 10.4324/9781032672458-10

in shaping a proactive and adaptive cybersecurity posture. Through this exploration, we aim to provide a comprehensive guide to building and maintaining cyber resilience in an increasingly volatile digital world.

10.2 THE EVOLVING IMPERATIVE OF CYBERSECURITY IN THE DIGITAL AGE

In today's rapidly advancing digital world, the necessity for robust cybersecurity measures has never been more critical. Businesses, regardless of their size or industry, are navigating a complex and constantly evolving threat landscape, where cyberattacks are becoming more frequent, sophisticated, and damaging. The proliferation of internet-connected devices, coupled with the growing expertise of cybercriminals, has broadened the array of cybersecurity risks that organisations must confront. From traditional malware attacks to sophisticated ransomware schemes, phishing scams, and hacking attempts, the tactics of threat actors are continually adapting, demanding that businesses remain vigilant and proactive in their defence strategies (Figure 10.1).

The implications of cybersecurity breaches for digital businesses extend far beyond immediate financial losses. A successful cyberattack can have a domino effect, leading to operational disruptions, damaged reputations, and, in some cases, legal or regulatory repercussions. Data breaches, in particular, expose sensitive information that can result in identity theft, financial fraud, and long-term reputational damage, significantly eroding customer trust. The recovery from such incidents is often resource-intensive, consuming valuable time and money while potentially paralysing day-to-day operations. The profound impact of cyberattacks highlights the necessity for businesses to view cybersecurity not just as a technical issue but as a critical business concern that affects every facet of their organisation.

Given the increasing severity and frequency of cyber threats, it is essential for businesses to develop and maintain a comprehensive cybersecurity strategy. Such a strategy should go far beyond basic compliance with legal requirements or industry standards; it must be a proactive, adaptive, and forward-looking approach to protecting digital assets

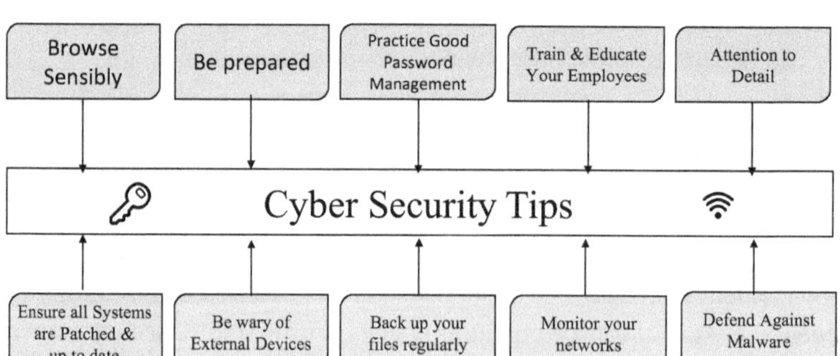

FIGURE 10.1 Top Cyber Security Tips to Help Protect Your Business

and sensitive information. Effective cybersecurity strategies require a multi-layered defence that includes risk assessment, threat intelligence, and the integration of technical solutions with human-centred approaches, such as employee training and clear incident response protocols. Furthermore, collaboration between internal teams and external cybersecurity networks enhances the overall strength of the strategy, allowing businesses to stay ahead of emerging threats.

A successful cybersecurity strategy is not a one-time investment but an ongoing commitment. As the digital landscape continues to shift and cyber threats become more sophisticated, businesses must ensure that their cybersecurity measures evolve accordingly. Regular testing, updating, and re-evaluating defence mechanisms are crucial in maintaining resilience against an ever-changing threat environment. In this light, cybersecurity becomes more than just a defence mechanism—it transforms into a strategic imperative for the long-term success and sustainability of any digital business. To thrive in this increasingly hostile digital landscape, businesses must prioritise the security of their digital assets and continuously work to strengthen their defences.

10.3 THE COMPLEX AND EVOLVING LANDSCAPE OF CYBERSECURITY THREATS

In the ever-expanding digital world, cybersecurity threats have become a prominent and persistent challenge, manifesting in diverse and increasingly sophisticated forms. These threats, ranging from direct cyberattacks to intricate schemes of social engineering, continually evolve, leaving businesses and individuals vulnerable to breaches, data theft, and significant operational disruptions.

At the core of this landscape are cyberattacks—deliberate attempts to compromise digital systems for malicious intent. These attacks can exploit weaknesses in software, target network infrastructure, or involve more complex methods to infiltrate secure systems. Cybercriminals, motivated by financial gain, frequently seek unauthorised access to valuable data, such as financial records, intellectual property, or personal information. With the advent of global digital connectivity, cybercrime has flourished, creating opportunities for illicit activities like identity theft, fraud, and the construction of botnets. The global nature of cybercrime means that no organisation or individual is immune to its reach, and tackling these threats requires an in-depth understanding of cybercriminal tactics paired with strong defence mechanisms.

One of the most common and dangerous forms of cyberthreats is malware, a term derived from "malicious software." Malware appears in various forms, each designed to compromise digital infrastructure in different ways. Viruses, one of the oldest and most pervasive forms of malware, attach themselves to legitimate files, spreading when these files are shared and often causing significant damage to systems. Another formidable type of malware is ransomware, which locks users out of their own systems or encrypts their data, demanding a ransom payment for its release. This particular strain of malware has caused severe financial and operational devastation for businesses globally, as the cost of recovery can be astronomical. Trojans, much like the ancient wooden horse of Greek mythology, disguise themselves as legitimate programs but carry malicious payloads. They infiltrate systems unnoticed, granting cybercriminals remote access or introducing more harmful malware. Defending against these multifaceted threats requires a comprehensive approach, including antivirus solutions, regular software updates, and user training on recognising suspicious activity.

While malware and cyberattacks involve direct technological compromise, some of the most effective threats exploit human vulnerabilities. Phishing and social engineering are examples of tactics that manipulate people rather than systems. Phishing involves the use of deceptive emails, websites, or messages that appear legitimate, tricking individuals into divulging sensitive information, such as usernames, passwords, or financial details. Social engineering, meanwhile, relies on psychological manipulation, exploiting trust, fear, or curiosity to persuade individuals into revealing confidential information or granting access to secure systems. These methods prey on the natural tendencies of people to trust communication that seems genuine. A successful phishing attack can lead to corporate breaches, the theft of sensitive data, or even financial loss.

The human element remains one of the most vulnerable entry points for cybercriminals. Combating phishing and social engineering requires more than technical solutions; it calls for a cultural shift within organisations. Employees must be trained to recognise suspicious communications, be aware of social engineering tactics, and maintain a sense of scepticism when handling sensitive information. Awareness campaigns, coupled with advanced filtering systems and security protocols, can go a long way in reducing the success rate of these attacks.

In conclusion, the diverse and complex nature of cybersecurity threats—from cyberattacks and malware to phishing and social engineering—demands a robust and multi-faceted approach to defence. As the digital landscape continues to expand and evolve, so must the strategies for securing it. Staying informed about the latest threats, strengthening both technological defences and human awareness, and adopting proactive cybersecurity measures will be key in safeguarding the integrity, confidentiality, and availability of digital systems. The digital age presents both opportunities and challenges, and ensuring the security of our online environments remains a top priority for businesses and individuals alike.

10.4 ESTABLISHING A ROBUST CYBERSECURITY FOUNDATION: A COMPREHENSIVE APPROACH

The bedrock of any effective cybersecurity strategy lies in the strength of its foundation, which must be meticulously built to withstand the complexities of the ever-evolving digital threat landscape. At the heart of this foundation is a holistic approach that incorporates risk assessment, the formulation of a cybersecurity framework, and strict adherence to data protection regulations. By addressing these core elements, organisations can establish a resilient defence capable of protecting their digital assets and sensitive information.

A key starting point in building this foundation is conducting a thorough risk assessment and vulnerability analysis. Organisations must take a proactive stance, systematically evaluating their digital ecosystems to identify potential risks and weaknesses. This involves analysing all possible points of exposure within their systems, networks, and applications.

By pinpointing vulnerabilities, businesses can anticipate how cybercriminals might exploit these gaps. Regular assessments, such as vulnerability scans and penetration testing, play an essential role in maintaining this vigilance. As threats continue to evolve, so too must the analysis and response to these risks. Understanding the overall risk profile allows organisations to allocate resources wisely, prioritising their efforts based on both the probability and potential impact of a security incident. In doing so, businesses ensure that their defences are strategically focused on the most significant vulnerabilities, mitigating the risks before they can be exploited.

With a clear understanding of the threat landscape, the next critical step is the development of a robust cybersecurity policy and framework. This framework serves as the strategic blueprint that governs how an organisation secures its digital environment. It provides structured guidance, setting out best practices, protocols for acceptable use, and comprehensive incident response procedures. More than just a set of technical specifications, the cybersecurity policy is a cultural imperative that embeds security into the very fabric of the organisation. This framework outlines specific roles and responsibilities, ensuring that every employee understands their part in maintaining security. Access controls are a vital component of this framework, dictating who can access certain systems and data, while encryption standards safeguard sensitive information from unauthorised access. Furthermore, employee training and ongoing education ensure that security practices evolve in line with emerging threats, reducing the risk of human error that could compromise security. The framework also extends to the software development lifecycle, ensuring that security is considered at every stage, from inception to deployment.

A comprehensive cybersecurity foundation cannot be complete without stringent compliance with data protection regulations. In today's interconnected world, the volume of sensitive data circulating within digital ecosystems is vast, and the consequences of a data breach can be catastrophic. Laws such as the General Data Protection Regulation in Europe, the Health Insurance Portability and Accountability Act in the United States, and various other regional or industry-specific regulations impose strict mandates on how organisations must handle sensitive data. Ensuring compliance with these regulations is not only a legal obligation but also a critical factor in preserving customer trust. To meet these requirements, organisations must implement protective measures such as data encryption, rigorous access controls, and regular compliance audits. Adhering to these standards mitigates the risk of legal penalties and, more importantly, demonstrates a commitment to safeguarding the privacy and integrity of customer data. This compliance also fosters an environment of transparency and accountability, which can significantly enhance an organisation's reputation and trustworthiness.

The combination of these elements—risk assessment, a strategic cybersecurity framework, and compliance with data protection regulations—forms the foundation upon which an organisation's security posture is built. By remaining proactive in identifying vulnerabilities, setting clear policies, and adhering to the highest regulatory standards, businesses not only protect themselves from immediate threats but also ensure long-term resilience in the face of an increasingly complex and interconnected digital world. This strong cybersecurity foundation is essential for maintaining operational integrity, protecting sensitive data, and fostering trust among stakeholders.

10.5 FORTIFYING NETWORK SECURITY: BUILDING A RESILIENT DIGITAL PERIMETER

In the increasingly interconnected digital world, securing an organisation's network infrastructure is paramount to maintaining the integrity and availability of its digital assets. Fortifying network security involves a multi-faceted approach that integrates advanced technologies, strategic architecture, and rigorous defence mechanisms to establish a resilient perimeter capable of withstanding sophisticated cyber threats. From firewalls and intrusion detection systems (IDS) to secure network architecture and Wi-Fi security, a comprehensive strategy is essential in protecting against the ever-evolving landscape of cyberattacks.

At the core of network security are firewalls and IDS/intrusion prevention systems (IPS), which function as the first line of defence against external threats. Firewalls act as gatekeepers, scrutinising incoming and outgoing traffic based on a set of predefined security rules, ensuring that only authorised data flow through the network. By creating a protective barrier between trusted internal systems and external, untrusted networks, firewalls are essential in preventing unauthorised access, whether through malicious actors or compromised devices. IDS and IPS further augment this line of defence by continuously monitoring network activities for signs of malicious behaviour or breaches in security protocols. While IDS is designed to detect and alert administrators to potential threats, IPS actively intervenes by blocking or mitigating attacks before they can cause harm. Together, these technologies form a robust perimeter that guards the network against a broad range of cyber threats, from malware to distributed denial-of-service attacks.

Beyond the implementation of protective technologies, the design of the network itself plays a critical role in safeguarding digital assets. Secure network architecture, which emphasises the minimisation of attack surfaces and the containment of potential breaches, is fundamental to enhancing network security. Central to this approach is network segmentation, which involves dividing the network into smaller, isolated segments. This strategy not only limits the spread of threats should a breach occur but also allows for tailored security measures to be applied to different segments, depending on the sensitivity of the data they contain. By adopting a "Zero Trust" model, in which no user or device is inherently trusted, organisations can ensure that all access is continuously verified, bolstering their security posture in the face of increasingly sophisticated threats. In a Zero Trust framework, each request for access to network resources, whether from internal or external sources, must be authenticated and authorised, thereby reducing the likelihood of a successful attack.

As the demand for wireless connectivity continues to rise, securing Wi-Fi networks has become an essential component of network security. Inadequate protection of wireless networks can open the door to unauthorised access, data interception, and other vulnerabilities. To mitigate these risks, organisations must implement strong encryption protocols, such as WPA3, which provide enhanced security for data in transit. Furthermore, robust authentication mechanisms ensure that only authorised devices and users can connect to the network, minimising the risk of intrusions. A key best practice is the establishment of a separate guest network, which isolates visitor devices from the organisation's internal systems. By doing so, organisations prevent unauthorised users from accessing sensitive resources or compromising critical infrastructure. The inclusion of a captive portal, which requires guest users to authenticate before accessing the network, adds an additional layer of security and control, ensuring that only legitimate users can connect.

In this multifaceted approach to network security, firewalls, IDS/IPS, secure network architecture, and Wi-Fi security collectively create a resilient defence against a diverse array of cyber threats. By integrating advanced technologies with strategic design principles, organisations can mitigate the risks posed by both internal and external threats, safeguarding their digital assets and ensuring the continued integrity and availability of their networks. As the digital threat landscape evolves, maintaining a strong network security posture will remain crucial to sustaining operational resilience and protecting against the growing complexities of cyber warfare.

10.6 SECURING CRITICAL ASSETS: THE ROLE OF DATA PROTECTION AND ENCRYPTION

In today's digital age, the safeguarding of data is more than just a technical necessity; it is a strategic imperative. Data, as one of the most valuable assets an organisation possesses, must be secured using a combination of precise, proactive measures that address both its classification and protection throughout its lifecycle. This complex challenge demands a holistic approach that includes data classification, data loss prevention (DLP) solutions, encryption strategies, and secure storage and backup processes.

The process begins with data classification, a critical step in understanding the varying levels of sensitivity and importance that different types of data hold. By categorising data, organisations can prioritise their security efforts, ensuring that the most sensitive information is afforded the highest levels of protection. Proper classification allows businesses to apply targeted security controls, such as restricting access to confidential data or applying stronger encryption protocols where needed. Equally important is the role of DLP solutions. These systems monitor data movement within the network, ensuring that sensitive information does not leave the organisation without authorisation, whether by accident or through malicious intent. DLP technologies enforce strict policies on how data can be shared or transmitted, helping to prevent data leaks and unauthorised disclosures. Regular audits and updates of both data classification and DLP policies are necessary to keep pace with the evolving business environment and to maintain compliance with ever-changing regulatory standards.

End-to-end encryption (E2EE) further reinforces data protection by ensuring that information is secure from the moment it is created until it reaches its intended recipient. E2EE guarantees that only those possessing the correct decryption keys can access the data, making it virtually impossible for unauthorised users to intercept or decipher it. This method encrypts data not only during transmission but also while it is stored, ensuring that it remains secure throughout its entire lifecycle. In an era where sensitive communications, such as financial transactions and personal data exchanges, are prime targets for cyberattacks, E2EE is indispensable. Its implementation provides confidence that even if intercepted, the data remain inaccessible to unauthorised parties, protecting businesses from the potential reputational and financial damage of a breach.

The protection of data does not end with encryption; secure storage and backup strategies are also paramount. Encrypted databases and file systems provide strong layers of protection for data at rest, guarding against unauthorised access or theft. Access controls, such as multi-factor authentication and stringent permission settings, ensure that only authorised personnel can access sensitive data. Beyond securing data in its primary location, reliable backup strategies are a critical component of an organisation's resilience. Regular, automated backups stored in secure, offsite locations create a fail-safe mechanism against data loss resulting from system failures, cyberattacks, or human error. These backups must be regularly tested for integrity and accessibility to guarantee that, in the event of a disaster or ransomware attack, the organisation can recover its critical data and resume operations with minimal disruption.

As the digital landscape continues to evolve, so too must an organisation's data security practices. Threat actors are constantly developing new techniques to exploit vulnerabilities, making it essential for businesses to adopt a forward-thinking, dynamic approach to protecting their data. The integration of data classification, DLP measures, E2EE, and secure storage and backup strategies provides a comprehensive defence framework. This multifaceted approach ensures that an organisation's most valuable asset—its data—remains secure, confidential, and available, even in the face of increasingly sophisticated cyber threats. As the importance of data security grows, so too must the commitment to maintaining a vigilant, adaptable posture to meet the challenges of a constantly shifting digital world.

10.7 NAVIGATING CYBERSECURITY CRISES: INCIDENT RESPONSE AND CRISIS MANAGEMENT

In today's fast-paced digital world, organisations must be prepared to respond quickly and effectively when faced with a cybersecurity breach. The key to mitigating the damage caused by such incidents lies in having a robust and well-structured approach to incident response and crisis management. This begins with developing a comprehensive incident response plan (IRP), ensuring that a trained and responsive Cybersecurity Incident Response Team (CIRT) is in place, and mastering the crucial phases of containment, eradication, and recovery.

At the heart of effective incident response lies the IRP. This critical document serves as a blueprint for the organisation's actions when faced with a security breach. The IRP establishes a structured, methodical approach to identifying, managing, and mitigating cyber incidents, ensuring a unified response across all departments. The plan clearly defines roles and responsibilities so that when an incident occurs, everyone knows their part in the response effort. This includes establishing detailed communication protocols that ensure swift internal reporting as well as coordinated external communication with stakeholders or regulatory bodies. The steps outlined in the IRP should cover the entire lifecycle of a cyber incident, from detection and analysis to containment, eradication, recovery, and post-incident evaluation. This ensures that all phases of the response are addressed methodically, minimising chaos and confusion during a critical time. Given the ever-evolving nature of cyber threats, it is crucial that the IRP undergo regular testing and updates, incorporating lessons from previous incidents and adjusting for new risks and vulnerabilities.

A cornerstone of any effective response is the creation of a specialised CIRT. This dedicated team is tasked with executing the IRP, coordinating efforts across different functions, and managing communication throughout the duration of the incident. Typically composed of specialists from various fields such as forensics, network security, legal, and communications, the CIRT ensures that the organisation's response is informed by expertise from across the business. However, assembling the team is only part of the equation; regular training, simulations, and drills are critical to ensuring the team's readiness. These exercises allow the CIRT to practice responding to diverse types of incidents, testing their agility and speed in handling a real-world crisis. By simulating attacks, organisations can foster a culture of readiness and continual improvement, enabling the team to respond more effectively to emerging threats. This consistent practice sharpens the team's skills and ensures that, when a breach occurs, the response is swift, coordinated, and effective.

When a cybersecurity incident occurs, time is of the essence, and the first priority is to contain the breach. The containment process involves quickly isolating compromised systems to prevent the spread of the attack. This could mean disabling user accounts, isolating servers, or implementing network segmentation to create barriers that stop the attack from affecting other parts of the infrastructure. Once containment is achieved, the focus shifts to eradication, where the root cause of the breach is identified and removed. A thorough forensic analysis is often conducted to understand how the breach occurred, what vulnerabilities were exploited, and what needs to be done to prevent a recurrence. This step may involve applying patches, correcting security flaws, or tightening controls to ensure the integrity of the system moving forward.

With the threat eliminated, attention turns to recovery. During this phase, affected systems are restored to normal operations, typically through the use of secure backups, while validating the integrity of those systems to ensure they are not still compromised. The recovery process is delicate, requiring careful planning to avoid reinfection or further vulnerabilities. It is essential not only to restore functionality but also to bolster security measures, ensuring the same incident does not recur. However, the process does not end once systems are back online. The post-incident phase is just as important, where organisations conduct a detailed post-mortem analysis to determine what went wrong and where improvements can be made. This review uncovers valuable insights, revealing gaps in the IRP or weaknesses in the overall cybersecurity framework. Armed with this information, businesses can refine their incident response strategies, ensuring they are better prepared for future incidents.

In a world where cyber threats are becoming increasingly sophisticated, having a robust incident response and crisis management strategy is not just an option—it is essential. A well-defined IRP, combined with a skilled and responsive CIRT, ensures that organisations are ready to tackle incidents as they arise. The critical steps of containment, eradication, and recovery provide a solid framework for managing the immediate aftermath of a breach, while continuous improvement ensures that future incidents are met with even greater resilience. As the threat landscape continues to evolve, organisations must remain vigilant and adaptive, ensuring their incident response strategies are capable of safeguarding their most valuable digital assets.

CASE STUDY 10

Target's Data Breach and Cybersecurity Overhaul

In 2013, Target, one of the largest retail chains in the United States, suffered a massive data breach that compromised the personal and financial information of over 40 million customers. The breach, which occurred during the busy holiday shopping season, exposed credit and debit card details, causing widespread concern about data security in retail businesses. Cybercriminals had gained access to Target's network through a third-party vendor, exploiting weak security measures to install malware on the company's payment system. This breach not only resulted in financial losses but also severely damaged Target's reputation, leading to a decline in customer trust and legal repercussions. The incident highlighted the urgent need for stronger cybersecurity measures in the digital business landscape.

In response to the breach, Target undertook a comprehensive cybersecurity overhaul to restore confidence among customers and stakeholders. The company appointed its first-ever Chief Information Security Officer (CISO) to lead a dedicated cybersecurity team and implemented E2EE for payment data to protect customer transactions. Additionally, Target invested in advanced threat detection systems and improved monitoring capabilities to identify and mitigate potential security threats in real time. The retailer also transitioned to chip-enabled EMV card technology, which provided enhanced protection against fraudulent transactions. Recognising the role of third-party vendors in the breach, Target strengthened its vendor security policies, requiring stricter compliance with cybersecurity protocols. Furthermore, the company provided customers with free credit monitoring services to help them safeguard their financial data.

The security enhancements significantly improved Target's cybersecurity resilience. By adopting advanced security technologies and strengthening its organisational commitment to data protection, Target successfully regained customer trust and restored its reputation. The financial impact of the breach, estimated at $162 million in legal settlements and remediation costs, underscored the importance of proactive cybersecurity investment. Additionally, Target's measures set a precedent for other retailers, prompting widespread adoption of stronger security protocols in the retail industry. The case demonstrated that while cyber threats remain a persistent challenge, businesses that prioritise cybersecurity can mitigate risks and protect their digital assets effectively.

Target's cybersecurity overhaul offers several key lessons for digital businesses. First, cybersecurity should be a top priority, with dedicated leadership and proactive measures in place to prevent breaches. Second, businesses must continuously monitor their security systems and adapt to emerging threats, rather than waiting for an attack to expose vulnerabilities. Third, collaboration with third-party vendors requires strict cybersecurity compliance to prevent security gaps. Finally, transparency and swift response following a breach are essential in maintaining customer trust and demonstrating accountability. The Target case serves as a cautionary tale and a blueprint for businesses aiming to strengthen their digital security infrastructure.

Discussion Questions for Students (with Indicative Answers)

1. **What were the primary weaknesses in Target's security system that led to the data breach?**
   Indicative Answer: Target's security vulnerabilities included weak third-party vendor access controls, inadequate threat detection systems, and a lack of proactive monitoring.
2. **How did Target rebuild customer trust following the data breach?**
   Indicative Answer: The company appointed a CISO, implemented stronger encryption, enhanced vendor security policies, and offered free credit monitoring services.
3. **Why is cybersecurity leadership important in digital businesses?**
   Indicative Answer: A dedicated cybersecurity leadership role, such as a CISO, ensures that security is a strategic priority, enabling businesses to prevent, detect, and respond effectively to cyber threats.
4. **What are the long-term impacts of a major data breach on a business?**
   Indicative Answer: Data breaches can result in financial losses, legal penalties, reputational damage, loss of customer trust, and increased regulatory scrutiny.
5. **How can businesses ensure third-party vendors do not pose security risks?**
   Indicative Answer: Businesses should enforce strict cybersecurity compliance, conduct regular security audits, and implement access control measures for third-party vendors.

10.8 STRENGTHENING CYBER RESILIENCE: SECURITY MONITORING AND THREAT INTELLIGENCE

In the ever-evolving realm of cybersecurity, maintaining a proactive stance through constant vigilance is critical to safeguarding digital assets. A comprehensive security monitoring strategy is essential, enabling organisations to detect and respond to potential threats in real time. Central to this approach is the implementation of Security Information and Event Management (SIEM) systems, which form the backbone of effective security monitoring. SIEM tools aggregate, analyse, and interpret log data from across an organisation's IT infrastructure, providing security professionals with invaluable insights into potential vulnerabilities. These systems serve as a centralised platform, monitoring a range of activities, from login attempts to network traffic, and identifying anomalies that could indicate malicious intent. By applying sophisticated correlation rules and machine learning (ML) algorithms, SIEM solutions can spot deviations from normal behaviour and generate alerts that warn of potential breaches or policy violations. Through this integration, organisations not only enhance their detection capabilities but also significantly improve their response times when dealing with cyber threats.

In tandem with SIEM, real-time monitoring and alerting stand as critical pillars of an organisation's cybersecurity defences. Cyber incidents can develop rapidly, and without swift detection, the damage can escalate significantly. To counter this, organisations need to deploy advanced monitoring tools capable of providing continuous, real-time visibility into network activities, system logins, and data access patterns. These tools are designed to detect suspicious behaviour as it happens, triggering automated alerts that immediately notify the relevant security teams. Prompt alerts allow for quick investigation and mitigation, often enabling organisations to neutralise a threat before it causes serious harm. This immediate reaction, combined with the heightened visibility offered by real-time monitoring, ensures a more agile and responsive cybersecurity posture, significantly reducing the window of opportunity for attackers.

Another vital layer of defence comes from the use of threat intelligence, which plays a key role in fortifying an organisation's security by providing timely and actionable insights into emerging cyber threats. Threat intelligence involves the collection and analysis of information about malicious activities, ranging from specific attack vectors to the tactics, techniques, and procedures used by cybercriminals. This intelligence is sourced from a variety of channels, including open-source intelligence, governmental agencies, and private security researchers, providing a holistic view of the threat landscape. When integrated with security monitoring systems, threat intelligence feeds empower organisations to not only detect known threats but also anticipate future ones. The actionable insights derived from this intelligence can be used to refine security controls, update firewall rules, and adjust IPSs, all based on the latest threat indicators. As a result, threat intelligence equips organisations with a proactive defence mechanism, enabling them to preemptively thwart potential attacks before they can materialise into full-blown incidents.

By combining these elements—SIEM solutions, real-time monitoring, and threat intelligence—organisations can build a resilient and adaptive cybersecurity framework. This holistic approach empowers them to detect and respond to threats swiftly while simultaneously strengthening their defences against emerging risks. In an environment where cyber threats are growing increasingly sophisticated, such proactive and layered defences are essential for staying ahead of potential breaches. As the digital landscape continues to shift, maintaining a robust security monitoring system, coupled with insightful threat intelligence, will be key to safeguarding sensitive data and ensuring the integrity of organisational assets.

10.9 STRENGTHENING CYBER DEFENCES THROUGH SECURE SOFTWARE DEVELOPMENT

In an increasingly interconnected digital world, the security of software applications is crucial for protecting organisational assets and mitigating the ever-growing risks posed by cyber threats. The foundation of secure software development lies in integrating security measures throughout the entire Software Development Life Cycle (SDLC). This holistic approach, often termed DevSecOps, recognises that security must be embedded into each phase of the software development process rather than being an afterthought or confined to a final step. From the initial stages of requirements gathering to the deployment and maintenance of the application, security is a priority.

Incorporating security into the SDLC begins with the collaborative efforts of developers and security professionals during the design phase. Together, they work to identify potential vulnerabilities and define security requirements that shape the project from its inception. Secure coding practices are then implemented to minimise the introduction of weaknesses that could later be exploited. This approach allows for early detection of risks and ensures that security is an ongoing consideration, thereby reducing the chances of vulnerabilities being embedded into the final product. By addressing potential threats from the outset, organisations can more effectively manage risks and deliver secure, reliable applications.

One of the critical pillars of secure software development is rigorous application security testing, designed to identify and address vulnerabilities in both the code and its runtime environment. Static Application Security Testing focuses on analysing the source code during development, scanning for security flaws and insecure coding practices before the application reaches production. This allows developers to correct issues early, ensuring more robust code and reducing the attack surface. Dynamic Application Security Testing, on the other hand, evaluates the application in its live environment, simulating real-world attack scenarios to uncover weaknesses that might not be visible during development. These testing methodologies, when applied in tandem, provide comprehensive coverage and significantly improve the security posture of the software.

Manual code reviews by seasoned developers and security experts further bolster the integrity of the codebase. While automated tools are invaluable for identifying many vulnerabilities, they can occasionally overlook complex issues that require human insight. Code reviews help fill this gap, offering a thorough assessment of the software to ensure compliance with security best practices, adherence to established coding standards, and identification of subtle flaws that may not be immediately apparent through automated testing alone. This meticulous scrutiny fosters a deeper understanding of the software's security and strengthens its resilience against potential threats.

As software ecosystems grow more connected, securing application programming interfaces (APIs) and managing third-party integrations become paramount in ensuring a secure application environment. APIs are essential for enabling seamless data exchange and functionality between different systems, but they also present new security challenges. Unsecured or poorly configured APIs can serve as entry points for attackers, exposing sensitive data or allowing unauthorised access to systems. To mitigate these risks, robust authentication mechanisms and authorisation controls must be implemented, alongside encryption to protect data in transit. Regular security assessments, including penetration testing, further ensure that APIs remain secure and resilient to emerging threats.

Third-party integrations, increasingly common in modern software development, also require careful scrutiny. External components and services can introduce vulnerabilities if they do not adhere to stringent security standards. Organisations must maintain vigilance when incorporating these elements, ensuring that all external services and applications are subject to the same rigorous security evaluations as their in-house systems. A failure in the security of a third-party integration could compromise the integrity of the entire system, making it crucial to assess and manage these risks proactively.

Incorporating security into every aspect of software development is essential for creating applications that are not only functionally sound but also resilient to the evolving threat landscape. By embedding security into the SDLC, conducting thorough application testing, and securing APIs and third-party integrations, organisations can build robust defences against cyber threats. This proactive approach ensures that security is a shared responsibility across development teams, fostering a culture of awareness and vigilance that is indispensable in today's digital environment. In doing so, organisations can confidently deliver applications that stand strong in the face of evolving cybersecurity challenges, safeguarding their digital assets and maintaining the trust of their users.

10.10 STRATEGIC LEADERSHIP AND GOVERNANCE IN CYBERSECURITY

Effective governance in cybersecurity begins with leadership, as those at the top play a vital role in embedding a culture of security and resilience across the organisation. The commitment of leadership is instrumental in shaping the attitude and actions of the entire workforce, reinforcing the necessity of safeguarding digital assets in an increasingly hostile digital landscape. Leadership's role extends well beyond endorsing security policies and procedures; it involves fostering a mindset where cybersecurity is considered an intrinsic component of all business operations. In doing so, leaders integrate cybersecurity considerations into strategic decision-making, ensuring that security measures are in harmony with broader business objectives. By visibly prioritising cybersecurity, leadership not only builds trust but also promotes a collective sense of responsibility among employees, encouraging everyone to play their part in protecting the organisation's digital infrastructure.

Beyond internal leadership, board-level engagement has become increasingly essential as cybersecurity has evolved into a top-tier business priority. In today's digital-first world, the potential damage caused by cybersecurity breaches can be catastrophic, impacting everything from a company's financial standing to its reputation. Recognising this, boards of directors are now expected to be actively involved in shaping cybersecurity strategy. This responsibility includes offering strategic direction, ensuring sufficient allocation of resources, and embedding cybersecurity within the wider risk management framework. To maintain effective oversight, it is critical that cybersecurity leaders communicate in a way that resonates with board members, translating complex technical issues into business terms that highlight the financial and reputational risks involved. Regular briefings on cybersecurity risks, combined with incident response simulations, provide board members with a clearer understanding of both the threat landscape and the organisation's preparedness, thus facilitating more informed decision-making.

A vital component of successful cybersecurity governance is the measurement and reporting of security effectiveness. Metrics serve as an essential tool in understanding the organisation's security posture, allowing leaders to assess the impact of their security initiatives, track improvements, and make data-driven decisions. Key performance indicators for cybersecurity can range from response times to security incidents, the robustness of security controls, or the frequency and effectiveness of employee security training. These metrics not only demonstrate the organisation's ongoing efforts to improve its security capabilities but also highlight areas that require further attention. Transparent and efficient reporting systems ensure that security data reach the appropriate stakeholders, from senior leadership and board members to external regulators, where applicable. Through clear and concise communication, decision-makers are better equipped to understand the evolving risk profile of the organisation, the success of security investments, and the potential threats looming on the horizon.

Ultimately, the strength of an organisation's cybersecurity lies in the synergy between governance and leadership. A proactive and engaged leadership team creates the foundation for a security-first culture, while the active involvement of the board ensures that cybersecurity is treated not as an operational afterthought but as a critical strategic priority. Robust measurement and reporting mechanisms further enhance this framework, providing ongoing visibility into security efforts and enabling continuous refinement of policies and controls. Together, these elements create a comprehensive and aligned cybersecurity governance structure, one that is capable of adapting to the shifting threat landscape while bolstering the organisation's resilience against cyberattacks. Through strong leadership and sound governance, organisations can ensure they are well-equipped to meet the demands of modern cybersecurity and protect their digital assets effectively.

10.11 THE FUTURE OF CYBERSECURITY: EMERGING TRENDS AND TECHNOLOGICAL ADVANCEMENTS

The field of cybersecurity is undergoing a significant transformation as advanced technologies like artificial intelligence (AI), ML, and Zero Trust Architecture (ZTA) reshape how organisations protect their digital environments. These innovations, coupled with the evolving nature of cyber threats, are pushing the boundaries of traditional security strategies, making adaptability and forward-thinking approaches essential for maintaining resilience in the face of an increasingly complex threat landscape.

The integration of AI and ML has brought about a fundamental shift in how cybersecurity operations are conducted. These technologies excel in their ability to process vast volumes of data at speeds far beyond human capabilities. Through advanced algorithms, AI and ML systems can identify patterns and anomalies in network behaviour, which may signal the presence of a cyber threat. ML models, continuously trained on historical and real-time data, can detect subtle changes that traditional security tools might overlook, providing enhanced accuracy in threat detection. Moreover, AI-powered automation significantly improves incident response times by automating routine tasks, enabling cybersecurity professionals to focus on addressing more complex and strategic threats. The self-learning nature of AI and ML also ensures that security systems evolve alongside emerging threats, adapting in real-time to new attack vectors, thereby strengthening overall cybersecurity resilience.

Concurrently, the ZTA has emerged as a critical framework for organisations, particularly as remote work becomes more prevalent. In stark contrast to the traditional security model, which relies on a defined network perimeter, Zero Trust operates on the assumption that threats can arise from both within and outside the organisation. It follows the principle of "never trust, always verify," requiring continuous authentication and authorisation for all users and devices attempting to access company resources. With remote work blurring the lines of the traditional network perimeter, ZTA ensures that employees, regardless of their location or device, are granted access only to the data and systems they need. Through multi-factor authentication, strict access controls, and continuous monitoring, ZTA reduces the attack surface, mitigates risks associated with remote access, and ensures that sensitive data remains secure, even in a decentralised work environment.

Looking ahead, the future of cybersecurity will be defined by a continuous struggle between malicious actors and defenders, with both sides increasingly leveraging cutting-edge technology. Ransomware attacks, for instance, are expected to grow in sophistication, with cybercriminals employing techniques like double extortion—where attackers not only encrypt data but also threaten to leak sensitive information unless a ransom is paid. Similarly, supply chain compromises have become a growing concern, as adversaries target third-party vendors to gain access to larger networks. This shift underscores the importance of a holistic approach to cybersecurity, where vigilance extends beyond the organisation's immediate infrastructure to encompass the entire ecosystem of connected partners and suppliers.

The IoT introduces another layer of complexity to the cybersecurity landscape. As the number of connected devices continues to surge, so too does the number of potential entry points for cyber threats. Each IoT device, from smart home gadgets to industrial sensors, represents a possible vulnerability that could be exploited by attackers. Securing these diverse endpoints requires the implementation of IoT-specific security protocols, robust device management practices, and ongoing monitoring to identify and neutralise threats before they can cause harm.

Additionally, the emergence of quantum computing has far-reaching implications for cybersecurity. While quantum computers have the potential to revolutionise fields like cryptography, they also pose a significant risk to current encryption standards. The exponential processing power of quantum computers could enable them to break encryption algorithms that are currently considered uncrackable. As a result, the development of quantum-resistant cryptographic algorithms is becoming a priority for cybersecurity researchers, as organisations must prepare for the eventual impact of quantum computing on data security.

To counter these evolving threats, future cybersecurity defence strategies will need to emphasise collaboration, information sharing, and a proactive approach to vulnerability management. Threat intelligence sharing among organisations, industries, and governments will become increasingly important in identifying emerging risks and coordinating responses. Furthermore, cybersecurity professionals must stay ahead of the curve, continuously adopting new technologies and refining their defence strategies to address the latest advancements in cybercrime tactics.

In conclusion, the landscape of cybersecurity is in constant flux, driven by the rapid evolution of both threats and technologies. The integration of AI and ML has empowered organisations with real-time detection and response capabilities, while ZTA provides a robust framework for securing increasingly decentralised networks. As we move forward, cybersecurity will continue to demand vigilance, adaptability, and innovation, with new technologies such as quantum computing and the proliferation of IoT devices shaping both the challenges and opportunities that lie ahead. By embracing these advancements and fostering a culture of security awareness, organisations can enhance their resilience against the ever-evolving threat landscape.

10.12 CHAPTER SUMMARY

In an era defined by digitalisation, where businesses are perpetually vulnerable to sophisticated and evolving cyber threats, a robust and comprehensive cybersecurity strategy is no longer optional but essential. The rise in data breaches, ransomware attacks, and advanced persistent threats has underscored the urgent need for organisations to protect their digital assets and maintain operational resilience. This chapter has outlined the critical steps organisations must take to secure their networks, safeguard sensitive data, and respond effectively to cybersecurity crises.

We have explored the importance of establishing a resilient cybersecurity foundation through the adoption of best practices in network security, data encryption, and secure software development. Ongoing security monitoring and the integration of threat intelligence were highlighted as crucial components for proactively identifying and neutralising emerging threats. Incident response and crisis management, when properly implemented, can significantly mitigate the impact of cyber incidents, allowing businesses to recover swiftly and maintain stakeholder trust. Finally, this chapter has stressed the role of leadership and governance in fostering a security-first culture and ensuring that cybersecurity is embedded into the strategic objectives of the organisation.

As technology continues to evolve, the future of cybersecurity will be shaped by new innovations such as AI, ML, and quantum computing. Vigilance, adaptability, and continuous improvement will be paramount as organisations face the challenges of an increasingly complex and interconnected digital world.

Key Questions for Discussion

1. As businesses increasingly adopt digital tools, why has cybersecurity become a critical component of business strategy? How can organisations balance the costs of cybersecurity with the potential risks of not investing in it?
2. With the rise of advanced threats like ransomware, phishing, and AI-powered cyberattacks, what proactive measures can businesses take to stay ahead of malicious actors? How can businesses educate employees about recognising and preventing cyber threats?
3. In the digital economy, data are often referred to as "the new oil." How can businesses effectively protect sensitive data using encryption, and what are the key challenges in doing so?
4. How should a business prepare for and respond to a cybersecurity breach? What key elements should be included in a robust incident response and crisis management plan?
5. With the emergence of technologies like quantum computing and AI, what are the upcoming trends in cybersecurity? How might these technologies both pose new threats and offer innovative solutions for protecting digital businesses?

BIBLIOGRAPHY

Andress, J. and Winterfeld, S. (2013). *Cyber Warfare: Techniques, Tactics and Tools for Security Practitioners*. Syngress.

Bayuk, J.L., Healey, J., Rohmeyer, P., Sachs, M., Schmidt, J. and Weiss, J. (2012). *Cyber Security Policy Guidebook*. Wiley.

Clinton, L. (2021). *Cybersecurity for Business*. GCS Network.

Cole, E. (2019). *Cyber Crisis: Protecting Your Business from Real Threats in the Virtual World*. BenBella Books.

Evans, A. (2021). *Enterprise Cybersecurity in Digital Business*. CRC Press.

Geer, D. (2020). *Cybersecurity Leadership: Powering the Modern Organization*. Apress.

Green, J. (2020). *Cybersecurity for Beginners*. CreateSpace Independent Publishing Platform.

Kaplan, J.M., Bailey, T., O'Halloran, D., Marcus, A. and Rezek, C. (2015). *Beyond Cybersecurity: Protecting Your Digital Business*. Wiley.

Lewis, J.A. (2021). *Cybersecurity and Cyberwar: What Everyone Needs to Know*. Oxford University Press.

Mitnick, K.D. and Simon, W.L. (2011). *Ghost in the Wires: My Adventures as the World's Most Wanted Hacker*. Little, Brown and Company.

Pease, A. (2021). *Threat Hunting with Elastic Stack*. Packt Publishing.

Peltier, T.R. (2016). *Information Security Policies, Procedures, and Standards: Guidelines for Effective Information Security Management*. CRC Press.

Schneier, B. (2020). *Click Here to Kill Everybody: Security and Survival in a Hyper-connected World*. W.W. Norton & Company.

Singer, P.W. and Friedman, A. (2014). *Cybersecurity and Cyberwar: What Everyone Needs to Know*. Oxford University Press.

Stallings, W. (2019). *Effective Cybersecurity: A Guide to Using Best Practices and Standards*. Addison-Wesley Professional.

CHAPTER 11

Building a Digital Team

Hiring and Managing Talent for a Digital World

Learning Outcomes

By the end of this chapter, you will be able to:

1. Explore the role of digital teams in driving innovation, efficiency, and business success in a technology-driven world.
2. Learn best practices for hiring, structuring, onboarding, and managing high-performing digital teams, including remote and virtual teams.
3. Examine strategies for cultivating a dynamic digital work environment, enhancing employee motivation, and leveraging diversity for competitive advantage.

11.1 INTRODUCTION

The digital world is advancing at an unprecedented rate, reshaping industries and transforming how businesses operate. As organisations undergo digital transformation, the need to build, manage, and nurture digital talent has become a strategic imperative. Successful businesses today understand that investing in digital teams is not just about staying relevant—it's about driving growth, innovation, and long-term success. The rise of artificial intelligence (AI), big data, cloud computing, and other digital technologies has significantly altered the types of skills and competencies organisations require. To remain competitive, companies must not only hire the right people but also ensure their teams are aligned with the organisation's strategic objectives.

This chapter explores the process of building high-performing digital teams from the ground up, starting with defining the strategic imperative. Understanding why and how digital teams contribute to organisational growth provides the framework for effective hiring, role structuring, and performance management. The next step is to craft roles within the team that optimise collaboration, creativity, and execution. This chapter will further delve into the recruitment of digital talent, identifying the competencies necessary for success, and navigating the unique challenges of managing remote and virtual teams in the digital era.

DOI: 10.4324/9781032672458-11

Additionally, fostering a culture of innovation and inclusivity is essential in maintaining a dynamic workforce. By offering comprehensive onboarding, training, and retention strategies, organisations can ensure their digital teams remain engaged, motivated, and prepared for future challenges. As we look towards the future, digital teams must stay adaptable to evolving trends and emerging technologies, making agility a key component of success in the digital age.

11.2 THE STRATEGIC IMPERATIVE OF BUILDING A DIGITAL TEAM

In today's rapidly changing digital landscape, the success of a business hinges on its ability to build and maintain a highly capable digital team. This section examines the crucial role such teams play in driving business success, reflecting on the evolution of digital roles and skills, and highlighting the significant impact that top-tier digital talent can have on an organisation's performance. A robust digital team is no longer a secondary component but a vital force behind a company's innovation, efficiency, and ability to adapt to the shifting demands of the digital era.

The need for a strong digital team has become a strategic necessity for businesses that seek to remain competitive. In a world where technological advancements dictate market trends, the digital team serves as the core engine that propels organisations forward, creating innovative solutions and streamlining business processes. These teams are not confined to traditional IT functions but extend across fields such as data science, digital marketing, user experience (UX) design, and cybersecurity. By aligning their technical expertise with broader business goals, they ensure that organisations are not merely reacting to technological shifts but are actively leveraging them to enhance performance and reach.

The roles and skills required of digital professionals have undergone a remarkable transformation. No longer are these roles restricted to narrow, siloed functions. Instead, there is a growing emphasis on cross-functional collaboration, where individuals must combine technical prowess with creativity, problem-solving, and adaptability. Data scientists, AI specialists, and cybersecurity experts now play integral roles in ensuring that businesses can navigate the complexities of the modern digital ecosystem. These professionals are not only expected to have expertise in their specific domains but also to possess the ability to communicate effectively, think creatively, and work agilely in an environment that demands continuous learning and evolution. As the digital landscape becomes increasingly interconnected, the ability to collaborate across different disciplines has become just as essential as technical proficiency (Figure 11.1).

The impact of digital talent on business success is profound, extending well beyond operational improvements. A strong digital team drives innovation by staying ahead of emerging trends, whether through harnessing big data, implementing AI solutions, or creating digital marketing strategies that resonate with consumers. These capabilities directly affect a business's competitive position, ensuring it remains relevant in the market and continues to grow. More than that, a digitally empowered team enhances customer experiences, an essential aspect of business in today's customer-centric environment. They can provide personalised,

FIGURE 11.1 Innovative Approaches to Improve Your HR and Talent Management in the Digital Era

data-driven interactions that meet consumer expectations and create lasting relationships with customers.

A well-constructed digital team also provides businesses with agility and scalability, enabling them to respond swiftly to changes in the market or technological advancements. Whether it's adopting new tools, entering unfamiliar markets, or adjusting business models to stay relevant, having the right digital talent allows organisations to be nimble in their approach. In this way, digital teams not only contribute to immediate operational success but also position businesses for long-term growth and adaptability in an ever-evolving landscape.

Ultimately, building a digital team is about more than just hiring the right people; it's about creating a foundation that will support ongoing innovation and resilience in the face of constant digital transformation. Understanding the evolving roles and skills required and recognising the critical impact digital talent has on overall business success is essential for any organisation hoping to thrive in the competitive digital world.

11.3 CRAFTING AND STRUCTURING DIGITAL TEAM ROLES FOR OPTIMAL PERFORMANCE

In today's digital landscape, identifying the right roles and defining their responsibilities are crucial to building a high-performing, cohesive digital team. A well-structured team not only ensures operational efficiency but also drives innovation and adaptability in an organisation. Central to this process is understanding the key roles essential for digital success, clarifying the responsibilities and skill sets required for each, and establishing a robust team structure that supports seamless collaboration and communication.

At the core of every successful digital team are a few indispensable roles. Digital marketers play a pivotal role in driving online visibility and fostering customer engagement through strategic campaigns. They are responsible for developing and executing marketing strategies across various digital channels, optimising content for SEO, and analysing campaign performance metrics to ensure ongoing improvement. Their ability to stay on top of industry trends and utilise digital marketing tools effectively is paramount to the success of any business in the digital age.

Equally essential are web developers, who form the backbone of an organisation's digital infrastructure. Their responsibilities encompass the creation and maintenance of websites, ensuring they function smoothly and securely while providing a seamless UX. Web developers must possess proficiency in programming languages such as HTML, CSS, and JavaScript, as well as an understanding of responsive design principles and content management systems. Their technical skills and attention to detail are crucial in ensuring a business's digital platforms are reliable and engaging.

Data analysts, with their expertise in extracting insights from vast amounts of data, are increasingly becoming an integral part of digital teams. They collect, interpret, and present data to inform strategic decisions and optimise digital initiatives. Skilled in tools such as SQL and Python, as well as statistical modelling, data analysts enable businesses to make data-driven decisions that enhance customer experiences and improve operational performance.

UX and user interface (UI) designers are the creative force behind the digital experience. They ensure that websites and applications are not only visually appealing but also user-friendly. UX/UI designers engage in activities like wireframing, prototyping, and collaborating with development teams to implement designs that align with user needs and business objectives. Their role requires a deep understanding of user behaviour, coupled with technical expertise in design tools such as Adobe XD and Figma.

Cybersecurity experts are tasked with safeguarding an organisation's digital assets. With the rising threat of cyberattacks, the need for these professionals has never been greater. Cybersecurity experts are responsible for conducting risk assessments, implementing security protocols, and responding to potential incidents. Their expertise in cybersecurity frameworks, ethical hacking, and evolving threat landscapes is vital in maintaining trust and data integrity within an organisation.

Defining the responsibilities and skills required for each role is crucial in ensuring the success of a digital team. For digital marketers, this includes crafting comprehensive digital marketing strategies, managing social media platforms, and optimising content for search engines. Web developers must ensure their work meets functional and aesthetic requirements while adhering to security protocols. Data analysts should possess a keen ability to interpret complex datasets, and UX/UI designers must create interfaces that enhance user engagement and satisfaction. Cybersecurity experts must constantly adapt to new threats and implement robust defensive measures to protect the organisation.

Once roles and responsibilities are clearly defined, establishing a structured team and reporting hierarchy becomes vital. A digital team leader or manager typically oversees the entire digital team, ensuring alignment with business goals, managing resources, and facilitating communication across departments. This leader often collaborates with specialised team leads, such as heads of marketing, development, or cybersecurity, who provide domain-specific guidance and mentorship to their respective teams.

Cross-functional teams composed of individuals from various digital disciplines are increasingly common in the digital space. These teams work together on specific projects, encouraging innovation and a holistic approach to problem-solving. Such collaborative efforts foster creativity and enhance the quality of outputs, as they combine diverse expertise and perspectives.

A clear reporting hierarchy is also essential for ensuring accountability and transparency within the team. Regular check-ins, progress reports, and feedback loops allow for efficient communication and help to address any challenges that arise promptly. This structured communication ensures that everyone is on the same page, working towards the organisation's broader digital goals, and enables the team to respond to changes swiftly and efficiently.

In conclusion, crafting a well-defined digital team structure, where roles are clear and the reporting hierarchy supports collaboration and efficiency, is critical for any organisation aiming to thrive in the digital world. By understanding the distinct roles and responsibilities required, ensuring the right skill sets are in place, and creating a framework that encourages seamless communication, businesses can build a digital team capable of driving innovation and long-term success.

11.4 CORE COMPETENCIES FOR HIGH-PERFORMING DIGITAL TEAMS

In the fast-paced digital landscape, the competencies and skills of team members are crucial for navigating the complexities of the ever-evolving digital world. The ability to blend technical proficiency, analytical thinking, and creative innovation sets digital teams apart and drives organisational success. At the heart of this lie three key pillars of expertise: digital literacy and technological proficiency, analytical and data-driven thinking, and creativity and innovation.

Digital literacy, particularly technological proficiency, is essential for effective collaboration and productivity within a digital team. In today's tech-driven era, team members must have an in-depth understanding of the digital tools, platforms, and emerging technologies relevant to their specific roles. Technological adaptability is key—digital team members must continuously stay on top of the latest advancements, from mastering new software to understanding the broader implications of emerging technologies such as AI, blockchain, and machine learning. An essential aspect of this is the ability to learn and adapt quickly, ensuring that the team remains agile in the face of rapid technological change. Depending on their role, platform proficiency is a necessity. For example, digital marketers must be skilled in social media management tools, while web developers require a solid command of content management systems and coding languages. In addition, cybersecurity awareness is vital across all roles. Every team member must understand best practices in securing digital assets and data, contributing to a robust organisational security posture. This includes basic principles of secure coding, safeguarding sensitive information, and recognising potential threats.

Beyond technical expertise, analytical and data-driven thinking has emerged as a foundational competency for all digital professionals. The digital environment generates vast amounts of data, and the ability to harness and interpret this information is indispensable. Data interpretation is the first step—team members must be able to distil complex datasets into meaningful insights that inform strategic decision-making. Understanding key performance indicators (KPIs) and leveraging analytics tools effectively enables them to evaluate the success of initiatives and identify areas for improvement. This data-driven approach extends to problem-solving. Whether optimising marketing campaigns, improving UX, or bolstering cybersecurity measures, digital team members must approach challenges with an analytical mindset. Constantly refining strategies through evidence-based decisions helps ensure the organisation remains competitive and agile. In addition, digital professionals must embrace continuous learning, as the digital landscape is constantly shifting. Keeping pace with industry developments, acquiring new analytical skills, and engaging in ongoing professional development are essential for staying ahead in this rapidly evolving field.

Creativity and innovation are equally critical components of a thriving digital team. While technical proficiency and data-driven decision-making are essential, it is the ability to think creatively that often differentiates exceptional teams from average ones. In the digital space, creativity must be user-centric, with a strong focus on understanding and addressing the needs, behaviours, and preferences of the target audience. UX/UI designers and digital marketers, in particular, must infuse creativity into their work to craft digital experiences that resonate with users. Whether designing a UI or developing content, these professionals should always seek to create meaningful, engaging, and intuitive experiences. However, creativity goes beyond just design—it is also key to innovative problem-solving. Digital team members must consistently think beyond the conventional and explore fresh, unorthodox approaches to challenges. This might involve streamlining internal processes, developing innovative product features, or crafting unique marketing strategies that set the organisation apart from its competitors. Finally, creativity thrives in an environment of agility and flexibility. Team members should be empowered to experiment, learn from their failures, and pivot quickly based on emerging trends or user feedback. A willingness to iterate and adapt is essential for fostering a culture of innovation.

Ultimately, the strength of a digital team is founded on the integration of these core competencies. Digital literacy and technological proficiency provide the necessary foundation, while analytical thinking enables informed decision-making, and creativity drives innovation. Organisations that nurture these competencies within their teams are well-positioned to not only meet the challenges of the digital age but to thrive in it. By fostering a culture of adaptability, continuous learning, and innovation, businesses can harness the full potential of their digital talent, ensuring sustainable growth and long-term success in the competitive digital landscape.

11.5 STRATEGIC RECRUITMENT AND HIRING OF DIGITAL TALENT

Recruiting and hiring digital talent is a carefully orchestrated process that demands both precision and foresight. In the rapidly evolving digital landscape, organisations must focus on attracting professionals with the right balance of technical expertise, creativity, and adaptability. The process begins with crafting engaging job descriptions that clearly define the roles and responsibilities, continues with identifying and sourcing the best candidates, and culminates in assessing their skillsets through thoughtful interview techniques.

The foundation of successful recruitment lies in the creation of compelling job descriptions. These descriptions should articulate the core responsibilities and expectations associated with each role in a clear and detailed manner. The tasks and skills required must be accurately outlined, ensuring that potential candidates have a comprehensive understanding of what is expected. For instance, when recruiting for a digital marketing role, it's essential to highlight specific areas of expertise such as search engine optimisation, social media management, and content creation, as well as any particular tools or platforms the candidate will need to be familiar with. However, beyond listing the necessary technical qualifications, job descriptions should also reflect the company's culture and values. It is vital to present a clear image of the organisational ethos, as this fosters alignment between candidates and the company, ensuring those who apply not only have the technical skills but also resonate with the values and vision of the business. Furthermore, in the competitive digital sector, professionals often seek opportunities that offer growth and career development. Employers must highlight the potential for progression within the company and emphasise the opportunities for continued learning and engagement with cutting-edge projects, thus making the role more appealing to ambitious candidates.

Once the job descriptions have been crafted, the next step involves identifying potential candidates through effective sourcing strategies. In today's digital world, online platforms have become indispensable tools for talent acquisition. Professional networking sites like LinkedIn, alongside industry-specific forums and job boards, provide access to a broad range of candidates actively seeking new roles. These platforms enable recruiters to search for professionals with specific skills and connect with them directly, casting a wide net in the hunt for top talent. However, sourcing candidates isn't just about scouring job boards; actively engaging with digital communities related to specific industries or skill sets can be an invaluable strategy. By building relationships within these forums, recruiters can establish a presence and tap into a pool of talent that may not be actively seeking new roles but would be open to the right opportunity. Participation in discussions, sharing expertise, and attending events in these digital spaces fosters trust and helps recruiters maintain a steady pipeline of potential candidates. In addition to these organic strategies, collaborating with digital agencies or leveraging freelance platforms can also yield impressive results. Many digital agencies and freelance professionals have highly specialised skills and a proven track record. Partnering with these entities offers a chance to access a diverse array of experts, whether on a permanent or project-based basis.

The final and arguably most critical stage in recruiting digital talent is the interview and assessment phase, where candidates' technical and behavioural capabilities are evaluated. Given the technical nature of many digital roles, it is essential to incorporate assessments of proficiency that go beyond the standard interview questions. Depending on the role, this could involve a variety of practical tasks. For example, a web developer might be asked to complete a coding exercise that tests their ability to solve real-world problems, while a digital marketer could be tasked with devising a sample campaign that demonstrates their understanding of current trends and platforms. Such exercises provide invaluable insights into a candidate's ability to perform under pressure and in a real working environment. However, technical proficiency alone does not guarantee a successful hire. Behavioural interviews play a key role in assessing a candidate's adaptability, communication skills, and overall cultural fit within the organisation. Exploring a candidate's past experiences, asking how they've handled challenges, and discussing their approach to teamwork helps the interviewer gauge whether the individual will thrive in the company's environment. Additionally, scenario-based questions that present candidates with hypothetical situations relevant to the role are effective in testing their problem-solving abilities. By asking how they would address particular challenges or issues that may arise in the workplace, interviewers can assess a candidate's ability to think critically and apply their knowledge in a practical and dynamic context.

The recruitment and hiring process for digital talent is crucial in shaping the success of a digital team. By thoughtfully crafting job descriptions, using strategic sourcing methods, and conducting thorough interviews, organisations can ensure they attract professionals with not only the necessary skills but also the right mindset and cultural fit. A careful, comprehensive approach to recruitment builds digital teams capable of navigating the demands of the current landscape while possessing the flexibility and foresight needed to adapt and thrive in the future.

11.6 CULTIVATING A DYNAMIC CULTURE OF DIGITAL INNOVATION

In today's rapidly evolving digital landscape, nurturing a culture of innovation is essential for unlocking the full potential of any digital team. Building an environment that fosters creativity, adaptability, and a willingness to experiment can drive meaningful advancements and allow teams to consistently push the boundaries of what is possible. This culture is shaped by several key elements, including fostering a collaborative and agile workspace, promoting continuous learning and development, and encouraging a mindset that embraces experimentation and risk-taking.

A truly collaborative and agile work environment is the foundation upon which innovation thrives. Open and transparent communication channels are crucial, as they allow team members to freely exchange ideas, share feedback, and voice concerns. This level of openness creates a culture where everyone feels comfortable contributing, knowing their input is valued. To support this, organisations often leverage a variety of digital tools—such as project management platforms and instant messaging apps—that facilitate real-time communication and streamline workflows. Furthermore, adopting agile methodologies enables teams to remain flexible and responsive in the face of changing priorities or challenges. Frameworks like Scrum and Kanban encourage iterative development, where regular stand-up meetings, sprint planning, and retrospectives ensure alignment with overarching project goals. This approach allows digital teams to deliver incremental improvements while remaining nimble enough to pivot when necessary. Cross-functional collaboration also plays a pivotal role in fostering innovation. Breaking down the silos that often exist between different departments—such as design, development, marketing, and data analysis—encourages a more holistic approach to problem-solving. By combining diverse skills and perspectives, teams can develop more creative and comprehensive solutions that drive greater impact.

Continuous learning and professional development are equally important in cultivating a culture of innovation. The digital space is constantly evolving, and to keep pace, team members must have access to resources that enable them to refine and expand their skillsets.

Providing access to online courses, webinars, and industry-specific workshops is a critical part of this process. Platforms like Udacity and Coursera, as well as more niche resources tailored to specific fields, offer team members opportunities to stay ahead of industry trends and technological advancements. Beyond informal learning, supporting formal certifications and skill enhancements can demonstrate the organisation's commitment to its team's professional growth. Whether it's obtaining qualifications in programming, mastering the latest digital marketing tools, or acquiring new data analysis techniques, such pursuits not only enhance the team's capabilities but also keep individuals engaged and motivated. Establishing mentorship programmes within the organisation is another effective way to foster development. By pairing less-experienced members with seasoned professionals, mentorship encourages knowledge transfer in a collaborative, supportive setting. This exchange of insights and best practices not only strengthens individual competencies but also reinforces the collective knowledge within the team.

Perhaps the most defining characteristic of a culture of innovation is a willingness to experiment and take risks. True innovation cannot flourish without the freedom to explore new ideas and the acceptance that failure is often part of the process. Cultivating an environment where failures are viewed as learning opportunities rather than setbacks encourages team members to think creatively and take calculated risks. After an unsuccessful project, conducting a thorough post-mortem analysis can uncover areas for improvement, helping the team grow from their experiences and refine their approach for future initiatives. Recognising and rewarding innovative thinking is another powerful way to drive a culture of experimentation. By introducing incentives—whether through recognition programmes, financial bonuses, or career advancement opportunities—organisations can motivate team members to think beyond conventional approaches and strive for innovation. This creates a sense of purpose and reinforces the idea that their contributions are valued. Allocating resources for prototyping and testing is also crucial. Giving teams the tools and support to develop prototypes allows them to explore new ideas and validate concepts before committing significant resources. Rapid prototyping and testing enable teams to iterate on ideas quickly, gather feedback, and refine solutions, ensuring that the most viable and impactful innovations are brought to life.

In cultivating a culture of digital innovation, organisations must be intentional in creating an environment where collaboration, learning, and experimentation are at the forefront. By fostering a dynamic workspace, continuously investing in professional development, and encouraging a mindset that embraces both risk and reward, digital teams are empowered to push boundaries and drive sustained innovation. Such a culture not only equips organisations to adapt to the fast-paced nature of the digital world but also positions them to lead in shaping the future of their industry.

11.7 BUILDING A FOUNDATION FOR SUCCESS: ONBOARDING AND TRAINING DIGITAL TEAMS

Effective onboarding and continuous training form the backbone of a successful digital team, ensuring that every member is seamlessly integrated into the organisation and remains equipped to meet evolving challenges. The process begins with the development of a comprehensive onboarding programme, which introduces new team members to the culture, tools, and structures that will shape their work. This is followed by ongoing training focused on familiarising them with the tools, technologies, and processes essential for success. Lastly, mentoring and coaching play a crucial role in enhancing individual skillsets and fostering collective growth, creating a collaborative learning environment.

A well-structured onboarding programme is fundamental to the smooth transition of new digital team members into the organisation. The first step is to immerse them in the organisation's culture and values, helping them understand the mission and guiding principles that inform every project. This cultural introduction is not simply about understanding policy; it is about cultivating a sense of belonging and alignment with the wider objectives of the organisation. By engaging new hires with the broader ethos, they are more likely to feel connected and committed to the goals that drive the team. Simultaneously, it is essential to provide a clear overview of the team structure and individual roles. A detailed understanding of the team dynamics, along with introductions to key collaborators and leaders, allows new members to see how their work will contribute to collective outcomes. This overview clarifies cross-functional relationships and demonstrates how diverse teams—such as marketing, development, and design—work in tandem to drive innovation. The final step in the onboarding process involves orienting new members to the digital tools and platforms they will use daily. Whether it's project management software, communication tools, or collaboration platforms, familiarising new hires with these systems early on ensures a seamless transition into the practical aspects of their role.

Beyond the initial onboarding, continuous training is vital to ensure that digital team members remain proficient in the tools, technologies, and processes required to excel in their roles. Hands-on training sessions are an integral part of this process, allowing new team members to gain practical experience with the technologies they will use. Workshops or simulations that mirror real-world scenarios provide the opportunity to apply theoretical knowledge in a tangible way, enhancing confidence and capability. As the digital landscape is in constant flux, it is equally important to provide regular updates on technological advancements. New tools and methodologies frequently emerge, and staying ahead of these developments ensures that the team can leverage cutting-edge technologies to enhance their work. In parallel, documenting processes and best practices is crucial for long-term efficiency and knowledge sharing. A centralised repository of resources, whether through internal wikis or shared collaboration platforms, allows all team members to access valuable information at any time, fostering a culture of continuous learning and skill development.

Mentoring and coaching are essential components of professional growth and the enhancement of individual skillsets within digital teams. Assigning mentorship relationships between new hires and experienced team members offers a structured support system, helping newcomers navigate the intricacies of both the organisation and their specific projects. These mentoring relationships are not only about skill-building but also about fostering a sense of belonging and offering guidance on professional development. Regular feedback and performance reviews are also critical in this process. Frequent, constructive feedback helps team members understand their strengths and areas for improvement, allowing them to adjust their approaches and focus on skill development where needed. By identifying specific areas for additional coaching or training, regular reviews ensure that every team member continues to grow and improve. Alongside formal mentoring and feedback, peer-to-peer learning plays a powerful role in collective skill enhancement. Informal knowledge sharing—through discussions, collaborative projects, or dedicated learning sessions—encourages team members to learn from one another, broadening their expertise and fostering a culture of continuous improvement.

In an ever-evolving digital landscape, the importance of a robust onboarding and training process cannot be overstated. A comprehensive onboarding programme that immerses new hires in the organisation's culture, introduces them to key tools and platforms, and clarifies their role within the team lays the groundwork for success. Coupled with ongoing, hands-on training and strong mentorship and coaching frameworks, digital teams can thrive and adapt to the rapid changes that define their industry. By prioritising continuous learning and skill enhancement, organisations not only strengthen individual capabilities but also ensure that their teams are prepared to meet the challenges of the future and continue contributing meaningfully to overall objectives.

CASE STUDY 11

IBM's Digital Transformation and Workforce Reskilling

IBM, one of the world's leading technology companies, embarked on a large-scale digital transformation to remain competitive in an era of rapid technological advancement. As cloud computing, AI, and automation reshaped the industry, IBM recognised the need to reskill its workforce and attract new digital talent. Many traditional job roles within the company were becoming obsolete, and there was a growing demand for expertise in emerging technologies. To stay ahead, IBM needed to ensure its employees could adapt to the evolving digital landscape while also fostering a culture of continuous learning and innovation.

To address these challenges, IBM implemented a comprehensive workforce reskilling initiative. The company invested heavily in training programmes that focused on AI, cybersecurity, cloud computing, and data science. Through its SkillsBuild platform, IBM provided employees with free access to digital courses, allowing them to upskill in high-demand areas. Additionally, the company launched partnerships with universities and online learning providers to create new certification programmes tailored to the digital economy. IBM also introduced an apprenticeship model that enabled employees to gain hands-on experience while transitioning into new tech-focused roles. Alongside reskilling existing employees, IBM actively recruited talent with expertise in digital technologies, ensuring that its workforce remained at the forefront of innovation.

The results of IBM's digital workforce strategy were significant. Over a three-year period, IBM reskilled more than 300,000 employees, equipping them with the necessary skills to thrive in the digital age. Employee engagement and job satisfaction improved as staff felt empowered to develop new competencies and remain relevant in a fast-changing industry. The company also strengthened its position in emerging technology sectors, securing major contracts in cloud computing and AI services. Furthermore, IBM's commitment to continuous learning fostered a culture of adaptability, allowing the organisation to respond effectively to technological disruptions. The initiative not only future-proofed IBM's workforce but also positioned the company as a leader in digital transformation within the corporate world.

IBM's reskilling and digital transformation strategy offers valuable lessons for businesses navigating similar challenges. Firstly, continuous learning is essential for maintaining a competitive workforce in the digital era. Companies must invest in training and development to ensure employees can adapt to evolving industry demands. Secondly, fostering a culture of innovation encourages employees to embrace technological advancements rather than fear them. Thirdly, businesses must balance internal reskilling efforts with external hiring to ensure they have the necessary expertise for future growth. Finally, digital transformation is not just about technology but also about people—successful change requires equipping employees with the skills and confidence to drive innovation.

Discussion Questions for Students (with Indicative Answers)

1. **Why was workforce reskilling a crucial part of IBM's digital transformation strategy?**
   Indicative Answer: IBM recognised that emerging technologies were changing job roles, and reskilling was essential to ensure employees remained relevant and could contribute to innovation.
2. **What steps did IBM take to upskill its workforce?**
   Indicative Answer: The company launched online learning platforms, formed partnerships with universities, introduced apprenticeship programmes, and focused on training in AI, cloud computing, and data science.

3. **How did IBM's digital transformation impact its business performance?**
Indicative Answer: The initiative improved employee engagement, enhanced IBM's capabilities in AI and cloud computing, and strengthened its position in the tech industry.
4. **What are the key benefits of fostering a culture of continuous learning in a digital business?**
Indicative Answer: A learning culture helps employees adapt to new technologies, improves job satisfaction, and ensures businesses remain competitive by keeping their workforce skilled.
5. **How can other companies apply IBM's approach to reskilling their employees?**
Indicative Answer: Companies should invest in accessible training programmes, encourage innovation, balance reskilling with external hiring, and create a culture that supports lifelong learning.

11.8 NAVIGATING REMOTE AND VIRTUAL TEAM MANAGEMENT IN THE DIGITAL ERA

In today's rapidly evolving digital landscape, the management of remote and virtual teams has become an integral aspect of organisational success. The rise of remote work, accelerated by technological advancements and changing workplace cultures, has reshaped the way digital teams operate, demanding new approaches to leadership, communication, and collaboration. Effective management of such teams requires embracing the unique opportunities remote work presents while also addressing the distinct challenges it brings. By focusing on fostering trust, implementing the right tools, and strategically addressing obstacles, organisations can ensure their digital teams remain productive, cohesive, and engaged.

Managing remote and distributed teams requires a fundamental shift in mindset, one that embraces the flexibility and opportunities provided by the digital nomad culture. This culture, which allows team members to work from anywhere in the world, has created an unprecedented level of freedom in how work is approached and completed. Team members are no longer bound by geographical constraints, opening up access to a global talent pool and enabling organisations to tap into diverse skill sets across different time zones and working styles. To effectively manage such teams, leaders must foster an environment that not only embraces this flexibility but also promotes adaptability, allowing individuals to tailor their work to fit their personal rhythms while still contributing to the collective goals of the organisation.

At the heart of successful remote team management lies the establishment of clear expectations and goals. Without the traditional office setting to provide structure, remote teams require well-defined tasks, deadlines, and KPIs to ensure alignment and accountability. When team members have a clear understanding of their roles, the projects they are working on, and the standards by which their success will be measured, they are far more likely to deliver quality results and remain engaged. This clarity is particularly crucial in a remote environment, where the absence of in-person interactions can sometimes lead to misunderstandings or misalignment.

Trust is another fundamental component in the management of remote teams. With team members dispersed across different locations, managers must cultivate a culture of trust built on transparent communication and a focus on outcomes rather than micromanagement. Trust allows team members to take ownership of their tasks, work independently, and feel confident in their contributions. When trust is established, remote teams thrive, as individuals are empowered to take initiative and collaborate effectively without the need for constant oversight.

Communication and collaboration tools are indispensable in bridging the gap created by physical distance. Unified communication platforms, such as Slack, Microsoft Teams, or Zoom, provide the foundation for seamless interaction, allowing team members to connect, share updates, and collaborate in real time. These tools are critical in maintaining fluid communication, especially in scenarios where teams are operating across different time zones. However, communication needs to go beyond task management. Video conferencing tools, for instance, play a vital role in fostering personal connections within remote teams. Regular virtual meetings provide the opportunity for face-to-face interactions, helping to reduce feelings of isolation and strengthening relationships among team members. These virtual touchpoints ensure that, despite the distance, the team remains cohesive and aligned.

Collaborative project management tools are equally essential in managing the logistics of remote work. Platforms such as Asana, Trello, or Jira enable digital teams to organise projects, allocate tasks, and track progress in a transparent and accountable manner. These tools serve as the digital equivalent of an office whiteboard, ensuring that everyone is on the same page regarding deadlines, responsibilities, and project goals. By centralising project information, managers and team members alike can monitor the status of various initiatives, preventing delays and maintaining momentum.

Despite the advantages of remote work, there are inherent challenges that must be addressed. One of the most common issues is communication gaps, which can arise due to the absence of spontaneous, in-person interactions. In a physical office, quick clarifications and impromptu discussions are part of the fabric of daily operations. In a remote setting, these informal exchanges are lost, potentially leading to misunderstandings or delays. To overcome this, managers must establish clear communication protocols and ensure that team members feel comfortable engaging in open dialogue. Encouraging the use of platforms for both formal and informal conversations can help bridge the gap, allowing team members to interact as they would in a traditional office setting.

Maintaining team cohesion in a virtual environment requires intentional effort. Virtual teams may struggle to build the same camaraderie as those who work side by side, but with the right strategies, a strong sense of connection can still be achieved. Team-building activities, whether professional or social, are invaluable in fostering relationships. Virtual coffee breaks, online games, or collaborative projects that focus on non-work-related tasks can help team members bond and develop a sense of camaraderie. By integrating these opportunities for personal connection, managers can cultivate a more united and engaged team.

Balancing flexibility with structure is another key challenge in remote work environments. While the appeal of remote work lies in its flexibility, too much freedom without clear processes can lead to inefficiencies and burnout. Maintaining structured workflows, regular check-ins, and a shared understanding of working hours helps prevent the blurring of boundaries between personal and professional life. This balance ensures that team members have the autonomy they need while still adhering to the discipline required to meet organisational goals.

The management of remote and virtual teams is a nuanced endeavour that requires a blend of trust, technology, and strategic oversight. By embracing the opportunities presented by remote work and addressing its inherent complexities, organisations can build high-performing digital teams capable of thriving in the modern landscape. The integration of clear communication practices, the use of collaborative tools, and a proactive approach to overcoming challenges create an environment where remote teams can flourish, contributing to the overall success of the organisation in this increasingly digital world.

11.9 STRATEGIES FOR MOTIVATING AND RETAINING DIGITAL TALENT IN A COMPETITIVE LANDSCAPE

In today's fiercely competitive digital landscape, motivating and retaining digital talent is not just a strategic consideration—it's a fundamental necessity for organisations aiming to succeed. The rapid pace of technological innovation, coupled with the growing demand for specialised digital skills, has heightened the importance of cultivating an environment where talent feels valued, inspired, and invested in the organisation's future. This involves creating a culture that embraces digital innovation, providing competitive compensation packages, and fostering opportunities for continuous career development. Together, these elements contribute to the establishment of a dynamic, engaging workplace where top talent can thrive and remain loyal to the organisation.

One of the key foundations for motivating and retaining digital professionals lies in the creation of a positive work environment that is underpinned by a strong company culture. This begins with embracing a digital-first mindset that encourages innovation and creativity. Digital teams perform best when given the freedom to explore new ideas, experiment with emerging technologies, and share insights in a collaborative atmosphere. A culture that champions agility, open communication, and a willingness to challenge the status quo not only enhances job satisfaction but also fosters a deep sense of engagement among employees. Moreover, this culture of innovation should be complemented by flexible work arrangements, recognising the shifting dynamics of the modern workplace. Offering remote work options, flexible hours, and a focus on outcomes rather than rigid schedules empowers digital professionals to manage their responsibilities while maintaining a healthy work-life balance. This flexibility is key to enhancing overall well-being and job satisfaction.

In addition to fostering a digital-first culture, prioritising employee well-being is crucial. Organisations that genuinely care about their workforce demonstrate this through mental health support, wellness programmes, and initiatives that encourage a healthy work-life balance. Such initiatives not only contribute to a more positive workplace but also show employees that their holistic well-being is valued. When employees feel cared for and supported, they are more likely to remain engaged, productive, and loyal to the organisation.

Beyond creating an inspiring work environment, offering competitive compensation and benefits is essential to attracting and retaining top digital talent. Staying abreast of industry standards and regularly benchmarking salaries ensures that employees are compensated fairly for their skills and expertise. Transparent communication around compensation policies fosters trust, which is especially critical in an era where the competition for digital talent is fierce. However, it's not just about base salary. Digital professionals often seek innovative benefits packages that align with their individual preferences and lifestyles. Organisations can stand out by offering health and wellness incentives, flexible spending accounts, and personalised benefits options that cater to the diverse needs of their workforce.

To further motivate digital talent, performance-linked bonuses are an effective tool. Tying financial rewards directly to individual or team performance establishes a clear link between effort and compensation, reinforcing a meritocratic culture. This not only encourages employees to excel in their roles but also ensures they feel recognised and rewarded for their contributions. A culture that promotes meritocracy motivates employees to push boundaries and innovate, knowing their efforts will be acknowledged both financially and professionally.

Career growth and advancement opportunities are another powerful driver in the retention of digital talent. Professionals in this field, often characterised by a desire for continuous learning, thrive when provided with opportunities to enhance their skills and advance their careers. Offering personalised development plans tailored to both the needs of the organisation and the aspirations of the individual allows employees to envision a future within the company. These plans might include the pursuit of industry certifications, attending conferences, or participating in ongoing training programmes. Supporting continuous learning in this way ensures that employees remain at the cutting edge of their fields while also feeling invested in their personal growth.

Mentorship and coaching programmes are also valuable tools for fostering skill development and career guidance. When less-experienced team members are paired with seasoned professionals, the transfer of knowledge and skills occurs organically, creating a supportive environment where employees feel encouraged to seek advice and guidance. This collaborative culture strengthens relationships within the team and contributes to a shared sense of purpose. Furthermore, these programmes offer invaluable insights into navigating challenges and identifying new growth opportunities, making them an essential element in creating a cohesive, high-performing digital team.

Providing clear career pathways is equally important in ensuring that digital professionals remain engaged and committed to the organisation. Employees are far more likely to stay when they can see a tangible progression in their career. Organisations should outline the steps required for advancement, define promotion criteria, and clearly communicate the opportunities for growth available within the company. Transparent and well-structured career pathways give employees a sense of purpose and long-term direction, ensuring they remain motivated and committed to the organisation's future success.

Ultimately, motivating and retaining digital talent requires a comprehensive, multifaceted approach that extends beyond traditional compensation models. It involves building a positive and flexible work environment, offering competitive and innovative benefits, and providing clear opportunities for career advancement. By fostering a digital-first culture, prioritising employee well-being, and empowering individuals to grow professionally, organisations can create a dynamic and engaging workplace that not only attracts top talent but also ensures they remain invested in the organisation's long-term success. As the digital landscape continues to evolve, companies that prioritise the motivation and retention of their digital talent will be better positioned to thrive in an ever-changing world.

11.10 THE STRATEGIC ADVANTAGE OF DIVERSITY AND INCLUSION IN DIGITAL TEAMS

In today's rapidly evolving digital landscape, diversity and inclusion are not just ethical considerations but also crucial strategic advantages. The complex and interconnected nature of digital business demands teams that reflect the diversity of the world they serve. By fostering a diverse and inclusive environment, organisations position themselves to innovate, respond to market demands, and solve problems more effectively. The value of diversity in digital teams extends far beyond representation; it fuels creativity, enhances market responsiveness, and strengthens a company's ability to navigate the multifaceted challenges inherent in the digital sphere.

The innovation that emerges from diversity is one of the most compelling reasons for its pursuit. A team comprised of individuals from varied backgrounds, perspectives, and experiences is inherently more dynamic. The richness of this diversity sparks creativity, enabling teams to approach problems from angles that would not have been apparent in a more homogenous group. In an industry that thrives on constant technological advancement, the ability to generate novel ideas and explore uncharted territories is a distinct advantage. This diversity of thought becomes the foundation of a culture of innovation, where new technologies, products, and solutions are continually created and refined to meet the demands of a fast-changing digital environment.

In addition to driving innovation, a diverse digital team significantly enhances a company's market responsiveness. In a global and interconnected marketplace, organisations must design products and services that resonate with a wide array of customers, each with distinct needs and preferences. A workforce that reflects the diversity of its target market is far more adept at anticipating and responding to these varied demands. When digital products and services are created by teams with a deep understanding of different cultural contexts, demographic factors, and user behaviours, the result is a product that is more relevant, inclusive, and competitive. The ability to tailor offerings to a broad spectrum of users strengthens a company's position in the market and opens doors to untapped opportunities.

The benefits of diversity extend even further into problem-solving. Digital challenges are often complex, requiring nuanced and multifaceted solutions. When a diverse team approaches a problem, each member brings unique insights and skills, drawing from their individual experiences. This diversity of thought leads to more comprehensive solutions, as problems are tackled from a variety of angles, with each team member offering a different perspective. The collaborative nature of such teams not only enhances problem-solving capabilities but also creates an environment where learning and growth are fostered through the exchange of ideas.

Creating an inclusive work environment is essential to unlocking the full potential of diversity. Inclusivity must be ingrained in the culture of the organisation, and this begins with leadership. Leaders play a critical role in championing inclusivity by modelling behaviours that prioritise openness, respect, and equity. They must ensure that all voices are heard and that diverse perspectives are valued, which in turn fosters a sense of belonging among team members. When leaders actively promote an inclusive environment, individuals feel empowered to contribute their best work, knowing their ideas will be respected and considered. This openness encourages innovation and enhances job satisfaction, making the team more cohesive and productive.

Visibility of diverse role models within the organisation is another crucial aspect of fostering inclusion. Diverse representation at all levels, particularly in leadership roles, sends a powerful message about the organisation's commitment to diversity and inclusion. Implementing mentorship programmes that connect underrepresented individuals with experienced mentors can provide invaluable guidance, support, and career development opportunities. These programmes also facilitate knowledge-sharing across different demographic groups, ensuring that all employees have access to the tools and resources they need to succeed. By bridging the gaps that often exist in career advancement for underrepresented groups, organisations can build a more equitable and supportive environment.

The establishment of inclusive policies and practices is vital to creating a culture that sustains diversity. This includes ensuring that professional development opportunities are accessible to all, promoting work-life balance, and addressing potential biases in performance evaluations. When organisations demonstrate their commitment to inclusion through transparent policies and practices, they reinforce trust and engagement within the workforce. Inclusive practices should be embedded in every aspect of the organisation, from recruitment and hiring to promotions and career development, ensuring that diversity is not just an ideal but a lived reality.

To fully embrace diversity, organisations must take concrete steps to mitigate bias in hiring and promotions. Structured and standardised hiring processes help reduce unconscious biases that can otherwise influence decisions. Clear criteria for evaluating candidates, combined with diverse hiring panels and blind recruitment practices, ensure that individuals are assessed based on their skills, experience, and qualifications rather than on superficial factors. This approach not only promotes fairness but also enhances the overall quality of hires by focusing on merit and potential.

Diverse interview panels contribute to more balanced and fair evaluations of candidates. When interviewers represent a variety of perspectives and backgrounds, they are better equipped to make informed decisions and are less likely to be influenced by unconscious biases. Furthermore, candidates are more likely to feel welcomed and comfortable when they see a diverse group of individuals conducting the interviews. This sense of connection during the hiring process can be a deciding factor for top talent considering multiple opportunities, making diversity in hiring panels a strategic advantage.

Merit-based promotions are another essential element of fostering diversity and inclusion. By establishing clear, objective criteria for promotions, organisations can ensure that decisions are based on skills, performance, and contributions rather than subjective factors. Regular performance reviews and constructive feedback help employees understand what is expected of them and what they need to achieve in order to advance. A transparent promotion process that aligns with the organisation's diversity and inclusion goals further reinforces fairness and trust, helping to retain top talent and maintain a motivated workforce.

In conclusion, diversity and inclusion within digital teams are more than just moral imperatives—they are strategic advantages that drive innovation, enhance market responsiveness, and improve problem-solving capabilities. By fostering an inclusive work environment, mitigating biases in hiring and promotions, and recognising the inherent value of diversity, organisations can harness the full potential of their digital teams. In doing so, they position themselves for sustained success in an increasingly diverse and complex digital landscape.

11.11 NAVIGATING THE FUTURE: BUILDING A DIGITAL TEAM FOR EVOLVING TRENDS AND TECHNOLOGIES

In a world where the digital landscape is in a state of constant flux, the ability to adapt swiftly to emerging trends and technologies is essential for any successful digital team. It is not enough to simply react to changes; proactive adaptation must be woven into the fabric of an organisation's strategy. By fostering a culture of continuous learning, anticipating and addressing skill gaps, and staying at the forefront of technological developments, digital teams can maintain their competitive edge and ensure long-term success. The key lies in creating an environment where innovation thrives and where teams are not only prepared for the future but are leading its charge.

The cornerstone of any adaptive digital team is a commitment to continuous learning. In an industry where technological advancements occur at an unprecedented rate, staying still is simply not an option. Digital leaders must prioritise the cultivation of an environment that encourages lifelong learning. This can be achieved by providing opportunities for team members to engage in ongoing education, whether through online platforms, workshops, industry conferences, or other learning initiatives. Such efforts are critical to ensuring that teams remain informed about the latest tools, trends, and methodologies that define the digital space. The ongoing pursuit of knowledge also helps instil a mindset of curiosity and growth, which is vital for both personal and organisational development.

Recognising that no two individuals learn in the same way is also paramount to fostering a learning-centric culture. Digital leaders must embrace the need for personalised learning paths, acknowledging the diverse skill sets, experiences, and learning preferences within their teams. By offering tailored learning opportunities—whether it's through mentoring programmes, flexible learning schedules, or a variety of training resources—organisations can empower their employees to take ownership of their professional development. Personalised learning not only helps individuals enhance the specific skills they need for their roles but also motivates them to pursue their own career aspirations, contributing to higher levels of engagement and satisfaction.

The ongoing investment in training programmes is an essential part of this continuous learning culture. Leaders must be proactive in identifying the key skills that are critical to the team's success and future growth. This involves both technical training on emerging tools and technologies and soft skills development that enhances teamwork, communication, and collaboration. By investing in comprehensive training initiatives, organisations equip their digital teams with the tools they need to thrive in an ever-evolving digital landscape. Such investments are not just about immediate gains; they are a long-term strategy for building a resilient and future-ready team.

Anticipating skill gaps and future talent needs is equally important in building a dynamic digital team. The rapid pace of change in digital industries means that today's skills may quickly become outdated. To stay ahead, digital leaders must engage in regular skills assessments, evaluating both the technical abilities and soft skills within their teams. This process allows for a clear understanding of where the team excels and where there may be deficiencies that need addressing. By identifying potential gaps early, organisations can implement strategies to either upskill existing team members or recruit new talent with the necessary expertise.

Staying attuned to the external talent landscape is also crucial. Leaders must keep their fingers on the pulse of industry trends, emerging technologies, and the skill sets that are becoming increasingly sought after. A deep understanding of the evolving demands of the digital workforce ensures that teams are always prepared to meet future challenges head-on. This knowledge enables digital leaders to position their teams strategically, ensuring they are well-equipped to tackle whatever comes next in the digital space.

Strategic workforce planning, informed by these skills assessments and industry insights, is the final piece of the puzzle. By aligning the team's skill sets with the organisation's long-term goals, leaders can ensure that their workforce remains agile and adaptable. This might involve hiring new talent, upskilling current employees, or even redefining roles to meet the demands of the shifting digital landscape. Strategic workforce planning allows organisations to remain future-focused, ensuring that their digital teams are not only responsive to change but are drivers of innovation and growth.

One of the most critical aspects of staying ahead of digital trends is embracing emerging technologies. Digital leaders must create an environment where experimentation with new tools and methodologies is encouraged. Pilot projects that explore these innovations in a controlled setting can provide valuable insights and allow teams to assess the potential of new technologies before fully integrating them into broader operations. This approach not only fosters a culture of innovation but also positions the team as early adopters, providing a competitive advantage in the marketplace.

Collaboration across different functions is often essential when adopting emerging technologies. Many of the most transformative digital trends require expertise from multiple disciplines, making cross-functional collaboration a vital strategy for success. Leaders must facilitate interdisciplinary projects that bring together diverse skill sets to tackle the challenges posed by new technologies. This collaborative approach not only strengthens the team's ability to integrate cutting-edge tools but also enhances adaptability, enabling the seamless incorporation of new technologies into existing workflows.

Beyond technical skills, fostering a tech-savvy mindset is critical to long-term success. This mindset is characterised by an openness to change, a curiosity about new technologies, and a willingness to explore innovative solutions. Leaders can cultivate such a mindset by encouraging regular knowledge-sharing sessions, promoting a culture of experimentation, and providing opportunities for team members to engage with the latest digital trends. When teams are comfortable with ambiguity and motivated by the prospect of exploring new frontiers, they become far more adept at navigating the complexities of the digital age.

Adapting to changing digital trends and technologies requires more than just technical competence; it demands a holistic approach that integrates continuous learning, forward-thinking talent management, and a fearless embrace of innovation. By committing to these principles, digital teams can build resilience, ensuring they are not only prepared for the future but are shaping it. In this way, they position themselves to lead in the adoption and application of the technologies that will define the next chapter of the digital revolution.

11.12 CHAPTER SUMMARY

In today's hyper-connected and rapidly evolving digital landscape, building a successful digital team requires more than just assembling individuals with technical expertise. It demands strategic foresight, thoughtful structuring, and ongoing management to create an environment where innovation can thrive. Throughout this chapter, we have explored how to effectively hire, manage, and nurture digital talent, emphasising the importance of aligning team roles with organisational goals to drive high performance. By investing in continuous learning, organisations can ensure their digital teams remain at the forefront of emerging trends and technologies while fostering a dynamic culture of innovation and inclusivity.

Key to long-term success is the ability to motivate and retain top talent. As competition for skilled digital professionals intensifies, businesses must provide a compelling employee experience—offering opportunities for growth, flexible working arrangements, and competitive benefits. A strong onboarding process and ongoing training initiatives are critical to setting the foundation for a team that is both cohesive and resilient. Moreover, diversity and inclusion should be prioritised, not only as a moral obligation but as a strategic advantage that fuels creativity, problem-solving, and market relevance.

Ultimately, the future belongs to agile, innovative digital teams that are equipped to adapt to rapidly changing technologies and market demands. By focusing on strategic recruitment, comprehensive management, and a forward-thinking approach, organisations can ensure their digital teams are primed for sustained success in the evolving digital world.

Key Questions for Discussion

1. In what ways has the rise of digital business changed the skills and roles required in a modern workforce? How can organisations ensure they are hiring for future digital needs rather than just current demands?
2. With competition for digital talent at an all-time high, what innovative strategies can businesses use to attract and retain top digital professionals? Should companies prioritise technical skills over adaptability and soft skills when hiring for digital roles?

3. The shift towards remote and hybrid working models has transformed team management. What are the key challenges in managing digital teams remotely, and how can businesses foster collaboration, productivity, and engagement in virtual environments?
4. How can fostering diversity and inclusion within digital teams contribute to innovation and business success? What steps can organisations take to ensure that their digital workforce reflects a broad range of perspectives and experiences?
5. As emerging technologies like AI, blockchain, and automation continue to reshape industries, how can businesses future-proof their digital teams to remain competitive? What strategies should leaders adopt to continuously upskill their workforce?

BIBLIOGRAPHY

Davenport, T.H. (2018). *The AI Advantage: How to Put the Artificial Intelligence Revolution to Work*. MIT Press.

Jesuthasan, R. and Boudreau, J.W. (2018). *Reinventing Jobs: A 4-Step Approach for Applying Automation to Work*. Harvard Business Review Press.

Johansen, B. (2017). *The New Leadership Literacies: Thriving in a Future of Extreme Disruption and Distributed Everything*. Berrett-Koehler Publishers.

Kane, G.C., Phillips, A.N., Copulsky, J.R. and Andrus, G.R. (2019). *The Technology Fallacy: How People Are the Real Key to Digital Transformation*. MIT Press.

McChrystal, S. (2015). *Team of Teams: New Rules of Engagement for a Complex World*. Portfolio.

Meyer-Cuno, D. (2021). *The Recipe for Empowered Leadership: 25 Ingredients for Creating Value & Empowering Others*. Greenleaf Book Group Press.

MIT Sloan Management Review (2018). *When Innovation Moves at Digital Speed: Strategies and Tactics to Provoke, Sustain, and Defend Innovation in Today's Unsettled Markets*. MIT Press.

Morgan, J. (2014). *The Future of Work: Attract New Talent, Build Better Leaders, and Create a Competitive Organization*. Wiley.

Rogers, D.L. (2016). *The Digital Transformation Playbook: Rethink Your Business for the Digital Age*. Columbia Business School Publishing.

Rugg-Gunn, M. (2022). *Managing Talent: A Short Guide for the Digital Age*. Routledge.

Sheninger, E. (2019). Digital Leadership: Changing Paradigms for Changing Times. Corwin.

Siebel, T.M. (2019). *Digital Transformation: Survive and Thrive in an Era of Mass Extinction*. RosettaBooks.

Wade, J. (2021). *The Human Team: So, You Created a Team but People Showed Up!* Greenleaf Book Group Press.

Westerman, G., Bonnet, D. and McAfee, A. (2014). *Leading Digital: Turning Technology into Business Transformation*. Harvard Business Review Press.

CHAPTER 12

Impact of Artificial Intelligence on Business and Society

Learning Outcomes

By the end of this chapter, you will be able to:

1. Understand how AI is reshaping modern business practices, automation, and efficiency, as well as its broader societal implications.
2. Explore key ethical concerns such as bias, transparency, and accountability, and assess the role of policy, regulation, and global cooperation in AI governance.
3. Investigate how AI is influencing workforce dynamics, human–AI collaboration, and emerging opportunities and challenges in an AI-powered future.

12.1 INTRODUCTION

Artificial intelligence (AI) has rapidly become one of the most transformative forces shaping the modern world, fundamentally altering the way businesses operate and society functions. Once confined to the realm of science fiction, AI has evolved into a powerful and practical tool that enhances decision-making, automates processes, and solves complex problems. Its impact extends across various sectors, from healthcare and finance to manufacturing and logistics, revolutionising industries through innovative applications and technologies. However, AI's growing integration into everyday life raises important questions about its societal implications, ethical considerations, and future trajectory.

This chapter explores the multi-faceted role of AI in transforming business and society. It begins by tracing the evolution of AI, examining its foundations and how its capabilities have developed over time to become a disruptive force. This chapter also delves into how AI has influenced modern business practices, driving efficiency, innovation, and competitiveness. With a focus on automation, the text investigates AI's role in streamlining business operations while acknowledging the ethical challenges that arise from AI implementation, such as bias and transparency. As AI reshapes the future of work, this chapter addresses its impact on employment and the growing need for collaboration between human intelligence and AI

DOI: 10.4324/9781032672458-12

systems. Lastly, it provides insights into the future of AI and the crucial role of governance and regulation in shaping a responsible and inclusive AI-driven future.

12.2 THE TRANSFORMATIVE POWER OF AI: FOUNDATIONS, EVOLUTION, AND SOCIETAL POTENTIAL

AI represents the pinnacle of technological advancement, bringing machines closer than ever to simulating human intelligence. At its essence, AI is about empowering systems to learn from data, adapt to new situations, and perform tasks traditionally requiring human cognition. The heart of AI lies in its ability to mimic human intelligence, with Machine Learning, a critical subset, enabling machines to learn and improve from experience without needing explicit programming. These interconnected technologies pave the way for a new era of automation, sophisticated decision-making, and complex problem-solving.

AI's power derives from the intricate relationship between data and algorithms. Algorithms, functioning as a set of instructions, drive the actions and decisions of AI systems. Through Machine Learning, these algorithms continuously evolve, improving their performance as they process more data. The basics of AI, therefore, revolve around understanding how algorithms interpret and analyse information, recognise patterns, and make predictions or decisions, much like the cognitive processes found in human reasoning. This foundational understanding is key to grasping AI's vast potential.

The evolution of AI is marked by significant advancements, transitioning from theoretical ideas to practical applications that have revolutionised various aspects of business and society. Initially, AI models were based on rule-based systems, operating solely on predefined instructions. However, the advent of Machine Learning, particularly with the development of neural networks and deep learning techniques, marked a radical transformation. These new AI models autonomously process vast datasets, uncover patterns, and make intricate decisions, mirroring the complexity of human thought. The leap from rule-based systems to learning models has ushered in a new age of AI capability.

Businesses have been quick to embrace AI, leveraging its potential to drive efficiency, streamline operations, and foster innovation. Across sectors as diverse as finance, healthcare, manufacturing, and retail, AI has permeated industries, fundamentally altering how they operate. It automates routine tasks, powers predictive analytics, and creates personalised customer experiences, transforming every level of business functionality. The integration of AI into business workflows enables organisations to extract valuable insights from massive data sets, make well-informed decisions based on those insights, and maintain a competitive edge in an increasingly data-driven economy.

Beyond business, AI offers extraordinary promise for society at large. Its potential applications stretch across numerous fields, presenting solutions to some of the most complex challenges facing humanity today. In healthcare, AI is already contributing to enhanced diagnostic accuracy, more efficient drug discovery, and the development of personalised treatment plans. In education, AI-powered tools enable tailored learning experiences that adapt to the needs and progress of individual students, helping to close educational gaps and improve outcomes.

Furthermore, AI plays a pivotal role in addressing global societal challenges such as climate change and sustainable resource management. Predictive modelling, powered by AI, equips scientists and policymakers with the tools to make data-informed decisions that promote sustainable development. Similarly, AI's influence extends into public safety, where technologies like predictive policing and disaster response systems help improve preparedness and response strategies, enhancing the safety and security of communities worldwide.

However, as AI continues to become more deeply embedded in the fabric of society, it raises important ethical questions that cannot be ignored. Ensuring fairness, transparency, and accountability in AI systems is crucial to their long-term positive impact. Striking a balance between the rapid pace of innovation and the ethical considerations that arise from its deployment is essential to making sure AI serves society responsibly. Issues such as algorithmic bias, privacy concerns, and the need for transparent decision-making processes must be addressed with care as AI becomes a more prevalent force in our lives.

The introduction of AI has undoubtedly ushered in a new era, transforming the way businesses operate and reshaping societal progress in profound ways. Understanding the foundations of AI, tracking its rapid evolution, and contemplating its potential for solving societal challenges are crucial first steps in navigating this complex landscape. As AI becomes more deeply intertwined with everyday life, the responsibility lies in its thoughtful and ethical integration, ensuring that its benefits can be fully realised by both business and society alike. The path forward for AI will be defined not just by its technological capabilities but by the wisdom with which it is applied.

12.3 THE TRANSFORMATIONAL IMPACT OF AI ON MODERN BUSINESS PRACTICES

AI has fundamentally altered the landscape of business operations, particularly in the realms of customer service, marketing, and sales. By integrating AI-driven technologies, companies are not only enhancing efficiency but also personalising customer experiences in ways previously unimaginable. AI's ability to process vast amounts of data in real time, draw insights, and automate processes is enabling businesses to operate more intelligently and with greater agility.

One of the most significant transformations has been in customer service and support. AI-powered systems such as chatbots, which are equipped with natural language processing (NLP) capabilities, now provide immediate and accurate responses to customer queries. These virtual assistants, accessible around the clock, have streamlined customer interactions, reducing response times and improving operational efficiency. As these AI-driven systems continuously learn from each interaction, they become increasingly adept at understanding customer needs, providing a more personalised and effective experience. In addition to direct interaction, AI is also revolutionising customer support through sentiment analysis. By assessing customer feedback, companies can swiftly detect trends in satisfaction, identifying potential issues before they escalate. This allows businesses to make data-driven improvements to their services, fostering stronger brand loyalty as customers value timely, tailored assistance.

The power of AI extends into the marketing domain, where it has redefined how businesses reach and engage their audiences. Machine learning algorithms are capable of analysing extensive datasets to uncover customer preferences, behaviours, and purchasing patterns. With these insights, businesses can create highly targeted and personalised marketing campaigns, delivering messages that resonate with individual customers. This approach not only maximises the effectiveness of marketing strategies but also fosters deeper connections with consumers by addressing their specific needs and interests. The use of AI-powered recommendation engines, particularly in e-commerce, exemplifies this shift. These engines offer personalised product suggestions based on users' browsing and purchasing history, significantly enhancing the shopping experience and boosting sales. The ability to anticipate and respond to customer desires has transformed marketing from a generic, one-size-fits-all method to a more refined and customer-centric approach, making businesses more competitive and responsive.

In the sales sector, AI has become a powerful tool for predictive analytics, driving more informed decision-making processes. AI models analyse historical sales data to identify patterns and predict future trends, allowing businesses to make strategic adjustments to inventory management, pricing, and sales forecasts. This analytical capability ensures that companies are not only optimising their resources but also responding proactively to market fluctuations. Furthermore, AI assists sales teams by automating routine tasks, such as lead generation and customer outreach. Chatbots, once again, play a crucial role in this area, engaging potential customers, answering their questions, and guiding them through the initial stages of the sales funnel. By automating these initial interactions, AI allows sales representatives to focus on more complex and high-value activities, ultimately improving both efficiency and customer satisfaction.

In addition, AI enables more strategic sales efforts through predictive lead scoring. By analysing a variety of factors, AI algorithms can rank potential leads according to their likelihood of conversion. This allows sales teams to prioritise their efforts on the most promising prospects, improving conversion rates and ensuring that resources are allocated where they can have the most impact. With AI's predictive capabilities, businesses are equipped to navigate the complexities of customer behaviour and market dynamics, ensuring they remain competitive in an increasingly data-driven world.

AI applications are not merely tools for improving individual business functions but represent a comprehensive shift in how companies operate and innovate. The integration of AI into customer service, marketing, and sales processes underscores the broad potential of this technology to transform business practices across the board. By automating routine tasks, personalising customer interactions, and providing predictive insights, AI enables businesses to operate more efficiently and with greater precision. As AI technology continues to evolve, its applications will undoubtedly broaden, presenting businesses with even more opportunities to innovate and thrive in an ever-changing digital economy.

12.4 THE TRANSFORMATIVE POWER OF AI IN BUSINESS AUTOMATION AND EFFICIENCY

AI has become a central force in driving automation and optimising business processes, reshaping the very foundations of operational efficiency and productivity. At its core, AI enhances businesses by automating routine, repetitive tasks, thus freeing human resources to concentrate on more complex, strategic, and creative endeavours. This not only reduces operational costs but significantly improves the speed, accuracy, and consistency of tasks that are often prone to human error.

In sectors such as finance and accounting, AI-powered automation has revolutionised traditional workflows. Tasks such as invoice processing, data entry, and financial reporting, once labour-intensive and time-consuming, are now seamlessly managed by intelligent systems. Through Machine Learning algorithms that refine their processes over time, AI ensures greater precision while requiring minimal manual oversight. This shift not only accelerates operational timelines but also enhances the overall accuracy of financial processes, enabling businesses to operate with increased confidence and security. The financial landscape is thus increasingly reliant on AI to manage high volumes of data with unparalleled efficiency (Figure 12.1).

Beyond internal processes, the integration of AI in supply chain and logistics has further transformed how businesses manage external operations. AI applications are driving smarter inventory management, more accurate demand forecasting, and optimised distribution networks. With the aid of predictive analytics, businesses can anticipate market fluctuations, adjusting their inventory levels accordingly to mitigate risks of shortages or overstocking. This proactive approach not only improves resource allocation but also reduces the financial waste associated with unsold stock or missed opportunities.

In logistics, AI has brought significant improvements through route optimisation and predictive maintenance. By analysing vast amounts of data, such as traffic patterns, weather conditions, and vehicle health, AI algorithms can recommend the most efficient delivery routes and predict when maintenance will be required. This predictive capability minimises downtime, reduces unexpected maintenance costs, and ensures timely deliveries, thus boosting the reliability and overall performance of supply chain networks. The application of AI in

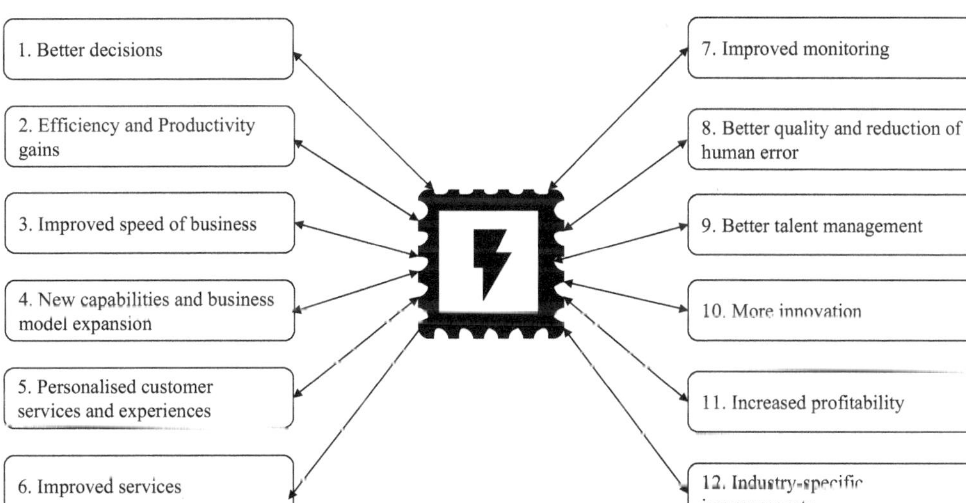

FIGURE 12.1 12 Important Benefits of AI for Businesses

logistics is proving to be a critical asset for businesses aiming to maintain a competitive edge in fast-paced, demand-driven markets.

However, while AI-driven automation offers undeniable benefits, it also has profound implications for the workforce. As more tasks become automated, there is an inevitable shift in job responsibilities, particularly in roles that involve routine and repetitive tasks. Workers must adapt to a rapidly evolving, technology-driven landscape, with an increasing emphasis on skills that complement, rather than compete with, AI capabilities. Critical thinking, creativity, and emotional intelligence are becoming more valuable, as these are areas where machines, for the moment, fall short.

Moreover, AI is not just reshaping existing jobs but also creating entirely new roles. The demand for AI specialists, data scientists, and machine learning engineers is surging as companies seek skilled professionals capable of designing, implementing, and optimising AI solutions. This shift signals the growing importance of continuous learning and upskilling, with a focus on emerging technologies, as essential strategies for maintaining relevance in an AI-dominated job market. As businesses increasingly integrate AI into their workflows, employees who invest in acquiring new technical skills will find themselves better positioned to navigate and thrive in this transformed employment landscape.

In conclusion, AI-driven automation is not just a tool for improving operational efficiency; it is a transformative force that is redefining how businesses function. From automating routine financial processes to optimising supply chains and logistics, AI allows for more intelligent, data-driven decision-making, leading to enhanced productivity and resource allocation. While automation is reshaping job roles, it also presents new opportunities for innovation, skill development, and specialisation. The future of work will be shaped by those who can effectively collaborate with AI systems, underlining the need for flexibility and adaptability in the workforce as AI continues to influence business dynamics.

12.5 THE SYNERGY OF AI AND HUMAN COLLABORATION: AUGMENTATION, OPPORTUNITIES, AND ETHICAL CONSIDERATIONS

The integration of AI into the workplace has initiated a fundamental shift from the notion of machines replacing human workers to a more collaborative relationship, where AI augments human abilities. This evolving synergy between AI systems and employees highlights the value of collaboration, with intelligent machines enhancing human capacity rather than supplanting it. In a variety of sectors, AI has become an indispensable tool, automating routine and repetitive tasks while allowing human workers to engage in more sophisticated roles that demand creativity, critical thinking, and emotional intelligence.

For instance, in customer service, AI-powered chatbots handle frequent, straightforward queries, freeing human agents to address more complex issues that require empathy and nuanced problem-solving. This collaborative approach to task management fosters an efficient work environment where humans and AI complement one another. In other domains, such as research and development or manufacturing, AI's capability to process vast amounts of data and perform high-speed calculations enables human workers to focus on innovation, strategic thinking, and refining operational processes. By amplifying human strengths through AI, businesses not only enhance their productivity but also promote an environment that values human creativity and ingenuity, aspects that machines are currently incapable of replicating.

However, this collaboration between humans and machines presents both opportunities and challenges. On the one hand, AI's ability to perform data-intensive tasks creates space for employees to concentrate on more strategic and relationship-driven activities. For example, in the finance industry, AI algorithms can swiftly analyse historical financial data and predict market trends, freeing financial professionals to focus on complex risk management and strategic decision-making. Similarly, in healthcare, AI supports medical professionals by analysing patient data, suggesting diagnoses, and even recommending treatment plans. Yet, it is the human expert who brings empathy, emotional intelligence, and a holistic understanding of patient care, resulting in a more comprehensive and compassionate healthcare experience.

On the other hand, the increasing reliance on AI poses significant challenges, particularly concerning job displacement. The automation of repetitive tasks has led to the reduction or elimination of certain roles, raising concerns about the future of employment in some sectors. Businesses must address this by investing in upskilling and reskilling programmes, ensuring that their workforce can thrive in an AI-augmented environment. By equipping employees with the knowledge and skills to work alongside AI systems, companies can smooth the transition, mitigate job displacement, and create opportunities for workers to engage in higher-level functions that require human judgement and expertise.

Human–machine collaboration also unlocks new possibilities for problem-solving, blending the analytical precision of AI with human intuition and creativity. In healthcare, for example, AI aids in diagnosing conditions with greater accuracy and speed, while medical professionals offer compassionate care and make judgement calls that take into account the unique context of each patient. Similarly, in sectors like law, AI can analyse large volumes of legal documents or past cases to provide insights, while human lawyers apply legal reasoning and creativity to develop strategies and arguments tailored to their clients' needs.

While the potential of AI–human collaboration is vast, it also brings important ethical considerations to the forefront. One of the most pressing concerns is the potential for AI systems to perpetuate biases present in the data on which they are trained. If historical data contain inherent biases—whether based on race, gender, or socioeconomic status—AI systems may inadvertently replicate these patterns, leading to unjust outcomes. In business, this could manifest in biased hiring processes, loan approvals, or even healthcare recommendations. To avoid such pitfalls, organisations must develop robust ethical frameworks that prioritise fairness and actively work to eliminate biases in AI-driven decision-making processes.

Moreover, transparency is critical in fostering trust between AI systems and their users. As AI increasingly influences decision-making in critical areas, such as finance, law, and healthcare, it becomes essential that users understand how these systems arrive at their conclusions. Explainability in AI models is vital, as it allows human oversight and provides clarity on the factors driving automated decisions. This transparency ensures accountability and empowers users to challenge AI outcomes when necessary.

In addition to transparency, AI systems must respect societal values and ensure the protection of sensitive data. Privacy concerns are particularly pertinent in sectors such as healthcare, where patient information is both highly confidential and deeply personal. The use of AI in diagnosing and treating patients requires strict adherence to medical ethics and data privacy regulations to maintain trust and safeguard patient rights. Failure to do so could erode confidence in AI technologies and hinder their potential benefits.

In conclusion, the collaboration between humans and AI represents a transformative force in the modern workplace, one that holds the potential to significantly augment human capabilities. By automating routine tasks and offering data-driven insights, AI enhances productivity and creativity, leading to more dynamic and adaptive work environments. However, addressing the ethical challenges of AI-driven decision-making and managing the societal impact of job displacement are essential for ensuring that this collaboration fosters positive outcomes for individuals, businesses, and society at large. As AI continues to evolve, the way humans and machines work together will be pivotal in shaping the future of work and business.

CASE STUDY 12

Aviva's AI-Powered Claims Processing—Transforming Insurance Operations

Aviva, a leading global insurance provider, recognised the need to modernise its claims process to improve efficiency and enhance customer satisfaction. Traditionally, insurance claims processing was a complex and time-consuming procedure, requiring extensive manual input, document verification, and multiple stages of approval. Customers often experienced long wait times for claim settlements, leading to frustration and dissatisfaction. The company sought to leverage AI to streamline operations and provide a faster, more seamless experience for its policyholders.

To address this challenge, Aviva introduced AI-driven automation into its claims processing system. The company implemented machine learning algorithms and NLP to analyse customer claims, verify documents, and assess damage with greater accuracy. AI-powered chatbots were deployed to handle initial customer enquiries, reducing the burden on human agents and enabling quicker claim submissions. Additionally, predictive analytics allowed Aviva to detect fraudulent claims more efficiently, ensuring that legitimate claims were prioritised. By integrating AI into its operations, the insurer significantly reduced manual workloads and enhanced decision-making capabilities.

The implementation of AI yielded impressive results. Claim processing times were reduced from several weeks to just a few hours in many cases, leading to increased customer satisfaction. Aviva reported a notable reduction in fraudulent claims, which improved overall cost efficiency. The automation of routine tasks also allowed employees to focus on more complex cases, enhancing service quality. As a result, customer trust in Aviva grew, and the company strengthened its reputation as an innovator in the insurance industry.

Aviva's successful adoption of AI in claims processing highlights several key insights into digital transformation. First, automation can significantly improve efficiency and reduce operational costs while enhancing the customer experience. Second, AI-driven fraud detection strengthens financial integrity and minimises losses. Thirdly, combining AI with human expertise allows businesses to balance automation with personalised service. Finally, embracing digital innovation is crucial for remaining competitive in rapidly evolving industries.

Discussion Questions for Students (with Indicative Answers)

1. **How did AI improve Aviva's claims processing system?**
   Indicative Answer: AI automated claim verification, document processing, and fraud detection, reducing settlement times and improving efficiency.
2. **What were the key benefits of implementing AI in Aviva's operations?**
   Indicative Answer: Faster claim settlements, enhanced fraud detection, improved customer satisfaction, and cost savings through automation.
3. **What challenges might companies face when integrating AI into their business processes?**
   Indicative Answer: High implementation costs, the need for employee training, potential data privacy concerns, and balancing automation with human oversight.
4. **Why is fraud detection an important application of AI in the insurance industry?**
   Indicative Answer: AI helps identify fraudulent claims quickly, reducing financial losses and ensuring that legitimate claims are processed efficiently.
5. **What lessons can other businesses learn from Aviva's AI transformation?**
   Indicative Answer: Companies can use AI to automate repetitive tasks, enhance customer service, improve decision-making, and stay competitive in a digital economy.

12.6 THE IMPERATIVE OF ETHICAL AI: ADDRESSING BIAS, ENSURING TRANSPARENCY, AND ESTABLISHING GOVERNANCE

As AI continues to permeate various aspects of society, its ethical implications have taken centre stage. Among the most pressing concerns is the potential for bias in AI algorithms, which, if left unchecked, can lead to unfair and discriminatory outcomes. AI systems, by their very nature, learn from historical data. If this data reflects societal prejudices, the algorithms can inadvertently perpetuate and even amplify these biases. Therefore, businesses, governments, and organisations must adopt proactive measures to identify, address, and mitigate bias to ensure fairness across AI applications.

A fundamental step in this process is the careful assessment of the data used to train AI models. Data form the backbone of AI decision-making, and its quality and diversity are critical in determining whether the outcomes are fair or biased. Organisations must rigorously examine datasets to identify any patterns that could introduce discrimination. This can involve diversifying data sources to encompass a broader spectrum of human experiences, ensuring that AI systems are not solely trained on data that reflects limited or biased viewpoints. By doing so, companies can minimise the risk of perpetuating inequalities and create AI systems that reflect a more inclusive reality.

However, addressing bias in the data is only one part of the equation. AI algorithms must also be subject to continuous scrutiny. As AI models learn and adapt over time, biases may emerge in ways that were not initially apparent. Regular audits and assessments, coupled with the implementation of bias detection tools, are essential in ensuring that the systems remain fair as they evolve. This commitment to ongoing evaluation is vital in maintaining the integrity and fairness of AI applications, whether in hiring processes, financial services, or law enforcement.

Beyond the technical aspects of mitigating bias, there is a growing demand for transparency in AI decision-making. As AI systems become more complex, their decision-making processes often resemble a "black box," making it difficult for users, stakeholders, and even the developers to understand how specific outcomes are reached. This opacity can lead to mistrust and hinder the acceptance of AI-driven solutions, especially when the decisions have significant implications for individuals or communities.

To address this, organisations must prioritise explainability in their AI systems. Explainable AI (XAI) aims to demystify how AI models operate by offering clear insights into the factors influencing a particular decision. By making AI's decision-making processes more transparent, organisations can foster trust and provide users with the information they need to challenge or question outcomes. This is especially important in sensitive areas like healthcare, criminal justice, and financial services, where AI-driven decisions can have profound consequences on people's lives. Additionally, enhancing transparency requires educating users and stakeholders about AI's limitations and capabilities, ensuring that everyone involved has a realistic understanding of what the technology can and cannot do.

Central to the development of ethical AI is the establishment of governance frameworks that set the standards for responsible AI use. Governments and regulatory bodies have a critical role to play in crafting policies that ensure AI systems are held to high ethical standards. Around the world, there is growing recognition of the need for comprehensive AI regulations.

These regulations may cover areas such as data privacy, transparency, and accountability, providing businesses with clear guidelines on how to deploy AI systems ethically.

For businesses, staying ahead of regulatory developments is not only a legal obligation but a strategic necessity. Engaging with policymakers and contributing to the development of these frameworks allows companies to shape regulations in ways that are both practical and effective. Beyond external regulation, businesses must also implement internal governance mechanisms tailored to their specific AI applications. Establishing internal policies on AI ethics, creating dedicated ethics committees, or appointing AI ethics officers are all steps organisations can take to ensure they navigate the ethical complexities of AI deployment responsibly.

As AI continues to evolve and become more deeply integrated into daily life, it is clear that a collective effort is required to uphold ethical standards and fairness. From addressing the biases inherent in historical data to ensuring that AI systems are transparent and governed by robust frameworks, the future of AI depends on the commitment of businesses, governments, and the wider technology community. Only by prioritising fairness, accountability, and ethics can we ensure that AI serves the best interests of society, fostering a more just and equitable world for all.

12.7 THE FUTURE OF WORK IN AN AI-DRIVEN WORLD

The rise of AI has profoundly altered the nature of work, ushering in a transformative era for industries across the globe. While AI offers immense potential for innovation, efficiency, and new opportunities, it also raises critical questions about job disruption and the evolving landscape of employment. As AI technologies continue to automate tasks traditionally performed by humans, the workforce is at a crossroads, requiring a rethinking of roles, responsibilities, and the skills necessary to thrive in an AI-augmented world.

The integration of AI into the workplace has led to significant changes in employment patterns, particularly in sectors that rely on manual, repetitive, and rule-based activities. Manufacturing, customer service, and data entry are just a few examples of industries that have seen the widespread adoption of AI-driven systems to perform tasks faster, more accurately, and more efficiently than their human counterparts. This has inevitably led to the displacement of certain job roles, sparking concerns about long-term employment security for workers in affected sectors. However, the impact of AI on employment is far more complex than simply replacing jobs with machines. While some roles may become obsolete, AI is simultaneously creating new opportunities, particularly in areas that require human ingenuity, emotional intelligence, and creative problem-solving. Jobs that involve managing, developing, and maintaining AI systems are becoming increasingly essential, with demand rising for AI specialists, data scientists, and engineers. The future of work will require a delicate balance between leveraging AI's efficiency and preserving human roles that remain critical to business innovation and strategic decision-making.

To navigate this shift effectively, businesses and workers alike must focus on reskilling and upskilling initiatives. As AI changes the nature of work, employees need to be equipped with new competencies that allow them to collaborate with AI technologies and adapt to evolving job roles. Reskilling involves retraining individuals for entirely new positions, aligning their abilities with the demands of an AI-driven workplace. Meanwhile, upskilling focuses on enhancing existing skill sets, often by incorporating AI-related knowledge into current roles. This dual approach will be crucial for organisations seeking to retain and redeploy their workforce in a rapidly changing environment.

Educational institutions, governments, and businesses all have a role to play in facilitating this transition. Schools and universities must update their curricula to include AI-related subjects, ensuring that future generations are prepared to enter an AI-centric workforce. Meanwhile, businesses should invest in internal training programmes that empower their employees with both technical and soft skills, such as critical thinking, adaptability, and communication. These skills will become increasingly valuable in a work environment where collaboration between humans and AI is the norm and where employees must navigate complex, often ambiguous situations that AI alone cannot handle. By fostering a culture of continuous learning, businesses can ensure that their employees remain competitive and resilient in the face of ongoing technological advancements.

Building AI-ready organisations requires more than just technological investment; it demands a cultural shift towards innovation, agility, and a commitment to learning. Leaders must champion AI as a core component of their organisation's strategic vision, fostering an environment where experimentation with new technologies is encouraged. This involves assembling cross-functional teams that bring together AI experts and domain specialists to ensure that AI solutions are integrated seamlessly into existing business processes. Creating an AI-ready organisation also means investing in the necessary infrastructure—such as user-friendly interfaces, training modules, and support systems—that allows employees to collaborate effectively with AI technologies.

However, the adoption of AI also brings with it a host of ethical considerations that cannot be ignored. Organisations must ensure that their AI systems are transparent, fair, and aligned with broader societal values. This requires the development of clear policies and ethical guidelines that govern the responsible use of AI, addressing concerns related to bias, privacy, and accountability. Ethical frameworks should not be viewed as constraints but as essential components that guide the organisation in using AI in a manner that upholds its values and fosters trust among its stakeholders.

In conclusion, the future of work in an AI-driven world presents both challenges and opportunities. While AI has the potential to disrupt traditional employment patterns, it also opens up new possibilities for human–machine collaboration, creativity, and innovation. By addressing the impact of AI on employment, investing in reskilling and upskilling initiatives, and fostering AI-ready organisations, businesses can position themselves to thrive in the evolving digital landscape. The successful integration of AI into the workplace will depend not just on the technology itself but on the ability of humans to adapt, collaborate, and push the boundaries of what is possible in an AI-augmented future.

12.8 AI GOVERNANCE: SHAPING THE FUTURE THROUGH POLICY, REGULATION, AND GLOBAL COOPERATION

The rapid and expansive development of AI has created an urgent need for governments and regulatory bodies across the world to establish robust governance frameworks. These structures are crucial in ensuring that AI technologies are deployed responsibly, adhering to ethical standards while mitigating potential risks. As AI becomes ever more pervasive, there is growing recognition of the need to strike a delicate balance between fostering innovation and protecting societal values. Across the globe, nations are actively engaged in developing and refining policies that address the profound implications of AI's integration into everyday life.

Governments worldwide have already begun to lay the groundwork for AI-specific regulations that tackle key issues such as bias, transparency, and accountability. In the absence of comprehensive governance, AI systems could unintentionally perpetuate harmful biases or lead to outcomes that disproportionately affect certain populations. To address these risks, many countries are crafting legal frameworks that set stringent guidelines for AI transparency, requiring that systems disclose their use and offer clear mechanisms for accountability in the case of adverse or unethical outcomes. This is particularly pertinent in sectors where AI decisions carry significant consequences, such as hiring practices, financial services, and the criminal justice system, where ensuring fairness and equitable outcomes is of paramount importance.

The regulatory landscape surrounding AI is far from uniform, with different regions adopting distinct approaches depending on their political, economic, and cultural contexts. The European Union has positioned itself as a leader in AI governance through its proposed AI Act. The Act provides a harmonised regulatory framework, classifying AI systems by their level of risk and placing rigorous requirements on high-risk applications. Central to the EU's approach is the prioritisation of transparency and accountability, alongside the prohibition of certain AI practices deemed too risky or unethical. This model aims to protect individual rights while promoting innovation across sectors.

In contrast, the United States has opted for a more decentralised, sector-specific strategy. Here, the regulatory focus often falls within the remit of individual agencies, such as the Federal Trade Commission, which concentrates on issues related to consumer protection and antitrust in the context of AI technologies. Simultaneously, the National Institute of Standards and Technology is working on developing technical standards that aim to increase trust in AI systems by ensuring their reliability and fairness. This multi-agency, sector-by-sector approach reflects the broader regulatory environment in the United States, where different industries face varying degrees of oversight depending on the potential societal impact of their AI applications.

Meanwhile, Asian nations, particularly China, are making considerable strides in both the development and regulation of AI technologies. China's ambitious AI agenda is matched by its growing focus on establishing guidelines that promote the responsible use of AI, particularly in relation to data security, algorithmic transparency, and accountability. However, the Chinese regulatory framework remains dynamic and subject to further refinement, reflecting the country's rapid AI advancements and the broader societal implications of such progress.

As AI knows no borders, its governance increasingly requires international collaboration to establish common standards and shared frameworks. Recognising the global nature of AI's challenges, initiatives such as the Global Partnership on Artificial Intelligence (GPAI) and the Organisation for Economic Co-operation and Development (OECD) AI Principles have emerged to foster such cooperation. The GPAI, formed by leading global economies, seeks to facilitate the responsible development and deployment of AI technologies through international collaboration. This initiative centres on themes such as AI's role in promoting human rights, fostering trust in AI systems, and ensuring inclusivity in the benefits AI offers.

Similarly, the OECD AI Principles provide a foundation for ethical AI development, which its member countries have committed to adopting. These principles encourage inclusive economic growth and the prioritisation of human-centred values, ensuring that AI technologies remain transparent and accountable. By fostering a global consensus on these guiding principles, the OECD provides a crucial platform for countries to align their AI policies with common ethical standards, creating a more cohesive and responsible global framework.

The regulation and governance of AI technologies represent a dynamic and evolving landscape, requiring constant attention and collaboration between governments, regulatory bodies, industry stakeholders, and international organisations. As AI continues to integrate more deeply into everyday life, it is clear that robust governance structures are essential not only for managing potential risks but also for promoting the responsible and ethical deployment of these transformative technologies. The future of AI governance reflects a global effort to ensure that AI's development remains aligned with societal values while also fostering innovation that benefits humanity as a whole.

12.9 THE FUTURE OF AI: NAVIGATING OPPORTUNITIES AND CHALLENGES

As we look ahead, the future of AI is filled with both immense opportunities and formidable challenges. The coming years will see AI shaping and transforming industries, societies, and global frameworks, as emerging trends and innovations push the boundaries of what technology can achieve. One of the most significant developments is the growing integration of AI with other cutting-edge technologies like the Internet of Things and 5G connectivity. This convergence allows AI to harness vast amounts of real-time data, vastly enhancing its ability to drive sophisticated automation and decision-making processes. In this interconnected ecosystem, AI systems will be able to anticipate and respond to human needs and environmental changes with increasing accuracy and speed.

Amongst the most exciting innovations is the ongoing evolution of machine learning, which continues to introduce groundbreaking approaches. For instance, federated learning allows AI models to be trained across decentralised devices without sacrificing individual privacy, enabling collaboration without the need to centralise sensitive data. Additionally, the rise of XAI is addressing the notorious "black box" problem associated with complex algorithms by providing more transparent insights into how decisions are made. This focus on interpretability enhances trust in AI, particularly in critical sectors like healthcare and finance. Even more transformative is the promise of quantum computing, which could exponentially increase AI's computational power, allowing it to solve complex problems and analyse large datasets at speeds previously unimaginable.

However, alongside these advancements come significant challenges. One of the foremost concerns is bias within AI systems. Bias can arise from the very data used to train AI models, leading to outcomes that reinforce social inequalities or discriminatory practices. In response, the AI community is actively developing techniques to detect and mitigate these biases, ensuring AI systems treat individuals equitably regardless of demographic factors. Fairness-aware machine learning models and ethical AI frameworks are becoming essential tools in addressing these issues, though the challenge of achieving true fairness remains daunting.

Furthermore, unintended consequences, particularly those related to job displacement and ethical dilemmas, are raising urgent questions about the societal impact of AI. As AI automates routine tasks and processes, many traditional job roles are at risk of becoming obsolete, leaving workers to face uncertain futures. Governments, corporations, and developers must work together to establish ethical guidelines and proactive regulations that address these concerns, ensuring that the deployment of AI does not deepen existing social disparities. This will require thoughtful dialogue and the creation of policies that reflect the complexity of AI's role in society, ensuring that its benefits are shared as widely as possible.

The transformative power of AI extends well beyond technological innovations, as it is set to play a pivotal role in the future of both business and society. In the world of business, AI is already driving automation, optimising processes, and enhancing efficiency across a wide range of industries—from manufacturing to customer service. Predictive analytics, driven by AI insights, are empowering organisations to make more informed decisions, foresee trends, and maintain a competitive edge. In fact, businesses that successfully embrace AI will likely find themselves at the forefront of their industries, as AI offers unprecedented opportunities to revolutionise operations and strategies.

In broader societal contexts, AI holds immense potential to address some of the world's most pressing challenges. In healthcare, for instance, AI is unlocking new frontiers in personalised medicine, early disease detection, and patient care. Its ability to process vast quantities of medical data and identify patterns invisible to the human eye makes AI an indispensable tool in the future of healthcare. Moreover, AI can play a crucial role in tackling environmental issues, aiding in climate change mitigation through its use in environmental monitoring and resource management. By predicting environmental trends and improving sustainability practices, AI can contribute to creating a more resilient and adaptive planet.

However, as AI becomes increasingly ingrained in our daily lives, ethical considerations become more critical. The responsible development and deployment of AI technologies require collaboration among technologists, policymakers, and the public at large. Ethical standards, privacy protections, and equitable access to AI resources must be at the forefront of AI innovation to ensure that it benefits all members of society. Striking this balance between advancing technology and upholding ethical responsibilities will be fundamental in harnessing AI's potential without succumbing to its risks.

In conclusion, the future of AI is a landscape brimming with possibilities but one that is equally marked by challenges. The emergence of new trends and innovations will undoubtedly bring about transformative changes in numerous sectors, yet these advancements must be tempered by a commitment to ethical responsibility. Addressing biases, safeguarding against unintended consequences, and promoting equitable outcomes will be essential as we strive to integrate AI into the fabric of society. As we navigate this complex future, a collaborative and forward-thinking approach will be key to unlocking the full potential of AI, ensuring that its impact is both positive and far-reaching.

12.10 CHAPTER SUMMARY

The transformative potential of AI is undeniable, and its impact on business and society is profound. As explored in this chapter, AI has evolved from a theoretical concept to a practical tool that influences almost every facet of modern life. In business, AI-driven automation, decision-making, and innovation are enhancing productivity, improving customer experiences, and creating new market opportunities. Yet, while AI brings remarkable efficiencies, it also raises critical ethical and societal challenges. Bias in AI systems, the need for transparency, and concerns over job displacement all underscore the necessity for responsible AI deployment.

Human–AI collaboration offers exciting opportunities for growth and augmentation. However, such integration also demands careful consideration of ethical frameworks that ensure fairness, accountability, and respect for individual rights. The governance of AI is an essential element in guiding its future development, and a global, cooperative approach is required to establish standards that promote the ethical use of AI technologies. Furthermore, as the future of work continues to shift, it is essential to invest in reskilling and preparing the workforce for an AI-driven world. Ultimately, the future of AI is rich with possibilities, but navigating its complexities requires a balanced approach that embraces innovation while safeguarding societal values, equity, and ethical responsibility.

Key Questions for Discussion

1. How is AI reshaping business decision-making, customer interactions, and operational efficiency? Are there specific industries that are more reliant on AI advancements than others?
2. AI is often perceived as a replacement for human labour, yet many argue that its true potential lies in augmenting human capabilities. How can businesses strike a balance between AI automation and human expertise to maximise productivity while maintaining ethical considerations?
3. AI systems have been criticised for reinforcing biases and lacking transparency. What steps should businesses and policymakers take to ensure AI is developed and deployed ethically, particularly in areas such as recruitment, financial services, and law enforcement?
4. As AI continues to automate tasks traditionally performed by humans, what new skills and competencies will be essential for the workforce of the future? Should governments and businesses invest in large-scale reskilling initiatives to prepare for an AI-dominated job market?
5. With AI influencing various aspects of society, there is growing debate around global AI regulation. Should AI governance be handled at a national level, or is an international framework necessary to ensure ethical and responsible AI development?

BIBLIOGRAPHY

Agrawal, A., Gans, J. and Goldfarb, A. (2018). *Prediction Machines: The Simple Economics of Artificial Intelligence*. Harvard Business Review Press.

Appio, F.P., La Torre, D., Lazzeri, F., Masri, H. and Schiavone, F. (Eds.). (2023). *Impact of Artificial Intelligence in Business and Society: Opportunities and Challenges*. Routledge.

Bostrom, N. (2014). *Superintelligence: Paths, Dangers, Strategies*. Oxford University Press.

Brynjolfsson, E. and McAfee, A. (2014). *The Second Machine Age: Work, Progress, and Prosperity in a Time of Brilliant Technologies*. W.W. Norton & Company.

Chui, M., Manyika, J. and Miremadi, M. (2016). *Where Machines Could Replace Humans—and Where They Can't (Yet)*. McKinsey Global Institute.

Davenport, T.H. and Kirby, J. (2016). *Only Humans Need Apply: Winners and Losers in the Age of Smart Machines*. Harper Business.

Domingos, P. (2015). *The Master Algorithm: How the Quest for the Ultimate Learning Machine Will Remake Our World*. Basic Books.

Ford, M. (2015). *Rise of the Robots: Technology and the Threat of a Jobless Future*. Basic Books.

Harari, Y.N. (2018). *21 Lessons for the 21st Century*. Jonathan Cape.

Kaplan, J. (2016). *Artificial Intelligence: What Everyone Needs to Know*. Oxford University Press.

Lee, K.-F. (2021). AI 2041: Ten Visions for Our Future. Currency.

Russell, S. and Norvig, P. (2020). *Artificial Intelligence: A Modern Approach*. 4th ed. Pearson.

Tegmark, M. (2017). *Life 3.0: Being Human in the Age of Artificial Intelligence*. Penguin Books.

Vardi, M.Y. (2019). *Artificial Intelligence: The Revolution Hasn't Happened Yet*. Communications of the ACM.

West, D.M. (2018). *The Future of Work: Robots, AI, and Automation*. Brookings Institution Press.

CHAPTER 13

Digital Ethics

Learning Outcomes

By the end of this chapter, you will be able to:

1. Understand the ethical issues surrounding data privacy, security, social media, digital marketing, and e-commerce and their impact on businesses and consumers.
2. Assess the ethical implications of big data, artificial intelligence, the Internet of Things, and other emerging technologies, focusing on fairness, transparency, and accountability.
3. Learn how to cultivate a culture of digital ethics within organisations, navigate ethical dilemmas, and align business practices with ethical standards and regulatory frameworks.

13.1 INTRODUCTION

As our lives become increasingly intertwined with digital technologies, the ethical implications of this integration demand urgent attention. Digital ethics encompasses a wide array of issues, including data privacy, security, and the responsibilities of various stakeholders in the digital ecosystem. With the proliferation of data-driven technologies and platforms, ethical considerations have emerged as fundamental to ensuring responsible practices that protect user rights and promote transparency. Navigating the ethical challenges associated with digital advertising and marketing is critical, as businesses seek to balance innovation with ethical standards that safeguard consumer interests. Moreover, social media and online platforms face heightened scrutiny regarding their role in shaping public discourse and the ethical responsibilities that come with user engagement.

In the realm of e-commerce, the protection of consumer rights is essential for fostering trust and promoting sustainable business practices. Additionally, the Internet of Things (IoT) presents unique ethical challenges related to privacy and data security, while the landscape of big data and analytics raises questions about fairness and accountability in data usage. As emerging technologies continue to reshape the digital environment, the need for ethical

DOI: 10.4324/9781032672458-13

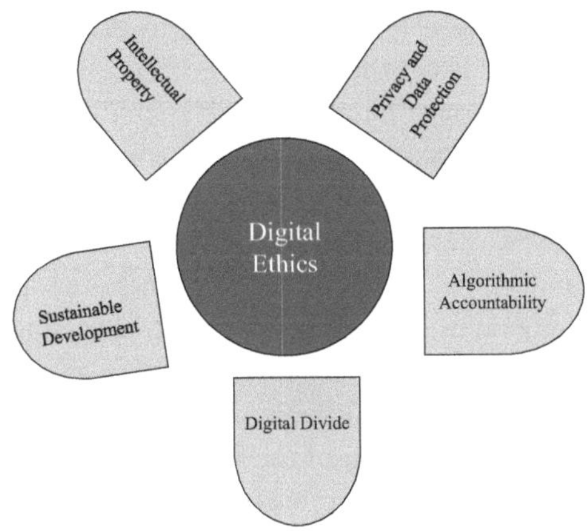

FIGURE 13.1 The Evolving Landscape of Digital Ethics

decision-making frameworks becomes increasingly urgent. By fostering a culture of digital ethics, organisations can better navigate the complexities of the digital landscape, contributing to a future where technology serves the public good (Figure 13.1).

13.2 NAVIGATING ETHICAL CHALLENGES IN DATA PRIVACY AND SECURITY

In today's digital age, the ethical management of data has become a critical concern, particularly in relation to privacy and consent. As individuals grow more aware of the significance of their personal information, they increasingly demand assurance that organisations are handling their data responsibly. Ensuring data privacy involves open and transparent communication with users about how their information will be collected, processed, and shared. Central to this is obtaining informed consent, which requires businesses to clearly explain the purposes for data collection and seek explicit permission from users. Consent mechanisms should be straightforward, avoiding complex legal jargon, and should empower users to make well-informed decisions about the use of their personal data. By respecting user choices and maintaining transparency, organisations can build and sustain trust, which is essential for maintaining strong relationships with their customers.

The rise of digital connectivity has unfortunately been accompanied by a corresponding increase in cyber threats, resulting in more frequent data breaches and cybersecurity incidents. Addressing these incidents ethically demands a swift, transparent, and accountable approach. Organisations must act quickly to notify affected individuals, regulators, and the public, offering clear information about the breach and detailing the steps taken to mitigate its impact. However, ethical cybersecurity practices should not be limited to reactive measures; they must also encompass preventative efforts. This includes investing in cutting-edge security technologies, ensuring systems are regularly updated, and cultivating a culture of cybersecurity awareness among employees. Given the potential harm that data breaches can cause to individuals, organisations hold a moral obligation to prioritise proactive cybersecurity measures, safeguarding personal data from unauthorised access or exposure.

Ethical data collection and usage hinge on establishing firm boundaries concerning the types of data gathered and the purposes for which it is employed. Striking the right balance between business objectives and respect for user privacy is paramount. Companies should collect only the data that are essential for their operations, steering clear of unnecessary invasions into individuals' private lives. Additionally, businesses should embrace transparency in communicating their data practices by providing clear, accessible privacy policies. These policies should outline how data are collected, processed, and shared, allowing individuals to better understand the lifecycle of their information. By equipping users with this knowledge, companies reinforce the ethical foundation of their data-handling processes and enable individuals to make informed choices about their data.

By addressing the ethical considerations surrounding data privacy and security, businesses not only ensure compliance with regulations but also foster a culture of trust and responsibility. Recognising the moral imperative to treat data with care allows organisations to position themselves as conscientious custodians of information. This approach contributes to a digital environment that prioritises both privacy and security while still embracing the innovations and possibilities offered by the digital age. In an ever-evolving landscape of digital ethics, these principles offer businesses a clear path to navigate the complex challenges of data privacy and security responsibly.

CASE STUDY 13

Facebook's Data Privacy Challenges—The Ethics of User Data

Facebook, one of the world's largest social media platforms, has faced significant scrutiny over its handling of user data. As a company that relies on targeted advertising for revenue, Facebook collects vast amounts of personal data from its users, including browsing habits, location data, and personal preferences. However, concerns over data privacy escalated when it was revealed that third-party organisations had gained access to users' private information without their explicit consent. This controversy highlighted broader ethical issues in digital business, particularly regarding transparency, user consent, and corporate responsibility in handling data.

The most notable challenge emerged in 2018 with the Cambridge Analytica scandal. It was discovered that the political consulting firm had harvested data from millions of Facebook profiles without users' knowledge, influencing political campaigns through targeted advertisements. The scandal exposed significant gaps in Facebook's data protection policies and raised global concerns about digital ethics, data privacy, and accountability. In response, regulators, including the European Union and the United States government, launched investigations, and Facebook was subjected to intense public and legal scrutiny. The company faced pressure to reform its data privacy practices and rebuild trust with users.

To address these challenges, Facebook implemented a series of privacy reforms. The company introduced clearer privacy controls, allowing users to manage their data more effectively and limit third-party access. It updated its terms of service to provide greater transparency on data collection practices and introduced stricter policies for third-party app developers. Additionally, Facebook strengthened its compliance with regulations such as the General Data Protection Regulation (GDPR) in Europe, which mandated greater user control over personal data. The company also launched campaigns to educate users on privacy settings, aiming to restore confidence in its platform.

Despite these efforts, Facebook suffered reputational damage, and the scandal led to significant financial consequences. The company was fined $5 billion by the U.S. Federal Trade Commission (FTC), one of the largest privacy-related fines in history. Regulators worldwide introduced stricter data protection laws, forcing digital companies to rethink their approach to ethical data management. Although Facebook remained a dominant player in social media, the case underscored the need for stronger digital ethics and highlighted the risks businesses face when failing to prioritise user privacy.

This case provides critical insights into the ethical responsibilities of digital businesses. First, transparency and user consent must be central to any data-driven business model. Second, regulatory compliance is crucial for long-term sustainability, as failure to meet legal standards can result in severe penalties. Third, businesses must proactively address ethical risks, ensuring that data protection is not merely a regulatory requirement but a core part of their corporate strategy. Finally, digital businesses must foster trust with users by prioritising privacy and maintaining ethical data practices.

Discussion Questions for Students (with Indicative Answers)

1. **What were the main ethical concerns in Facebook's data privacy scandal?**
   Indicative Answer: The lack of transparency, unauthorised data collection, third-party misuse of personal data, and the impact on political manipulation.

2. **How did regulatory bodies respond to Facebook's data privacy failures?**
   Indicative Answer: Governments and regulators, including the U.S. FTC and EU GDPR authorities, imposed heavy fines, launched investigations, and introduced stricter data privacy laws.
3. **What steps did Facebook take to improve its data privacy policies?**
   Indicative Answer: It introduced clearer privacy controls, updated its terms of service, strengthened third-party app regulations, and improved compliance with global privacy laws.
4. **Why is user trust important for digital businesses, and how did the scandal impact Facebook's reputation?**
   Indicative Answer: Trust is essential for user engagement and platform sustainability. Facebook's reputation suffered as users became more sceptical of its data practices, leading to increased regulatory scrutiny.
5. **What lessons can other businesses learn from Facebook's experience with data privacy and digital ethics?**
   Indicative Answer: Companies should prioritise ethical data practices, ensure transparency, comply with regulations, and proactively address potential privacy concerns to maintain user trust.

13.3 UPHOLDING ETHICAL STANDARDS IN DIGITAL ADVERTISING AND MARKETING

In the era of pervasive digital communication, maintaining ethical standards in advertising and marketing has never been more critical. The rise of digital platforms has provided businesses with unprecedented opportunities to reach consumers, but it has also amplified the risks of deceptive practices. Deceptive advertising, where companies deliberately mislead consumers with false or ambiguous claims, can significantly undermine the trust between businesses and their customers. This erosion of trust not only harms consumer confidence but also jeopardises the long-term reputation of companies. To counter this, businesses must commit to transparency and truthfulness in their advertising practices, ensuring that their messages accurately reflect the value and capabilities of their products or services. It is crucial to comply with industry regulations and guidelines, implementing clear, easily understood disclosures that empower consumers to make well-informed decisions. This commitment to honesty fosters trust and cultivates lasting relationships with customers, underpinned by credibility and integrity.

The proliferation of targeted advertising, driven by sophisticated data analytics and user profiling, has transformed how businesses engage with consumers. While personalised content can enhance user experience, it simultaneously raises significant ethical concerns, particularly regarding privacy. Targeted advertising requires marketers to tread carefully, balancing the desire to deliver tailored messages with the need to safeguard user privacy. This ethical balance is best achieved by obtaining explicit, informed consent from users before collecting their data. Furthermore, businesses must be transparent about the extent of data collection and its intended use. Ethical data usage not only involves securing user consent but also necessitates implementing stringent security measures to protect sensitive information from potential breaches. Marketers should prioritise data anonymisation and aggregation techniques to mitigate the risk of exposing personal details, thereby reducing privacy infringement. Offering users the option to opt out of targeted advertising and ensuring they retain control over their data are essential steps in cultivating a responsible and ethical digital marketing environment.

Central to ethical marketing is the responsible use of customer data, which has become a cornerstone of modern digital strategies. The collection and application of customer data must align with both legal requirements and ethical principles. Businesses are duty-bound to seek explicit consent from customers before gathering their personal information, making certain that customers understand how their data will be used. Transparent communication about data usage is imperative in fostering a trusting relationship between businesses and their customers. Equally important is the protection of customer data from unauthorised access or breaches, which can have devastating effects on both the individual and the company involved. Adopting robust cybersecurity practices and conducting regular audits of data-handling processes can help maintain the ethical integrity of digital marketing efforts.

Ultimately, ethical digital marketing transcends mere compliance with legal regulations. It embodies a commitment to prioritising the well-being of customers, ensuring that businesses not only meet the expectations of their audience but also act in their best interests. By embracing transparency, respecting user privacy, and responsibly managing customer data, companies can cultivate a positive brand image that endures. In an increasingly interconnected world where consumer trust is paramount, ethical advertising and marketing practices are not only a moral obligation but also a strategic necessity for long-term success.

13.4 NAVIGATING THE ETHICAL RESPONSIBILITIES OF SOCIAL MEDIA AND ONLINE PLATFORMS

The digital age has revolutionised communication, placing social media and online platforms at the heart of global interactions. However, with this immense influence comes significant ethical responsibility. One of the most pressing challenges is the pervasive spread of misinformation and fake news. The speed at which false narratives can proliferate across these platforms presents a serious ethical dilemma. It is essential for platforms to actively confront this issue by adopting rigorous fact-checking protocols and collaborating with credible sources to ensure the dissemination of accurate information. Leveraging artificial intelligence (AI) to detect and flag misleading content is a necessary step, but this must be coupled with human oversight to maintain credibility. Transparency in algorithms is also crucial, allowing users to understand how content is prioritised and ensuring that the platform operates in the public's best interest. By empowering users with the tools to identify trustworthy information, platforms foster a more informed and ethically sound digital society.

Beyond combating misinformation, social media and online platforms face the complex challenge of moderating content without infringing on freedom of expression. The delicate balance between curbing harmful material and upholding free speech is at the heart of ethical content moderation. Platforms must craft clear and consistent content guidelines, taking into account the cultural diversity of their global user base. This not only ensures fairness but also helps users navigate what is deemed acceptable behaviour on the platform. Ethical moderation requires that platforms safeguard their users from hate speech, violence, and other damaging content, but this can only be achieved with well-designed reporting systems and a dedicated, trained moderation team. Furthermore, these guidelines must evolve, keeping pace with societal changes and emerging ethical standards, ensuring that platforms remain responsible digital stewards.

The rise of social media has also led to an increase in online harassment and cyberbullying, underscoring the need for platforms to take robust ethical measures in protecting users. The anonymity and reach provided by the digital sphere often embolden harmful behaviour, making it imperative for platforms to be proactive in addressing these issues. Ethical guidelines demand swift and effective responses to reports of harassment, with clear mechanisms in place for users to seek help and protection. Beyond reactionary measures, platforms should develop and implement preventive strategies, such as AI-driven content monitoring and collaboration with mental health organisations, to reduce the prevalence of such harmful interactions. By fostering a culture of safety and respect, platforms can enhance user trust and contribute to a more supportive online environment.

In fulfilling their ethical responsibilities, social media and online platforms play a pivotal role in shaping the digital world. From addressing misinformation to ensuring balanced content moderation and combating online harassment, these platforms are instrumental in maintaining the integrity of online spaces. By investing in transparent processes, adopting cutting-edge technology, and remaining actively engaged with their users, platforms can build a more responsible and ethical digital ecosystem that prioritises safety, respect, and truth.

13.5 UPHOLDING ETHICAL STANDARDS IN E-COMMERCE AND CONSUMER RIGHTS

In the rapidly evolving world of e-commerce, ethical considerations have become central to maintaining trust and safeguarding consumer rights. One of the primary pillars of ethical e-commerce is ensuring transparency in pricing and product information. Online retailers must provide consumers with accurate, comprehensive details about the goods they offer, including clear pricing, precise specifications, and terms of sale. Any form of ambiguity in these areas erodes consumer trust, making it essential that pricing is upfront, with no hidden charges or misleading tactics. Ethical online retailers avoid dubious practices, such as presenting products at deceptively low prices only to introduce unexpected fees later in the purchasing process. Additionally, promotions and discounts must be communicated with clarity, ensuring consumers understand the terms and conditions without being misled.

A related issue in maintaining ethical standards in e-commerce is the need to avoid bait-and-switch tactics, where the advertised product fails to match the item actually being offered. This unethical practice undermines the integrity of the platform and damages consumer trust. Ethical retailers and platforms must commit to fair business practices that respect consumer rights, providing customers with accurate descriptions and honest representations of their products. This approach fosters an environment where customers can make informed, confident decisions about their purchases, contributing to a fairer, more transparent digital marketplace.

Handling customer data responsibly is another critical ethical consideration in the e-commerce sector. As consumers engage with digital platforms, they leave behind a wealth of personal information, from contact details to purchase histories. With such vast amounts of sensitive data at their disposal, online retailers are ethically obligated to protect consumer privacy and ensure the security of this information. Robust data protection measures, such as encryption and secure storage, must be employed to safeguard customer data from breaches or unauthorised access. Transparency in how these data are collected, stored, and used is essential. Platforms must clearly communicate their data-handling practices through user-friendly privacy policies and obtain explicit consent from customers. Moreover, consumers should have the option to control their data preferences, including the ability to opt out of data collection or request that their information be deleted.

An integral part of digital ethics in e-commerce is combating the sale of counterfeit products and preventing fraud. Online platforms have a duty to protect their customers from these unethical practices by implementing stringent verification processes for sellers and products. Employing technologies such as AI and machine learning (ML), platforms can monitor listings and swiftly detect counterfeit items, removing them before they reach unsuspecting consumers. Ethical e-commerce platforms also work to prevent fraud by maintaining rigorous oversight of their sellers and ensuring that fair competition is upheld. By fostering a marketplace where honest business practices prevail, platforms can create a safe space for consumers and sellers alike.

In cases of suspected fraudulent activity or counterfeit products, e-commerce platforms must establish clear and transparent reporting mechanisms that allow customers to flag suspicious listings. Such transparency, coupled with active collaboration with law enforcement and regulatory bodies, ensures that online platforms remain vigilant in protecting their users. In doing so, they build stronger, more accountable relationships with their customers, grounded in trust and fairness.

Upholding digital ethics in e-commerce goes beyond merely complying with regulations; it is about fostering a marketplace where consumer rights are respected and prioritised. By adhering to ethical guidelines, including transparent pricing, responsible data handling, and robust measures to combat counterfeiting and fraud, e-commerce platforms contribute to a sustainable, consumer-centric digital economy. In this environment, businesses and consumers alike can thrive, confident in the knowledge that ethical practices form the foundation of their interactions.

13.6 SAFEGUARDING PRIVACY AND UPHOLDING ETHICS IN THE IOT

As the IoT becomes an increasingly integral part of modern life, the ethical management of privacy and security has become essential in ensuring the responsible use of connected devices. Protecting user privacy in this digital ecosystem requires a commitment to safeguarding the personal data that IoT devices inevitably collect. Businesses that deploy IoT systems must adopt clear and transparent privacy policies, ensuring that users are fully informed about what data are being gathered, how it will be used, and for what purpose. Consent mechanisms must be designed in a way that is easy for users to understand, enabling them to make informed decisions about the extent to which they are willing to share their personal information.

Central to these ethical practices is the principle of data minimisation, where only the data necessary for a device's function are collected. This ensures that users' privacy is respected without the intrusion of excessive data gathering. Anonymisation and encryption techniques are essential tools in this regard, providing a layer of protection to shield users' identities and prevent sensitive data from falling into the wrong hands. Moreover, empowering users with control over their privacy settings is a crucial ethical responsibility for businesses operating in the IoT space, allowing individuals to have a direct say in how their data are shared or stored.

In addition to privacy, security remains one of the most critical ethical considerations for IoT. Given the vast interconnected networks that IoT devices operate within, they are particularly vulnerable to cyberattacks and other security threats. Developers and manufacturers of these devices must prioritise security from the design phase, building devices that are secure by default. This means incorporating strong encryption protocols and ensuring that devices are regularly updated with the latest firmware to patch any vulnerabilities that may emerge over time. It is equally important that users are provided with clear guidance on how to protect their devices, such as using strong passwords and regularly updating software. However, the responsibility cannot solely rest on the user; manufacturers must also engage in ongoing monitoring of security issues and be prepared to respond swiftly to any incidents, ensuring that potential risks are contained before they lead to significant harm.

The ethical use of data derived from IoT devices extends beyond privacy and security concerns. Companies that collect insights from connected devices must handle this information responsibly, ensuring that data are used for legitimate purposes that ultimately benefit users. This involves adopting transparent data practices, allowing users to make informed decisions about how their data are used and providing them with the option to opt out of certain forms of data sharing. It is also essential that businesses refrain from engaging in unethical profiling or discriminatory practices, ensuring that all users are treated fairly and equitably regardless of the data collected.

Ethical considerations must also guide how companies share and store IoT data. Without explicit user consent, businesses should avoid selling or disclosing sensitive information to third parties. Moreover, IoT data should not be stored indefinitely; companies need clear policies that define how long data are retained and how they will be securely disposed of once they are no longer needed. By managing data retention responsibly, businesses can minimise the risk of unauthorised access or data breaches, further strengthening the trust between users and the IoT devices they rely on.

In the broader context of the IoT revolution, upholding these ethical principles—protecting user privacy, ensuring robust security, and using data responsibly—creates a foundation of trust between consumers and the businesses that provide connected technologies. As the IoT continues to evolve, adhering to these ethical standards will be pivotal in shaping a responsible and sustainable future for digital innovation.

13.7 NAVIGATING THE ETHICAL LANDSCAPE OF BIG DATA AND ANALYTICS

The expansive potential of big data and analytics has revolutionised how organisations operate, but it also brings significant ethical challenges that require careful navigation. One of the fundamental aspects of ethical big data practices lies in the way data are collected. Organisations must establish clear and transparent guidelines for how they acquire data, ensuring that individuals are fully informed about what information is being gathered and why. Informed consent is not just a formality but a cornerstone of ethical data collection, where users are made aware of the potential implications of sharing their data. This transparency extends beyond mere acknowledgement, demanding that businesses regularly reassess their data collection methods in light of evolving ethical standards and societal expectations. Sensitive information, in particular, should never be collected without explicit and informed consent. Incorporating privacy-enhancing technologies, such as differential privacy, can help balance the need for valuable data insights with the necessity of respecting individual privacy.

As the use of big data continues to grow, ensuring that data are properly anonymised and aggregated becomes a critical ethical obligation. Simply removing personally identifiable information is not enough; organisations must adopt robust anonymisation techniques that offer strong protection against the re-identification of individuals, even in large datasets. This not only protects users from privacy violations but also preserves the integrity of the data in a way that allows for meaningful analysis. Ethical data management further necessitates aggregation, where information is combined and processed in a way that focuses on trends and patterns rather than individual-level details. This approach helps mitigate the risk of privacy breaches while still enabling organisations to derive actionable insights from their data. The challenge lies in striking a balance between the utility of the data and the protection of individual privacy, ensuring that neither is compromised.

However, the ethical responsibilities do not end with the collection and anonymisation of data. How organisations use and act upon the insights generated from big data is equally important. Ethical decision-making in this context requires a deliberate focus on fairness, transparency, and accountability. The insights gleaned from data should be used in ways that avoid perpetuating discrimination or bias, particularly when algorithms are involved in the decision-making process. Bias in data interpretation or algorithmic decision-making can reinforce existing societal inequalities, making it imperative that organisations adopt a conscientious and inclusive approach when designing and deploying their models. Regular audits of algorithms to check for fairness and bias are essential, as is the use of diverse datasets to train ML systems. Human oversight remains a crucial component in these processes, ensuring that automated decisions do not drift into ethically dubious territory without checks and balances.

In order to foster trust, organisations must also be transparent with stakeholders about the ethical considerations that underpin their use of big data. This includes clear communication about the potential social impacts of their data-driven decisions, as well as a commitment to ongoing accountability. Ethical data use is not only about compliance with regulations but about building a foundation of trust between businesses and users, where data are treated with the respect it deserves. Ultimately, responsible stewardship of big data can contribute positively to society, but it requires a commitment to ethical principles at every stage—from collection to analysis, decision-making, and beyond.

13.8 NAVIGATING THE ETHICAL DIMENSIONS OF EMERGING TECHNOLOGIES

The rapid advancement of emerging technologies, including blockchain, virtual and augmented reality, and biometrics, has introduced a host of ethical challenges that organisations must address as they integrate these innovations into everyday life. Blockchain, celebrated for its transparency, immutability, and decentralisation, presents ethical dilemmas concerning data ownership, consent, and individual rights. The very features that make blockchain appealing—its permanent record-keeping and distributed nature—also raise questions about governance and control. Ethical practice in blockchain involves establishing transparent governance structures within networks to ensure that participants are fully aware of their roles, responsibilities, and the data stored on the ledger. Furthermore, inclusivity must be maintained to prevent a concentration of power among a few actors, undermining the foundational ethos of decentralisation. Organisations must also grapple with challenges like the right to be forgotten, an issue at odds with blockchain's immutability. By navigating these complexities with a commitment to ethical governance, organisations can responsibly harness the potential of decentralised systems.

Similarly, virtual and augmented reality technologies, while providing innovative and immersive experiences, also bring forward new ethical considerations, particularly around privacy and user autonomy. These technologies have the capacity to reshape user experiences in unprecedented ways, yet they simultaneously open avenues for invasive data collection and surveillance. As users engage with virtual environments, developers must ensure that individuals are fully informed about the scope and nature of the data being collected and that they have control over how much they choose to share. The immersive nature of these technologies also necessitates a careful focus on user well-being, given the potential psychological impacts of prolonged engagement with virtual worlds. Developers must avoid perpetuating harmful content, biases, or manipulative design that could exploit users' vulnerabilities. In this context, ethical frameworks for virtual and augmented reality stress the importance of transparency, consent, and the protection of user autonomy, while also ensuring that the virtual spaces created are inclusive, safe, and reflective of societal values.

Biometric technologies, such as facial recognition and fingerprint scanning, add yet another layer of complexity to the ethical landscape. As these systems become increasingly ubiquitous, the balance between innovation and individual privacy becomes more tenuous. Biometrics, by their nature, involve the collection of highly personal and unique data, making it critical that such data are handled with the utmost care. Ethical considerations centre on securing clear and informed consent from individuals, as well as ensuring that the data collected is accurate and not subject to misuse. The potential for biased or inaccurate results, particularly in the context of facial recognition technologies that may disproportionately affect certain demographic groups, underscores the need for rigorous standards in both development and deployment. Furthermore, concerns about surveillance and tracking without user consent highlight the importance of strong safeguards against the misuse of biometric data. Transparency in how biometric data are collected, stored, and used, coupled with robust security measures, is essential for maintaining public trust and ensuring that these technologies do not infringe upon individual rights.

In essence, the ethical implications of emerging technologies like blockchain, virtual and augmented reality, and biometrics are vast and multifaceted. While these innovations hold immense promise, they also carry significant responsibilities for organisations to uphold ethical standards that prioritise user rights, privacy, and societal well-being. Navigating these ethical challenges requires a steadfast commitment to transparency, consent, and inclusivity, ensuring that technological progress benefits all members of society without compromising fundamental ethical principles.

13.9 NAVIGATING ETHICAL DECISION-MAKING IN THE DIGITAL BUSINESS LANDSCAPE

In the rapidly evolving environment of digital business, ethical decision-making is essential for steering organisations through complex situations while maintaining responsible practices. To ensure their actions align with ethical principles, businesses must adopt comprehensive frameworks that guide their decision-making processes. A widely recognised model is the "Principles of Ethical Decision-Making," which provides a structured approach for assessing situations. This framework involves clearly identifying the issue, considering the interests and impact on various stakeholders, evaluating potential alternatives, and ultimately making a well-informed decision that adheres to ethical standards.

Such frameworks are indispensable for digital businesses, particularly when facing challenges such as safeguarding data privacy, mitigating algorithmic bias, or managing the social and environmental implications of technological innovation. By embedding these frameworks into their operations, organisations cultivate a culture where ethical considerations are integrated into every aspect of the decision-making process. This not only ensures compliance with regulatory requirements but also fosters an environment of accountability and transparency, which is increasingly critical in the digital age.

Central to this ethical foundation is the role of leadership. Ethical leadership in digital organisations serves as a cornerstone for building and sustaining an ethical business culture. Leaders are responsible for setting the standard of behaviour within their organisations, and their approach to ethical decision-making directly influences the actions of their employees. In an era where the choices surrounding technological deployment can have profound consequences on society, it is vital for leaders to demonstrate a steadfast commitment to transparency, fairness, and the overall well-being of all stakeholders.

Ethical leaders go beyond mere compliance, actively fostering an environment in which integrity and accountability are the norm. They encourage teams to prioritise ethical considerations during the development and application of digital technologies, ensuring that the pursuit of innovation does not come at the cost of ethical compromise. By modelling such behaviour, these leaders inspire trust within their organisations, gaining the confidence of employees, customers, and the broader community. The presence of ethical leadership strengthens the organisation's ability to navigate the complexities of the digital landscape with a moral compass, ensuring that decisions made today do not create unforeseen challenges tomorrow.

Despite the best intentions, ethical dilemmas and conflicts are inevitable in the digital realm, given the pace of technological advancements and the intricate nature of digital business operations. The very complexity of these operations can often blur the lines between what is legally permissible and what is ethically right. Organisations must, therefore, take a proactive stance in addressing these dilemmas by establishing robust mechanisms for identifying and resolving ethical conflicts as they arise.

To effectively manage such challenges, digital businesses must create an open, supportive environment where employees feel empowered to raise ethical concerns without fear of reprisal. This can be achieved through clearly defined channels for reporting ethical issues, alongside formal structures such as ethics committees or the appointment of ethics officers tasked with overseeing the organisation's ethical integrity. These committees can play a critical role in reviewing decision-making processes and ensuring that all choices are scrutinised through a comprehensive ethical lens.

Additionally, fostering a culture that encourages open dialogue around ethical disagreements is essential. When conflicts do arise, organisations should prioritise transparent communication and establish clear protocols for resolving disputes. Ethical concerns should not be viewed as hindrances to progress but as valuable opportunities for reflection and improvement. By addressing ethical challenges in this way, businesses not only enhance their decision-making processes but also reinforce their commitment to responsible innovation and ethical accountability.

In conclusion, navigating the ethical landscape of digital business requires more than just adherence to rules and regulations. It calls for the consistent application of ethical frameworks, strong ethical leadership, and a proactive approach to resolving dilemmas and conflicts. When these elements come together, they form the foundation upon which digital businesses can build trust, foster integrity, and operate with a sense of responsibility that ensures long-term success in an increasingly interconnected and scrutinised digital world.

13.10 CULTIVATING A CULTURE OF DIGITAL ETHICS

In today's digital landscape, fostering a culture of digital ethics within an organisation is crucial for ensuring responsible business practices. A foundational element in this endeavour is the establishment of an Ethical Code of Conduct specifically designed to address the unique challenges posed by the digital realm. This code should clearly outline the ethical principles, values, and guidelines that employees are expected to uphold in their digital interactions and responsibilities.

The Ethical Code of Conduct acts as a guiding framework, providing a coherent roadmap for ethical decision-making across various digital contexts, including data management, technology implementation, and interactions with stakeholders. By articulating the organisation's unwavering commitment to integrity, transparency, and respect for all parties involved, the code fosters a collective understanding of ethical expectations throughout the digital workforce. This shared commitment serves not only to unify employees under a common ethical framework but also to reinforce the importance of ethical considerations in their daily operations.

However, simply having a code in place is not enough to ensure a culture of digital ethics. To deeply embed these principles within the organisation's DNA, robust training and education programmes focused on digital ethics are essential. These initiatives equip employees with the necessary knowledge and skills to effectively navigate the ethical challenges they may encounter in their specific roles. Training should encompass critical topics such as data privacy, algorithmic accountability, and the responsible use of emerging technologies.

Moreover, continuous education is vital to keeping employees informed about the evolving ethical landscape in the digital domain. This can be achieved through a variety of means, including workshops, seminars, and online courses that utilise real-world case studies to provide practical insights into ethical decision-making. By investing in the ethical development of its workforce, an organisation nurtures a community of informed and conscientious digital professionals who are well-equipped to tackle ethical dilemmas as they arise.

Beyond the establishment of policies and training programmes, actively encouraging ethical behaviour is integral to cultivating a culture of digital ethics. Leaders and managers hold a crucial responsibility in setting ethical expectations and reinforcing a commitment to ethical conduct within their teams. Recognising and rewarding ethical behaviour sends a strong signal regarding the organisation's dedication to digital ethics, reinforcing its importance at every level.

Additionally, digital organisations can incorporate ethical considerations into performance evaluations, making adherence to ethical standards a vital criterion in employee assessments. By linking ethical behaviour to career advancement and recognition, organisations incentivise employees to prioritise ethical considerations in their professional undertakings.

Open communication is also paramount in creating an environment where ethical behaviour thrives. Employees should feel empowered to raise ethical concerns without the fear of reprisal. Establishing mechanisms for anonymous reporting and conducting regular discussions on ethical issues contribute significantly to the development of a workplace culture that values and celebrates ethical behaviour.

In essence, cultivating a culture of digital ethics necessitates the creation of a comprehensive Ethical Code of Conduct, the implementation of robust ethics training, and the active encouragement of ethical behaviour throughout the organisation. This multifaceted approach ensures that digital ethics is not merely a set of guidelines but rather an intrinsic part of the organisational ethos, ultimately contributing to responsible and sustainable practices in the ever-evolving digital landscape.

13.11 THE FUTURE LANDSCAPE OF DIGITAL ETHICS

The trajectory of digital ethics is shaped by a host of dynamic trends and emerging challenges as technology advances at an unprecedented pace. A significant development is the growing integration of AI and ML within digital systems, which raises profound ethical questions surrounding automated decision-making. As algorithms become increasingly sophisticated, the pressing need to ensure fairness, transparency, and accountability in their outcomes emerges as a pivotal challenge for stakeholders in the digital realm.

Data privacy remains a critical issue, and the rise of new technologies, particularly the IoT, introduces additional layers of complexity. Striking a balance between harnessing the benefits of data-driven insights and safeguarding user privacy is likely to be an ongoing struggle in this ever-evolving digital landscape. Furthermore, the advent of biometric technologies brings with it ethical considerations concerning the responsible handling of sensitive personal information, necessitating careful deliberation on how such data should be collected, stored, and used.

In this context, technology companies occupy a central position in shaping the ethical fabric of the digital era. As the architects and distributors of digital solutions, these organisations bear the responsibility of prioritising ethical considerations throughout the lifecycle of their products, from development and deployment to user engagement. Adopting a proactive approach to issues such as data privacy, algorithmic bias, and cybersecurity is essential for fostering trust and accountability.

Transparency and openness are fundamental principles that technology companies must embrace to effectively promote ethical practices. This entails clearly communicating data usage policies, providing users with control over their personal information, and addressing any ethical concerns raised by users or regulatory authorities in a timely and responsible manner. Moreover, fostering collaborative efforts within the industry—such as sharing best practices and collectively tackling ethical challenges—will contribute to the establishment of a more responsible and sustainable digital ecosystem.

As the technological landscape continues to evolve, so too must the ethical guidelines that govern it. Regulatory bodies, industry associations, and advocacy groups play vital roles in the ongoing development and refinement of ethical frameworks that align with contemporary challenges. These guidelines must be dynamic and responsive, ensuring that ethical considerations keep pace with rapid technological advancements.

Importantly, ethical guidelines should not only address the issues of today but also anticipate the challenges of tomorrow. As new technologies emerge and societal expectations shift, ethical frameworks must adapt to confront novel dilemmas. Engaging in open dialogues with a diverse range of stakeholders—including users, policymakers, and ethicists—will be essential for crafting comprehensive and adaptable ethical guidelines that reflect the complexities of the digital age.

In navigating the future of digital ethics, stakeholders must remain vigilant and proactive, addressing emerging trends and challenges while acknowledging the influential role of technology companies in fostering ethical practices. By ensuring that ethical guidelines evolve alongside technological advancements, we can collectively contribute to the responsible and sustainable development of technology, ultimately benefiting society as a whole.

13.12 CHAPTER SUMMARY

The journey through the ethical landscape of the digital world highlights the pressing need for organisations and individuals alike to engage with ethical principles in their technological practices. As we have explored, the challenges associated with data privacy and security, digital advertising, and the responsibilities of social media platforms necessitate a proactive approach to ethical decision-making. Upholding ethical standards in e-commerce and protecting consumer rights further illustrate the crucial role that ethical considerations play in building trust within the digital ecosystem.

Emerging technologies, including the IoT and big data analytics, present new ethical dilemmas that demand ongoing dialogue and vigilance. The implications of these technologies necessitate robust ethical frameworks that adapt to the rapidly changing digital landscape. As organisations strive to cultivate a culture of digital ethics, they not only enhance their own practices but also contribute to the broader societal discourse on ethical technology use.

Looking ahead, the future of digital ethics is poised for evolution, requiring collaboration among stakeholders to establish and refine ethical guidelines that reflect contemporary challenges. By prioritising ethics in the digital realm, we can navigate the complexities of technological advancement responsibly, ensuring that innovations serve the best interests of individuals and society as a whole. In this way, digital ethics emerges not merely as a set of rules, but as a foundational ethos guiding the development and implementation of technology for the greater good.

Key Questions for Discussion

1. In an era where personal data are constantly collected and analysed, what ethical obligations do businesses have in ensuring data privacy? Should consumers have more control over how their data are used, and if so, how can this be achieved?
2. Many digital marketing strategies rely on personal data to target consumers effectively. Where should businesses draw the line between personalisation and intrusion, and how can ethical advertising be maintained in an increasingly data-driven world?
3. Social media platforms have been criticised for spreading misinformation, amplifying harmful content, and violating user privacy. What ethical responsibilities should these platforms uphold, and what measures can be put in place to promote ethical content governance?
4. With smart devices collecting vast amounts of user data, how can businesses ensure ethical IoT usage? Should stricter regulations be enforced to prevent privacy violations, and what role should consumers play in protecting their own data?
5. As emerging technologies like AI, blockchain, and biometric surveillance continue to evolve, what are the key ethical challenges that businesses and policymakers must address? How can organisations foster a culture of digital ethics to navigate these challenges responsibly?

BIBLIOGRAPHY

Beever, J., McDaniel, R. and Stanlick, N.A. (2020). *Understanding Digital Ethics: Cases and Contexts.* Routledge.

Coeckelbergh, M. (2020). *AI Ethics.* MIT Press.

Müller, V.C. (Ed.). (2020). *Ethics of Artificial Intelligence and Robotics.* Routledge.

Newport, C. (2019). *Digital Minimalism: Choosing a Focused Life in a Noisy World*. Portfolio.
Noble, S.U. (2018). *Algorithms of Oppression: How Search Engines Reinforce Racism*. New York University Press.
O'Neil, C. (2016). *Weapons of Math Destruction: How Big Data Increases Inequality and Threatens Democracy*. Crown Publishing Group.
Véliz, C. (2020). *Privacy Is Power: Why and How You Should Take Back Control of Your Data*. Bantam Press.
Véliz, C. (Ed.). (2021). *The Oxford Handbook of Digital Ethics*. Oxford University Press.
Wylie, C. (2019). *Mindfck: Inside Cambridge Analytica's Plot to Break the World**. Random House.
Zuboff, S. (2019). *The Age of Surveillance Capitalism: The Fight for a Human Future at the New Frontier of Power*. PublicAffairs.

CHAPTER 14

The Future of Digital Business

Emerging Technologies and Trends to Watch

> **Learning Objectives**
>
> By the end of this chapter, you will be able to:
>
> 1. Understand how innovations such as AI, blockchain, IoT, and 5G are transforming digital business models, operations, and consumer interactions.
> 2. Explore the cybersecurity risks, data privacy challenges, and ethical implications associated with advanced technologies in digital business.
> 3. Identify potential business opportunities and strategic challenges posed by robotics, automation, extended reality, and other cutting-edge technologies in a rapidly evolving digital landscape.

14.1 INTRODUCTION

The digital business landscape is undergoing a profound transformation, driven by a wave of emerging technologies that redefine the way companies operate and engage with consumers. In this dynamic environment, organisations must adapt to rapidly changing technological advancements to remain competitive and relevant. Emerging technologies, such as artificial intelligence (AI), machine learning, blockchain, the Internet of Things (IoT), and extended reality (XR), are not only enhancing operational efficiencies but also enabling innovative business models and creating new avenues for customer engagement.

The integration of these technologies facilitates greater transparency, decentralisation, and interconnectivity, leading to improved decision-making and enhanced consumer experiences. For instance, AI and machine learning enable businesses to harness vast amounts of data for predictive analytics, while blockchain technology pioneers secure and transparent transactions. Simultaneously, 5G connectivity promises unprecedented speed and reliability, paving the way for seamless communication and interaction across digital platforms.

DOI: 10.4324/9781032672458-14

However, alongside these transformative opportunities lie significant challenges. Cybersecurity threats, data privacy issues, and ethical considerations present complex dilemmas that organisations must navigate in their pursuit of technological advancement. This chapter aims to explore the multifaceted implications of emerging technologies on digital business, examining their potential to revolutionise industries while addressing the critical considerations that come with such rapid change.

14.2 THE TRANSFORMATIVE POWER OF EMERGING TECHNOLOGIES

The digital business landscape is evolving at an unprecedented rate, driven by the rapid advancement of emerging technologies. Innovations such as AI, blockchain, machine learning, and the IoT are revolutionising the way businesses operate, transforming customer interactions, and reshaping entire industries. The relentless pace of these technological breakthroughs not only redefines existing business models but also opens up new possibilities for how organisations create value. As we enter an era where digital transformation is a prerequisite for success, the challenge lies in staying abreast of these developments and integrating them effectively.

Recent years have witnessed the widespread adoption of advanced technologies that offer businesses unprecedented capabilities. Machine learning, for instance, has given organisations the ability to make data-driven decisions with greater precision, while IoT has provided real-time insights into operational efficiency. The advent of 5G connectivity, with its promise of faster and more reliable communication, is set to enhance digital applications across industries, facilitating everything from autonomous vehicles to smart cities. In parallel, blockchain technology is fostering transparency and security in transactions, while quantum computing promises to unlock new dimensions of data processing, making previously insurmountable problems solvable (Figure 14.1).

The profound impact of these emerging technologies on digital business cannot be overstated. AI is increasingly automating routine tasks, streamlining processes, and delivering personalised customer experiences at scale. Predictive analytics is enabling businesses to anticipate consumer needs and optimise supply chains with greater accuracy. Blockchain is not only ensuring secure, transparent transactions but is also transforming industries like finance, supply chain, and healthcare by removing intermediaries and reducing fraud. Furthermore, augmented reality (AR) is changing the retail experience, allowing consumers to interact with products virtually, while the rise of edge computing is reducing latency by processing data closer to the source, thereby improving operational efficiency.

While the opportunities that these emerging technologies offer are immense, they come with significant challenges that businesses must navigate. Cybersecurity remains a critical concern as the adoption of digital tools increases, making organisations more vulnerable to data breaches and attacks. Ethical considerations surrounding AI, data privacy, and automated decision-making demand careful scrutiny to prevent unintended biases and protect consumer rights. Additionally, the need for a highly skilled workforce to harness these innovations is more pressing than ever. Organisations must invest in upskilling their employees and

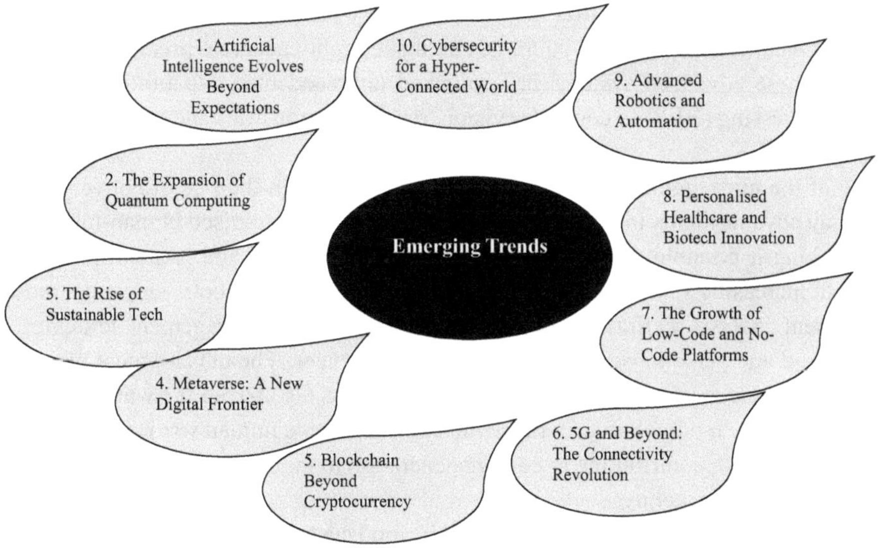

FIGURE 14.1 Emerging Trends Shaping the Future of Technology and Business

fostering a culture of continuous learning to fully leverage the potential of these technological advancements.

At the same time, businesses that are agile enough to embrace these technologies will find themselves well-positioned to capitalise on the opportunities they present. The integration of sustainable technologies is opening new avenues for environmentally conscious business practices, aligning profitability with corporate social responsibility. Augmented and virtual reality (VR) are creating immersive experiences that deepen customer engagement, while IoT is enabling smart, data-driven decisions that enhance operational performance. The future of digital business will depend on how adeptly organisations can balance innovation with the management of associated risks, positioning themselves for long-term success in an increasingly digital world.

To thrive in this rapidly changing environment, businesses must not only adopt the latest technologies but also cultivate resilience and adaptability. The digital transformation journey involves continuously rethinking strategies, fostering innovation, and embracing new models of operation. As organisations navigate this evolving landscape, their ability to integrate emerging technologies into their operations, while addressing the ethical and practical challenges, will be key to securing a competitive edge and sustaining success in the future of digital business.

14.3 THE TRANSFORMATIVE INFLUENCE OF AI AND MACHINE LEARNING ON DIGITAL BUSINESS

AI and machine learning have dramatically transformed the digital business landscape, with deep learning leading the charge in this technological revolution. At the core of deep learning are neural networks, modelled after the human brain, which enable machines to process vast amounts of data, discern intricate patterns, and make highly accurate predictions. The development of these advanced systems has unlocked unprecedented capabilities, from natural language processing (NLP) to computer vision, reshaping industries and redefining how businesses operate.

One of the most significant breakthroughs in AI has been the rise of conversational AI, powered by advancements in NLP. This technology has revolutionised human-machine interaction, making it possible for machines to understand, process, and respond to human language with increasing sophistication. AI-driven tools, such as chatbots, language translators, and sentiment analysis platforms, are now integral to customer engagement strategies, offering more fluid and personalised communication experiences. The development of generative models, such as Generative Pre-trained Transformers, has also paved the way for creative AI applications. These models can generate coherent text, mimic human writing styles, and even create visual content, contributing to content generation in industries as diverse as journalism, entertainment, and marketing.

AI's transformative potential extends well beyond customer service and content creation, with its influence now permeating every industry. In healthcare, AI is revolutionising diagnostic processes, accelerating drug discovery, and enhancing patient care through the use of computer vision, which powers highly accurate medical imaging analysis. This, in turn, facilitates early disease detection and more effective treatment plans. AI's predictive analytics capabilities are also enabling more proactive healthcare management, identifying potential health risks before they escalate.

In the financial sector, AI is streamlining risk management, fraud detection, and customer service. By employing predictive algorithms to analyse market trends, financial institutions are making more informed investment decisions and optimising their portfolios. AI-driven chatbots are also transforming customer interactions, delivering faster and more efficient responses to queries and support requests while simultaneously reducing operational costs. Meanwhile, manufacturing industries are using AI for process optimisation, predictive maintenance, and quality control. Machine learning models analyse vast amounts of production data to predict equipment failures, minimising downtime and maximising productivity. Autonomous AI-powered robots are now integral to warehouse operations and assembly lines, boosting efficiency across supply chains.

As we look to the future, the role of AI in business automation and decision-making will become even more pronounced. Robotic process automation (RPA), driven by AI, is already automating routine tasks, allowing human workers to focus on strategic initiatives that add greater value to their organisations. AI's integration into supply chain management is transforming logistics, inventory control, and demand forecasting, optimising business operations at every level.

Crucially, AI is also reshaping decision-making processes, moving beyond automating simple, repetitive tasks to influencing more complex and strategic business decisions. The rise of explainable AI models is providing businesses with transparency and accountability in the decision-making process, reducing concerns over the "black box" nature of AI. These models enable organisations to better understand how decisions are made, fostering trust in AI systems and ensuring more ethical and informed decision-making. Moreover, the combination of AI and data analytics is empowering businesses to extract actionable insights from vast data sets, driving a more data-driven culture across sectors.

However, as AI continues to shape the future of business, the ethical implications of its use must be addressed. The development of responsible AI practices is essential to mitigate biases and ensure fairness in AI-driven outcomes. As businesses become more reliant on AI technologies, regulations and industry standards must evolve to ensure that these systems are used in a way that benefits society as a whole.

Ultimately, the future of AI and machine learning in digital business promises to be transformative. From automating tasks to enhancing decision-making capabilities and creating new opportunities for innovation, AI will continue to play an essential role in shaping the trajectory of modern business. Companies that strategically integrate AI into their operations will not only drive efficiency and innovation but also gain a competitive edge in a rapidly evolving digital landscape.

14.4 BLOCKCHAIN: PIONEERING TRANSPARENCY AND DECENTRALISATION IN THE DIGITAL ERA

Blockchain and distributed ledger technology (DLT) are redefining the foundations of digital business, offering transformative solutions across a wide range of industries. Central to this revolution is blockchain's capacity to create transparent, decentralised, and secure systems, which are rapidly displacing traditional, centralised structures. Cryptocurrencies, such as Bitcoin and Ethereum, stand as the most prominent examples of this shift, leveraging blockchain technology to facilitate secure, peer-to-peer financial transactions without the need for intermediaries. At its heart, blockchain is a distributed ledger, maintained by a network of participants, where each party has real-time access to an identical copy of the ledger. Cryptographic techniques ensure the security and immutability of the data stored, preventing tampering and providing a trustworthy and permanent record. Smart contracts, self-executing agreements embedded within the blockchain, further elevate this technology by automating processes and reducing the need for human intervention. Once certain predefined conditions are met, these contracts execute automatically, streamlining operations and reducing inefficiencies.

The impact of blockchain is perhaps most visibly felt in supply chain management, where it addresses long-standing challenges such as product provenance and transparency. With blockchain, each step of the supply chain—from the sourcing of raw materials to the final delivery of the product—is recorded in an immutable ledger, providing an unalterable and verifiable record. This transparency mitigates the risk of counterfeiting, enhances trust, and streamlines logistical processes. By allowing every participant in the supply chain to access the same information in real-time, blockchain reduces the complexities of coordination, improves efficiency, and ensures accountability. In sectors such as food production, pharmaceuticals, and luxury goods, where authenticity and safety are paramount, blockchain technology is proving invaluable by offering a clear and accessible audit trail of product origins and transactions.

In the financial sector, blockchain's potential to disrupt traditional banking systems is profound. The rise of decentralised finance (DeFi) platforms highlights this shift, offering financial services such as lending, borrowing, and trading without the need for centralised institutions like banks. By utilising blockchain technology, DeFi platforms are able to deliver secure, transparent, and efficient financial transactions, often at lower costs and with fewer barriers to entry. Smart contracts play a critical role in these platforms, facilitating peer-to-peer transactions that are automatic and trustworthy. This reduction in reliance on intermediaries not only decreases transaction costs but also increases accessibility for individuals and businesses, particularly those in regions with limited access to traditional banking services. The adoption of blockchain in finance is enabling faster settlements, reducing fraud, and enhancing the overall efficiency of the financial ecosystem.

However, the potential of blockchain extends far beyond supply chains and finance. The healthcare sector is increasingly turning to blockchain to ensure the secure and seamless exchange of patient data between authorised parties. By decentralising data storage, blockchain enhances patient privacy and security while simultaneously improving the interoperability of healthcare systems. Medical records can be safely shared among healthcare providers, enabling better collaboration and continuity of care, without the risk of data breaches or unauthorised access. Moreover, blockchain's application in clinical trials and pharmaceutical supply chains ensures the integrity and traceability of medical products, further enhancing patient safety.

Governments, too, are exploring the potential of blockchain to transform public services. In areas such as voting, record-keeping, and public transactions, blockchain provides an incorruptible and transparent mechanism that reduces the risk of fraud and fosters greater trust in government processes. Secure voting systems based on blockchain can ensure the authenticity of each vote while maintaining voter anonymity, thus addressing many of the concerns associated with traditional voting methods. Additionally, blockchain's ability to create tamper-proof records is invaluable for land registries, tax systems, and public spending, where transparency and accountability are crucial.

One of the most exciting prospects of blockchain lies in decentralised identity management. In a digital world where personal data is frequently collected, stored, and sometimes misused by centralised entities, blockchain offers individuals the opportunity to regain control over their personal information. Through decentralised identity solutions, individuals can store their credentials on a blockchain and decide when, how, and with whom they share these data. This not only improves online security but also reduces the need for multiple usernames and passwords, simplifying digital interactions while preserving privacy. As digital identity becomes increasingly important in areas such as e-commerce, online banking, and social media, blockchain's decentralised approach is likely to play a pivotal role in shaping the future of online authentication.

In conclusion, blockchain and DLT are at the forefront of a paradigm shift in the digital business world. By introducing transparency, security, and decentralisation into industries ranging from finance to healthcare, blockchain is enabling new, innovative approaches to solving long-standing challenges. As the technology continues to mature, its applications will only broaden, offering businesses and governments the tools they need to create more resilient, efficient, and trustworthy systems. With its potential to revolutionise industries and reimagine the structure of digital ecosystems, blockchain is positioned to remain a cornerstone in the evolution of digital business. The ongoing exploration of blockchain's capabilities, alongside the emergence of new use cases, underscores its significance as a transformative force in the digital era.

14.5 THE FUSION OF IOT AND EDGE COMPUTING: SHAPING THE FUTURE OF INTERCONNECTED SYSTEMS

The proliferation of the IoT has transformed the digital landscape, establishing a vast network of interconnected devices that communicate and share data across a range of industries. From smart home appliances and wearable health monitors to industrial sensors and autonomous vehicles, IoT is reshaping the way businesses, governments, and individuals interact with the digital world. This explosion of IoT devices has been fuelled by advancements in sensor technologies, more efficient communication protocols, and an ever-growing demand for automation and data-driven decision-making. The result is a web of interconnected devices that collectively generate unprecedented amounts of data, allowing for smarter, more responsive systems that have far-reaching implications for efficiency, security, and personalisation.

As IoT expands, its applications are becoming integral to digital business operations. The ability of IoT devices to seamlessly gather and exchange data in real time offers businesses significant opportunities to enhance operational efficiency, monitor and predict equipment health, and gain valuable insights into consumer behaviour. The integration of IoT into business operations, from logistics and manufacturing to retail and service industries, is fostering a new era of data-driven decision-making and automation, enabling organisations to remain agile and competitive. As the number of connected devices grows exponentially, the role of IoT is becoming increasingly indispensable to the future of digital business, embedding itself deeply within the fabric of both private and public sectors.

The influence of IoT, however, extends far beyond individual devices and corporate settings. Its transformative power is seen in the development of smart cities, where IoT is being leveraged to create more sustainable, efficient urban environments. IoT sensors embedded in city infrastructure, such as traffic lights, streetlights, and waste management systems, enable real-time monitoring and management of public resources. Smart traffic systems, for instance, can adjust signals based on real-time traffic flow, reducing congestion and improving the efficiency of transport networks. Similarly, smart energy grids can monitor and adjust energy consumption, optimising power distribution and reducing wastage. These applications not only contribute to the sustainability of urban environments but also improve the overall quality of life for residents by reducing pollution, enhancing public safety, and streamlining the management of public services.

In the healthcare sector, IoT is revolutionising the way care is delivered and managed. Wearable health devices equipped with sensors collect real-time data on patients' vital signs, enabling healthcare providers to monitor conditions remotely and provide preventive care. This is particularly valuable for managing chronic conditions, where real-time monitoring can detect potential health risks before they escalate, thus improving patient outcomes and reducing hospital admissions. The ability of IoT to facilitate personalised medicine, through continuous data collection and analysis, offers a more targeted approach to healthcare, allowing treatments to be tailored to individual patients' needs. By integrating IoT into healthcare systems, providers can not only enhance patient care but also alleviate the strain on healthcare infrastructures by reducing unnecessary hospital visits and streamlining care delivery.

However, the rapid growth of IoT and the data it generates have introduced new challenges related to data processing and latency. With vast amounts of data being transmitted across networks, the traditional model of sending all information to centralised cloud servers for processing can lead to delays, particularly in scenarios where real-time responses are critical. This is where edge computing comes into play. Edge computing involves processing data closer to the source—at the "edge" of the network—allowing for quicker decision-making and reducing the latency associated with cloud-based processing. By processing data locally, edge computing ensures that time-sensitive applications, such as autonomous vehicles, industrial automation, and AR, can operate efficiently and respond to real-time events without delay.

The integration of edge computing with IoT is particularly vital in industries where immediacy is crucial. Autonomous vehicles, for example, require split-second decision-making based on real-time data from sensors monitoring the vehicle's surroundings. Any delay in processing this data could result in dangerous situations. Similarly, in industrial settings, predictive maintenance systems powered by IoT sensors can detect potential equipment failures and immediately trigger actions to prevent downtime, all thanks to edge computing's ability to process the data where they are generated. This minimisation of latency not only improves safety and efficiency but also reduces the strain on centralised data centres by offloading some of the processing burden.

As businesses and industries increasingly adopt IoT and edge computing, the synergy between these technologies is set to drive significant innovation and reshape the digital business environment. The fusion of IoT's expansive data collection capabilities with edge computing's real-time processing power offers a powerful framework for creating more agile, efficient, and responsive systems. Whether in the context of smart cities, healthcare, manufacturing, or retail, this combination is unlocking new possibilities for automation, data analysis, and intelligent decision-making.

In conclusion, the ongoing expansion of IoT and the rise of edge computing mark a new era of interconnected, intelligent systems that are transforming how businesses and industries operate. As IoT devices continue to proliferate and the demand for real-time data processing increases, edge computing will play an ever-more critical role in ensuring the responsiveness and efficiency of these systems. Together, IoT and edge computing are reshaping the future of digital business, driving innovation across industries, and offering new opportunities for businesses to thrive in an increasingly connected world. As these technologies evolve, their ability to revolutionise everything from urban living to healthcare will solidify their place at the heart of the digital transformation.

CASE STUDY 14

Tesla's Integration of AI and IoT in Autonomous Vehicles

Tesla has become a leader in the automotive industry by pioneering the integration of AI and the IoT into self-driving technology. The company's vision for autonomous vehicles is built on a sophisticated network of sensors, real-time data analysis, and machine learning, enabling cars to make complex driving decisions without human intervention. By combining AI-driven decision-making with IoT connectivity, Tesla has pushed the boundaries of innovation in digital business, transforming the future of mobility and smart transportation.

One of the primary challenges Tesla faced in developing autonomous vehicles was ensuring safety, reliability, and regulatory compliance. Unlike traditional vehicles, self-driving cars must process vast amounts of data in real-time, reacting to unpredictable road conditions, pedestrians, and other vehicles. Additionally, legal and ethical concerns regarding AI-driven decision-making posed significant hurdles in gaining public and governmental trust. Many regions had yet to establish clear regulations for fully autonomous vehicles, making widespread adoption difficult.

To overcome these challenges, Tesla developed its Autopilot and Full Self-Driving systems, which use AI-powered neural networks to continuously learn from real-world driving scenarios. The company equipped its vehicles with a suite of cameras, radar, and ultrasonic sensors to gather data from the environment. This data is processed using Tesla's AI algorithms, allowing vehicles to detect obstacles, navigate roads, and make split-second driving decisions. Additionally, Tesla's over-the-air (OTA) software updates ensure that every car on the road can receive real-time improvements, making the fleet progressively smarter. Through cloud-based connectivity, Tesla vehicles also share insights with one another, creating a continuously evolving and improving AI model.

The integration of AI and IoT in Tesla's vehicles has led to remarkable results. The company has significantly improved the performance of its self-driving systems, reducing accident rates when compared to human-driven vehicles. Tesla's data-driven approach has enabled the development of predictive maintenance, helping to detect and resolve mechanical issues before they escalate. Moreover, by harnessing IoT connectivity, Tesla has enhanced vehicle security and driver convenience, allowing users to control various functions remotely via smartphone applications. Financially, Tesla's AI-driven strategy has strengthened its position as a market leader, with soaring stock valuations and increased consumer demand for smart electric vehicles.

This case study highlights key lessons about the future of digital business. Firstly, AI and IoT are reshaping industries by enabling automation, efficiency, and continuous learning. Secondly, real-time data collection and AI-driven decision-making are critical for businesses looking to stay ahead in a fast-evolving technological landscape. Thirdly, regulatory and ethical considerations must be addressed when implementing disruptive technologies. Tesla's approach demonstrates the importance of innovation, adaptability, and a data-centric strategy in driving the future of digital business and mobility.

Discussion Questions for Students (with Indicative Answers)

1. **What role does AI play in Tesla's self-driving technology?**
   Indicative Answer: AI enables Tesla vehicles to process real-time data, detect objects, make driving decisions, and continuously improve through machine learning.
2. **How does IoT contribute to the functionality of Tesla's autonomous vehicles?**
   Indicative Answer: IoT connects Tesla cars to the cloud, allowing for real-time data sharing, software updates, remote control features, and predictive maintenance.
3. **What are some of the key challenges Tesla faced in developing autonomous vehicles?**
   Indicative Answer: Challenges included ensuring road safety, handling unpredictable driving conditions, complying with regulations, and gaining public trust in AI-driven cars.
4. **How has Tesla's approach to AI and IoT influenced the automotive industry?**
   Indicative Answer: Tesla has set a precedent for smart vehicles, leading other automakers to invest in AI, IoT, and connected car technology to enhance automation and user experience.
5. **What are the ethical considerations surrounding AI in self-driving cars?**
   Indicative Answer: Ethical concerns include AI decision-making in accident scenarios, data privacy, cybersecurity risks, and accountability in cases of system failure.

14.6 5G CONNECTIVITY: PAVING THE WAY FOR THE FUTURE OF DIGITAL COMMUNICATION

The arrival of 5G connectivity represents a monumental leap forward in communication technology, introducing a new era of speed, efficiency, and capacity that has the potential to transform the digital landscape for businesses across all sectors. Unlike its predecessor, 4G, which had limitations in terms of data speed and network capacity, 5G brings with it a host of advantages that revolutionise the way organisations operate, communicate, and innovate. The technology boasts exponentially faster data transfer speeds, ultra-low latency, and the ability to support far more connected devices, providing a platform for businesses to fully exploit advanced applications and services that were previously constrained by bandwidth and communication delays.

For businesses, one of the most immediate and tangible benefits of 5G is the enhancement of connectivity, which underpins a more seamless flow of information and enables unprecedented levels of efficiency in communication and data exchange. The ultra-fast data transfer rates make it possible for companies to use real-time collaboration tools without disruption, allowing for smooth video conferencing, instantaneous data sharing, and advanced AR applications. This acceleration of communication fosters an environment where decisions can be made more swiftly and with greater accuracy, improving productivity and optimising workflows. Whether it's enabling real-time updates for project management software or facilitating remote team collaboration across the globe, 5G empowers businesses to function more fluidly in an increasingly interconnected world.

Beyond enhancing traditional forms of communication, 5G serves as the critical infrastructure needed to accelerate the growth and functionality of the IoT, as well as the development of AR and VR technologies. The combination of low latency and high bandwidth that 5G offers is crucial for ensuring that IoT devices can operate synchronously, in real time, across various settings. From industrial manufacturing plants using smart sensors for predictive maintenance to interconnected transportation systems in smart cities, 5G enables an unprecedented level of responsiveness and integration. The technology makes it possible to create environments in which everything, from machinery to public infrastructure, is linked together in an intelligent, cohesive network that can adapt and respond dynamically to real-time data.

In the realms of AR and VR, 5G unlocks new opportunities for creating more immersive and interactive experiences that were simply not feasible with previous generations of network technology. The reduced latency provided by 5G ensures that AR and VR applications can react instantaneously to user input, making these experiences more lifelike and responsive. This has significant implications for industries such as education, where AR can be used to create interactive learning experiences, or healthcare, where VR simulations can be employed for training surgeons or guiding patients through therapeutic exercises. In entertainment, 5G enables richer, more immersive virtual environments that can transform gaming, film, and live event experiences, offering users a level of interactivity and engagement never before seen.

As businesses prepare for the full-scale rollout of 5G, it is essential for them to consider how best to position themselves to take advantage of the capabilities that this new technology offers. One of the first steps is to ensure that current digital infrastructure is prepared for 5G compatibility. This may involve upgrading existing networks and devices to handle the faster speeds and larger data loads that 5G will bring. Businesses must also begin exploring how they can innovate within their specific industries by developing applications and services that utilise the unique characteristics of 5G, such as its support for edge computing or its ability to facilitate real-time, data-driven decision-making.

Security is another crucial consideration in the era of 5G, as the expanded network capacity and rapid data transfer capabilities also present new risks. With more devices connected to the network and a larger volume of data in transit, the potential for cyberattacks increases. Therefore, it is imperative for businesses to implement strong cybersecurity protocols, including encryption, advanced authentication methods, and continuous network monitoring, to safeguard their communications and ensure that sensitive data is protected.

The advent of 5G connectivity heralds a new chapter in the evolution of digital business, one where the speed, reliability, and scope of communication and data exchange will set the stage for unprecedented technological innovation. As 5G enables faster and more responsive interactions across both digital and physical domains, businesses will have the opportunity to drive efficiencies, develop new products and services, and create richer experiences for customers. Those who strategically prepare for the 5G revolution by upgrading their infrastructure, investing in innovation, and strengthening security will find themselves well-positioned to seize the immense opportunities that this transformative technology presents. The future of communication is being shaped by 5G, and with it comes the promise of a more connected, intelligent, and dynamic world.

14.7 THE IMMERSIVE WORLD OF XR: SHAPING THE FUTURE OF BUSINESS

XR technologies, which encompass AR, VR, and Mixed Reality (MR), are revolutionising the way businesses interact with both their environments and their customers. These immersive technologies are transforming industries by blurring the lines between the digital and physical worlds, creating new opportunities for innovation, engagement, and efficiency.

At the forefront of XR is AR, a technology that seamlessly overlays digital information onto the real world, enriching the user's perception of their physical surroundings. AR has made significant strides across a variety of sectors, providing businesses with innovative ways to engage with customers and optimise operations. In retail, for instance, AR allows consumers to visualise products within their own space before purchasing, bridging the gap between online shopping and the in-store experience. This integration of digital elements into the consumer journey has not only enhanced customer satisfaction but has also increased conversion rates for businesses adopting AR solutions.

Beyond retail, AR plays a pivotal role in employee training, offering immersive, hands-on experiences that translate theoretical knowledge into practical application. Industries such as healthcare benefit enormously from AR's ability to provide real-time data during complex procedures, enabling surgeons to make more precise decisions and reduce the risk of error. The potential of AR to reshape business processes is vast, and as the technology continues to evolve, its applications across sectors will only become more prominent and varied.

While AR enhances the physical world with digital information, VR creates entirely immersive digital environments, transporting users beyond their immediate surroundings. VR's potential for businesses is vast, particularly in training and development. Through realistic simulations, employees can practise skills in a controlled virtual environment, experiencing scenarios that would be difficult, expensive, or even impossible to replicate in real life. This not only improves learning outcomes but also reduces the risks associated with on-the-job training, especially in high-stakes fields such as aviation, healthcare, and heavy industry.

Architectural firms are also harnessing VR's immersive capabilities, allowing clients to step inside and experience proposed building designs before they are constructed.

These virtual walkthroughs provide an unparalleled preview of future spaces, making the design process more interactive and intuitive. Moreover, the entertainment industry has fully embraced VR, creating immersive gaming worlds and interactive storytelling experiences that captivate audiences and offer new ways to engage with content. As VR becomes more accessible and refined, its influence on business strategies, particularly in sectors such as marketing, entertainment, and education, will continue to expand, reshaping traditional practices and creating new avenues for consumer engagement.

MR takes the concept of XR even further by merging the digital and physical worlds into one cohesive experience. By combining elements of both AR and VR, MR allows users to interact with both digital content and physical objects simultaneously. This interaction is especially valuable in collaborative settings, where teams can visualise and manipulate holographic data in real-time, facilitating creativity and problem-solving across different locations. In this way, MR breaks down geographical barriers, enabling more dynamic and productive remote collaboration, whether in boardrooms or across global teams.

The manufacturing and design industries have also found tremendous value in MR, particularly in the context of visualising and interacting with 3D models. Engineers and designers can superimpose digital prototypes onto real-world spaces, providing them with a more comprehensive understanding of how a product will function within a given environment. This ability to assess designs in context streamlines the development process and reduces the time and cost associated with prototyping. Additionally, MR's applications in healthcare, such as real-time surgical planning, further illustrate how this technology is enabling professionals to make more informed, data-driven decisions.

As XR technologies continue to advance, the integration of AR, VR, and MR into everyday business operations will become increasingly widespread. The convergence of these technologies is not only reshaping the way businesses operate but also redefining the ways in which we work, learn, and engage with the world. XR empowers businesses to create richer, more immersive experiences for both their employees and their customers, pushing the boundaries of innovation and efficiency.

In a rapidly evolving digital landscape, the strategic adoption of XR technologies is crucial for businesses looking to remain competitive and forward-thinking. The ability to blend digital and physical experiences allows for unprecedented opportunities to rethink traditional workflows, engage customers in novel ways, and foster creativity and collaboration across industries. As businesses continue to explore and implement XR, they place themselves at the forefront of a technological revolution that is set to reshape the future of work and interaction in profound ways.

14.8 NAVIGATING CYBERSECURITY IN THE ERA OF ADVANCED TECHNOLOGY

In an age where technological advancements continue to accelerate, cybersecurity faces ever-evolving challenges. The rapid expansion of digital ecosystems, coupled with the increasing sophistication of technology, has created a broader and more complex attack surface for cyber threats. As organisations increasingly rely on interconnected networks, such as the IoT and cloud computing infrastructures, the risks multiply, with businesses now more vulnerable to a diverse array of cyberattacks. These range from traditional malware to advanced persistent threats and zero-day vulnerabilities, each presenting a significant risk to the integrity and security of digital systems.

To tackle these growing threats, businesses must shift towards a proactive and resilient approach to cybersecurity. Rather than relying solely on reactive measures, it is crucial to implement continuous risk assessments and conduct regular security audits. This process allows organisations to identify vulnerabilities before they are exploited. Additionally, robust cybersecurity policies and frameworks need to be embedded within company operations to ensure that security is treated as an ongoing priority, not an afterthought. Yet, even with the most advanced systems in place, human error remains a considerable risk, as many breaches result from insider mistakes or negligence. Therefore, educating employees through comprehensive cybersecurity awareness training is vital. Ensuring that everyone within an organisation understands their role in maintaining security is often the first line of defence against potential breaches.

AI has emerged as a pivotal force in enhancing cybersecurity defences, offering solutions that would have been unimaginable just a few years ago. AI's ability to process and analyse vast datasets enables it to identify patterns and predict potential threats with remarkable accuracy. By using machine learning algorithms, AI systems can autonomously detect anomalies and respond to suspicious activities in real time, drastically reducing the window of opportunity for malicious actors. These AI-powered solutions can identify even the most subtle deviations from normal network traffic or user behaviour, providing a robust line of defence against both known and emerging threats.

AI's adaptive nature allows it to continuously improve, learning from new data to become more effective at thwarting cybercriminals who frequently evolve their attack methods. The dynamic nature of AI's machine learning capabilities means that it can adjust in response to new and previously unseen tactics employed by cyber adversaries. However, the very power of AI poses a double-edged sword. Just as cybersecurity professionals harness AI to strengthen defences, threat actors are increasingly turning to AI themselves, using it to develop more advanced and sophisticated attacks. This creates a constant arms race between defenders and attackers, necessitating an ongoing cycle of innovation and adaptation in the cybersecurity space. Organisations must be prepared to invest in advanced AI-driven technologies and stay ahead of the evolving tactics of cybercriminals.

The rise of quantum computing adds another layer of complexity to the cybersecurity landscape. While quantum computers hold enormous promise due to their unprecedented computational power, they also pose a substantial threat to existing cryptographic methods. Most current encryption systems, particularly those that rely on the difficulty of factoring large prime numbers, are likely to be rendered obsolete by quantum computers capable of performing such calculations exponentially faster than today's most powerful machines.

In anticipation of this emerging threat, the field of quantum-safe cryptography, or post-quantum cryptography, has gained increasing prominence. Researchers and cybersecurity experts are actively developing cryptographic algorithms designed to withstand the processing power of quantum computers. These quantum-resistant algorithms include lattice-based, hash-based, and code-based cryptography, among others. As quantum computing advances towards commercialisation, businesses are encouraged to assess their cryptographic infrastructures and begin transitioning to quantum-safe algorithms. This forward-thinking approach ensures that security protocols are future-proofed against the inevitable challenges that quantum computing will bring.

Integrating quantum-resistant encryption methods is not just a precautionary measure; it is quickly becoming an essential component of any comprehensive cybersecurity strategy. Organisations that fail to make this transition risk being caught unprepared when quantum technologies reach maturity, exposing them to potentially catastrophic breaches. As quantum-safe cryptography continues to develop, its implementation will be critical in safeguarding sensitive data and ensuring secure communications in the quantum era.

In this advancing technological landscape, maintaining strong cybersecurity requires a multi-faceted and forward-looking approach. The adoption of AI-powered defences significantly enhances an organisation's ability to detect and respond to cyber threats in real time, while quantum-safe cryptography prepares systems for the looming challenges posed by quantum computing. For businesses navigating the complexities of the digital age, staying informed about emerging technologies, and adapting to the constantly shifting cybersecurity landscape is not just advantageous but essential. By fostering a proactive security culture and embracing cutting-edge solutions, organisations can build a resilient digital future, better protected from the ever-present dangers of cyber threats.

14.9 THE EVOLUTION OF ROBOTICS AND AUTOMATION: REDEFINING INDUSTRIES AND WORK

The integration of robotics into manufacturing has heralded a new age known as Industry 4.0, characterised by the profound transformation of production processes. In this era, robotics serves as a cornerstone for automating various manufacturing tasks, significantly enhancing efficiency and productivity. The introduction of collaborative robots, or cobots, has redefined human–machine interaction, facilitating a new paradigm where these machines work alongside human operators. Cobots take on repetitive and physically demanding tasks, freeing human workers to engage in more complex activities that require creativity, problem-solving, and decision-making skills.

The scope of automation extends well beyond traditional robotics, encompassing interconnected systems enabled by the Industrial Internet of Things. By deploying sensors and smart devices, businesses can collect real-time data that offer valuable insights into production processes. This data-driven methodology not only facilitates predictive maintenance—thus minimising downtime and optimising resource use—but also contributes to sustainability efforts by reducing waste and energy consumption.

In addition to manufacturing, service robots have begun to revolutionise various sectors, particularly in healthcare and customer service. In healthcare environments, robots support medical professionals by executing routine tasks such as medication delivery and sanitisation, allowing healthcare workers to dedicate more time to direct patient care. Telepresence robots also facilitate remote consultations, bridging geographical distances between patients and healthcare providers, thereby improving access to essential medical services.

The customer service sector is similarly undergoing a transformation through the adoption of service robots. From chatbots that deliver instant responses to customer enquiries to humanoid robots assisting shoppers in retail spaces, automation is enhancing the overall customer experience. These service robots offer improved efficiency and round-the-clock availability, catering to the increasing demands of today's digitally connected consumers.

As robotics and automation advance, they are instigating a significant shift in the nature of work. While fears regarding job displacement are prevalent, the integration of robotics often results in the creation of new roles and opportunities. Workers are increasingly collaborating with robots, focusing on tasks that demand emotional intelligence, creativity, and critical thinking—attributes that machines have yet to master. The gig economy is also experiencing the effects of automation, particularly with the rise of RPA and autonomous vehicles. By automating routine and repetitive tasks like data entry and transportation, gig workers are liberated to concentrate on activities that require human ingenuity and innovation.

In this rapidly changing landscape, upskilling and reskilling initiatives are essential for the workforce to adapt and remain competitive in an automated job market. The synergy between humans and robots is poised to define a new era of work, where the complementary strengths of both are leveraged to foster a more efficient, innovative, and dynamic workforce. However, ethical considerations surrounding this technological shift must not be overlooked. Ensuring responsible implementation and equitable distribution of the benefits of robotics and automation across society will be crucial as we navigate the implications of this evolving landscape.

14.10 NAVIGATING DATA PRIVACY IN A CHANGING REGULATORY LANDSCAPE

In a world where data have become an invaluable commodity, the protection of individuals' privacy has emerged as a critical concern. The landscape of data privacy regulations is in a constant state of flux, as governments globally acknowledge the necessity for robust frameworks designed to safeguard personal information. The European Union's General Data Protection Regulation (GDPR) serves as a benchmark, establishing stringent standards for the collection, processing, and storage of personal data. Its key principles, including the right to be forgotten and the requirement for explicit consent prior to data processing, have profoundly influenced data protection laws across the globe.

In response to the rapidly expanding digital ecosystem, nations outside the EU are either enacting new data privacy regulations or updating existing ones. Notable examples include the California Consumer Privacy Act in the United States and Brazil's General Data Protection Law (LGPD). These regulations empower individuals with increased control over their personal information, compelling businesses to maintain transparency about their data practices and providing users with mechanisms to manage and delete their data.

The impact of GDPR, implemented in 2018, extends well beyond Europe, affecting how organisations manage personal data on a global scale. Its extraterritorial reach mandates that companies worldwide must comply with its provisions when processing the data of EU citizens. This regulation has set a precedent for comprehensive data protection, inspiring the development of similar frameworks in other jurisdictions. Central tenets of GDPR, such as privacy by design and default, data breach notification obligations, and the appointment of data protection officers, have become critical elements of global privacy standards.

As data effortlessly traverse borders in the digital age, there is a growing consensus on the need for a harmonised approach to privacy. Initiatives like the Privacy Shield, an agreement between the EU and the U.S. aimed at facilitating transatlantic data transfers while adhering to GDPR standards, have highlighted the complexities involved. However, the invalidation of this agreement in 2020 has underscored the necessity for more robust and sustainable mechanisms to ensure uninterrupted data flows between regions.

Looking ahead, the future of data protection presents various challenges stemming from rapid technological advancements, evolving business models, and the ever-increasing volume of data generated daily. The rise of AI and machine learning introduces intricate considerations surrounding ethical and transparent data processing. Striking a balance between fostering innovation and ensuring privacy will be essential, demanding ethical considerations in algorithmic decision-making and AI-driven insights.

Emerging technologies such as edge computing, quantum computing, and the IoT also bring unique challenges to data privacy. Edge computing, which processes data nearer to its source, raises concerns regarding decentralised data governance and security. Meanwhile, the potential of quantum computing to undermine traditional encryption methods necessitates the development of quantum-safe cryptographic solutions to safeguard sensitive information.

The future of data privacy will hinge on the adaptability of regulatory frameworks to the rapidly evolving digital landscape. The evolution of regulations inspired by GDPR lays the groundwork for establishing a global privacy standard. Addressing future challenges will require a proactive approach to regulatory development, fostering collaboration among nations, and ensuring a delicate balance between innovation and the protection of individuals' digital rights. Organisations must remain vigilant, cultivating a culture of privacy compliance that enables them to navigate the shifting terrain of data protection effectively.

14.11 ETHICAL AND SOCIETAL CONSIDERATIONS IN THE AGE OF EMERGING TECHNOLOGIES

The swift advancement of emerging technologies necessitates a critical focus on their ethical utilisation across various sectors. As innovations such as AI, blockchain, and biotechnology become integral to everyday life, it is essential to establish comprehensive frameworks and guidelines that govern their ethical development, deployment, and use. This landscape of ethical considerations encompasses a variety of issues, including privacy, bias, transparency, and accountability. A key aspect is the imperative to ensure that AI algorithms are devoid of bias and do not produce discriminatory outcomes. Developers and organisations must prioritise the ethical management of data, reflecting on the broader implications of technology on individuals and communities. Achieving a balance between innovation and ethical integrity calls for a concerted effort from industry leaders, policymakers, and technology experts.

Moreover, the widespread adoption of these technologies carries the risk of exacerbating societal inequalities if not managed with care. The digital divide remains a pressing issue, where specific populations lack access to essential technologies, risking the deepening of existing disparities. The automation of jobs through robotics and AI poses additional challenges, as it may lead to significant job displacement. This necessitates proactive measures to retrain and upskill the workforce, ensuring that individuals can adapt to an evolving job landscape. Societal impacts extend to concerns about privacy, security, and the potential misuse of advanced technologies, highlighting the need for a comprehensive approach to reconcile technological innovation with societal well-being. Policymakers play a vital role in crafting regulations that promote the responsible deployment of technology, safeguarding the interests of all citizens. Concurrently, businesses should embrace ethical practices that prioritise long-term societal benefits over immediate financial gains.

Given the global nature of emerging technologies, international collaboration is crucial for effectively addressing ethical and societal considerations. Policymakers, industry leaders, and researchers must unite to establish global standards and guidelines that facilitate the ethical development and deployment of these technologies. This collaborative effort can help prevent a fragmented approach to technology governance, fostering a cohesive global strategy. Additionally, ethical technology development must promote inclusivity in the design and implementation of innovations. Engaging diverse voices from various cultures, backgrounds, and perspectives is vital to creating technologies that are universally beneficial and free from unintentional biases. Initiatives that encourage diversity within the tech industry and advocate for ethical considerations in research and development will contribute to a more responsible and inclusive technological future.

As we navigate the complexities of emerging technologies, prioritising ethical and societal considerations is of utmost importance. The responsible utilisation of advanced technologies requires a multi-stakeholder approach, engaging governments, businesses, academia, and civil society. By championing ethical practices, addressing societal impacts, and fostering global collaboration, we can harness the transformative power of technology for the greater good while effectively mitigating potential risks and challenges.

14.12 CHAPTER SUMMARY

As we look towards the future of digital business, it is evident that emerging technologies hold the key to transformative growth and innovation. The advancements in AI and machine learning are reshaping decision-making processes and driving efficiencies across various sectors. Blockchain technology introduces a new paradigm of transparency and decentralisation, fostering trust and security in digital transactions. Additionally, the fusion of IoT and edge computing facilitates real-time data processing and interconnected systems that enhance operational capabilities.

However, the rapid pace of these technological advancements does not come without its challenges. Cybersecurity remains a pressing concern as businesses become increasingly reliant on digital infrastructures. Furthermore, the evolving regulatory landscape necessitates a careful approach to data privacy, ensuring compliance while safeguarding consumer trust. Ethical considerations in the deployment of these technologies must also be at the forefront of organisational strategies to mitigate societal impacts and ensure equitable access.

In conclusion, the future of digital business is a complex tapestry woven from the threads of innovation, opportunity, and responsibility. To thrive in this new era, organisations must not only embrace emerging technologies but also adopt a holistic approach that prioritises ethical practices and addresses the challenges associated with rapid technological change. By doing so, businesses can harness the transformative power of these innovations, paving the way for a more interconnected and sustainable future.

Key Questions for Discussion

1. As AI and machine learning continue to reshape industries, what are the potential risks and ethical dilemmas businesses must navigate? Should there be stricter regulations to ensure responsible AI development and deployment?
2. Beyond cryptocurrencies, how can blockchain technology enhance business transparency, security, and trust? What challenges do organisations face in adopting blockchain at scale?
3. With IoT devices increasingly integrated into daily life and business operations, how can organisations balance efficiency with data privacy concerns? What role does edge computing play in addressing security and latency issues?
4. The rollout of 5G is expected to revolutionise digital communication, smart cities, and business operations. What opportunities and challenges does 5G present for businesses, particularly in terms of security, accessibility, and infrastructure investment?
5. As emerging technologies like AI, robotics, and XR become more advanced, how can businesses ensure they are developed and used ethically? What societal impacts should policymakers and business leaders anticipate and address?

BIBLIOGRAPHY

Ball, M. (2024). *The Metaverse Fully Revised and Updated Edition: Building the Spatial Internet.* HarperCollins.

Bodell, L. (2021). *Make Room for Innovation: "Wildcards"*. Wiley.

Faistické Kolaboranty, N. (2024). *20 Best New Technology Books to Read in 2024.* BookAuthority.

Kissinger, H., Schmidt, E. and Huttenlocher, D. (2021). *The Age of A.I.* Little, Brown and Company.

Klein, E. (2021). *Automation Apocalypse: Too Many Robots? More Like Not Enough.* Avid Reader Press.

Sanders, K. (2023). *10 Must-Read Tech Books for 2023.* The Enterprisers Project.

Index

FSC
www.fsc.org
MIX
Papier | Fördert
gute Waldnutzung
FSC® C083411

Kolibri 360 GmbH
Ferdinand-Jühlke-Straße 7
99095 Erfurt, Deutschland
produktsicherheit@kolibri360.de